Free DVD   Free   Free DVD

From Stress to Success DVD from Trivium Test Prep

Dear Customer,

Thank you for purchasing from Cirrus Test Prep! Whether you're looking to join the military, get into college, or advance your career, we're honored to be a part of your journey.

To show our appreciation (and to help you relieve a little of that test-prep stress), we're offering a **FREE *Praxis Essential Test Tips DVD**** by Cirrus Test Prep. Our DVD includes 35 test preparation strategies that will help keep you calm and collected before and during your big exam. All we ask is that you email us your feedback and describe your experience with our product. Amazing, awful, or just so-so: we want to hear what you have to say!

To receive your **FREE *Praxis Essential Test Tips DVD***, please email us at 5star@cirrustestprep.com. Include "Free 5 Star" in the subject line and the following information in your email:

1. The title of the product you purchased.
2. Your rating from 1 – 5 (with 5 being the best).
3. Your feedback about the product, including how our materials helped you meet your goals and ways in which we can improve our products.
4. Your full name and shipping address so we can send your **FREE *Praxis Essential Test Tips DVD***.

If you have any questions or concerns please feel free to contact us directly at 5star@cirrustestprep.com.

Thank you, and good luck with your studies!

* Please note that the free DVD is <u>not included</u> with this book. To receive the free DVD, please follow the instructions above.

Praxis II Elementary Education Curriculum, Instruction, and Assessment (5017) Study Guide:

COMPREHENSIVE REVIEW WITH PRACTICE TEST QUESTIONS

J.G. Cox

Copyright © 2021 by Cirrus Test Prep

ISBN-13: 9781635309928

ALL RIGHTS RESERVED. By purchase of this book, you have been licensed one copy for personal use only. No part of this work may be reproduced, redistributed, or used in any form or by any means without prior written permission of the publisher and copyright owner. Cirrus Test Prep; Trivium Test Prep; Accepted, Inc.; and Ascencia Test Prep are all imprints of Trivium Test Prep, LLC.

ETS was not involved in the creation or production of this product, is not in any way affiliated with Cirrus Test Prep, and does not sponsor or endorse this product. All test names (and their acronyms) are trademarks of their respective owners. This study guide is for general information only and does not claim endorsement by any third party.

Table of Contents

Introduction i

Part I: Teaching Theory and Practice 1
    CURRICULUM 3
    INSTRUCTION 15
    ASSESSMENT 29

Part II: Reading and Language Arts 49
    CONTENT KNOWLEDGE 51
    CURRICULUM 75

Part III: Mathematics 97
    CONTENT KNOWLEDGE 99
    CURRICULUM 123

Part IV: Social Studies 137
    CONTENT KNOWLEDGE 139
    CURRICULUM 183

Part V: Science 207
    CONTENT KNOWLEDGE 209
    CURRICULUM 243

Part VI: Art, Music, and Physical Education 259
Curriculum and Instruction 261
Assessment 279

Part VII: Practice 287
Reading and Language Arts Practice 289
Mathematics Practice 321
Social Studies Practice 351
Science Practice.. 383
Art, Music, and Physical Education Practice 405

Introduction

Congratulations on choosing to take the Praxis Elementary Education: Curriculum, Instruction, and Assessment (5017) exam! By purchasing this book, you've taken the first step toward becoming an elementary school educator.

This guide will provide you with a detailed overview of the Praxis Elementary Education exam, so you know exactly what to expect on test day. We'll take you through all the concepts covered on the test and give you the opportunity to test your knowledge with practice questions. Even if it's been a while since you last took a major test, don't worry; we'll make sure you're more than ready!

What is the Praxis?

Praxis Series tests are a part of teaching licensure in approximately forty states. Each state uses the tests and scores in different ways, so be sure to check the certification requirements in your state by going to www.ets.org/praxis/states. There, you will find information detailing the role of the Praxis tests in determining teaching certification in your state, what scores are required, and how to transfer Praxis scores from one state to another.

What's on the Praxis?

The content in this guide will prepare you for the Praxis Elementary Education: Curriculum, Instruction, and Assessment (5017) exam. This multiple-choice test assesses whether you possess the knowledge and skills necessary to become an elementary educator. You have a maximum of 130 minutes to complete the entire test. The test always has a total of 120 multiple-choice questions; however, the number of questions specific to each subject is approximate (see the table on the following page).

Each subject area in the test will cover three aspects: curriculum, instruction, and assessment. Curriculum questions will assess your ability to appropriately plan curriculum for each subject. Knowledge of effective evaluation of instruction in each subject is covered by assessment questions. The instruction questions will vary more by each subject area.

Praxis Elementary Education: Curriculum, Instruction, and Assessment (5017)

Subjects	Approximate Number of Questions	Percentage
Reading and Language Arts	37	31%
Mathematics	31	26%
Science	20	16%
Social Studies	17	14%
Art, Music, and Physical Education	15	13%
Total	120 questions 130 minutes	

You will answer approximately thirty-seven multiple-choice questions (31 percent of the test) on reading and language arts. Instruction questions in this section will cover writing, language, and reading foundational skills; literature; and informational texts. Teachers should be able to use instruction that develops students' proficiencies in these areas.

You will answer approximately thirty-one multiple-choice questions (26 percent of the test) on mathematics. You should expect instruction questions to cover three major areas: numbers and operations, algebraic thinking, and geometry and measurement. This set of questions will assess your ability to design instruction that conveys and teaches these concepts. You will not be permitted the use of a calculator on this portion of the test.

You will answer approximately twenty multiple-choice questions (16 percent of the test) on science. This section assesses your ability to teach about scientific fundamentals in a wide spectrum of the sciences, including Earth, life, and physical sciences; science in personal and social perspectives; and science as inquiry. Questions will explore the structure of systems, such as matter, living systems, and Earth systems. Be sure to familiarize yourself with the unifying processes of science and science as a process and human endeavor.

You will answer approximately seventeen multiple-choice questions (14 percent of the test) on social studies. Social studies instruction is interdisciplinary; it will test your ability to teach relationships among fields in social studies. These include geography, anthropology, sociology, world and US history, government/civics/democracy, economics, and social studies as inquiry. You'll need knowledge of all of these subjects in order to answer the questions correctly.

You will answer approximately fifteen multiple-choice questions (13 percent of the test) on art, music, and physical education. Instruction questions in this section will cover art and design media, techniques and concepts, elements of music, and physical education concepts.

How is the Praxis Scored?

The questions are equally weighted. Keep in mind that some multiple-choice questions are experimental questions for the purpose of the Praxis test-writers and will not count toward your overall score. However, since those questions are not indicated on the test, you must respond to every question. There is no penalty for guessing on Praxis tests, so be sure to eliminate answer choices and answer every question. If you still do not know the answer, guess; you may get it right!

Your score report will be available on your Praxis account for one year, but you can also opt for a paper report. The score report includes your score and the passing score for the states you identified as score recipients. Your score will be available immediately after the test.

How is the Praxis Administered?

The Praxis Series tests are available at testing centers across the nation. To find a testing center near you, go to http://www.ets.org/praxis/register. At this site, you can create a Praxis account, check testing dates, register for a test, or find instructions for registering via mail or phone. The Praxis Elementary Education: Curriculum, Instruction, and Assessment (5017) exam is administered as a computerized test. The Praxis website allows you to take a practice test to acclimate yourself to the computerized format.

On the day of your test, be sure to bring your admission ticket (which is provided when you register) and photo ID. The testing facility will provide pencils and erasers and an area outside of the testing room to store your personal belongings. You are allowed no personal effects in the testing area. Cellphones and other electronic, photographic, recording, or listening devices are not permitted in the testing center at all, and bringing those items may be cause for dismissal, forfeiture of your testing fees, and cancellation of your scores. For details on what is and is not permitted at your testing center, refer to http://www.ets.org/praxis/test_day/bring.

About Cirrus Test Prep

Cirrus Test Prep study guides are designed by current and former educators and are tailored to meet your needs as an incoming educator. Our guides offer all of the resources necessary to help you pass teacher certification tests across the nation.

Cirrus clouds are graceful, wispy clouds characterized by their high altitude. Just like cirrus clouds, Cirrus Test Prep's goal is to help educators "aim high" when it comes to obtaining their teacher certification and entering the classroom.

About This Guide

This guide will help you master the most important test topics and also develop critical test-taking skills. We have built features into our books to prepare you for your tests and increase your score. Along with a detailed summary of the test's format, content, and scoring, we offer an in-depth overview of the content knowledge required to pass the test. Our sidebars provide interesting information, highlight key concepts, and review content so that you can solidify your understanding of the exam's concepts. Test your knowledge with sample questions and detailed answer explanations in the text that help you think through the problems on the exam as well as practice test questions that reflect the content and format of the Praxis. We're pleased you've chosen Cirrus to be a part of your professional journey!

Part I: Teaching Theory and Practice

Curriculum

State and National Standards

In the 1990s, states began to create formalized standards around which districts, schools, and teachers were required to build their curriculum. This trend became known as the **Standards and Accountability Movement**, and it resulted in a patchwork of standards that varied from state to state. These standards were designed to ensure that all students attained certain content knowledge and certain skills at each grade level. A shift in pedagogy occurred: students' learning goals—the standards—were established first, and the curriculum was built around them. This **standards-based curriculum** planning was the precursor to the **outcomes-based curriculum** planning that is widely accepted today.

Common Core Standards

By 1996, state governors had begun considering the need for a cohesive set of standards that could be used across the country. In 2009, development of the **Common Core Standards** began, and the Math and English Language standards were released in 2010. The standards are designed to be more comprehensive and more specific than previous state standards. For example, the Writing standards list specific types of writing students must master at various grade levels.

Since that time, forty-two states and the District of Columbia have adopted the standards. It is important to note that the Common Core standards are not federal standards, nor are they enforced by the federal government in any way. While funding from the No Child Left Behind Act was tied to adoption of the standards, the 2015 Every Student Succeeds Act expressly forbids the federal government from coercing or encouraging states to adopt the standards. While some states have pulled away from them or modified them, the Common Core standards are still the predominant learning standards used across the United States.

ELA Standards

The English and Language Arts (ELA) standards for the Common Core are designed to ensure that students are college and career ready. They differ from previous state standards in that they include literacy in history/social studies, science, and technical subjects. The standards are divided into five components: Reading, Writing, Speaking and Listening, Language, and Media and Technology. The Reading and Writing standards expect students to be able to read increasingly difficult texts and to articulate increasingly complex logical arguments through their writing. The Language standards focus on vocabulary and the cultivation of formal language, as well as the ability to adjust language to fit differing circumstances.

The Speaking and Listening standards did not previously exist in most states. They assume that articulation of complex ideas does not only happen in writing. In fact, particularly in their careers, students will more often be asked to present information orally than in writing. Similarly, the Media and Technology standards focus on ways in which students will be asked to communicate in the twenty-first century workplace.

Mathematics Standards

Unlike the previous ELA standards, which were primarily critiqued for being out of date and irrelevant to real-world skills, the previous Math standards across the country were criticized for being too scattered and too shallow. As a result, the Common Core Math standards attempt to create a coherent and focused set of standards for teachers to use. The standards outline eight mandated mathematical principles:

- problem solving
- abstract and quantitative reasoning
- construction and critique of arguments and their reasoning
- mathematical models
- appropriate and strategic usage of mathematical tools
- precision in mathematical thinking and work
- identification and use of structure
- identification and use of regularity in repeated reasoning

While they are modified to be developmentally appropriate for each grade level, these eight principles are the basis of the standards at every level. The standards also identify the mathematical content that should be learned at each grade level, emphasizing the cumulative nature of mathematical learning. They do not, however, dictate the order in which topics should be taught, leaving that decision to the teachers or school.

The mathematical content standards are organized into eleven **domains**, each containing several **clusters** of standards. The goal of this structure is to show how various mathematical concepts relate to each other, allowing for a more cohesive curriculum.

SOCIAL STUDIES AND SCIENCE STANDARDS

The Common Core does not contain specific standards for Social Studies or Science, although both are covered as literacy topics in the ELA standards. As a result, these standards are still written on a state-by-state basis.

In 2012, the **Next Generation Science Standards** (NGSS) were released. Spearheaded in part by the same group behind the Common Core standards, NGSS are similar in style and purpose to Common Core, and have been aligned with them at the grade level. In addition to outlining content at each grade level, the NGSS have three dimensions that are included across the grades: core ideas, science and engineering practices, and "cross-cutting" concepts—ideas that are relevant to multiple topics. They have been adopted by sixteen states.

Curriculum Planning

When organizing the school year, teachers must first establish year-long learning goals for their students, derived from national and state standards. These goals will guide all subsequent curriculum planning and will be the benchmark by which teachers determine the extent of student learning. A teacher must then determine how these goals will be achieved. The first step is to create unit plans.

A unit plan is a plan for a defined period of time within the school year, usually four to six weeks, which focuses on a particular area of study. When planning a unit, it is important to consider the goals of the specific unit, their place in the broader framework of year-long goals, and what students have mastered at the end of the previous unit. Essentially, a unit plan is guided by these questions: Where are we coming from, and how do we get to our target destination?

While there are many theories of unit planning, the following is a general guideline of the process.

DETERMINE STUDENT READINESS

As stated earlier, it is important to first determine students' progress toward learning goals before creating a new unit. What skills or concepts did students previously master that the teacher can now use as a foundation for building new knowledge? What skills or concepts were students still struggling with at the end of the last unit that must be reinforced in the next? While many teachers prefer to plan out units for the whole year at the beginning of the year, it is important to allow flexibility for adaptation throughout the year. A unit plan should not be finalized until near the end of the preceding unit. Even then, teachers should leave room to change plans during the course of the unit based on student learning needs.

Effective teachers use beginning-of-unit diagnostic tools to determine student knowledge and skill levels. There are two ways to approach this kind of assessment. Readiness tools allow teachers to determine if students have the skills needed to attain the objectives in the unit. Even with scaffolding, students are sometimes not ready. For example, if a student does not have basic number sense, no amount of scaffolding will help him or her achieve the learning goal of multiplying and dividing fractions. In order to use a readiness tool, the teacher must first determine the skills students will need in order to take on the challenges of the unit. Pre-tests, on the other hand, indicate whether students have already mastered the content in the unit. If a teacher is planning a unit on government, a pre-test would allow the teacher to determine students' current understanding of government in order to tailor the unit accordingly. So, whereas a readiness tool assesses skills necessary to understand the unit, pre-tests are based on the content of the unit itself.

> **HELPFUL HINT**
>
> To *scaffold* is to provide support for student learning, enabling them to complete tasks they could not do on their own.

DEVELOP UNIT OBJECTIVES

After determining student status, the teacher must then determine student objectives. What is the overarching goal (or goals) for this unit of study? State and national standards, while excellent guidelines, are not concrete enough for the development of an effective curriculum. The broad goals of the standards must be turned into specific learning objectives, which can then be implemented in specific lessons and easily and clearly measured. Remember, the unit objective (or objectives) must further the established year-long goals. For example, if a year-long goal is that "students will be able to articulate their ideas in three forms of writing," then perhaps a unit objective would be to ensure that "students will be able to write a 500-word persuasive essay."

TYPES OF OBJECTIVES

There are three types of learning objectives: psychomotor, cognitive, and affective. **Psychomotor** objectives focus on student skills—tasks or actions they can execute. For example, "students will be able to tell time from an analog clock" is a psychomotor objective. **Cognitive** objectives focus on student learning: "Students will be able to explain how a bill becomes a law." **Affective** objectives focus on student feelings and values: "Students demonstrate respect for ideas different from their own."

> **HELPFUL HINT**
>
> Remember the three types of objectives in this way: *motor* is related to *action*, so *psychomotor* deals with what students do. *Affective* refers to what *affects* them, what they feel. And *cognition* corresponds to how the *cogs* in their brain turn (how they think).

It is important to note that all of these objectives are student-centered. The most common mistake teachers make is to build objectives around the activities of either the teacher or students during the course of the unit. For example, a teacher might develop the learning objective, "Talk about the parts of the human body" or "Draw and label a picture of the human body." These are not true learning objectives. Learning objectives must address what students will be able to do at the end of the unit, not during it.

A good tool for ensuring student achievement-based goals is to use the acronym *SWBAT* (**S**tudents **W**ill **B**e **A**ble **T**o) when writing objectives. This will keep the teacher focused on the end goal ("Students will be able to independently identify ten major body parts") instead of the process ("Students will use differently-shaped noodles to make a model of the human skeleton").

All learning goals should also be *SMART* goals, meaning they are

- **S**pecific: Goals should not simply name a content or skill area but specifically state what students will be able to do.
- **M**easurable: Goals should be written so that a teacher can determine if the goal was actually achieved.
- **A**chievable: Goals should be realistic, taking into account student maturity and development as well as the time constraints of the classroom.
- **R**elevant: Goals should directly link to the broader overarching goals for the year.
- **T**ime-bound: Goals should list a specific time frame (e.g. by the end of the unit) in which they will be achieved.

Often the most difficult of these criteria to meet is *measurable*. The key to creating a measurable objective is to use the correct verb. Vague verbs like *understand*, *learn*, *enjoy*, and *appreciate* cannot be measured. How can a teacher measure a student's enjoyment? How can student understanding be quantified or qualified? Instead, learning objectives should use verbs that describe an action the students can perform. Strong verbs include:

- list
- identify
- name
- explain
- define
- order
- calculate
- compare
- contrast
- evaluate
- write
- draw

A teacher can measure if a student has named all of the parts of the body, but not if he or she has actually learned all of the parts of the body. A measurable learning objective takes into account how the teacher will determine if students have mastered the content or skill.

TYPES OF UNIT ORGANIZATION

While all units must be objective-based, there are three types of unit organization. The first is a goals-based unit. This is a unit that focuses on a group of standards in the same content area. A unit on fractions would be a goals-based unit. A thematic unit, on the other hand, draws on standards from multiple content or subject areas. A unit on math in art would be a thematic unit. The final type of unit organization is a project-based unit. This type of unit focuses on the creation of a specific end product that demonstrates mastery of the objectives. So, a unit in which students create a math-based art museum would be a project-based unit. Projects can include anything from books to plays to individual presentations to field trips. The primary criterion is an activity that acts as a summation of the unit.

Evaluate Alignment

An important step in the unit-planning process is to reflect on objectives and ensure they are relevant and attainable. To do this, teachers must review their unit objectives in light of their year-long goals and the national and state standards. Will attaining the chosen objectives lead to achieving the year-long goals? If so, how? If the teacher is unable to answer either of these questions, a misalignment in the curriculum has been identified and must be corrected.

To ascertain whether objectives are attainable, the teacher must ensure that they reflect developmentally appropriate practice. This means that teachers must determine the skills and capabilities students are actually able to achieve given their developmental stage. There are multiple developmental theories relevant to education and curriculum structure. The two most important are Jean Piaget's stages of cognitive development and Lee Vygotsky's zones of proximal development.

PIAGET'S THEORY OF DEVELOPMENT

Through his study of child development, Piaget theorized that human development occurs in four general stages: sensorimotor, preoperational, concrete operational and formal operational. With each new stage, the individual has a greater capacity to comprehend and to make sense of the world. Piaget argued that this course of development was essentially biological; the process could not be accelerated, nor could stages be skipped. He also argued that, until a person entered the appropriate stage, it was not possible for him or her to perform certain functions. Of course, Piaget's theory had a significant impact on education. For example, a child in the preoperational stage (from approximately two to seven years of age) cannot yet understand concrete logic and struggles to see a situation from a different point of view. Therefore, an objective stating that "students will compare the motivations of the British and the colonists in the American Revolution" is not an attainable objective for a child of this age.

VYGOTSKY'S ZONES OF PROXIMAL DEVELOPMENT

In his study of the impact of classroom instruction on students, Lee Vygotsky determined that learning occurs through two distinct processes: development and teaching. Development occurs spontaneously and naturally, but teaching is an active, intentional process. While development is important, according to Vygotsky, it can only take students so far. For example, a student's linguistic ability will improve over the course of early and middle childhood through natural development. However, the development of a large vocabulary and critical thinking skills occurs only through active teaching.

Vygotsky also concluded that teaching occurs in the zone of proximal development. This is the difference between what a student can do independently—or what the student has mastered—and what the student can do with help—what the student is developmentally capable of, but has not yet been taught. The teacher's job in creating unit objectives, then, is to find that zone and scaffold student learning to help students learn how to complete tasks on their own. For example, a six-year-old is developmentally capable of adding and subtracting numbers. However, he or she cannot naturally do this independently (at least not in a formal way). The teacher must scaffold the child's learning with related activities and practice exercises.

> **QUICK REVIEW**
>
> How does Vygotsky's theory build on Piaget's theory?

BLOOM'S TAXONOMY

The most useful tool for teachers evaluating the alignment and appropriateness of objectives is Bloom's Taxonomy. Originally published in 1956 by Benjamin Bloom and collaborators, Bloom's Taxonomy is a framework for categorizing educational goals. The framework identifies six categories based on the three domains of learning (psychomotor, affective, and cognitive). Each of these categories is then further divided into subcategories. The categories and subcategories are organized on a continuum from simple and concrete to complex and abstract. In 2001, the taxonomy was revised to more clearly present the categories as a dynamic classification, rather than a static one. To do this, the category names—nouns—were replaced with verbs. Below, the original category name is listed in parentheses next to the revised name. The revised version uses gerunds for the subcategories:

Remember (Knowledge): recalling specific factual information, patterns or processes

- ▶ Recognizing
- ▶ Recalling

Understand (Comprehension): understanding presented material and can use it without necessarily understanding all of its implications

- Interpreting
- Exemplifying
- Classifying
- Summarizing
- Inferring
- Comparing
- Explaining

Apply (Application): using abstract concepts in appropriate specific and concrete situations

- Executing
- Implementing

Analyze (Analysis): breaking down material into its parts and determining the hierarchy and relationship of those parts

- Differentiating
- Organizing
- Attributing

(Synthesis: combining information and material to form a whole)—*does not exist in the revised taxonomy.*

Evaluate (Evaluation): articulating judgments about values and methods presented

- Checking
- Critiquing

Create (*was not in the original framework*): drawing on information learned to produce something new

- Generating
- Planning
- Producing

When planning a unit, the teacher should first determine where the overall learning goal is on Bloom's Taxonomy, ensuring it is developmentally appropriate. The unit objectives must be inclusive of this level. This means that the objectives for the unit that have the highest cognitive level must be equivalent on Bloom's to the overall learning goal. Not all unit objectives, however, will be at this level. The teacher must determine the level of his or her students on the taxonomy and then create objectives that guide students from their starting position on the taxonomy to that of the overall goal.

> **QUICK REVIEW**
>
> The objective "Students will explain the process of a butterfly's metamorphosis" aligns with which level of Bloom's Taxonomy?

Again, verb choice is important in ensuring objectives are aligned to the proper categories on the taxonomy. The following chart provides verbs for each category:

Table 1.1. Verbs Applicable to Bloom's Taxonomy

Category	Verbs
Remember/Knowledge	list, match, tell, label, name, locate, memorize, repeat
Understand/Comprehension	describe, explain, summarize, restate, identify, translate
Apply/Application	solve, classify, demonstrate, dramatize, manipulate
Analyze/Analysis	debate, compare, differentiate, separate, group, research
Create/Synthesis	create, produce, reconstruct, arrange, pretend, assemble, organize, blend, generate
Evaluate/Evaluation	assess, justify, rate, revise, defend, support

SEQUENCE CONTENT

All unit learning objectives must then be broken down into specific lesson objectives that move students upwards on Bloom's Taxonomy. Not only must teachers consider what objectives each unit must meet to achieve the year-long goals, they must also determine which objectives each lesson must meet to achieve the unit objectives. Then, they must also determine the proper order, or **sequence**, of those objectives. When sequencing content, the goal should be to scaffold objectives, providing support to help move students towards attainment of the unit objectives, and ultimately of the year-long goals. Proper sequencing builds on increasing student understanding as a unit progresses, beginning with lower level concepts and moving on towards more complex ones. A well-sequenced unit should build logically and conceptually.

> **HELPFUL HINT**
>
> The sequence of objectives in a lesson or unit should align with the hierarchy of Bloom's Taxonomy.

For example, in a unit on ancient Egypt, a unit objective might be for students to create a model of an Egyptian city. The first lessons of the unit would have objectives like "Students will label the major cities of ancient Egypt" and "Students will define the various buildings in ancient Egypt." Later lessons will have higher-order thinking objectives like "Students will describe the functions of the major structures in ancient Egyptian cities," followed by "Students will compare and contrast the importance of religious and economic institutions in ancient Egypt." Each objective builds on the knowledge developed through the preceding objectives. Students would not be able to compare the importance of religious and economic institutions without first knowing what those institutions are. Each lesson objective, however, is also clearly connected to the ultimate goal: for students to create a representation of an Egyptian city.

Another important consideration is **instructional pacing**, or how quickly a teacher moves through the content and related activities. Teachers must consider how long it will take for students to understand a new concept and how much practice a new skill requires. Pacing lessons too quickly will not foster any learning; objectives will not be reached. Yet if pacing is too slow, the teacher is scaffolding past the point of mastery, ultimately resulting in failure to attain all of the unit goals. Proper pacing requires the teacher to obtain frequent feedback from students on their comprehension of the material, using **curriculum-based measures**. These measures determine student progress and performance based on specific lessons presented in the unit. The teacher must then adapt lessons and pacing to accommodate students' needs.

CREATE MEASUREMENT TOOLS

In order to effectively sequence content, it is important for teachers to take an outcomes-based approach to lesson and unit planning. Teachers should develop their summative assessment before planning any lessons within a unit. This assessment will shape and reflect the goals for the unit, which will ultimately translate into specific, relevant lesson objectives. It is also important for teachers to then develop a tool or tracking system for monitoring and assessing student growth. While the details of assessment are discussed elsewhere in this text, it is important to note that simply developing the assessments is not enough if the teacher does not have a tool that organizes the assessment data into an understandable format.

EXAMPLE QUESTIONS

1) Which of the following objectives is the most effective?

    A. Students will read three books about wild cats.

    B. Talk to students about different types of wild cats.

    C. Students will appreciate the diversity of wild cats that exist.

    D. Students will compare and contrast three different types of wild cats.

    Answers:

    A. Incorrect. This objective describes what the students will do during the lesson or unit, not the skill or knowledge they will be able to demonstrate.

    B. Incorrect. This objective is teacher-focused instead of student-focused.

    C. Incorrect. The students' appreciation for wild cats cannot be measured.

    D. **Correct.** This objective is measurable, student-focused, and based on student outcomes, not process.

2) A first-grade class cannot meet the unit's objective of writing a reflective essay on the book *Roll of Thunder, Hear My Cry* by Mildred Taylor. What is most likely the problem?

   A. The objective is developmentally inappropriate for these students.

   B. The teacher's instructional pacing was too fast, preventing mastery.

   C. The students are not engaged in the content; the teacher should select a different text.

   D. The teacher most likely did not sequence lessons within the unit effectively.

   Answers:

   A. Correct. The concepts in the novel are too difficult for first-grade students to fully understand, as are the skills required for writing an essay.

   B. Incorrect. Because the objective is developmentally inappropriate, there is no instructional pacing that would lead to a positive outcome.

   C. Incorrect. There is no indication that lack of engagement is an issue.

   D. Incorrect. While ineffective sequencing can lead to an unachieved objective, in this case there was no sequencing that would enable the students to achieve this goal.

3) **According to Vygotsky, teaching occurs when**

   A. students undergo natural cognitive developments.

   B. teachers provide students with the support needed to complete tasks they would otherwise be unable to finish on their own.

   C. students demonstrate mastery of a new skill or concept.

   D. teachers offer students the independence to explore tasks on their own.

   Answers:

   A. Incorrect. While natural cognitive developments are a form of learning, according to Vygotsky, they are not related to teaching.

   B. Correct. According to Vygotsky, teaching occurs in the zone of proximal development, between what a student can do independently and what he or she needs help to accomplish. Teachers are teaching when they provide the assistance that eventually allows a student to complete the task independently.

   C. Incorrect. Demonstration of mastery shows that learning has already occurred, but it does not indicate how the student learned the concept or skill—whether through development or teaching.

   D. Incorrect. Teaching, according to Vygotsky, is an active process of helping students to bridge the gap between what they can and cannot do. Independent exploration does not involve a teacher's help.

Instruction

Learning Theories

Effective teachers understand how students learn. At its core, learning is receiving, absorbing, processing, and retaining new and unfamiliar information. The information children learn in the elementary school years can be placed into five categories:

- **Cognitive**: Comprehension of the world around them, including cause and effect, reasoning, and patterns
- **Language**: Alphabetic and phonemic awareness; written and oral language
- **Physical**: gross and fine motor skills
- **Social-emotional**: Also called affective; social interactions, development of empathy, kindness, and respect for others
- **Adaptive**: Self-care skills and increasing independence

While it is important to consider what content will be delivered in a lesson, it is equally important to consider *how* it will be delivered. There are multiple frameworks for this process, and teachers must be familiar with all of them.

COGNITIVE LEARNING THEORIES

Cognitive learning theories focus on how students think about the world around them. **Jean Piaget**, discussed previously, is the most prominent cognitive theorist. In addition to his model of development, Piaget identified two processes whereby individuals perceive and process new information. Piaget theorized that all people have **schemata**, rules by which they understand the world around them. These schemata are developed through an individual's experiences and interactions with the world. When presented with new information, a person has a choice. She can either incorporate it into her existing schemata—**assimilation**—or adjust her schemata to fit the new information—**accommodation**. For example, when a student learning to read encounters a new word like *pig*, he assimilates it into his schemata. He has already learned the letters corresponding to the relevant sounds in the word, so he must simply connect those sounds to learn this new word. However, when he learns a word like *knight*, he must adjust his schemata, or accommodate, to understand that sometimes letters (like *k*, *g* and *h*) can be silent in a word.

Piaget argues that an individual's ability to assimilate or accommodate new information depends on his or her stage of development. For example, a child in the preoperational stage (from ages two through seven) is just beginning to understand and master language. This child, then, would not be able to articulate a hypothesis about the outcome of a science experiment. Such capability does not develop until the final stage of development, formal operations. However, many theorists now question Piaget's stages, arguing that they are too rigid and provide a slower developmental model than is typical. Some even posit that stages in general are not a useful model for understanding development, which—according to these psychologists—occurs on a continuing basis.

An alternative is **Lee Vygotsky's cultural-historical theory**. Vygotsky argued that Piaget's stages did not properly take into account the influence of culture and society on a student's learning. His theory of **zones of proximal development** is based on the assumption that children learn through their interactions with adults. For example, before a child even begins to try to sound out words, he or she must learn to sit and hold a book; they the child learns to turn the pages based on watching an adult. In the same way, a child's understanding that the symbols in the book can be translated into words comes from watching the adults in the surrounding environment. Therefore, Vygotsky argues, the role of the teacher in the learning process is essential. The teacher must properly **scaffold** activities and information to aid in successful learning.

> **HELPFUL HINT**
>
> A discussion of Piaget's developmental stages as well as more information on Vygotsky's zones of proximal development can be found in the curriculum chapter of this book.

Behavioral Learning Theories

Behavioral theorists argue that humans learn through external positive and negative responses to their behavior, rather than through internal processes. So, according to behaviorists, learning is a way in which certain behaviors are either acquired or lost, rather than a shift in understanding of the world.

The most famous behavioral learning study was Ivan Pavlov's study of salivation in dogs. In fact, Pavlov was studying digestion in dogs when he discovered that the dogs salivated when they heard sounds associated with the places where they were fed. Upon further study, he concluded that animals (including humans) respond to some stimuli naturally, but that they can be trained to respond to other stimuli in the same way by linking it to the original stimulus. For example, the dogs salivated when they saw their dog food. That is a natural response. After the experimenter rang a bell whenever the dog food was presented, the dogs eventually began to salivate simply upon hearing the bell ring. This is called **classical conditioning**.

While classical conditioning is an important learning theory, it simply trains an individual in reflexive responses. Therefore it is not particularly useful in the classroom. **Operant conditioning**, on the other hand, is a method of learning in which consequences are associated with behaviors. **B. F. Skinner** conducted experiments to learn how to train animals to make certain behavior choices through positive and negative reinforcement. **Positive reinforcement** provides the subject with a reward for his or her behavior, whereas **negative reinforcement** removes something unpleasant in response to certain behavior. Skinner found that reinforcement is more effective than punishment (receiving a negative consequence or removing a positive one in response to undesirable behavior).

Imagine a teacher trying to teach a class to be quiet when the lights are turned off. According to Skinner's methodology, the teacher should not respond in any way when students continue to talk when the lights are turned off. However, every time the students become quiet when the lights go off, the teacher could give them each a sticker. This is positive reinforcement. Alternatively, the teacher could play a loud noise when the lights turn off that stops whenever the students become quiet (but continues to play when the students are loud). This would be negative reinforcement.

> **HELPFUL HINT**
>
> Operant conditioning is also called *instrumental conditioning*. This is because the behavior becomes an *instrument* to solve a problem (like earning a reward or eliminating a negative factor such as loud noise).

Because operant conditioning focuses on behavior, it is a particularly useful concept to understand for behavior management in the classroom. It has less of an impact on the implementation of lessons.

Social Learning Theory

Albert Bandura extended Pavlov's and Skinner's theories of conditioning, arguing that—for humans—there is a social element to learning as well. In his **social learning theory**, Bandura states that children learn by observing others and **encode** their behaviors. These people—adults, peers, and fictional characters—are called **models** because they provide a model of behavior for the child to imitate. Bandura argues that children are most likely to imitate behaviors in people they see as most similar to themselves and to continue behavior that is rewarded or reinforced, either positively or negatively (just like in operant conditioning). Behaviors can also be taught through **vicarious reinforcement**, the reinforcing of behavior in someone else. So, if one student is praised for being prepared when class starts, other students in the class might start to be prepared as well.

Reinforcement in Bandura's model, however, can be given either externally—by parents, teachers, or peers—or internally through self-praise or increased feelings of self-worth. For example, consider a student who acts out in class. If the student's peers laugh, he or she may receive positive reinforcement, thus continuing to act out. On the other hand, if the student's peers do not react, the student is more likely to stop the behavior. This student's behavior is being reinforced externally. On the other hand, a student who studies for a test and does well, and then feels smarter as a result, will most likely study the next time because of the internal reward of feeling smarter.

Psychodynamic Theory

The psychodynamic theory is one of the fundamental theories of psychology, although its legitimacy has been called into question. Focused more on the internal workings of the mind than hard science, psychodynamic psychologists see the development of the mind as a series of internal struggles. The theorist who most greatly impacted education and schooling was **Erik Erikson** with his **psychosocial development theory**.

Erikson argued that there were eight stages in human development, with each stage centered on a different social conflict. The resolution of each conflict will either move the individual forward in development or stunt his or her growth, resulting in negative emotions and behaviors. Only stages three, four, and five are relevant to schooling:

> **Stage Three (ages 3 – 5) Initiative vs. Guilt**: This is the *why* stage in a child's development when the child begins to question the structure of the surrounding environment. If this questioning is encouraged and validated, the child will develop initiative and a sense of purpose and curiosity moving forward. If not, the child will feel guilt and resist asking questions.
>
> **Stage Four (ages 6 – 11) Industry vs. Inferiority**: As students enter into formal education, they will begin to compare themselves to their academic peers. If they feel equal to those peers in intelligence and ability, they will develop confidence and an innate sense of industry. If not, they will feel permanently inferior and incompetent. As a result, it is important for teachers to create atmospheres encouraging respect, collaboration, and growth in their classrooms; they must also structure lessons addressing the diverse strengths of the students in the classroom. So, while one assessment might be an essay—allowing strong writers to shine—another assessment should be a presentation in which outgoing students can demonstrate their creative abilities.
>
> **Stage Five (12 – 18) Identity vs. Role Confusion**: In this adolescent stage, children attempt to find their most comfortable

social identity. If they find one in which they are accepted and at ease, they will develop a stable sense of self. If not, they will experience the extreme confusion of an identity crisis. For teachers, this calls attention to the importance of social-emotional instruction in the classroom, in addition to academic instruction. It is important to provide safe spaces for students to explore multiple identities and to accept the changing identities of their peers.

> **QUICK REVIEW**
>
> What is the primary difference between the behavioral and psychodynamic theories of learning?

ECOLOGICAL SYSTEMS THEORY

Other psychologists argue that an individual's environment has a significant impact on their development and subsequent learning. **Urie Bronfenbrenner** developed **ecological systems theory** which consists of five environmental systems that impact individual development. The five systems are:

- **Microsystem**: The connections between the child and the groups that are closest to the child: family, school, peers, neighborhood, etc.
- **Mesosystem**: The connections between the various groups of the microsystem (e.g. the relationship between family and school, etc.)
- **Exosystem**: The larger social system surrounding the child (e.g. parent work schedules or neighborhood safety). While the child does not directly take part in this system, the exosystem directly impacts children by either empowering them or degrading them.
- **Macrosystem**: Cultural values, customs, and laws that govern the society in which the child lives. This level impacts all of the other levels of a child's ecosystem.
- **Chronosystem**: The patterns of significant events and transitions throughout a child's life (e.g. puberty, divorce of parents, birth of a sibling, etc.)

Each ecological system provides challenges and benefits. The particular combination of systems determines the development of the individual. For example, an only child living in a poor neighborhood in which he is of the majority race will have a very different experience than a child from an affluent family with many siblings who lives in a neighborhood in which she is the minority. These differing experiences will shape how each student develops and is able to learn.

Instructional Methods

There are two main categories of instructional methods: **teacher-directed instruction** and **student-centered instruction**. Each aligns with a different theory of learning.

Teacher-Directed Instruction

In the teacher-directed model, the teacher presents the information to the students. The most common teacher-directed strategy is **direct instruction**, in which the teacher stands in front of the class and relays information. Students are expected to take notes or internalize the information independently. Traditionally, all instruction was direct instruction. There are times when this method is still appropriate, particularly when providing finite chunks of factual information (rather than explaining processes).

Another form of teacher-directed instruction is **task analysis**. In task analysis, the teacher takes a larger, complex goal and breaks it down into smaller, concrete components that lead to the ultimate goal. For example, one goal may be for students to improve their reading by one grade level by the end of the year. Using task analysis, the teacher would then break that goal down into concrete tasks: for example, to create a reading list including books of increasing difficulty and to develop a series of vocabulary lists for students to master.

The **Socratic Method**, or **questioning**, is another teacher-directed method of instruction. Here, the students, not the teacher, are expected to provide the information. However, the teacher still leads the process by asking a series of questions. Constructing useful questions in this setting can be challenging. Question structures should follow Bloom's Taxonomy, falling into one of two major categories:

Lower-level questions check student comprehension, determine students' strengths and weaknesses, and help review or summarize content. **Higher-level questions** encourage critical thinking, problem solving, and discussion; they lead students to seek out information independently.

> **QUICK REVIEW**
>
> Provide one example of a lower-level question and one of a higher-level question.

Effective teachers vary the level of questions they ask in a particular class period. Lower-level questions may be used as stepping stones to higher-level questions; they may also be used to scaffold students' learning or to gauge student knowledge when higher-level questions fail.

Student-Centered Instruction

Constructivist learning theory shifted approaches to instruction in the classroom. Understanding how children process new information led to practices that emphasized learning through experience rather than instruction. Education reformers

John Dewey and Maria Montessori advocated **experiential learning**, a process by which students actively seek out and construct knowledge for themselves. This can be done in several ways.

The most direct implementation of Dewey's theories is **discovery learning**. Articulated by Jerome Bruner in the 1950s, this form of instruction emphasizes learning by doing. The teacher provides materials that students can independently use to find their own answers to academic questions, rather than being provided with an answer or even with a clear path to an answer. Critics of this method point out that students risk developing incomplete or inaccurate explanations or understanding of academic concepts.

Drawing on Vygotsky's arguments about the importance of adults in the learning process, Robert Manzano developed **enhanced discovery learning**, in which the teacher provides the students with knowledge ahead of time to prepare them for tackling a task. Teachers may use direct instruction.

A variation on discovery learning is the **inquiry method**, in which students are encouraged to ask questions that are meaningful to them. Teachers are discouraged from providing answers; instead, they should ask more questions to stimulate student thinking and inquiry. This draws, in part, on the psychodynamic emphasis on initiative: the process of questioning and seeking is ultimately more important to a child's development than any particular static knowledge.

When implementing **cooperative learning**, the teacher places students into small groups and gives them a task to complete together. It is important to note that cooperative learning is not simply grouping students to have them complete the same tasks they would do independently. Instead, it is the intentional practice of fostering positive interdependence between academic peers. Cooperative learning emphasizes collaboration, and the interpersonal skills that develop are equally important as the academic skills learned. Effective cooperative learning activities are cognitively demanding, creative, and open-ended. They allow for multiple approaches and paths, so that groups are not trying to identify the proper way to complete the task; rather, they are absorbing the content and developing interpersonal skills.

Group formation in cooperative learning must also be intentional. Groups can be organized either as **homogenous groups**, meaning students are grouped by skill and ability, or as **heterogeneous groups**, intentionally mixed so that all ability levels are represented. In order to determine which type of grouping is best, the teacher must consider the purpose of the activity. If the goal is to improve collaboration skills and encourage students to learn how to work and communicate with a wide range of people, heterogeneous groups are best. If the goal is to build certain skills based on student ability, homogenous groups are the better choice, as they allow the teacher to differentiate expectations and scaffolding by group.

Either way, it is important for students to be given clear expectations when working in groups, and to be assigned clear—and differing—roles. For example, in a math class constructing a graph of student-collected data, one student might be assigned to check arithmetic, a second will be the illustrator, a third will write a description of the graph, and a fourth will present the findings to the class. This division of labor prevents any one student from being burdened with (or taking over) all of the work.

Teachers may assign specific types of group activities. In **jigsaws**, students work in a group to develop expertise in a particular section of the content. Then, they form new groups with other students who focused on other sections of the content to teach and learn from each other. In **think pair shares**, students reflect on a question individually and then turn to other students nearby to share and discuss their responses.

Cooperative learning is also often used in project-based lessons or units, a type of instruction called **project-based learning**. Rather than organize instruction around a specific set of content, students create a project. The actual process of creating the project guides students toward achieving the unit objectives. While project-based learning can be implemented individually, teachers often find it more productive and effective to use a cooperative learning model.

> **HELPFUL HINT**
>
> To determine if an activity is teacher-led or student-centered, consider where students will be looking during the activity—at the teacher or at other students.

While student-centered learning relies in great part on group work, this approach can also be effective on a single-student basis. For example, the inquiry method can be used for students completing an **independent study**, an independent investigation into a question of their own choosing conducted at their own pace (although with deadlines created by the teacher). A science project is one example of an independent study.

Instructional Support

Knowing how to properly scaffold a student's learning is a key skill for an effective teacher. According to Vygotsky, teachers are essential in the learning process, moving students from ignorance to mastery of a skill or content. While both student-centered and teacher-directed instructional practices can be useful in this process, teachers also need tools to enhance student understanding.

Some instructional practices that can help scaffold student learning follow. **Instructional pacing** is modifying the speed at which content or skills are covered in a class period or a unit, based on the comprehension and mastery of the students. For example, if students are struggling with a concept, pacing should be slowed. If students master it more quickly than expected, the teacher should alter the pacing accordingly.

Another key element of pacing is **wait time**. It is important that teachers pause after asking a question before calling on a student for an answer. This time allows students who do not process information quickly or who need time to gain confidence to participate more fully in class.

Feedback is consistent, frequent, and prompt information that teachers provide students regarding how they are progressing in relation to the learning goals. Such information allows students to modify their understanding and approach to content and skills.

Teachers should tailor instruction based on the abilities, needs, and development of students, whether they are working in groups or independently. This is **differentiated instruction**. While psychologists have identified stages of development, in reality students develop at different paces and come into the classroom with different abilities. To find each student's zone of proximal development, the teacher must address each student as an individual learner.

Effective teachers **model** skills for students. For example, if asking students to write a descriptive paragraph, the teacher should provide an example—from an age-appropriate published work, a strong student example, or one of their own creation—in order to show students what they are aiming to do.

Providing students pictorial depictions of concepts or processes can help them understand abstract concepts in a concrete fashion. Mind maps, concept mapping, and entity relationship charts—are types of **graphic organizers** that can be used across content areas.

Classroom Management

In order to effectively implement a curriculum, the teacher must maintain a classroom environment conducive to learning. **Classroom management** involves active management of the physical classroom space, the culture of the classroom, and individual student behavior.

ORGANIZING THE CLASSROOM

The setup of the classroom strongly impacts learning; teachers should choose a classroom setup consistent with the learning approach to be used. For example, if students spend much of their time in small, cooperative groups, desks may be arranged in pods of four or five; conversely, a classroom reliant on direct instruction would benefit from rows facing the front.

It is also important that the walls of the classroom reflect a positive and focused learning environment. Displaying key ideas or rules the class will refer to throughout the year, classroom rules or guidelines, and exemplary student work all set a positive and productive tone.

Classroom Culture

The old adage "don't smile until Christmas" comes from the need to establish a clear and defined culture of learning in the classroom. Most student behavior problems can be avoided if the classroom culture is already one of focus and respect for learning and for each other. There are multiple theories and approaches to establishing a strong classroom culture.

Also known as the *take-control* approach to discipline, **assertive discipline** is a classroom management technique in which the teacher takes clear control over the classroom and its dynamics. This does not mean that instruction must be teacher-led; rather, the teacher establishes the boundaries of appropriate behavior by laying out clear and concrete rules. Teachers also incorporate those rules into instruction and the physical classroom space, communicate the rules to administrators and parents, and solicit their help in reinforcing them.

An effective assertive discipline practice includes the establishment of daily procedures and consistent classroom routines. For example, students should know that they should always have their folder and a pencil on their desk and be seated when class begins. Furthermore, behavior descriptions should be objective and concrete. For instance, instead of insisting that "students should show respect to each other," a classroom rule would be that "students should only use positive words with each other."

The assumption in assertive discipline is that students will misbehave, so consequences should be articulated and anticipated. These consequences should be defined before any infractions take place and should escalate based on the severity of the misbehavior. This way, when a student misbehaves, the teacher does not waste time devising a consequence, nor does the consequence feel personal to the student. The teacher responds to the behavior, not the student, and learning can continue. It is also important for the teacher to give prompt positive feedback to students who are following the rules.

In his **choice theory**, William Glasser posits that behavior is not separate from choice. He divides behavior into four categories: acting, thinking, feeling, and physiology. While the latter two categories are instinctual and cannot be controlled, the first two are directly in an individual's control. The student chooses to sit quietly in class, chooses to raise his or her hand, and chooses to run down the hallway. The second, equally important part of his theory is that while an individual chooses her or his own behavior, she or he cannot control that of anyone else. The teacher's job, then, is to help students envision a **quality existence** in school; one filled with positive archetypes and goals. Moreover, teachers must help students plan behavior choices that achieve those goals.

Rather than the top-down approach to behavior management advocated by assertive discipline, choice theory favors a more collaborative approach. Glasser encourages teachers to communicate frequently and deliberately with students through class meetings where concerns can be aired and the teacher can help students draw clear connections between their goals and their behavior.

Another approach, **withitness**, coined by the theorist Jacob Kounin, describes a teacher's awareness of what is happening everywhere in the classroom, regardless of his or her immediate activity. A form of **preventative discipline**, *withitness* emphasizes the importance of a teacher's ability to manage the demands of multiple students at once, read the engagement level or mastery level of students, and adjust accordingly. Like assertive discipline, this is a teacher-centered approach to classroom management as the teacher bears the responsibility of ensuring that all students are behaving accordingly in the classroom. Teachers who demonstrate *withitness* use effective transitions to move between activities without losing student interest, easily and quickly identify off-task behavior, use non-verbal behavior checks like **proximity** (standing close to a student in order to correct behavior), and generally give students the perception that they have "eyes in the back of their head."

INDIVIDUAL STUDENT BEHAVIOR

There are two main effective techniques used to manage individual student misbehavior. The first, **applied behavior analysis (ABA)** uses the principles of classical and operant conditioning to change student behavior. For example, if a student continually stands up in the middle of class, the teacher could use positive reinforcement to modify the student's behavior so he or she remains seated. This could be as simple as offering praise every time the teacher notices the student remaining in her seat.

The second method, **positive behavioral supports (PBS)**, provides a social learning approach. Instead of behavior modification, the aim of PBS is to determine the cause of the behavior. This system assumes all persistent behavior choices are logical, so a persistent misbehavior must serve some kind of purpose. The misbehavior is also reinforced by the attention—albeit negative—it receives from adults. So, the student who gets up and walks around the room continues to do so because the teacher provides the student undivided attention in telling him or her to sit back down. A teacher using PBS would conduct a **functional behavior assessment** to determine what behaviors are occurring and in what context, attempt to predict when the behavior will occur, and prevent reinforcement. Following this assessment, the teacher can then construct a plan to address the needs of the particular student and modify the behavior.

Student Motivation

A key element in the learning process is the individual's **motivation**. As Glasser states, behavior is a choice, so to engage students in productive behavior, the teacher must help students find a reason, or motivation, to behave appropriately.

Maslow's Hierarchy of Needs

Psychologist Abraham Maslow defined motivation as the desire to fulfill a need. He posited that while people have a range of needs, those needs are not equal: the higher priority needs must be met before lower priority needs can be addressed. He identifies five levels of need in his hierarchy: physiological, safety, love/belonging, esteem, and self-actualization. An effective teacher understands how this hierarchy impacts student motivation and achievement. Academic achievement is an aspect of esteem and self-actualization. So, if, for example, a student does not have a secure source of food or does not feel safe in their home, the student will be unable to focus on schoolwork. In the same way, if the classroom is not a safe space for students, they will be unable to move to the higher-level needs.

Glasser follows a similar model, identifying several related needs a teacher must help students fulfill in order for them to be successful: autonomy, arousal (having their interest piqued), competence, relatedness, and self-determination. Instruction that addresses these needs will be more successful. For example, a teacher might give students jobs in the classroom—handing back papers, watering the plants, or distributing and collecting tools (like calculators)—that they can perform regularly and independently to build a sense of autonomy. Students, then, are more likely to take risks in their academic work as autonomous individuals.

Sources of Motivation

Effective teachers recognize that students are driven by both **extrinsic motivation**—motivation that comes from outside of themselves—and **intrinsic motivation**—motivation that comes from within themselves. Extrinsic motivators include grades, rewards, and praise. While these can be effective in encouraging desired behaviors, the behavior also tends to stop when the motivator stops. For example, if a teacher offers students a piece of candy every time they bring in their homework, the students will most likely begin to regularly turn in their homework. However, once she stops offering the candy, students will return to their previous levels of completion.

Situated motivation is also a form of extrinsic motivation. This is when a student is motivated, but only within the particular context of the situation. For example, a student may be motivated to engage in work when grouped with certain students in the class, but off-task and distracted with others.

Achievement motivation is the desire to continually seek greater challenges; it includes the desire to increase one's sense of competency, self-esteem, or self-actualization—all intrinsic motivators. Because it is not associated with the approval of others, intrinsic motivation is more effective in the long-term. A student who completes assignments because he or she enjoys the feeling of accomplishment and competency is likely to continue that behavior.

Extrinsic motivation works well for short-term goals or to bridge the gap while intrinsic motivation develops. Again, a teacher might begin by offering a piece of candy to motivate students to complete their homework. Once they start fulfilling assignments, students might develop an appreciation for the sense of competency and confidence they derive from being prepared, which in turn motivates them to continue even after the candy stops.

> **QUICK REVIEW**
>
> Why is intrinsic motivation preferable to extrinsic motivation?

EXAMPLE QUESTIONS

1) A fourth-grade teacher places students into groups of four to six for reading activities. Each group works together to pick a book. They read each chapter independently, and then discuss the chapter as a group. The teacher assigns each member of the group a different role in the discussion. Which instructional method is this teacher using?

    A. direct instruction
    B. cooperative learning
    C. jigsaw
    D. Socratic Method

    Answers:

    A. Incorrect. In direct instruction, the teacher conveys information to the students. However, in this case the teacher is not directly involved in the activity.
    B. Correct. Group and student-led learning are the key markers of cooperative learning.
    C. Incorrect. When jigsawing, students focus on one element of a concept and then switch groups to teach each other.
    D. Incorrect. The Socratic Method is a teacher-led technique in which the teacher pushes students toward understanding by asking a series of questions.

2) A second-grade student repeatedly throws wads of papers across the room. A teacher using positive behavior supports would respond in which of the following ways?

    A. The teacher reminds the student of this classroom rule: "No throwing objects."
    B. The teacher stops class to discipline the student.
    C. The teacher makes the student stand in the corner of the room for the remainder of the day.
    D. The teacher monitors the student to determine why he or she was throwing the paper.

Answers:

- A. Incorrect. Focusing on clearly established rules is an element of assertive discipline, not positive behavior supports.
- B. Incorrect. This would reinforce the student's misbehavior, only increasing the likelihood he or she will continue to throw paper.
- C. Incorrect. Making the student stand in the corner of the room is an inappropriately harsh response to the misbehavior; this punishment provides reinforcing attention, and it does not address the causes of the misbehavior.
- D. **Correct.** Positive behavior supports is based on the idea that all behavior is rational. Therefore, the teacher focuses on addressing the root of the behavior rather than the behavior itself.

3) Matthew, a fourth-grade teacher, gives his students ten minutes of computer time whenever they turn an assignment in on time. Matthew is using what kind of motivation?

- A. extrinsic motivation
- B. intrinsic motivation
- C. situated motivation
- D. achievement motivation

Answers:

- A. **Correct.** The computer time is an external motivator, encouraging students to choose to complete their homework on time.
- B. Incorrect. Intrinsic motivation refers to instances when students make choices based on internal motivating factors (such as a sense of satisfaction).
- C. Incorrect. Situated motivation is based on the student's circumstances. Matthew is not changing the situation to try to change behavior.
- D. Incorrect. Achievement motivation is based on a desire for ever-increasing challenges. This is a form of intrinsic motivation.

Assessment

Why are there so many different assessments in education? Each type of test uses different criteria for item-selection as well as grading strategies that match the intent. This chapter explores different types of assessments that are used for educational purposes. Assessments are designed to measure student mastery; some are intended for teachers to use in the classroom to make instructional decisions, while other tests provide data for accountability or student-placement decisions. Teachers need to clearly understand the purpose of each test, the grading strategy, and basic statistical information that is provided on score reports to be able to articulate results to stakeholders and make sound educational decisions with the information provided.

Assessment and Evaluation Strategies

Throughout the learning process, teachers use a variety of assessments for various purposes: to evaluate student's progress against a statistical average of other students of the same age; to make instructional decisions; to assess background knowledge; to monitor student progress; and for accountability purposes and grades.

In addition to the type and purpose of the test, the format of a test should be based on the type of evidence the teacher hopes to glean from the assessment. For example, essay tests give students the freedom to creatively articulate their learning at a deep level; however, they are time-consuming both to take and to grade. Selected responses cover a great deal of material and are easier to grade, but students may guess some answers and error-analysis is difficult. Certain subjects lend themselves to specific assessment formats; these are discussed in more detail below.

Peer assessment and self-assessment are tools for helping students internalize the criteria for quality work. These assessment methods help students use their critical thinking skills to evaluate work products and articulate feedback.

Formal and Informal Assessments

Some assessments that are used for educational purposes are considered formal and some are informal. **Formal assessments** measure student progress using standardized measures. Both achievement and aptitude tests are examples of formal assessments. Formal assessments may be oral, written, or computer-based. For example, annual state tests and Wechsler Scales are commonly used formal assessments. Generally, formal assessments are purchased from a publisher who has specified both administration and scoring procedures. An advantage to using a formal test is that a great deal of effort has gone into making sure that it accurately measures what it claims to measure; however, formal assessments are expensive and time-consuming, and therefore are not practical for daily application.

Informal assessments are regularly used to assess classroom performance and drive instruction. Certain teacher-made tests, anecdotal records, portfolio assessments, conferences, and project-based assessments are all examples of informal assessments that may be used in the classroom. Typically, informal assessments are created by teachers or committees of teachers, but have not gone through the rigorous validation processes of formal assessments. Most districts use informal benchmark tests, but provide some degree of standardization in the administration and scoring of the test.

> **QUICK REVIEW**
>
> What is the difference between formal and informal assessments?

Formal assessments are frequently used to make educational placement decisions and measure the effectiveness of educational programs, while informal tests are used to help districts, schools, and teachers make informed classroom decisions.

EXAMPLE QUESTIONS

1) Which of the following is an example of an informal assessment?

   A. annual state testing
   B. college admissions tests
   C. IQ tests
   D. portfolio assessments

   Answers:

   A. Incorrect. Annual state testing is a formal test that is used primarily for accountability purposes.
   B. Incorrect. College admissions tests are standardized, formal assessments.
   C. Incorrect. IQ tests are formal assessments.

D. **Correct.** Portfolio assessments are informal tests that are used by teachers to make instructional decisions.

2) Mr. Clayborne wants to gather information about Charity's progress in reading to help him target her small group instruction. Which assessment is most appropriate for him to use?

A. state standardized test
B. aptitude test
C. anecdotal records
D. intelligence test

Answers:

A. Incorrect. Standardized tests provide accountability information to agencies.
B. Incorrect. Aptitude tests help determine student's strengths in comparison to other students of the same age.
C. **Correct.** Anecdotal records are an informal assessment that helps guide instruction.
D. Incorrect. Intelligence tests help diagnose exceptionalities.

FORMATIVE, SUMMATIVE, AND DIAGNOSTIC ASSESSMENTS

Depending on the goal of the assessment instrument, teachers may use formative, summative, or diagnostic assessments. **Diagnostic assessments** are formal or informal assessments given before a learning experience that provide teachers with a baseline of student's skills. Formal diagnostic assessments include Developmental Reading Assessments (DRA), Dynamic Indicator of Basic Early Learning Skills (DIBELS), and Comprehension Attitude Strategies Interests (CASI). Each of these formal diagnostic assessments provide teachers with information about student reading levels; however diagnostic assessments may also be used in other content areas. Informal diagnostic assessments include student self-assessments, anticipation guides, KWL charts, and pre-tests. Anticipation guides ask students questions about the content to spark student interest and activate prior knowledge; they can be used as a diagnostic assessment as they reveal what students already know before launching a new unit. KWL charts are graphic organizers that may be used both before and after a unit. Three columns are drawn, each labeled *K*, *W*, or *L*. Under *K*, students list what they already know, activating prior knowledge and helping the teacher measure it. Under *W*, students list what they want to know. This section is used to set learning goals for the unit. Under *L*, students list what they have learned; this section can be used at the end of the unit as part of a summative assessment.

Formative assessments are used throughout the learning experience to help teachers make instructional decisions and to provide feedback to students. Examples of formative assessments include anecdotal records, questioning techniques, and pop quizzes. Generally, formative assessments do not provide quantifiable data, but they are valuable for providing teachers with information to tailor instruction to specific student needs.

Table 3.1. Examples of Formative Assessments	
anecdotal records	Teachers keep notes that indicate student performance according to learning or behavior goals.
observation	The instructor watches students perform a learning activity to determine strengths and weaknesses so that students may receive targeted remediation.
pop quiz	A pop quiz is a short, unexpected assessment used to indicate student strengths and weaknesses regarding newly learned material. These are more useful for giving the teacher and student feedback rather than for grades.
ticket out the door (exit ticket)	Exit tickets are open-ended questions that students must answer in ending a lesson; these provide insight about student strengths and challenges in relation to new learning.
think/pair/share	In a think/pair/share, all students think about a question related to content and then articulate their answers to a partner, allowing them to practice active listening and learn from one another. This serves as a formative assessment when teachers observe discussions and ask partner groups to share their answers.
journals/ learning logs	Students keep learning logs throughout a learning experience to journal their thoughts and questions. Teachers can use these to assess student understanding.
discussion	Discussions inform the teacher about general understanding of learning topics. Care must be taken during a discussion to prevent some students from dominating the conversation as others avoid participation.
questioning	Asking questions helps teachers gain insight into student understanding. However, care must be taken to maintain student engagement by calling on students at random and giving ample think time to the class.
signaled responses	In a signaled response, a student performs a gesture to answer a question. Gestures could include giving a thumbs up or thumbs down, standing up or sitting down, or walking to a certain corner of the classroom. Signaled responses require everyone to engage on a physical level; however, some students will copy one another rather than think independently.

choral responses In a choral response, everyone in the class gives the answer at the same time. For short answer questions, choral response can improve student engagement. Students must be explicitly told prior to each learning experience whether the expectation is to raise their hand or call out answers.

Summative assessments may be formal or informal and evaluate student achievement after learning takes place. Standardized state tests are an example of a formal summative assessment. End-of-unit tests and benchmark tests are examples of informal summative assessments. Summative assessments may be used for accountability and grades as they are a measure of student performance in relation to the objectives.

Regardless of type, an assessment will only be accurate if it is aligned with the instructional objectives and learning activities. Therefore, how the teacher will use formative and summative assessments is a crucial part of the planning process that should not be overlooked.

> **QUICK REVIEW**
>
> Why would a teacher use a diagnostic assessment?

EXAMPLE QUESTIONS

3) Miss Randle is gathering information about her students at the beginning of the school year to determine their reading levels. She wants to find out what skills they are entering school with. Which assessment tool should she choose?

   A. diagnostic assessment
   B. formative assessment
   C. summative assessment
   D. aptitude test

   Answers:

   A. **Correct.** Diagnostic assessments pre-test students before a learning experience.
   B. Incorrect. Formative assessments take place throughout a learning experience to provide information for instructional decisions.
   C. Incorrect. Summative assessments take place after a learning experience to evaluate learning.
   D. Incorrect. Aptitude tests measure student talents.

Go on

4) Mr. Ferguson's students are taking an end-of-course exam that they must pass as a graduation requirement. Which type of assessment are they taking?

   A. diagnostic assessment
   B. formative assessment
   C. summative assessment
   D. intelligence test

Answers:

   A. Incorrect. Diagnostic assessments determine background knowledge and skills before a learning experience.
   B. Incorrect. Formative assessments provide information that guides instruction.
   C. **Correct.** Summative assessments evaluate what students have learned.
   D. Incorrect. Intelligence tests help diagnose exceptionalities.

Assessment Formats

For each type of assessment, there are a variety of formats that may be used to evaluate student learning.

Convergent questions may be used as summative tests. These are questions that have a clear, correct answer. **Selected response**, or multiple-choice questions, are the most common example of convergent questions. They can be used in any subject to provide information about student content knowledge; however, they have limitations.

Convergent questions are beneficial in assessing a student's literal and interpretive comprehension. They are also versatile and easy to grade, making them a popular choice among educators. For example, in reading, a teacher might give a test with convergent questions to assess a student's understanding of the plot of a book or of lower-order, concrete skills like spelling or grammar; in math, a teacher may present a series of math problems.

The majority of district- and state-administered assessments primarily use convergent questions. However, convergent questions can be difficult to write; furthermore, they do not allow for creativity and have limited analytical possibilities, as it is also difficult to determine the reason for student error, making remediation a challenge. They are not well suited to all subjects and most appropriate where there is only one right answer, for example, in math, science, grammar, vocabulary, and certain instances in social studies.

In reading and writing assessment, **cloze questions** are often used in addition to multiple-choice questions. Also called **fill-in-the-blanks**, these are questions in which certain words or phrases are left out of a text. Students must then fill in the appropriate word or phrase. Cloze tests are primarily used to assess students' vocabulary and their ability to use context for comprehension. Depending on the objectives of the assessment, cloze tests can be objective—meaning they have one specific correct answer—or subjective—meaning there are multiple ways to correctly complete the text.

To assess a student's critical or creative comprehension and writing skills, teachers should use **divergent questions**. Divergent questions are open ended and designed to assess a student's ability to analyze, evaluate, and create. These typically come in the form of **constructed responses** in which the teacher gives the students a prompt to which the students respond. Essay tests are easy to write, but time-consuming and subjective to grade, and so are more practical to use either as a summative assessment or in conjunction with other types of questions. They may also be used as a formative assessment that can be quickly reviewed. Such divergent questions are best suited to English and language arts and social studies.

It is important that when designing a prompt, the teacher considers the objectives to assess. Test directions should clearly focus students on those objectives. For example, when completing a unit on descriptive language, the teacher may give the students the prompt, "Write a paragraph about the first day of school." The teacher should also include a statement like, "Include at least three examples of descriptive language" or, more effectively, the teacher should provide a rubric that describes the criteria of assessment in detail (see below for more information on rubrics). Otherwise, students might focus more on factual accuracy, plot development, or grammar than on developing effective descriptive language.

A similar assessment tool is the **one-minute essay**. In this formative assessment, the teacher provides students with a question that can be answered in approximately one minute. The question must be open ended and not so simple it can be answered in just a word or two; however, it must be possible to address it in a very short period of time. For example, after reading a book, the teacher may assign a one-minute descriptive essay, asking the student to describe the main character. These short essays can serve as the basis for discussion in the next day's class or simply as a way to determine the extent of student comprehension and mastery.

An ongoing formative assessment tool, a **journal** is a specialized notebook students utilize to record what they are thinking or doing in particular tasks or activities throughout a unit or even the whole school year. Journals are a particularly good assessment tool for measuring growth because students return to them regularly. They also allow students to ask questions, express uncertainty or frustration, and celebrate their successes more openly because they write without having to worry about being corrected or exposing themselves to embarrassment in front of their peers. They may be used in any subject, but are especially suited to language arts, science, and social studies.

Journal entry topics can be open ended or based on questions, statements, and issues provided by the teacher. Although a teacher should read journals with set criteria in mind—similar to making classroom observations—she or he should not grade a journal entry. Instead, the teacher can record information about the journal entry in a separate location like an observation log and simply mark the student for completeness. The teacher should, however, respond to the journal entry in a way that validates the student's experience. This can be done with simple and short—but specific—responses to the student. For example, if a student writes in his or her journal that the vocabulary of a text was particularly challenging, the teacher might acknowledge that experience by writing, "The vocabulary in this text was a step harder than what we have been doing so far, but you did really well with it!" or "We can keep working on this kind of vocabulary moving forward." In addition, the teacher might suggest a specific strategy for handling challenging vocabulary.

Both **writing** and **reading** journals are used in language arts assessment. Writing journals typically give students the opportunity to practice writing without evaluation. Teachers can direct students to utilize a new skill in their journal entry or engage in a timed or untimed **freewrite**, an unstructured writing period designed to increase students' fluency and comfort with writing. Reading journals allow students to respond to a specific book or text by recording their questions and analysis. Like with writing journals, the teacher may supply specific prompts or allow students to choose their own topics. This can be a very useful tool in helping students prepare for a book talk.

In science and social studies, **reflective journal entries** can be very helpful when the teacher is trying to assess a student's overall comfort with the content, the student's ability to make connections, or identify multiple areas of misunderstanding. Reflective journal entries should have a guiding question. This can change from lesson to lesson or be a consistent question used each time the students journal, like "What content do you feel confident about?" "What content do you have questions about?" or "How does this relate to one other thing we have studied previously in this unit (or a past unit)?" Changing the question each time allows for more directed assessment based on the specific content of the unit. Furthermore, keeping a consistent question allows the teacher to assess growth in students' reflective abilities.

There are also means for teachers to quickly assess student learning. An **exit ticket** is a useful tool for teachers to assess student understanding at the end of a lesson in order to better shape future lessons. An exit ticket is a small piece of paper that includes two to three short, literal comprehension questions; these may be multiple choice, open ended, or short answer questions. These may be used in all subjects. The teacher can have students sign their exit tickets in order to assess students individually, or leave them unsigned to gather data on the class's comprehension as a whole. Like journaling, this technique gives quiet students the chance to articulate questions without exposing themselves to the entire class.

Single sentence formative assessments allow the teacher to very quickly measure student comprehension and are effective for all subjects. These are best used as bell-ringers to start the class period, or as exit tickets to end the class period. A few examples of single sentence formative assessments follow.

At the end of the class period, the teacher has each student write a **question** she or he still has after the lesson. The goal of this assessment is for students to practice self-assessment and for teachers to quickly identify areas needing re-teaching or clarification. It is important the teacher considers both the actual content of the questions and how well students were able to identify a significant area of misunderstanding. This assessment applies to any subject.

Another quick formative assessment is the **newspaper headline**, especially effective in social studies, but applicable in other subjects. Students write a newspaper headline based on the content from the day's lesson or a series of lessons. Alternatively, the teacher could have the students write a headline based on the previous night's reading (for students in the older grades). The headline allows the teacher to assess both the student's understanding of the content and their ability to identify the main idea.

Finally, the **big idea** is best used at the end of a unit. Students write down a **big idea**—a major theme—from the unit that can be applied beyond the unit. For example, if students are studying urbanization in a geography unit, the big idea might be, "The more people in a place, the more resources they need." This activity allows teachers to assess the students' ability to analyze as well as their preparedness for civic engagement.

Short answer formative assessments can range from a few sentences in length to a full paragraph (although they generally should not exceed this length). These provide teachers more in-depth data about student comprehension. Whereas single sentence assessments are good for determining if students understand the main concepts, short answer formative assessments are best for assessing understanding of details and analytical skill development. Examples of short answer formative assessments include short answer questions, primary source analysis, and document-based questions (DBQs).

Short answer questions based on secondary text readings or in-class activities like stations activities or videos allow teachers to assess student depth of understanding of the specific content covered in a lesson. These questions can be a combination of convergent (content-based) and divergent (analytical), organized in a way that moves students from lower order to higher order thinking. By having both types of questions, the teacher will be better able to determine where any misunderstandings occurred (whether in content or in interpretation), and be able to assess both content comprehension and analytical skills. For example, if students are looking at both a physical and political map of North America, the short answer questions might proceed like this:

1. List three major bodies of water.
2. How many cities or towns are located near each body of water?
3. Identify one desert.
4. How many cities or towns are located in the desert?
5. Using your maps, explain how water impacts the location of cities.

Short answer questions can also tie the lesson's content to that of previous lessons or the overall objectives of the unit.

Organizing formative assessments around **primary sources** is most useful when focusing on students' analytical skills. This type of assessment can be done with short answer questions or with a guiding acronym like SOAPS (subject, occasion, audience, purpose, speaker) or APPARTS (author, place in time, previous knowledge, audience, reason, the main idea, significance).

Document-based questions (DBQs) are an important assessment tool in social studies because they assess student reading comprehension, comprehension of unit content, and ability to analyze and apply information. An effectively structured DBQ contains three to fifteen primary and secondary source documents that all relate to a single question. That question should align with the objectives of the unit, and can even be the unit's essential question (if one was used). The question should be divergent, with multiple possible responses, and the documents should also provide evidence for a wide range of responses. The teacher might also find it helpful to scaffold student analysis by providing multiple questions—moving from lower order to higher order—which lead into the essential question for the DBQ. It is important that the teacher select documents which are in line, also, with the students' reading level, both in terms of lexile score and difficulty of the concepts included.

While most often used with older students, DBQs can be adapted for younger learners as well by limiting the number and difficulty of documents used, providing clear and concrete questions, having students answer orally, or incorporating older students as aides in the writing process.

Teachers can also assess reading and writing through end-of-unit or end-of-semester **projects**. These can be particularly effective assessments: in social studies and science, students taking on independent research projects should be directed to develop their own analytical question based on the larger objectives of the unit, while in language arts, they measure a student's creative comprehension. However, they also contain many pitfalls. Projects also include skills beyond writing and reading such as multimedia and oral presentation. The teacher must consider objectives specific to these skills at the beginning of the unit as well and incorporate them into the final assessment. Moreover, creativity is an important element of most projects, and teachers must create a system for actively measuring it. Finally, the outcome of a project measures a student's creative comprehension without giving any information about his or her other levels of comprehension. A well-designed project will have formative assessments built in along with the summative assessment portion to ensure the other levels of comprehension are mastered before the final project is completed. A project summative assessment must be part of a project-based unit or curriculum to be effective; it cannot replace a test.

In social studies and science independent research projects, upon generating the question, students must determine the types of sources needed to answer their question, read and interpret those resources, and finally use evidence from them to develop an argument, or thesis, in response to their question. The final presentation of their thesis and evidence can vary: a paper, an oral presentation, or a visual project. Independent research projects can range in length and depth depending on the content and the level of a student's ability. However, although they are summative assessments, they should be incorporated into the length of a unit, not simply included at the end. Effective teachers also scaffold student research and analysis by providing multiple milestones and formative assessments throughout the length of the research project. By allowing students to select their own course of research, student engagement also increases throughout the unit as a whole.

Teachers can also meet with students in a one-on-one **conference**, meetings between the teacher and student in which learning is orally assessed and evaluated. Conferences are generally private between the student and the teacher, putting the student at ease and allowing for more individualized assessment and immediate feedback. They also allow teachers to ask follow-up questions and clarify student language to get a more accurate view of the student's comprehension. To minimize disruption to the flow of the curriculum and to minimize student anxiety, it is best to keep conferences short: 5 minutes or less. Conferences can be difficult to grade and do not provide a trail of evidence to justify a grade, therefore it is suggested that some type of checklist or rubric is used when using a conference as part of a student's grade.

In science and social studies, **student-teacher conferences** permit the teacher a deeper assessment of a student's content knowledge. Because students and teachers meet individually, the teacher can ask follow-up questions tailored to each student. This type of formative assessment is most useful when folded into long-term projects like a research paper or presentation. The teacher can then make sure the student is on track with research and analysis.

In language arts, teachers can also conduct spontaneous **over-the-shoulder conferences** with a student after reading some of the student's writing or listening to him or her read. These questions could be based on literal comprehension of the text a student is reading or on higher order comprehension, asking for the interpretation or judgment of the tests. Similar steps can be taken in mathematics.

Although conferences are typically one-on-one, teachers can also use **group conferences**, in which they meet with several students at once. This technique is very useful for assessing the work of reading circles or reading groups. Even without reading groups, group conferences take place more quickly. It is important, though, that the teacher ensures all students are heard. A quick whip around is helpful for this, asking each student to quickly share an example or a response to a question.

Conferences should take place when other students are working independently on an activity. For greatest impact, conferences should be conducted regularly. This encourages students to develop their reflection skills, and—like journals—provides for ongoing assessment. When conducted effectively, conferences should eliminate recurring behaviors like repetitive grammar, organizational mistakes in their writing, or systematic mathematical errors.

A variation on the conference for daily classroom use is **Meet the Teacher**, a technique in which students individually decide on the main idea for a lesson. They each then take turns coming up and presenting it to the teacher. This gives the teacher a chance to quickly and effectively measure the impact of an individual lesson.

Another common technique used is the **think/pair/share technique**. This is a good tool for measuring student analysis. Students develop an individual answer to a challenging divergent question, then share that answer with a partner. This allows all students to speak up in a less intimidating environment, avoiding the pressures of speaking in front of the whole class.

Like informal questioning and discussion, formal and organized **questioning** allows the teacher to gather plentiful useful data. It is important that questions are well-crafted to provide the teacher information relevant to the objective. To be a true formative tool, questions and discussions must be guided by clear objectives and criteria that allow teachers to assess student comprehension. Questions also should not have single, direct answers. Instead, questions should be open-ended and provide room for students to demonstrate both mastery of content and areas of misunderstanding. The effective teacher also is comfortable correcting students and pointing out areas of confusion or misunderstanding. It is beneficial for students to hear the teacher's assessment process.

In **discussions**, the teacher assesses by facilitating conversation about a text between members of the class. The teacher should minimize his or her direct involvement and, instead, evaluate via observation. Discussions can be quick (like a **think-pair-share** activity mentioned above) or a whole class activity like a **Socratic seminar**, in which students engage in an in-depth discussion of a particular text. While it is good to allow the discussion to follow the interest of the students to an extent, it is important to also keep it in line with the lesson's objectives.

Students can be assessed orally in small groups using **structured discussions**. These discussions can be short: they may be 5 to 10 minutes in length and built around a specific question generated from the lesson, or they can last the length of a class period and be the vehicle through which content is taught. In a structured discussion, the teacher establishes clear expectations and guidelines and assigns students specific roles. To evaluate students, the teacher should circulate between groups, keeping a running record of the discussions or using a checklist to check for specific objectives. Assessing students orally in small groups allows the teacher to assess students more efficiently than in one-on-one interactions. Teachers also can assess students' collaborative skills. Structured discussions may be used in many different subjects, but especially lend themselves to social studies.

In social studies, whole class oral assessments are best used to assess students' analytical skills and their civic engagement. This is done by having students engage in discussions or debates on the content. For example, a teacher could use a **mini-debate** format to have students tackle a real-world question related to the content. Or they could use a four corners activity in which students are asked a question and then move to one of the four corners of the room based on their response. Once in the corners, students explain their choice by supporting their argument with evidence from the content covered.

It is still important to distinguish between formative and summative assessments here. For example, the mini-debate is not intended to measure students' final understanding of the content, but to evaluate the ways in which they are applying new information and to uncover areas where understanding needs to be strengthened.

Observation is when a teacher watches a student engaged in a learning activity to find evidence of learning. Like conferences, observation does not leave a paper trail and is difficult to grade, but can provide information to make instructional decisions. Anecdotal records, checklists, or rubrics should be used when employing this method of assessment. Observation is effective in all subjects.

In all subjects, **graphic organizers** provide a visual representation of students' thinking process. While there are many formats for graphic organizers, teachers must consider the objectives of the lesson and unit. Graphic organizers are helpful to students as they provide a concrete structure to organize their thoughts and think explicitly about reading strategies and literary elements they have learned. The graphic organizer should have room for the student to write the steps of their process and the conclusions to which those steps brought them.

For graphic organizers to be effective, the teacher must model their proper use for students. It is important that the teacher assesses student mastery of the objectives, not simply student understanding of the organizer's structure.

Portfolio assessments are especially effective in art, although they may also be used in language arts and potentially other subjects. Students collect a variety of artifacts as evidence of learning to be evaluated when using **portfolio** assessments. Written work, photographs of projects, and video evidence may all be used as artifacts in a portfolio. Portfolios have the advantage of providing a holistic view of student learning, but are time-consuming and difficult to grade. An example of a portfolio assessment might be used in a technology class where students are asked to submit their best work from each of the applications used.

Performances give students the opportunity to present their learning while teachers watch to assess mastery of learning goals. Performances provide students the opportunity to present skills in ways that cannot be assessed in other ways. Performances do not work for all subject areas, but are a great way to demonstrate abilities in athletics, music, and the arts. Performances can be time-consuming and difficult to grade, but provide opportunities for students to tap into an area of intelligence that may be neglected using other assessment formats.

Providing students some choice in which evaluation method they may use to demonstrate their knowledge can be motivating. Choice provides opportunities for students to take advantage of their learning style and express creative and critical thinking. However, there may be challenges in providing consistent scoring when a variety of assessment methods are used in a summative assessment. Checklists that outline which information must be included can help create more consistent outcomes.

> **QUICK REVIEW**
>
> Consider the best assessments for your specialty.

EXAMPLE QUESTIONS

5) Mrs. Franco's students meet with her individually so that she can ask them questions about what they have learned. Which assessment format is Mrs. Franco using?

   A. performance
   B. observation
   C. conference
   D. portfolio

   Answers:

   A. Incorrect. Performances give students the opportunity to present their learning as teachers watch to assess mastery of learning goals.
   B. Incorrect. Observation is when a teacher watches a student engaged in a learning activity to find evidence of learning.
   C. **Correct.** Conferences are meetings between teacher and student in which learning is orally assessed and evaluated.
   D. Incorrect. Students collect a variety of artifacts as evidence of learning to be evaluated when using portfolio assessments.

6) Mr. Diego, the history teacher, will be giving a final test the day before grades are due for the semester. He needs an assessment that will cover all of the information that has been learned so far this year in a format that will be quick and easy to grade. Which format would work best for Mr. Diego?

   A. essay
   B. selected response
   C. conferences
   D. portfolios

   Answers:

   A. Incorrect. Essay tests do not cover as much information as other types of tests, therefore could not cover an entire semester of instruction.

B. **Correct.** Selected response are easy to grade and cover a breadth of information.

C. Incorrect. Conferences are time-consuming and difficult to grade.

D. Incorrect. Portfolios take a great deal of time to grade.

Assessment Tools

Teachers use a variety of assessment tools to gather the information they need. Different tools lend themselves to different subjects in elementary education.

Rubrics are fixed scales that measure performance, offering detailed descriptions of criteria that define each level of performance. Rubrics set the expectations of an assignment, thereby clarifying the standards of quality work and improving consistency and reliability in evaluations. Rubrics work best with writing, projects, and performance-based learning activities.

Analytical checklists outline student performance criteria; as students show mastery of each required skill in standards-based education, teachers can mark off that skill. Checklists should be written in language easily understood by students and their parents but should be based on state standards. Analytical checklists only note if a student has mastered a skill; they do not provide information regarding the degree to which the student has met proficiency. Typically, the teacher would date the checklist so that progression can be seen over time. Checklists work best in activities that require the incremental mastery of skills, such as athletics, instrumental music, languages, math fluency, and pre-reading skills.

Table 3.2. Sample Analytical Checklist: Pre-K

Objective	Date of Mastery
Rides a tricycle.	
Matches objects by shape.	
Matches objects by color.	

Frequently, anecdotal notes will accompany checklists. **Anecdotal notes** are written records of the teacher's observations of a student. Records should be specific, objective, and focused on outlined criteria. Anecdotal notes provide cumulative information about how each individual performs and may include information about learning and/or behavior. Anecdotal notes are particularly useful for targeting remediation; however it can be overwhelming for a teacher to attempt to observe every action of every student in this way.

Scoring guides are similar to a rubric because they outline criteria for quality work and define levels of proficiency; however, they differ from rubrics in that each criteria is weighted with a multiplier. For example, a rubric may measure writing scores based on mechanics, word choice, and organization. On the other hand, a scoring guide may indicate that word choice is more important than mechanics, so the score on the word choice portion of the rubric will be multiplied by two.

As students make progress, they proceed on a continuum. A **continuum** is a progression of learning. Sometimes while moving through the continuum, students will reach a plateau or even regress slightly before continuing to move forward. Computer-based programs are available that adapt to student progress and regression by providing questions slightly more difficult than the question they just answered correctly or one slightly less complex than the question they missed.

Rating scales are used to rate attitudes and opinions on a continuum. Typically a **rating scale** will ask participants to rate an idea or an experience on a number scale or a category, such as *strongly agree, agree, neutral, disagree,* and *strongly disagree*. The most commonly used rating scale is the Likert Scale. A Likert Scale should be interpreted using the mode rather than the mean and then displayed using a bar graph. The advantage of using rating scales is that students are required to rate the degree to which they feel a certain way. However, students are not always honest. Rating scales can be used for self-assessment, peer assessment, or to gain student input to evaluate learning activities and overall understanding of concepts. For example, the teacher may ask students to rate the participation of their peers during a cooperative learning activity.

To gather information about challenging behaviors, a teacher can develop a **behavior scale**. To create a behavior scale, the teacher should clearly identify the behavior to be observed. Typically, a teacher targets between one and three behaviors. Next, a method for measuring the behavior must be developed. Is information about frequency, duration, and/or intensity going to be part of the data collected? Then, a baseline is established by measuring the behavior before any interventions begin. From there, goals are set. For example, if a student typically has three temper tantrums every hour, the first goal might be to reduce the number of temper tantrums to one per hour.

EXAMPLE QUESTIONS

7) Ms. Frisillo notates the progress of her kindergarten students by indicating the date at which a child is able to master skills such as writing his or her name, identifying basic shapes, and memorizing his or her phone number. Which assessment tool is Ms. Frisillo using?

   A. rubric
   B. checklist
   C. anecdotal notes
   D. portfolio

   Answers:

   A. Incorrect. Rubrics are fixed scales that measure performance with detailed descriptions of criteria that define each level of performance.

B. **Correct.** Checklists outline student performance criteria that teachers mark as students show mastery of each required skill.

C. Incorrect. Anecdotal notes are written records of the teacher's observations of a student. They are specific, objective, and focused on outlined criteria.

D. Incorrect. Students collect a variety of artifacts as evidence of learning to be evaluated when using portfolio assessments.

8) Mr. Amendt, the English teacher, provides students with detailed descriptions of criteria that define each level of writing performance. Students use the descriptions to learn what they can do to be better writers and then the student's level of performance is graded according to the criteria. Which assessment tool is Mr. Amendt using?

   A. rubric
   B. selected response
   C. checklist
   D. anecdotal notes

   Answers:

   A. **Correct.** Rubrics are a fixed scale that measures performance with detailed descriptions of criteria that define each level of performance. Rubrics can be used to guide students and to grade performance.

   B. Incorrect. Selected response are multiple-choice tests.

   C. Incorrect. Checklists outline criteria of student performance that teachers are able to mark as students show mastery of each required skill.

   D. Incorrect. Anecdotal notes are written records of the teacher's observations of a student in relation to a learning standard.

SELF-ASSESSMENT AND PEER ASSESSMENT

Who evaluates student work? The teacher is the primary evaluator, but there are times when training students to be evaluators will improve outcomes. When students evaluate their own work and the work of their peers, they are using metacognitive skills that help them to internalize the distinguishing characteristics of a quality work product from one of lesser quality. Students become active participants in the evaluation process and develop into autonomous learners.

Self-assessment describes methods by which students monitor their own progress towards learning goals. Students must have a clear understanding of their learning goals to be able to determine if they are making adequate progress. Goals should follow the SMART goal format. In other words, they should be specific, measurable, attainable, relevant, and time-bound. With the use of learning contracts, students and teachers work together to determine how the student will monitor their own progress. Students may use checklists or rubrics as they develop a portfolio to document their growth. Self-assessment is frequently used with writing assignments and projects to help students internalize the criteria outlined for their assignment. Self-assessment gives students the opportunity to reflect on their work and use critical thinking skills to evaluate their work product. Are there any drawbacks to self-assessment? It takes a great deal of effort on the part of the teacher to effectively train students to be reliable evaluators as the tendency of students is to inflate their own grades. Self-assessment helps to motivate students to learn as they see themselves moving toward their learning goals.

Many of the same benefits of self-assessment occur with peer assessment. **Peer assessment** is when students evaluate one another and offer feedback. Students need a great deal of training to properly use peer assessment as they are unable to help one another if they do not have a clear understanding of what constitutes quality performance. It is recommended that students participate in guided practice using a sample of writing provided by the teacher prior to their first independent peer assessment. Rubrics, checklists, and rating scales may be used as a guide to help students evaluate one another. Peer assessment requires a safe learning atmosphere in which students trust one another and feel comfortable providing and receiving critical feedback. Frequently, peer assessment is used as part of group work and may improve participation of all group members. Peer assessment improves critical thinking skills as students must not only be able to evaluate one another's work, but articulate and defend the reasons behind the scores they assign. Students involved in peer assessment feel a greater sense of responsibility for the achievement of their classmates. Teachers should be mindful that students may feel peer pressure to mark students higher or lower than the accurate score or may be reluctant to provide any type of feedback to their peers. Peer assessment should be used cautiously to prevent embarrassment or confidentiality issues.

The goal of both self- and peer assessment should be to improve student performance and help students critically evaluate what constitutes quality work, rather than assigning grades.

Table 3.3. Self–Assessment vs. Peer Assessment

	Self-Assessment	Peer Assessment
Students gain clear understanding of learning objectives.	✓	✓
Students use critical thinking skills to evaluate work.	✓	✓
Teachers must train students to be effective evaluators.	✓	✓
Students feel responsible for making sure all students are successful.		✓

	Self-Assessment	Peer Assessment
Students may feel uncomfortable sharing feedback.		✓
Students may give inaccurate scores.	✓	✓

EXAMPLE QUESTIONS

9) Ms. DiCristafaro is considering using peer assessment to help students edit their writing assignments. Which of the following steps should she take first?

    A. establish a safe learning environment

    B. pair students by ability level

    C. teach students active listening skills

    D. remind students of the importance of grades

    Answers:

    A. **Correct.** Students must feel safe and trust their peers to be able to participate in peer assessment.

    B. Incorrect. Students will not be paired for editing until after all students have had a chance to practice their editing skills with teacher support.

    C. Incorrect. Active listening skills will be helpful when receiving feedback, but that is the last step in the editing process.

    D. Incorrect. Peer assessment should be used to improve learning, not assign grades.

10) Mr. Patrick would like his students to self-assess their history projects before turning them in. Prior to beginning the project, which of the following should take place?

    A. set learning goals

    B. locate resources

    C. critically evaluate their work

    D. articulate learning

    Answers:

    A. **Correct.** Students should write SMART goals to drive their learning experience.

    B. Incorrect. Resources will not be selected until after the goals are set.

    C. Incorrect. Once the project is complete, students will evaluate their work.

    D. Incorrect. By the end of the project, students will be able to articulate their learning.

Part II: Reading and Language Arts

Content Knowledge

Reading, writing, speaking, and listening are the four cornerstones of a language arts curriculum in elementary education. Teacher content knowledge is demonstrated in the following areas: reading foundational skills, student comprehension of literature and informational texts, the stages and characteristics of the writing process and effective writing, and techniques for oral communication and collaboration.

Reading: Foundational Skills

PHONOLOGICAL AWARENESS

Phonological Awareness is an understanding of how sounds, syllables, words, and word parts can be orally manipulated to break apart words, make new words, and create rhymes. It is an important foundational skill for learning to read and literacy development. **Phonemic awareness** is a type of phonological awareness that focuses on the sounds in a language. It is an understanding of how each small unit of sound, or **phoneme**, forms the language by creating differences in the meanings of words. For example, the phonemes /m/ and /s/ determine the difference in meaning between the words *mat* and *sat*. There are forty-four different phonemes in the English language. These includes letter combinations such as consonant diagraphs like /sh/ and vowel dipthongs like /oi/ where the letters work together to produce one sound. Teachers build phonemic awareness in their students using a variety of techniques such as phoneme blending, phoneme segmentation, phoneme substitution, and phoneme deletion.

Table 4.1. Phoneme Chart

s	t	p	n	m	a	e	i	o
sun	tan	paint	now	mark	apple	edge	innertube	obvious
g	d	c k	r	h	u	ai	ee	igh
girl	dark	cat, kite	ring	heat	under	pain	flee	night
b	f	l	j	v	oa	oo	oo	ar
buy	find	lamb	joy	vehicle	float	foot	scoot	far
w	x	y	z	qu	or	ur	ow	oi
wipe	exit	yellow	zip	quiet	port	turn	brow	foil
ch	sh	th	th	ng	ear	air	ure	er
sandwich	sharp	thick	them	ring	fear	flair	lure	driver

Phoneme blending is combining phonemes to make a word; for example, /m/ /a/ /t/ combines to form *mat*. In contrast, **phoneme substitution** is the replacement of phonemes in words to make new words; removing the /m/ from the beginning of the word *mat* and replacing it with /s/ creates the word *sat*. **Phoneme segmentation** is separating phonemes in words; separating the sounds in the word *mat* isolates the phonemes /m/ /a/ /t/. Finally, in **phoneme deletion**, phonemes are removed from words to make new words. Removing /m/ from *mat* leaves the word *at*.

> **DID YOU KNOW?**
>
> *The Reading Teacher's Book of Lists* by Edward Fry and Jacqueline Kress is an excellent resource for becoming familiar with the range of phonemes formed by two letters in addition to recommended teaching tactics.

Building phonemic awareness in students is the latter part of a developmental sequence that contributes to a strong foundation in phonological awareness. Prior to focusing on phonemic awareness, teachers build phonological awareness with exercises that task students with orally manipulating the phonological units of spoken **syllables**. These phonological units are defined as onsets and rimes and can be blended, substituted, segmented, and deleted just like phonemes. The **onset** of a syllable is the beginning consonant or consonant blend. The **rime** includes the syllable's vowel and its remaining consonants. For example, in the word *block*, the consonant blend /bl/ is the onset, and the remainder of the word *–ock* is the rime.

> **STUDY TIP**
>
> Remember that phonological and phonemic awareness are auditory skills that do not involve printed letter or word recognition.

Once students have a solid foundation in phonological awareness, they are ready to begin phonics instruction. **Phonics** is the study of the relationship between the spoken sounds in words and the printed letters that correspond to those sounds, or **letter-sound correspondence**. In explicit phonics instruction, letters and their corresponding sounds are first taught in isolation, then blended into words, and finally applied to decodable text. Initially, the most common sounds for each letter and **high frequency** letter-sound correspondences, or those that occur most often in the English language, are introduced. In order to assist students beginning to read simple VC (vowel-consonant), VCC (vowel-consonant-consonant), CVCC (consonant-vowel-consonant-consonant), and CVC (consonant-vowel-consonant) words early on, a few short vowel sounds are introduced as well. Letters with names that bear a strong relationship to their sounds are introduced before letters that do not. For example, the sound of the letter *s* can be heard at the end of its name.

> **DID YOU KNOW?**
>
> A majority of words used to build phonological awareness are one-syllable words, or words made up of only one onset and one rime.

Phonics instruction progresses from simple to more complex letter-sound correspondences and sound/spellings (or the spelling of words based on letter-sound correspondences). Short-vowel sound spellings are introduced before long-vowel sound/spellings, and letters that are similar in appearance (e.g., *b* and *d*) or sound (e.g., /m/ and /n/) are taught separately along the instructional continuum. As students move through kindergarten and the primary grades, they progress from decoding two- or three-phoneme words with letters representing their most common sounds to longer words and more complex sound/spelling patterns.

Sight words, words that are repeated most often in text, are taught in conjunction with phonics. These are words that students need to learn to recognize by sight, such as *a*, *in*, *the*, *at*, and *I*, in order to read sentences with optimal fluency. As with letter-sound correspondences and sound/spellings, sight word instruction begins with the most common words, or highest frequency words. Teachers develop sight word lists for students using either the *Dolch List of Basic Sight Words* or *Fry's Numerical List of Instant Words*. These lists change and evolve across grade levels so that students build a large repertoire of instantly recognizable words as they move through the primary grades.

ROOTS AND AFFIXES

Beginning in second grade, language arts students also receive instruction in identifying and understanding roots and affixes in order to determine the meanings of unfamiliar words. **Roots** are typically derived from Latin or Greek and establish the basis of new words. *Cent* is a Latin root meaning "one hundred." **Affixes** are added to words or roots to change their meanings. They consist of prefixes, added to the beginning of a word or root, and suffixes, added to the end of a word or root. For example, the prefix *per-* can be added to *cent* to make the word *percent*, effectively changing the meaning to "one part in a hundred." Likewise, the suffix *–ury* can be added to *cent* to make the word *century*, effectively changing the meaning to "a period of one hundred years." By understanding how roots and affixes work together to form words and change the meanings of words, students can steadily add new words to their automatic memory banks of known words and decode unfamiliar words with greater ease and precision. As with instruction in phonics and sight words, elementary language arts teachers begin with the most common prefixes and suffixes and progress from simple to complex combinations of roots and affixes.

> **QUICK REVIEW**
>
> How many different words can you make from the Greek root *san* (meaning "health") and the Latin root *fig* (meaning "form") by adding affixes?

Table 4.2. Common Roots and Affixes

Root	Definition	Example
ast(er)	star	asteroid, astronomy
audi	hear	audience, audible
auto	self	automatic, autograph
bene	good	beneficent, benign
bio	life	biology, biorhythm
cap	take	capture
ced	yield	secede
chrono	time	chronometer, chronic
corp	body	corporeal
crac or crat	rule	autocrat
demo	people	democracy
dict	say	dictionary, dictation
duc	lead or make	ductile, produce
gen	give birth	generation, genetics
geo	earth	geography, geometry
grad	step	graduate
graph	write	graphical, autograph
ject	throw	eject
jur or jus	law	justice, jurisdiction
log or logue	thought	logic, logarithm
luc	light	lucidity
man	hand	manual
mand	order	remand
mis	send	transmission
mono	one	monotone
omni	all	omnivore
path	feel	pathology
phil	love	philanthropy

phon	sound	phonograph
port	carry	export
qui	rest	quiet
scrib or script	write	scribe, transcript
sense or sent	feel	sentiment
tele	far away	telephone
terr	earth	terrace
uni	single	unicode
vac	empty	vacant
vid	see	video
vis	see	vision

Table 4.3. Common Prefixes

Prefix	Definition	Example
a- (also an-)	not, without; to, toward; of, completely	atheist, anemic, aside, aback, anew, abashed
ante-	before, preceding	antecedent, anteroom
anti-	opposing, against	antibiotic, anticlimax
com- (also co-, col-, con-, cor-)	with, jointly, completely	combat, codriver, collude, confide
dis- (also di-)	negation, removal	disadvantage, disbar
en- (also em-)	put into or on; bring into the condition of; intensify	engulf, entomb
hypo-	under	hypoglycemic, hypothermia
in- (also il-, im-, ir-)	not, without; in, into, toward, inside	infertile, impossible, influence, include
intra-	inside, within	intravenous, intrapersonal
out-	surpassing, exceeding; external, away from	outperform, outdoor
over-	excessively, completely; upper, outer, over, above	overconfident, overcast
pre-	before	precondition, preadolescent, prelude
re-	again	reapply, remake
semi-	half, partly	semicircle, semiconscious
syn- (also sym-)	in union, acting together	synthesis, symbiotic
trans-	across, beyond	transatlantic
trans-	into a different state	translate
under-	beneath, below	underarm, undersecretary
under-	not enough	underdeveloped

Reading Fluency

Language arts teachers apply strategic phonics, sight word, and word analysis strategies to help students become fluent readers who can use their reading skills as a means of accessing literature and deriving information from printed text. In other words, reading to learn is the end-all goal of learning to read and **fluency**, or the ability to read with ease and automaticity, is the key. Reading fluency is composed of three factors: rate, accuracy, and prosody.

Reading **rate** is the speed and fluidity with which a student can read. It is determined by the number of words read correctly per minute or the length of time it takes for a student to read a selected passage. A steady, fluid reading rate is important because it allows the reader to focus on constructing meaning from text without being distracted by the effort it takes to slowly plod through word pronunciations.

Reading **accuracy** refers to a student's ability to recognize or decode words correctly. Meaningful comprehension of reading material is dependent on reading accuracy, which in turn depends upon the reader having a significant inventory of known sight words and an ability to decode words effortlessly. Without accuracy, a student is unlikely to understand what an author or text is communicating. By examining patterns in word-identification errors, the elementary language arts teacher can identify decoding strategies that a student is not using and provide appropriate instruction.

Prosody encompasses the range of vocal expressions a reader uses when reading aloud. It includes rhythm, intonation, and stress patterns. Being able to read text orally while conveying the meaning of what is being read with appropriate vocal cues is evidence of reading prosody. In other words, when a student reads out loud, the spoken words should reflect natural speech patterns. Typically, when prosody is lacking, a student will read in a stilted, monotone voice, which often means the student does not understand the words.

Teaching English to Speakers of Other Languages

Many elementary language arts classrooms include both students whose first language is English and students who are learning English as a second language. Five **stages of language acquisition** have been identified for students learning a second language. These stages are defined as preproduction, early production, speech emergence, intermediate fluency, and advanced fluency. These stages correlate to five **levels of language proficiency**, L1 through L5, which are L1) Entering, L2) Beginning, L3) Developing, L4) Expanding, and L5) Bridging.

Table 4.4. Stages of Second-Language Acquisition

Stage	Characteristics
Preproduction	Preproduction is also known as the silent period. Though these learners may have close to 500 words in their receptive vocabulary, they refrain from speaking but will listen and may copy words down. They can respond to visual cues such as pictures and gestures, and they will communicate their comprehension. However, sometimes students will repeat back what they have heard in a process referred to as parroting. This can aid them in adding to their receptive vocabulary, but it should not be mistaken for producing language.
Early Production	In this stage learners have achieved a 1000-word receptive and active vocabulary. They now produce single-word and two- to three-word phrases and can respond to questions and statements. Many learners in this stage enjoy engaging in musical games or word plays that help them to memorize language chunks that they can use later.
Speech Emergence	English language learners have a vocabulary of about 3000 words by the time they reach this stage of second-language acquisition. They are able to chunk simple words and phrases into sentences that may or may not be grammatically correct. They respond to modeling of correct responses better than direct correction. At this stage, learners also are more likely to participate in conversations with native English speakers, as they are gaining confidence in their language skills. These learners can understand simple readings when reinforced by graphics or pictures and can complete some content work with support.
Intermediate Fluency	By the intermediate fluency stage, English language learners have acquired a vocabulary of about 6000 words. They are able to speak in more complex sentences and catch and correct many of their errors. They are also willing to ask questions to clarify what they do not understand. Learners at this stage may sound fluent, but they have large gaps in their vocabulary as well as in their grammatical and syntactical understanding of the language. They are often comfortable speaking in group conversation that avoids heavy academic language.
Advanced Fluency	Second-language learners who reach advanced fluency have achieved cognitive language proficiency in their learned language. They demonstrate near-native ability and use complex, multi phrase and clause sentences to convey their ideas. Though accents are still detectable and idiomatic expressions are sometimes used incorrectly, the language learner has become essentially fluent.

The **preproduction stage** of language acquisition is defined as the silent stage during which a student is primarily absorbing new input. At this proficiency level—L1 Entering—a student rarely uses English to communicate and responds nonverbally to instruction, constructing meaning primarily from illustrations, graphs, and charts. This is followed by the early production stage in which a student begins to speak a few words and simple phrases. At this proficiency level—L2 Beginning—a student can communicate basic information in a limited manner but exhibits a number of predictable errors.

During the **emergence of speech stage**, the student begins to speak more clearly and accurately and increases his or her spoken vocabulary. It is during this stage that the student takes steps toward reading and writing in the second language. At this proficiency level—L3 Developing—a student understands more complex speech and can communicate spontaneously in simple sentences. However, the student's vocabulary and comprehension of language structure remains limited.

During the **intermediate fluency stage**, the student gains competency speaking in more complex sentences and demonstrates a larger vocabulary. This is the stage at which a student can begin to think in the second language as well as speak it. At this proficiency level—L4 Expanding—a student can read in the second language with demonstrated fluency, but may still struggle with comprehending text that describes complex or abstract concepts.

Finally, the student enters the **advanced fluency stage** in which he or she can converse fluently and think clearly in the second language. At this proficiency level—L5 Bridging—a student requires only minimal language support and can function at the same level as peers with a first language of English. Progression through these five stages of language acquisition typically takes around two years. It is important for language arts teachers to recognize these stages and proficiency levels in order to best facilitate and recognize student understanding and internalization of both the new language and new content.

SAMPLE QUESTIONS

1) A teacher says *hat* and instructs students to produce the sounds they hear in the word. Which strategy is the teacher using to build phoneme awareness?

   A. phoneme blending
   B. phoneme deletion
   C. phoneme segmentation
   D. phoneme substitution

   Answers:

   A. Incorrect. The strategy of phoneme blending requires students to combine phonemes to make a word.

B. Incorrect. The strategy of phoneme deletion requires students to remove phonemes in words to make new words.

C. Correct. The strategy of phoneme segmentation requires students to separate the phonemes in a word.

D. Incorrect. The strategy of phoneme substitution requires students to replace phonemes in words to make new words.

2) **Which of the following is an example of prosody?**
   A. using appropriate vocal cues when reading aloud
   B. decoding words correctly when reading aloud
   C. reading at an appropriate speed when reading aloud
   D. reading smoothly and steadily when reading aloud

Answers:

A. Correct. Prosody is a reader's ability to use appropriate vocal expressions when reading aloud.

B. Incorrect. Decoding words correctly while reading aloud is an example of reading accuracy.

C. Incorrect. Reading aloud at an appropriate speed is an example of reading rate.

D. Incorrect. Reading smoothly and steadily when reading aloud is an example of reading rate.

Reading Literature and Informational Text

In order to effectively teach students to comprehend the literature and informational text they are tasked with reading, the elementary language arts teacher needs to demonstrate an understanding of comprehension strategies, point of view, comparing information from a variety of texts and multimedia sources, and the role of text complexity in reading development.

COMPREHENSION STRATEGIES

Expertise in language arts requires an ability to use key ideas and details from literary or informational text to determine the moral, theme, or central idea; make inferences; and summarize information. Readers must also be able to analyze characters, setting, plot, and relationships among ideas, events, and concepts. The **theme** of a literary text is the basic idea that the author wants to convey. It weaves in and out of the text as the story, play, or poem unfolds. It expresses an underlying opinion related to the text's subject. On the other hand, the **moral** of a literary text is the lesson the author wants to teach the reader. It is more direct than a theme. The basic underlying idea of informational text is referred to as the **central idea**. This is the major focus of the information provided in the text.

The key purpose of reading text is to obtain information or experience a story. In order to do this, readers must have the ability to comprehend what is being read. Without comprehension, reading is simply an exercise in making sounds that have no meaning. Being able to comprehend what is being read is what connects the words an author writes to the reader's experience of the world; it is what gives text meaning and makes it relatable. Elementary language arts teachers help students to comprehend what is being read by teaching students a variety of comprehension strategies. One of these strategies is the ability to make **inferences**, or determine what an author is suggesting by using clues in text. It is the ability to understand what is not directly stated by an author.

> **QUICK REVIEW**
>
> In other words, the reader studies the text to discern what the writer is saying "between the lines."

Summarization is the distillation and condensation of a text into its main idea and key details. It is a short encapsulation of what the text is about to clarify the general message. However, to properly summarize, it is important to **identify story elements**. More specifically, this is identifying the characters (e.g., main, minor, protagonist, antagonist, dynamic, static), **setting** (where the story takes place), and **plot** development (e.g., exposition, rising action, problem/climax, falling action, resolution) in a text. Understanding the role of a character in a story via the character's actions, traits, relationship, and personality is **character analysis**. Analyzing how a character thinks and behaves allows a reader to understand his or her motivations and beliefs.

Recognizing genre is the ability to name the genre of a text (e.g., poetry, drama, picture book, graphic novel, folktale, myth, fairy tale, tall tale, historical fiction, science fiction) and the features of that genre. Readers who understand and recognize the characteristics of a variety of genres can gain additional insights into an author's purpose or message. For example, a reader is able to comprehend a text with a greater depth and breadth if he or she knows how the **rhyme scheme** (e.g., abab, aabb, aabba) and **meter** (basic rhythmic structure of the lines or verses in poetry) of a poem affect its tone or how **stage directions** develop the rising action in a play.

> **DID YOU KNOW?**
>
> Most genres have defining characteristics that elementary language arts teachers need to know. What are the similarities and differences between folktales, tall tales, fairy tales, fables, myths, and legends?

An author uses a specific point of view to tell a story. When **identifying point of view**, readers use genre and pronoun clues to identify who is telling a story to best form accurate conclusions about the events of the story. Typically, authors use one of five points of view: first-person, second-person, third-person objective, third-person limited omniscient, and third-person omniscient. In **first-person** point of view, one character tells the story from his or her direct experience using pronouns such as *I, my, mine*, and *we*. In **second-person** point of view, the perspective of the text is from an external "you," whether that be the reader or unknown other. In **third-person objective** point of view, a detached narrator relates the actions and dialogue of the story, but not the thoughts or feelings of any characters. In **third-person limited omniscient** point of view, a detached narrator tells the story from one character's point of view including that character's internal thoughts and feelings. In **third-person omniscient** point of view, a detached and all-knowing narrator tells the story from the point of view of all of the characters, including all of their thoughts and feelings. Any text told from a third-person point of view includes pronouns such as *he, she, it*, and *they*.

Some texts offer supplemental information outside of the main text. These **text features** include imagery like photographs, drawings, maps, charts, graphs. They also include organizational features like chapter **headings**, titles, **sidebars** (boxes of explanatory or additional information set aside from main text), and **hyperlinks** (highlighted sections or words in digital text that take a reader to another digital location or document for additional information). Readers should be able to **analyze text features** to better comprehend an author's message.

Finally, **analyzing text organization** is the ability to analyze the way a text is organized in order to better comprehend an author's purpose for writing. Different forms of textual organization facilitate an author's message. Some of the more common organizational structures are cause and effect, problem and solution, sequence of events or steps-in-a-process, compare and contrast, and description. Each **text structure** can be identified by the use of particular signal words (words that provide clues to how the author has organized information) and features.

Text Complexity

The teaching of reading comprehension strategies is best facilitated when students are reading text that is at developmentally appropriate reading levels. Students improve their reading skills best when the text provided is neither too easy nor too difficult. **Text leveling**, or complexity, is determined by three factors: quantitative measures, qualitative measures, and reader and task considerations. **Quantitative measures** include readability scores determined by computer algorithms that evaluate text elements such as word frequency and sentence length. **Qualitative measures** include analysis of text elements such as structure (i.e., low or high complexity), language clarity (i.e., literal vs. figurative or familiar vs. unfamiliar), and knowledge demands (i.e., assumptions about what a reader already knows). **Reader and task considerations** are determined by the professional judgment of educators who match texts to particular students, classes, and/or tasks based on their inherent needs.

SAMPLE QUESTIONS

3) Which of the following is true of quantitative measures of text complexity?

   A. They are task considerations determined by professional judgment.
   B. They are analytical measurements determined by knowledge demands.
   C. They are statistical measurements determined by computer algorithms.
   D. They are leveling measurements determined by text structure.

   Answers:

   A. Incorrect. Quantitative measures of text complexity are free of human judgment.
   B. Incorrect. The analysis of knowledge demands is a qualitative measure of text complexity.
   C. Correct. Quantitative measures are objective and based on statistics.
   D. Incorrect. Leveling measurements based on text structure are qualitative measures.

4) Read the excerpt from *Treasure Island* by Robert Louis Stevenson.

   I remember him as if it were yesterday, as he came plodding to the inn door, his sea-chest following behind him in a hand-barrow—a tall, strong, heavy, nut-brown man, his tarry pigtail falling over the shoulder of his soiled blue coat, his hands ragged and scarred, with black, broken nails, and the sabre cut across one cheek, a dirty, livid white.

   This text is written from which point of view?

   A. second-person
   B. first-person
   C. third-person objective
   D. third-person omniscient

   Answers:

   A. Incorrect. Second person point of view is written from the perspective of an external "you."
   B. Correct. First person point of view is written directly from the perspective of one character.
   C. Incorrect. Third-person objective point of view is written from the perspective of a detached narrator.
   D. Incorrect. Third-person omniscient point of view is written from the perspective of an all-knowing, detached narrator.

Writing

Elementary school is where students establish a solid foundation of writing skills that lead to a lifelong ability to communicate ideas, opinions, experiences, and beliefs. Language arts teachers across the grades are tasked with building student understanding of writing styles, purposes, and practices.

Table 4.5. Developmental Stages of Writing

Stage	Age	Students in this stage...
Preconventional	3 – 5	▸ are aware that print conveys meaning, but rely on pictures to communicate visually. ▸ include recognizable shapes and letters on drawings. ▸ can describe the significance of the objects in their drawings.
Emerging	4 – 6	▸ use pictures when drawing, but may also label objects. ▸ can match some letters to sounds. ▸ copy print they see in their environment.
Developing	5 – 7	▸ write sentences and no longer rely mainly on pictures. ▸ attempt to use punctuation and capitalization. ▸ spell words based on sound.
Beginning	6 – 8	▸ write several related sentences on a topic. ▸ use word spacing, punctuation, and capitalization correctly. ▸ create writing that others can read.
Expanding	7 – 9	▸ organize sentences logically and use more complex sentence structures. ▸ spell high frequency words correctly. ▸ respond to guidance and criticism from others.
Bridging	8 – 10	▸ write about a particular topic with a clear beginning, middle, and end. ▸ begin to use paragraphs. ▸ consult outside resources (e.g., dictionaries).
Fluent	9 – 11	▸ write both fiction and nonfiction with guidance. ▸ experiment with sentence length and complexity. ▸ edit for punctuation, spelling, and grammar.

Stage	Age	Students in this stage...
Proficient	10 – 13	▸ write well-developed fiction and nonfiction. ▸ use transitional sentences and descriptive language. ▸ edit for organization and style.
Connecting	11 – 14	▸ write in a number of different genres. ▸ develop a personal voice when writing. ▸ use complex punctuation.
Independent	13 and older	▸ explore topics in depth in fiction and nonfiction. ▸ incorporate literary devices in their writing. ▸ revise writing through multiple drafts.

In order to best facilitate student progress, elementary language arts teachers must have a firm understanding of the characteristics and stages of common types of writing, strategies for producing effective writing, digital tools for writing, and the research process.

Types of Writing

There are four main writing **styles** that students learn in elementary school. Each style is selected based on an author's **purpose** for writing—to explain, to entertain, to describe, or to persuade—and the needs of the **audience**, the people reading the material. Different audiences have different needs. For example, people reading a humor blog will most likely prefer an informal style, while the audience for a magazine article explaining environmental problems caused by deforestation will appreciate writing with a well-organized structure and paragraphs that expand on key issues. The four main styles of writing are as follows:

▸ **Expository Writing**: This style of writing is primarily used to explain an idea or concept or inform the reader about a topic. It is most often used in formal essays that include a main idea and supporting details based on fact.

▸ **Narrative Writing**: This style of writing is primarily used to tell a personal or fictional story that entertains the reader. The author includes descriptive details and figurative language in order to maintain the reader's attention with dynamic characters, interesting settings, and captivating plots. Poems that tell stories, or **narrative poems**, also use this writing style.

▸ **Descriptive Writing**: This style of writing emphasizes the production of imagery using words and figurative language that appeal to the reader's five senses. It is a writing style that produces vivid pictures in the reader's imagination and is often used to write poetry or detailed descriptions of experiences or events.

- **Persuasive Writing**: This style of writing is used to convince, or persuade, a reader to subscribe to the author's opinion or point of view. It follows a formal progression that aims to sway the reader into accepting the author's stance and often plays on the reader's emotions to achieve its goal. Persuasive writing is often used for **speeches** and **advertisements**.

THE WRITING PROCESS

Elementary students also need to learn that writing is a process that begins with an idea and ends with a final draft. The writing process is made up of five key stages: prewriting, drafting, **revising/editing**, rewriting, and publishing. This process allows students to experience writing as it takes place in the profession. It is a process that enables students to capture the inspiration of the initial idea and then carefully shape and polish that idea until it can best capture a reader's interest. During the prewriting phase of the writing process, authors brainstorm ideas for writing by organizing them in charts, lists, or by other means. This **organization** of ideas is used to write the first draft of a writing piece. During the next stage of the process, a writer reviews the first draft for **coherence** by identifying sections that need elaboration, correction, and/or reorganization. The original draft is revised based on these observations and those of peer editors. Once the **revisions** have been determined, the first draft is rewritten with corrections and changes made. It is only after the first draft has been carefully examined and rewritten that it is ready for an audience during the publishing phase of the writing process.

USING SOURCES

As students grow as writers, they begin to learn how to cite sources to support their ideas in research papers. The research paper is an expository essay that contains references to outside materials that legitimize claims made in the essay. Students learn to **paraphrase** supporting information, or briefly restate it in their own words, in order to avoid **plagiarism**, the intentional copying and credit-taking of another person's work. They also learn to include **citations** that name original sources of new information and are taught how to differentiate between primary sources, secondary sources, reliable sources, and unreliable sources.

Primary sources are original materials representative of an event, experience, place, or time period. They are direct or firsthand accounts in the form of text, image, record, sound, or item. **Secondary sources** inform about events, experiences, places, or time periods, but the information is provided by someone who was not directly involved and who used primary sources to discuss the material.

Reliable sources are trustworthy materials that come from experts in the field of study. These sources have **credibility** because they include extensive bibliographies listing the sources used to support the information provided. Some examples of reliable sources are published books, articles in credible magazines, and research studies provided by educational institutions. **Unreliable sources** are untrustworthy materials from a person or institution that does not have the educational background, expertise, or evidence of legitimate sources to support a claim. Some examples of unreliable sources are self-published materials, studies done to sell products, and opinion pieces.

SAMPLE QUESTIONS

5) Which of the following can be classified as persuasive writing?

   A. an advertisement for a new product
   B. a research paper on the effects of climate on ecosystems
   C. a poem about the ocean on a foggy day
   D. a short story with a suspenseful plot

   Answers:

   A. **Correct.** Persuasive writing aims to influence the reader to agree with what is stated and to act accordingly.
   B. Incorrect. A research paper is an example of expository writing and is often neutral in tone.
   C. Incorrect. A poem using sensory imagery is an example of descriptive writing.
   D. Incorrect. A short story with a plot arc is an example of narrative writing.

6) Which of the following is considered a reliable source for research about California?

   A. a personal blog about living in California
   B. a research paper published by the State of California
   C. an advertisement for California real estate
   D. a letter to the editor about California roadways

   Answers:

   A. Incorrect. A personal blog is an unreliable source for research on a broad topic.
   B. **Correct.** A published study by a government institution is a reliable research source.
   C. Incorrect. Advertisements present biased information and are therefore unreliable sources of information.
   D. Incorrect. Letters to the editors of newspapers typically include opinions, which are unreliable sources of information.

Language

Throughout elementary school, students are introduced to the conventions of Standard English grammar, usage, mechanics, and spelling as tools to facilitate communication and comprehension when writing, speaking, reading, and listening. They learn how to utilize the English language in both formal and informal contexts through exposure to conversational, academic, and content area language. In addition, they build vocabulary by learning how to use context and word structure to determine the meanings of unknown words and phrases. Elementary language arts teachers are responsible for implementing a curriculum and providing feedback that best help students develop and strengthen these language skills.

GRAMMAR

Grammar refers to how parts of speech work together in sentences and how words are grouped to make meaning such as in phrases or clauses. Students learn the functions of nouns, verbs, adjectives, adverbs, prepositions, pronouns, and articles. They also learn about subject-verb agreement, verb tense, and how to identify, construct, and use simple sentences, compound sentences, complex sentences, and compound-complex sentences. Knowing how to order words, select appropriate verbs, and vary sentence structure are significant factors in learning how to write proficiently in elementary school.

- **Simple sentence**: A simple sentence is the most basic type of sentence. It is short and contains a subject, a verb, and a completed thought. Simple sentences can also act as independent clauses in compound or complex sentences.

- **Compound sentence**: A compound sentence is made up of two independent clauses (or simple sentences) joined by a coordinating conjunction such as *for, and, nor, but, or, yet*, and *so*. A comma is used before the coordinating conjunction to separate the two clauses.

- **Complex sentence**: A complex sentence is made up of an independent clause and one or more dependent clauses, which cannot stand alone as simple sentences. Dependent clauses can be subordinate or relative. Subordinate clauses are preceded by subordinating conjunctions such as *because, if*, and *after*. Relative clauses are preceded by relative pronouns such as *who, which*, and *that*. If the dependent clause comes first in the sentence, it is separated from the independent clause by a comma. However, if the dependent clause comes *within* the independent clause, it may need to be set off with commas on either side if the information it contains is not essential to comprehension of the independent clause. If the information in the dependent clause is essential to understanding the independent clause, no commas are used.

- **Compound-complex sentence**: A compound-complex sentence has two or more independent clauses joined by coordinating conjunctions and one or more dependent clauses that begin with subordinating conjunctions.

Modifiers are words or phrases that change the meanings of or add details to other words or phrases in a sentence. They can cause problems when a reader is unable to understand a sentence's meaning because the modifier has not been used correctly. A **misplaced modifier** is one that causes confusion because it does not modify its intended word or phrase. This happens when the modifier is placed in the wrong part of a sentence. For example, in the sentence, "I rose from my seat after the sad movie I saw slowly," the modifier *slowly* is misplaced. Instead of modifying "rose," it modifies "saw," which makes it seem as though the writer watched the movie slowly instead of rising slowly after watching it. A **dangling modifier** is one that has no clear connection to any other part of a sentence. It can cause a sentence to mean something other than intended. For example, in the sentence, "After putting on my socks, the doorbell rang," the phrase "after putting on my socks" dangles because the subject it is supposed to modify (*I*) is missing. It ends up modifying "the doorbell" instead, which is nonsensical because a doorbell doesn't put on socks.

> **STUDY TIP**
>
> The word *FANBOYS* is a mnemonic device for remembering the following coordinating conjunctions: **F**or, **A**nd, **N**or, **B**ut, **O**r, **Y**et, **S**o.

Mechanics

Mechanics are the conventions of print that are not necessary in spoken language, such as punctuation, capitalization, and indentation. These conventions allow a reader to easily follow and understand what a writer is communicating. For example, the correct **punctuation** in a sentence (e.g., period, comma, question mark, exclamation mark) helps a reader know when to change pace or read with inflection. **Spelling** is a component of mechanics but is treated as a separate category in elementary school. In the earlier grades, it begins with the use of phonics to "invent" spellings in writing assignments and becomes more formalized as students move up through the grades.

> **DID YOU KNOW?**
>
> Emergent writers "invent" spellings by listening for the sounds they hear in a word and transferring those sounds to paper using written letters. The focus is more on creating writing than on using conventional spellings.

An understanding of **syntax**, or the grammatical formations and patterns of sentences, not only is a necessary concept for elementary students to master with respect to writing clearly and effectively but also is one that aids in reading comprehension. It can be utilized to determine the **literal** meanings, or most basic or exact meanings, of unknown words encountered while reading. It is a source of knowledge taught in elementary school that empowers students to decipher word meanings in **context**—to use the construction of sentences immediately surrounding a difficult word or phrase to determine its meaning. Another method elementary students learn for decoding unknown words in text is **structural analysis**, or an analysis of the roots and affixes of words.

Roots are the most basic forms of words and therefore form the basis of many new words. Affixes, in the form of prefixes or suffixes, are additions to a root word that change its meaning. Many roots and affixes derived from Greek and Latin are used fairly consistently throughout the English language and are responsible for a large percentage of its vocabulary. By learning a repertoire of roots, prefixes, and suffixes, students can analyze words they come across by deconstructing the parts in order to uncover meaning. For example, if a student knows that the Latin root *-port-* means "carry," he or she will know that words containing that root are related to "carry" in some way. By knowing that the prefix *trans-* means "across," the word *transport* can be determined to mean "carry across." By knowing that the prefix *ex-* means "out" and the suffix *-ation* means "process," the word *exportation* can be determined to mean "a carry out process." Roots and affixes are examples of *morphemes*, or the smallest units of language that contain meaning.

> **FOR REFERENCE**
>
> See Table 4.2 for a list of common roots and affixes.

USAGE

Usage refers to the agreed-upon rules for how language is used under certain conditions or within particular styles. It concerns itself with how English varies depending upon regional, historical, societal, and contextual factors. Such things as dialect, register, academic language, and conversational language fall under this category as does the study of how an author's **word choice** contributes to the **tone**, or attitude, of a text. Writers use and manipulate words to engender reactions in their readers that cross a whole range of human feeling: surprise, calm, joy, fear, anger, etc. As elementary students become familiar with concepts such as figurative language and connotation, they can comprehend not only the words used but also the unstated impressions writers include in text, or that which is "between the lines."

> **DID YOU KNOW?**
>
> The register for the field of medicine includes medical terms and particular ways of communicating information, such as "The hospital board has decided to explore an ambulatory model that supports outpatients and attendances at A&E."

Dialect is language that is particular to a geographical location or consolidated social group. Characters in novels may speak in dialect to give a story authenticity.

Nonregional, **register** refers to particular styles of language determined by purpose, audience, and social context. Registers include specialized vocabulary and specific language structures depending on the lexicon of a particular subset of people. Register can also be used to reference formal and informal language.

> **DID YOU KNOW?**
>
> Academic language is the language of school that students must internalize in order to achieve success in educational and professional institutions.

Academic language is language used in formal settings and academic writing. It includes professional standards, discipline-specific vocabulary, conventions of etiquette, and proper formats for specific types of presentations. In contrast, **conversational language** is familiar and informal, the language used with friends, to convey humor, and to communicate in nonacademic contexts.

Language also conveys general impression and meaning. **Figurative language** is constructed to convey images and ideas separate from the actual meanings of the words used. It includes several types of literary devices that add expression, sensory appeal, impact, and insight to text. A few of these devices are simile, metaphor, personification, onomatopoeia, hyperbole, and alliteration. On the other hand, **connotation** is the intended meaning of a word beyond its literal meaning, or detonation. It is a suggested response attached to a particular word selected by a writer. The connotations of words hold emotional or cultural associations that can contribute positive or negative tones to writing. For example, to cast an immature character in a positive light, a writer may describe the character as *childlike*, invoking a sensation of protectiveness or compassion in the reader. However, to cast that same character in a negative light, the writer may describe the character as *childish*, invoking a feeling of distaste or contempt in the reader.

SAMPLE QUESTIONS

7) Andre will study in the school library, while his brother auditions for the school play.

   What error has been made in the sentence above?

   A. The sentence is a run-on sentence.
   B. No comma is necessary.
   C. The dependent clause always comes first.
   D. The adverb phrases belong before the verbs.

   Answers:

   A. Incorrect. The sentence is a complex sentence with incorrect punctuation between the independent clause and the dependent clause.

B. **Correct.** When a dependent clause follows an independent clause in a complex sentence, a comma is not used before the subordinating conjunction.

C. Incorrect. A dependent clause can come before or after an independent clause in a complex sentence.

D. Incorrect. In this sentence, the adverb phrases work best by following the verbs they modify.

8) Read the sentence from *The Wonderful Wizard of Oz* by Frank Baum.

There now came a sharp whistling in the air from the south, and as they turned their eyes that way they saw ripples in the grass coming from that direction also.

How would the tone of the sentence change if *sharp* were replaced by *gentle*?

A. The tone of the sentence would remain about the same.

B. The tone of the sentence would become more negative.

C. The tone of the sentence would be indistinguishable.

D. The tone of the sentence would become more positive.

Answers:

A. Incorrect. The word *gentle* has a more positive connotation than *sharp*, so the tone of the sentence would change to one that is positive instead of negative.

B. Incorrect. The word *gentle* has a more positive connotation than *sharp*, so the tone of the sentence changes to suggest that the storm is more playful than sinister.

C. Incorrect. A writer's word choice always gives text a recognizable tone.

D. **Correct.** The use of *gentle* instead of *sharp* would change the tone of the sentence by making the storm seem less threatening and more playful.

Listening and Speaking

Listening and speaking are a child's first pathway to literacy. Children typically enter elementary school with an ability to orally communicate ideas, experiences, and concepts. The role of the elementary language arts teacher is to help students hone this skill set for academic and social growth. Students learn how to use strategies for listening and speaking that contribute to their abilities to listen carefully, think critically, differentiate relevant from irrelevant information, articulate clearly, and use appropriate vocal cues and word choice. Students are tasked with communicating for a variety of purposes, audiences, and contexts and have opportunities to engage in active listening during discussions of text, topics, and community.

Active listening is listening that is focused and empathetic. It is listening to authentically "hear" a perspective, feeling, or point of view. The following characteristics make up active listening:

- **Focusing**: Students practice keeping their attention on the person who is speaking.
- **Using positive nonverbal cues**: Students demonstrate interest by looking at the speaker and by using appropriate facial expressions and body language.
- **Allowing speaker to finish uninterrupted**: Students wait for a speaker to finish and concentrate on the message before formulating a response.
- **Not judging**: Students listen and respond with respect for the speaker's views and feelings. They agree or disagree using methods that maintain respect within the whole group.
- **Paraphrasing**: Students verify understanding by restating the speaker's main points concisely and in different words.

Students in elementary school also learn how to prepare and engage in small group and individual oral presentations. They learn the steps necessary to organize the information they want to present and techniques for presenting the information in ways that capture and maintain the attention of the audience. The following oral presentation skills provide an overview of what elementary school students need to know in order to effectively communicate with their audience:

- **Logical structure**: Ideas follow a logical line of reasoning.
- **Supporting evidence**: Information is supported by relevant evidence.
- **Word choice**: Only necessary and relevant words and sentences are included.
- **Collaboration**: Group presentations are creative, cohesive, and logical.
- **Eye contact**: Eyes are directed at the audience to the extent possible.
- **Articulation**: Enunciation is clear.
- **Volume**: Intonation is natural and neither too soft nor too loud.
- **Audience**: The style of presentation matches the needs of the audience.
- **Displays**: Visuals, props, and/or sounds that enhance presentation are used.

SAMPLE QUESTIONS

9) Which of the following quotes is a demonstration of active listening?
    A. "If I understand correctly, you think the classroom needs a pet."
    B. "I think you meant to say that you wish you had a pet at home."
    C. "You didn't talk about the kind of pet our classroom should have."
    D. "There's no way the principal will let us have a classroom pet."

Answers:

- **A. Correct.** This quote demonstrates active listening because the listener is paraphrasing the message to clarify understanding.
- B. Incorrect. This quote does not demonstrate active listening because the message is changed to what the listener thinks instead of remaining as the speaker intended.
- C. Incorrect. This quote does not demonstrate active listening because the listener changes the topic; furthermore, the listener speaks in a critical manner.
- D. Incorrect. This quote does not demonstrate active listening because the listener dismisses the message.

10) **Students have been placed in small groups to prepare reader's theater presentations that they will perform for each other. How might each group best meet the needs of its audience?**

- A. by reciting their lines in quiet voices during the performance
- B. by passing around a script to read from during the performance
- C. by using classroom materials as props during the performance
- D. by skipping some parts of the story during the performance

Answers:

- A. Incorrect. Reciting lines in quiet voices makes it difficult for an audience to hear important details.
- B. Incorrect. Reading from a shared script interrupts the flow of a performance and causes the audience to become restless.
- **C. Correct.** Props add interesting visuals to a performance and reinforce comprehension.
- D. Incorrect. Skipping some parts of a story is confusing to an audience.

Curriculum and Instruction

In elementary language arts, curriculum design and planning builds upon students' prior knowledge via logical progressions of lessons that increase content mastery in reading, writing, speaking, and listening. An in-depth understanding of diverse learning styles and developmental needs is necessary in order to best match students to tasks, materials, strategies, and resources that meet the needs of both the whole group and individuals within the group. Elementary language arts teachers are thus able to assess the learning behaviors and outcomes of their students and adapt curriculum accordingly.

Reading Foundational Skills

At the emergent literacy stage, students are provided with lessons and tasks that increase their understanding of how language works in order to facilitate their transition to reading and writing. Elementary language arts teachers understand that learning to read is a developmental process. Initially, students are provided with tasks and activities that build phonological awareness and print concepts.

Concepts of print are taught to familiarize students with the structures and purposes of books and other reading materials. Students learn that books have a front cover, a back cover, an author, and often an illustrator. They learn that letters, words, and sentences convey messages to readers about different topics, both real and imaginary. They gain an understanding of how books are read from top to bottom, left to right, one line after the next. Teachers demonstrate these concepts by reading a variety of texts aloud and displaying the texts of poems and songs on charts, allowing students to follow along as the teacher points to words as they are spoken. They model appropriate reading behaviors, which students practice by looking through books independently, both individually and in small groups. A selection of developmentally appropriate strategies that reinforce print concepts is presented on the following page.

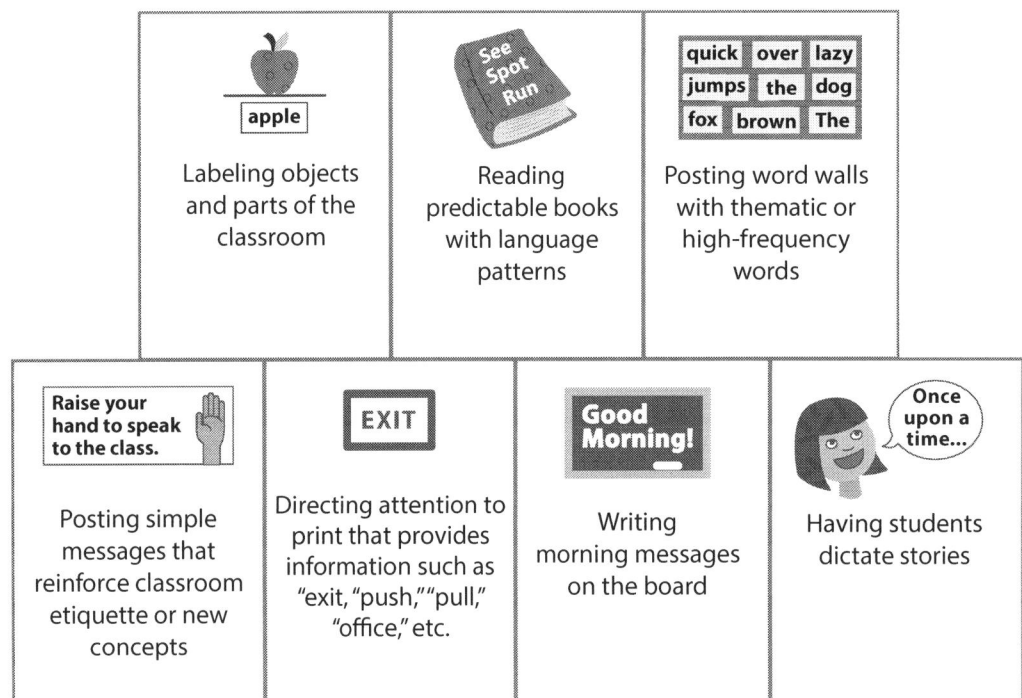

Figure 5.1. Concepts of Print Strategies

At the early literacy stage, teachers provide opportunities for students to internalize the link between oral and written language with exercises that reinforce phonological awareness. Such exercises also introduce students to the **alphabetic principle**, or the way that sounds and letters work together to create a decipherable

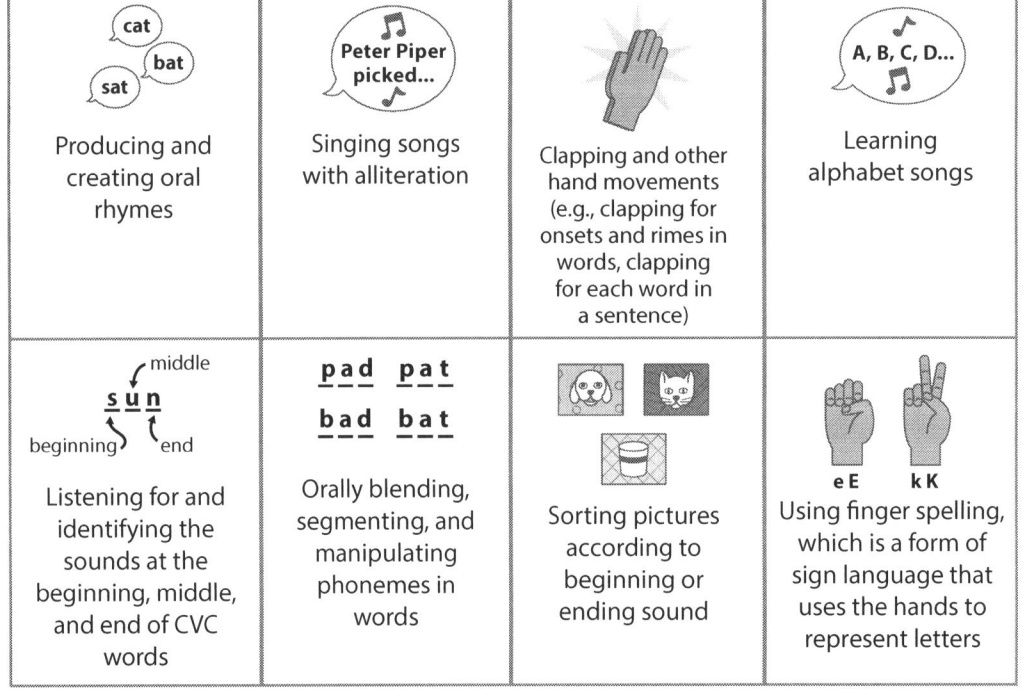

Figure 5.2. Phonological Awareness Strategies

code for giving and receiving messages. Teachers utilize rhyming books, books with repetitive text, engaging poems, play, and music to focus student attention on the sound units, or phonemes, that make up words. Please see Figure 5.2. for a selection of developmentally appropriate strategies; these reinforce phonological awareness and introduce the alphabetic principle.

Once students have a solid understanding of the link between the sounds in words and the letters that represent those sounds, they receive systematic instruction in phonics. Beginning with one-to-one letter-sound correspondences, teachers focus students on making connections between letter sounds and printed letters. This is followed by teaching techniques for **decoding** text (pronouncing written words based on knowledge of letter-sound relationships) such as word pattern recognition and blending and segmenting sounds in printed words. Initial lessons focus on sounding out and manipulating the letters in names, signs, and labels, and progress from there. Teachers complement phonics instruction with word study activities in order to establish a foundational reading vocabulary of recognizable words, including high-frequency words and sight words. Teachers use a variety of strategies and approaches to implement phonics and word study lessons, some of which are provided below.

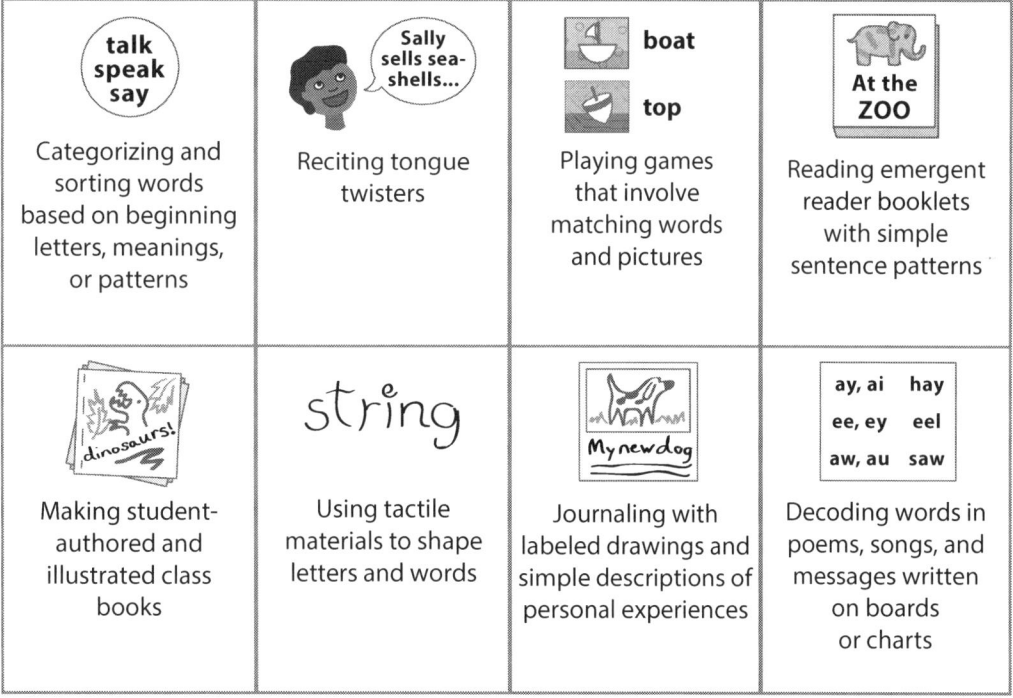

Figure 5.3. Phonics Strategies

Fluency, or the ability to automatically recognize words in print and recite them in a fluid, expressive manner, is critical to reading **comprehension**, or the ability to make meaning from text. For this reason, elementary language arts teachers model reading at an appropriate rate with accuracy and meaningful expression. In order to help students learn how reading with fluency sounds and feels, teachers engage in repeated readings of familiar picture books with patterns, rhymes, and engaging illustrations. They encourage students to read with them, or **choral read**, during the predictable parts of books or while following along in copies of the book, reciting each word in unison.

Guided reading is another technique teachers use to model the behaviors of readers who read for meaning. During guided reading, teachers pause during reading to ask questions about the words, pictures, characters, events, and information encountered in text in order to maximize understanding of content. Teachers may ask students to identify and pronounce words, make predictions, analyze character behaviors, use pictures as clues to meaning, and make inferences. Students should also practice restating information in their own words and make connections to themselves, other books, and the outside world. As students transition to independent readers, guided reading is used to monitor progress in small groups as students take turns reading aloud. **Repeated reading**, or reading the same section of text over and over until errors are eliminated, is used to increase fluency.

Another component of reading instruction that contributes to a strong reading foundation is an understanding of **morphology**, or how the forms and structures of words contribute to their meanings. One aspect of morphology pertains to the segmenting of words into affixes (prefixes and suffixes) and roots, which teaches students how word parts provide clues to the meanings of whole words and their functions in sentences. The attachment and detachment of affixes to roots changes, or morphs, word meanings and allows students to acquire collections of related vocabulary words that mean different things and interact in different ways with surrounding text. By participating in **word analysis** exercises, students learn how to break words apart into smaller units in order to ascertain their meanings and build vocabulary.

EXAMPLE QUESTIONS

1) Mr. Falls is reading aloud from a predictable picture book. He has written a refrain from the story on a sentence strip that is displayed on a pocket chart. Each time the refrain occurs in the story, Mr. Fall signals his students to read aloud with him as he points to each word. Which of the following is Mr. Falls demonstrating?

    A. decoding

    B. predicting

    C. concepts of print

    D. word analysis

    Answers:

    A. Incorrect. In decoding, Mr. Falls would model how to pronounce words using knowledge of letter-sound relationships.

B. Incorrect. To demonstrate predicting, Mr. Falls would pause to ask students what they think might happen next in the story's plot development.

C. **Correct.** By having students listen to predictable text and chant the refrain with him as he points to individual words, Mr. Falls is reinforcing concepts of print, clarifying that words and letters convey meaning, words are constructed of letters, and text is read from left to right.

D. Incorrect. Mr. Falls is not demonstrating word analysis because he is not asking students to break apart words into roots and affixes in order to determine the words' meanings.

2) Which of the following concepts involves understanding how the forms and structures of words contribute to their meanings?

   A. phonology
   B. mechanics
   C. paraphrasing
   D. morphology

   Answers:

   A. Incorrect. Phonology focuses on the relationships between the oral sounds that make up a language.

   B. Incorrect. Mechanics is concerned with the conventions of print, such as punctuation, that are used to provide pacing and expression cues in written text.

   C. Incorrect. Paraphrasing is the ability to restate a spoken or written message in one's own words.

   D. **Correct.** Morphology investigates how the forms and structures of words contribute to their meanings.

Reading Literature and Informational Text

A student becomes a reader when he or she is able to describe and analyze the content being read. Elementary language arts teachers **scaffold** reading comprehension strategies so that students can progress toward independent reading proficiency at developmentally appropriate levels with tasks that challenge without overwhelming. Teachers break reading tasks into manageable chunks and provide students with tools and strategies for mastering each chunk. Because students enter classrooms at a variety of reading levels, teachers must be able to assess a diverse set of reading needs and differentiate lessons accordingly for both struggling and advanced readers. The tools and strategies employed in an optimal reading comprehension curriculum provide pathways for students to **think critically** (actively and explicitly conceptualize, apply, analyze, synthesize, and/or evaluate information in order to form a conclusion) in order to interpret the purposes and meanings of written text across a variety of genres and styles. Exercises in reading comprehension take place before, during, and after reading.

Before reading, teachers have students make observations, connections, and predictions related to book titles, cover illustrations, text features, and background knowledge. They activate prior knowledge and pre-teach new vocabulary. To generate interest, teachers may choose **literature** (fiction and nonfiction in story form) and **informational text** (academic nonfiction) that relates to themes or topics that students are learning about in other subject areas. By connecting text to student experience, teachers can build on what is already known about a topic and increase understanding by challenging students to interpret new information.

During reading, teachers monitor understanding by pausing to ask questions about characters, setting, theme, figures of speech, vocabulary, main ideas, supporting details, points of view, plot development, and text organization. They also ask questions that require students to make inferences related to dialogue, behavior, word choice, and the author's intentions. In so doing, teachers model **thinking aloud**, or verbalizing thoughts and insights, so that students learn to pause and reflect during reading to maximize and facilitate comprehension. **Graphics**, such as maps, tables, photographs, and graphs, can be provided and analyzed to clarify difficult academic concepts, historical eras, or author motivations.

After reading, teachers provide opportunities for students to summarize text and **draw conclusions** about the author's message. Students participate in activities in which they consider new text in relation to other materials on the same topic (print and multimedia) in order to make **informed judgments** about personal, local, and global subjects and situations. Students are also provided opportunities to participate in creative and collaborative activities (e.g., writing, art, reader's theater, field trips, research, or debate) that reinforce comprehension and extend learning.

> **CONSIDER THIS**
>
> How would you scaffold an instructional unit on making inferences during reading?

Charts and graphic organizers are used as tools to support students as they draw meaning from content. **Graphic organizers** provide ways of organizing ideas and information in order to clarify thinking. Some of the main types of reading comprehension graphic organizers are listed below:

- **KWL Chart**: This is a three-column chart with the headings *K*, *W*, and *L*. The first column lists what students already *know* (K) about a topic, the second column lists what students *want* (W) to know about a topic, and the third column lists what students *learned* (L) from reading about the topic.

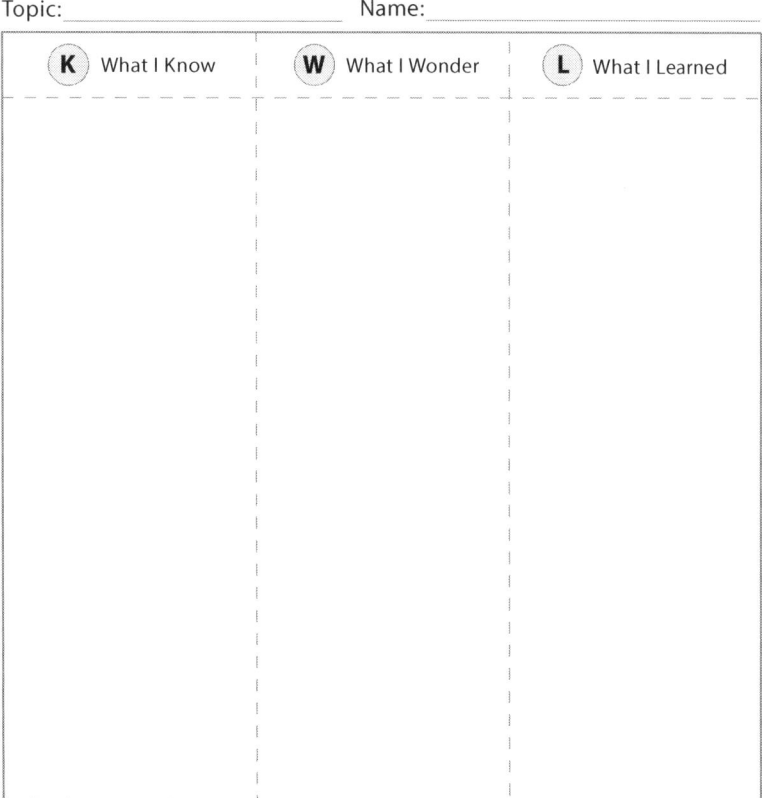

Figure 5.4. KWL Chart

- **Venn Diagram**: This is a diagram that is used to compare and contrast texts that treat similar stories or topics in different ways. For example, a teacher may read the same fairy tale told by two different authors. Students could then use Venn diagrams to organize the similarities and differences of the two stories.

- **Sequencing Chart**: This organizer is used by students to correctly order the events in a story or the steps in a procedure. Students either arrange picture cards or sentences, or draw pictures and write sentences.

- **Main Idea/Key Detail Chart**: This chart is an organizational aid for recording the main idea of an informational text and the key details that support the main idea. Prior to using the organizer, students learn how to search introductory and concluding paragraphs for main ideas and body paragraphs for supporting details.

- **Fact and Opinion Chart**: This organizer provides columns where students construct lists of facts and opinions encountered in text. Students learn that facts are truths proven with hard evidence, while opinions are thoughts or beliefs that are unproven. Students learn to look for numerical clues to determine facts and word clues such as *believe* and *should* to determine opinions. In later grades, student use their knowledge of facts and opinions to identify **reasoned judgments**, or points of view supported by reasons and evidence.

▸ **Problem and Solution Diagram**: This diagram is an organizational aid for recording the central problem in a story and the events that lead to its resolution.

▸ **Plot Pyramid**: This visual is an organizational aid for identifying the plot development in a story. With an understanding of the characteristics of exposition, rising action, climax, falling action, and resolution, students can delve deeper into an author's reasons for using particular events, dialogue, and literary devices to move a story forward.

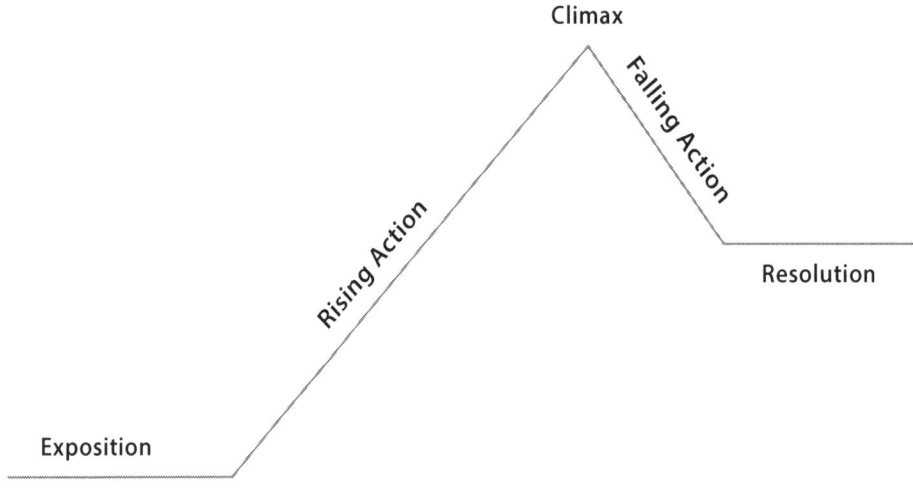

Figure 5.5. Plot Pyramid

▸ **Text Structure Chart**: This is a tool that prompts students to identify the relationships between ideas in a text and the signal words that reveal those relationships. Signal words provide clues to the structure an author is using to present information. For example, a sequencing text structure will include signal words such as *first*, *next*, and *last*; a cause-and-effect structure will include signal words and terms such as *consequently*, *as a result*, and *in order to*.

EXAMPLE QUESTIONS

3) Before students begin a new literature book, Ms. Bean introduces them to a list of vocabulary words from the book and has them work in groups to develop skits that demonstrate the meaning of each word. Which of the following is Ms. Bean demonstrating?

    A. thinking aloud
    B. scaffolding
    C. identification of signal words
    D. informed judgment

Answers:

- A. Incorrect. Thinking aloud is when a teacher verbalizes thoughts and insights to model pausing and reflecting during reading to maximize and facilitate comprehension.
- B. **Correct.** Ms. Bean is scaffolding instruction by pre-teaching difficult vocabulary so that meanings are easily accessed during reading. In this way, the teacher can focus student attention on another reading comprehension strategy (beyond vocabulary development) during reading.
- C. Incorrect. The identification of signal words is a reading comprehension strategy related to text structure.
- D. Incorrect. Students are prompted to make informed judgments on a topic after the topic has been thoroughly investigated via different materials and sources.

4) A teacher notices that a group of students who have just finished reading the same novel are having difficulty identifying how the story transitions from one stage to another. Which of the following is the best graphic organizer to help students understand the story's development?

- A. a plot pyramid
- B. a Venn diagram
- C. a main idea/key details chart
- D. a sequencing chart

Answers:

- A. **Correct.** A plot pyramid helps students identify and visualize how an author moves a story forward in clear stages with specific characteristics: exposition, rising action, climax, falling action, and resolution.
- B. Incorrect. A Venn diagram is used to organize the similarities and differences between two texts.
- C. Incorrect. Students would use a main idea/key details chart to identify the main idea of an informational text and the most significant details supporting that idea.
- D. Incorrect. A sequencing chart helps students order events in a story, but it does not task them with identifying how the events work together to move the story forward as elements of plot structure.

Writing

In elementary school, students learn how to write in a variety of genres (e.g., personal narrative, tall tales, correspondence, poetry, science fiction, short stories, essays, research papers) and styles (e.g., descriptive, narrative, expository, persuasive).

Teachers select writing tasks to correlate with content knowledge goals assigned to grade levels via district and state standards.

> **QUICK REVIEW**
>
> Can you develop a writing task appropriate for fourth-grade students?

In the earliest grades, elementary school students are provided with open-ended opportunities to develop as writers through both collaborative and independent writing activities such as lists, names, thematic vocabulary, pages for class books, individual books, journal entries, and responses to daily writing prompts. In addition, they practice forming letters using tactile and paper/pencil materials. Writer's workshops, in which students peer review, edit, and share writing, allow students to learn the writing process in small groups under a teacher's guidance.

As students move upward through the grades, writing assignments become more structured, and students learn the characteristics and conventions of writing using different forms, structures, and literary devices. As with reading comprehension, teachers use a number of strategies and tools to guide students as they work to attain writing proficiency. **Graphic organizers** provide ways for students to organize their ideas and clarify thinking at the beginning of the writing process. Some examples are listed below:

▸ **Concept Map**: Using boxes and/or circles and lines, students begin with a main idea and draw links to supporting ideas, adding additional links and cross-links as necessary.

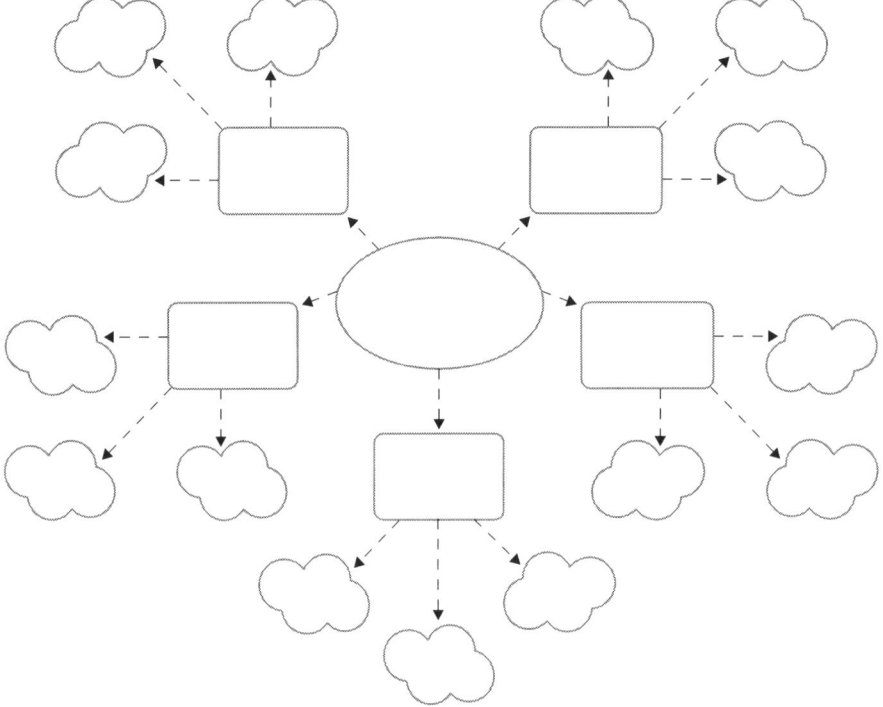

Figure 5.6. Concept Map

- **Story Map**: Students brainstorm story elements and plan out the plot development of a story.
- **Lists**: Students brainstorm writing topics, story ideas, sensory words, rhyming words, alliterative words, etc.
- **Outlines**: Students create and revise formal working outlines as guides to writing expository essays and research papers.
- **Sequence Maps**: Students draw or write events in the order they will occur in a text.
- **Beginning, Middle, and End Organizers**: Students plan the main structure of a writing piece by noting how it will begin (introduction), what is needed in the middle (body), and how it will end (conclusion).

Creative writing assignments provide opportunities for students to focus on concepts taught across the language arts curriculum. Reading and language concepts such as figurative language and word choice are naturally integrated into the writing process, as are literary elements such as character, setting, point of view, and plot.

In addition, **poetry** writing provides a wealth of opportunities for reinforcing concepts such as syllabification, spelling, vocabulary, parts of speech, and rhyming words. Some forms of poetry that may be accessible to students include the following:

- inquain: a five-line poem with a 2-4-6-8-2 syllable pattern
- haiku: a three-line poem with a 5-7-5 syllable pattern
- acrostic: a poem written for each letter in a word or phrase, reflecting its meaning
- diamante: a seven-line diamond-shaped poem requiring different parts of speech on each line
- quatrain: a four-line stanza with a rhyme scheme

Teaching students how to do **research** and prepare reports based on that research is a fundamental role of elementary language arts teachers. Beginning in the early grades, students learn how to use print and multimedia sources to find out information and develop presentations—visual, written, and spoken—to share what they learned. Students learn how to navigate text and digital features, formulate questions, locate information, evaluate sources for reliability, identify primary and secondary sources, take notes, and paraphrase to avoid plagiarism. The research process is approached in a series of clear, focused, and manageable steps over a specified duration.

EXAMPLE QUESTIONS

5) Ms. Jules has read and discussed several alliterative poems with her students. As a follow-up assignment, each student will write and illustrate an alliterative sentence for a class book. Which prewriting activity will best help students prepare for the assignment?

- A. drawing a concept map
- B. making a list of words
- C. developing a story map
- D. planning an outline

Answers:

- A. Incorrect. Concept maps are best used before writing work that includes a main idea and supporting ideas.
- **B. Correct.** A list of words that begin with the same letter can be used as a reference when writing an alliterative sentence.
- C. Incorrect. Plot development is not necessary for this writing assignment.
- D. Incorrect. An outline is too formal for this writing assignment. It would be used for more substantial research assignments.

6) A teacher has just provided students a general overview of a research project due at the end of the semester. Which of the following is most appropriate as a first task?

- A. to select a topic and locate some general information on the topic
- B. to develop an outline listing the main idea and supporting details
- C. to choose reliable primary and secondary resources
- D. to formulate an appropriate research question on a topic

Answers:

- **A. Correct.** The first step in any research project is to select a topic of interest and acquire background knowledge about it. Once general information on a topic is understood, a relevant question can be formulated.
- B. Incorrect. Prior to developing an outline, students need to select topics and formulate appropriate research questions.
- C. Incorrect. Resources should be selected after a topic has been selected and an appropriate research question has been formulated.
- D. Incorrect. Research questions are best formulated after a topic has been selected and background knowledge acquired. Having a general idea of the issues surrounding a topic makes it easier to narrow the focus of a research project and formulate a relevant research question.

Language

Within the contexts of reading comprehension and writing, elementary language arts teachers design instruction and select strategies and resources to develop students' understanding of Standard English conventions, vocabulary, and figurative language.

Editing checklists correlate to writing assignments; students use them to review and edit their work. These checklists include specific criteria for each assignment and bullet points such as *I used a capital at the beginning of each sentence, I fixed words that do not look right, Each sentence contains a noun and a verb,* and *I used punctuation at the end of each sentence.* Similarly, **peer editing checklists** are used by peers to edit classmates' writing. In a common three-part strategy, peers provide compliments, suggestions, and corrections.

In addition to checklists, visual aids can be used in instruction. **Word investigations** are graphic organizers used for in-depth word study. Students determine a word's definition, structural parts, part of speech, related words, and examples of the word used in context. Students may also use **figurative language graphic organizers** to find and interpret figurative language found in text. Students identify the type of figurative language used and use context to determine its meaning.

Finally, teachers can always resort to strategic **mini-lessons on common errors** which address common errors in English conventions that they may notice occurring with frequency among a large percentage of students.

EXAMPLE QUESTIONS

7) Which strategy would best help Mr. Green develop his students' reading vocabularies?

   A. having students peer edit each other's short stories
   B. conducting a mini-lesson on using a dictionary
   C. providing weekly opportunities for word investigations
   D. brainstorming a list of words in a particular category

Answers:

A. Incorrect. Peer editing is used during the revision stage of the writing process as a form of feedback before rewriting. Vocabulary development may occur, but it is not the focus of the task.

B. Incorrect. Learning how to use a dictionary is an important skill, but it does not necessarily increase vocabulary development over time in a systematic way.

C. Correct. Consistently providing opportunities for students to investigate words in-depth increases the probability that they will retain comprehension of the words over time.

D. Incorrect. Brainstorming a list of words in a particular category is a good prewriting strategy, but it is unlikely that it would significantly increase students' reading vocabularies because students are most likely suggesting words they already know.

8) While reading the first drafts from a writing assignment, Mrs. Hamm notices that her students have a poor grasp of the proper use of commas. Which strategy would best serve Mrs. Hamm's goal of improving her students' understanding of comma usage?

- A. peer editing
- B. a mini-lesson
- C. a word investigation
- D. rewriting

Answers:

- A. Incorrect. Peer editing is used during the revision stage of the writing process as a form of feedback before rewriting. However, if most students do not understand how to use commas correctly, they will not be able to edit for commas effectively.
- B. **Correct.** A mini-lesson on using commas correctly would best serve the needs of the group and fill in the gaps of missing information.
- C. Incorrect. A word investigation would not help students understand the conventions of comma usage.
- D. Incorrect. Providing a mini-lesson on the conventions of comma usage is the best strategy to ensure that students use commas correctly during the rewriting stage of the writing process.

Listening and Speaking

Elementary language arts teachers design curriculum to develop students' speaking and listening skills in conjunction with reading and writing skills. Specific strategies are used to develop proficiency in the areas of active listening, oral presentation, and the use of **multimedia** (combined mediums of expression) to support speech. As they do with other language arts skills that students are expected to acquire in elementary school, teachers chart the key elements of listening and speaking assignments and guide students through the process of preparing oral presentations in chunks or detailed steps. Across the duration of an oral presentation assignment, teachers cover the following material:

- **Delivery**: Posture, intonation, volume, eye contact, and expression
- **Organization**: A logical presentation structure with:
  - a brief, attention-grabbing hook that captures the audience's interest (e.g., an amusing thought, an interesting prop, an intriguing fact, or a thought-provoking statement).

- ▷ an introduction that states the topic and gives a brief overview of what will be covered.
- ▷ a body of evidence and/or details that correlate to and support the topic.
- ▷ a conclusion that summarizes the presentation's main points.

▸ **Audience Awareness**: Preparedness, appropriateness, and ability to hold audience attention

▸ **Visuals and/or Audio**: Supporting materials that reinforce content such as props, posters, digital media, photographs, music, etc.

Students are provided with opportunities to strengthen listening skills during classmates' oral presentations. They are tasked with providing **constructive feedback**—positively worded suggestions—derived from previously agreed-upon criteria for active listening: focus, respect, objectivity, and paraphrasing.

> **QUICK REVIEW**
>
> How would you design an oral presentation research project for first grade students?

EXAMPLE QUESTIONS

9) Mr. Couch has his students take turns doing show-and-tell presentations every Friday afternoon. Which of the following is a primary benefit of show-and-tell opportunities for students?

   A. Students make decisions about what to share.
   B. Students rest at the end of a busy week.
   C. Students practice speaking in front of an audience.
   D. Students are rewarded for doing their homework.

   Answers:

   A. Incorrect. While students do make decisions about what to share, this is secondary to the practice they receive speaking in front of an audience using proper delivery and audience awareness.

   B. Incorrect. While students may enjoy show-and-tell, it is still an academic practice when the teacher applies expectations for speaking in front of an audience and active listening.

   C. Correct. Opportunities for show-and-tell provide students with practice speaking in front of an audience. The audience members also receive practice exercising their active listening skills.

   D. Incorrect. Show-and-tell benefits students by giving them practice speaking in front of an audience, which is an important skill, as opposed to an appropriate reward.

10) Which strategy is most typically used to grab the audience's attention at the beginning of an oral presentation?

- A. eye contact
- B. a statement of topic
- C. a loud voice
- D. an engaging hook

Answers:

- A. Incorrect. Eye contact is a strategy for maintaining an audience's interest during an oral presentation, but it is not the most effective strategy for gaining the audience's attention.
- B. Incorrect. The introduction of an oral presentation must include a statement of topic, but it is best introduced by an engaging hook to gain the audience's attention.
- C. Incorrect. Using a loud voice is not the best strategy for grabbing an audience's attention because it could be received as unprofessional or ill-mannered.
- **D. Correct.** An engaging hook prior to the introduction of an oral presentation is typically used to grab the audience's attention.

Terms

academic language: language used in formal settings and academic writing

active listening: listening that is focused and empathetic

advanced fluency stage of language acquisition: learners demonstrate near-native ability and use complex, multiphrase and multiclause sentences to convey their ideas

affixes: added to words or roots to change their meanings; include prefixes (added to the beginning of a word or root) and suffixes (added to the end of a word or root)

analyzing text organization: analyzing how a text is organized in order to better comprehend an author's purpose for writing

audience: the reader/readers

central idea: the basic underlying idea of informational text

character analysis: understanding the role of a character in a story via the character's actions, traits, relationships, and personality

citations: identification of original sources of outside information

complex sentence: a sentence made up of an independent clause and one or more dependent clauses

compound sentence: a sentence made up of two independent clauses (or simple sentences)

compound-complex sentence: a sentence that has two or more independent clauses and one or more dependent clauses

connotation: the intended meaning of a word beyond its literal meaning

conversational language: familiar and informal language

credibility: proof of the reliability of a source

denotation: the literal meaning of a word

descriptive writing: a writing style that emphasizes the production of imagery using words and figurative language that appeal to the reader's five senses

dialect: language that is particular to a geographical location or consolidated social group

early production stage of language acquisition: learners produce single-word and two- to three-word phrases and can respond to questions and statements

expository writing: a writing style that explains an idea or concept or informs the reader about a topic

figurative language: language that conveys images and ideas separate from the actual meanings of the words used

first-person point of view: one character tells the story from his or her direct experience using pronouns such as *I*, *my*, *mine*, and *we*

fluency: the ability to read with ease and automaticity

genre: type of a text (e.g., poetry, drama, picture book, graphic novel, folktale, myth, fairy tale, tall tale, historical fiction, science fiction)

grammar: the way parts of speech work together in sentences and how words are grouped to make meaning such as in phrases or clauses

high frequency letter-sound correspondences: letter-sound correspondences that occur most often in the English language

identifying point of view: using genre and pronoun clues to identify who is telling a story to best form accurate conclusions about the events of the story

inferences: conclusions about what an author suggests in a text based on context clues

intermediate fluency stage of language acquisition: learners are able to speak in more complex sentences and catch and correct many of their errors

letter-sound correspondence: the relationship between the spoken sounds in words and the printed letters that correspond to those sounds

levels of language proficiency: L1) entering, L2) beginning, L3) developing, L4) expanding, and L5) bridging

literal: the most basic or exact meaning of a word

mechanics: the conventions of print that are not necessary in spoken language, such as punctuation, capitalization, and indentation (spelling is a component of mechanics but is treated as a separate category in elementary school)

meter: the basic rhythmic structure of the lines or verses in poetry

misplaced modifier: a modifier that causes confusion because it does not modify its intended word or phrase

modifiers: words or phrases that change the meanings of or add details to other words or phrases in a sentence

moral: the lesson the author intends to teach the reader in a literary text

morphemes: the smallest units of language that contain meaning

narrative poems: poems that tell stories

narrative writing: a writing style that tells a personal or fictional story that entertains the reader

onset: the beginning consonant or consonant blend of a syllable

paraphrasing: briefly restating information in one's own words

persuasive writing: a writing style that convinces, or persuades, a reader to subscribe to the author's opinion or point of view (often used for speeches and advertisements)

phoneme: each small unit of sound in a language

phoneme blending: combining phonemes to make a word

phoneme deletion: removing phonemes from words to make new words

phoneme segmentation: separating phonemes in words

phoneme substitution: replacing phonemes in words to make new words

phonemic awareness: a type of phonological awareness; an understanding of how phonemes form a language by creating differences in the meanings of words

phonics: the study of the relationship between the spoken sounds in words and the printed letters that correspond to those sounds

phonological awareness: an understanding of how sounds, syllables, words, and word parts can be orally manipulated to break apart words, make new words, and create rhymes

plagiarism: intentionally copying and taking credit for another person's work

plot development: the exposition, rising action, problem/climax, falling action, and resolution

preproduction stage of language acquisition: the silent period; learners refrain from speaking but will listen, may copy words down, and can respond to visual cues

primary sources: original materials representative of an event, experience, place, or time period

prosody: the range of vocal expressions a reader uses when reading aloud, including rhythm, intonation, and stress patterns

punctuation: periods, commas, question marks, exclamation marks, and other markings that divide text or help a reader know when to change pace or read with inflection

qualitative measures: contributors to text leveling that include analysis of text elements such as structure, language clarity, and knowledge demands

quantitative measures: contributors to text leveling that include readability scores determined by computer algorithms that evaluate text elements such as word frequency and sentence length

reader and task considerations: matching texts to particular students, classes, and/or tasks based on their inherent needs as determined by the professional judgment of educators

reading accuracy: the ability to recognize or decode words correctly

reading rate: the speed and fluidity with which a reader can read

register: particular styles of language determined by purpose, audience, and social context

reliable sources: trustworthy materials that come from experts in the field of study

rhyme scheme: rhyme pattern in a poem; may be represented as letters (e.g., *abab*, *aabb*, *aabba*)

rime: a syllable's vowel and its remaining consonants (not including the onset)

roots: the basis of many words in the English language, typically derived from Latin or Greek

second-person point of view: a narrative perspective from an external "you," whether that be the reader or unknown other

secondary sources: sources that inform about events, experiences, places, or time periods using primary sources but that were not directly involved in the event in any way

setting: where a story takes place

sight words: words that are repeated most often in text

silent period: the preproduction stage of language acquisition

simple sentence: a sentence that contains a subject, a verb, and a completed thought

speech emergence stage of language acquisition: learners can chunk simple words and phrases into sentences that may or may not be grammatically correct and can understand simple readings when reinforced by graphics or pictures

stages of language acquisition: preproduction, early production, speech emergence, intermediate fluency, and advanced fluency

structural analysis: an analysis of the roots and affixes of words

summarization: distilling and condensing a text into its main idea and key details by identifying story elements

syllables: phonological units composed of onsets and rimes that can be blended, substituted, segmented, and deleted like phonemes

syntax: the grammatical formations and patterns of sentences

text features: supplemental information outside of the main text such as chapter headings, titles, sidebars (boxes of explanatory or additional information set aside from main text) and hyperlinks

text leveling: complexity of text as determined by quantitative measures, qualitative measures, and reader and task considerations

text structure: organizational structures like cause and effect, problem and solution, sequence of events or steps-in-a-process, compare and contrast, and description

theme: the basic idea that the author wants to convey in a literary text

third-person limited omniscient point of view: a narrative perspective in which a detached narrator tells the story from one character's point of view, including that character's internal thoughts and feelings

third-person objective point of view: a narrative perspective in which a detached narrator relates the actions and dialogue of the story, but not the thoughts or feelings of any characters

third-person omniscient point of view: a narrative perspective in which a detached and all-knowing narrator tells the story from the point of view of all of the characters, including all of their thoughts and feelings

tone: the attitude of a text

unreliable sources: untrustworthy materials from a person or institution that does not have the educational background, expertise, or evidence of legitimate sources to support a claim

usage: common rules for how language is used under certain conditions or within particular styles

writing styles: specific types of writing that convey the author's purpose for writing—to explain, to entertain, to describe, or to persuade

Part III: Mathematics

Content Knowledge

Numbers and Operations

PLACE VALUE

While historically some civilizations have used other numbering systems, today most of the world uses the base-10 system. In the **base-10** system, each **digit** (the numeric symbols 0 – 9) in a number is worth 10 times as much as the number to the right of it.

Table 6.1 Place Value Chart

1,000,000	10^6	millions
100,000	10^5	hundred thousands
10,000	10^4	ten thousands
1,000	10^3	thousands
100	10^2	hundreds
10	10^1	tens
1	10^0	ones
.		decimal
$\frac{1}{10}$	10^{-1}	tenths
$\frac{1}{100}$	10^{-2}	hundredths

For example, in the number 321, each digit has a different value based on its location. This is called **place value**. Knowing the place value of each digit allows students to write a number in expanded form. **Expanded form** is breaking up a number by the value of each digit. For example, the expanded form of 321 is written as 300 + 20 + 1.

Figure 6.1. Expanded Form

Number Theory

A basic foundation in numeracy is vital for establishing the groundwork for understanding advanced mathematical concepts. Students begin working with **natural numbers**, which are used when counting (e.g., 1, 2, 3, etc.). Once a basic understanding of natural numbers is achieved, more advanced concepts, such as whole numbers and integers, can be introduced. **Whole numbers** are similar to natural numbers, except that whole numbers include 0. **Integers** are positive or negative whole numbers (not fractions or decimals).

> **QUICK REVIEW**
>
> What are some examples of concrete objects that could be used to teach numeracy in the classroom?

Rational numbers are numbers that can be made by dividing two integers. Rational numbers must be expressed as a terminating or a repeating decimal, such as 0.125 or $0.\overline{66}$. Pi (π) is not a rational number because it does not terminate or repeat (π = 3.14159265...); instead, pi goes on forever with no repeating pattern. Integers are rational numbers because they can be written as a fraction with a denominator of 1.

Every whole number (except 1) is either a prime number or a composite number. A **prime number** is a natural number greater than 1 which can only be divided evenly by 1 and itself. For example 7 is a prime number because it can only be divided by the numbers 1 and 7.

On the other hand, a **composite number** is a natural number greater than 1 which can be evenly divided by at least one other number besides 1 and itself. For example, 6 is a composite number because it can be divided by 1, 2, 3, and 6.

Composite numbers can be broken down into prime numbers using factor trees. For example, the number 54 is 2 × 27, and 27 is 3 × 9, and 9 is 3 × 3, as shown in the figure on the right.

Once the number has been broken down into its simplest form, the composite number can be expressed using exponents. An **exponent** shows how many times a number should be multiplied by itself. In the factor tree, the number 54 can be written as 2 × 3 × 3 × 3 or 2 × 3^3.

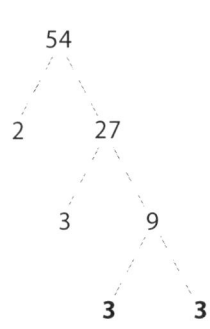

Figure 6.2. Factor Tree

OPERATIONS WITH WHOLE NUMBERS

Rational numbers can be used to perform mathematical operations. **Addition** is combining numbers, while **subtraction** requires finding the difference between numbers. **Multiplication** is the repeated addition of the same number to itself; in contrast, **division** is splitting a number into equal parts. Addition and subtraction are considered **inverse operations** because each operation cancels out the other operation. For example, 2 + 3 = 5 is true, and so is the inverse, 5 − 3 = 2. Multiplication and division are also inverse operations because 2 × 3 = 6, and the inverse, 6 ÷ 3 = 2, are both true. Knowing inverse operations allows students to check their answers.

In multiplication, the two numbers multiplied together are called **factors**. The answer is called the **product**. For example, in the operation 3 × 2 = 6 (3 added to itself 2 times), the numbers 3 and 2 are factors and the number 6 is the product.

Multiplication may be presented in a number of ways. One way to visually present a multiplication problem is with an **array**, such as the one shown below. In an array, each of the two factors is represented by the appropriate number of rows or columns, and the product will be the total number of boxes in the array.

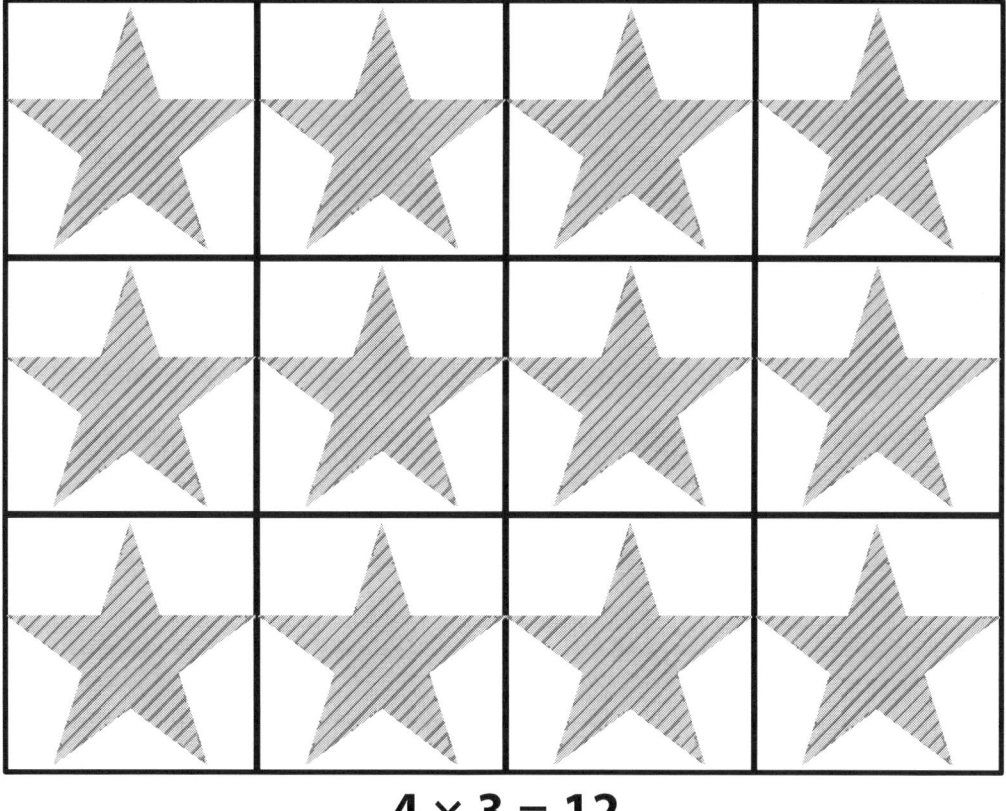

Figure 6.3. Array

Another way to represent multiplication is by using **area models** (also called the box method). Although this is a nontraditional approach to multiplication, it promotes the understanding of place value.

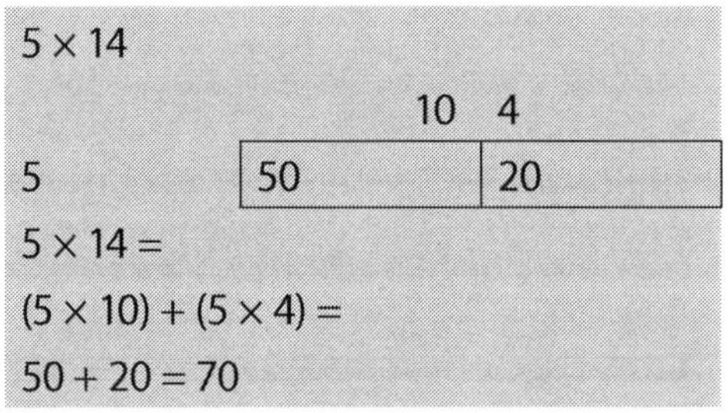

```
5 × 14
                    10   4
5            50          20
5 × 14 =
(5 × 10) + (5 × 4) =
50 + 20 = 70
```

Figure 6.4. Area Models

In division, the number that is being divided into groups is called the **dividend**. The number by which the number is divided is the **divisor**. The answer is called the **quotient**. For example, in the operation 12 ÷ 3 = 4, 12 is the dividend, 3 is the divisor, and 4 is the quotient.

Sometimes in a division problem, the dividend cannot be divided equally. The number that is left over when a number does not divide evenly into another number is called the **remainder**. For example, when twelve items are divided into five groups, each group will have two items in it, and there will be two items left over, meaning the remainder is 2.

In the figure below, 12 squares are divided into 5 different groups, each represented by a different color. There are 2 squares in each group (the quotient). Two squares are left, meaning there are not enough squares to put 3 squares in each group. Thus, the remainder is 2.

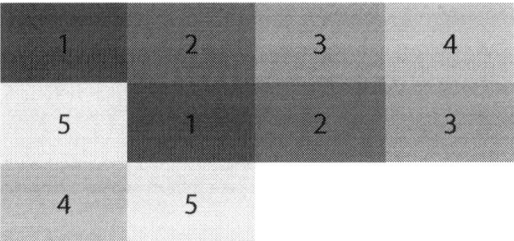

Figure 6.5. Remainder

An **algorithm** is a set of steps to follow when performing mathematical operations. Even the simplest of computations has an algorithm. As problems become more complicated, there are rules, or properties, that guide the problem solver.

Table 6.2. Mathematical Properties

Name	Description	Applies to	Example
commutative property	The order of the operation doesn't matter.	addition multiplication	$a + b = b + a$ $ab = ba$
associative property	Grouping of numbers doesn't matter.	addition multiplication	$(a + b) + c = a + (b + c)$ $(a \times b) \times c = a \times (b \times c)$
distributive property	Multiply a value by all the values inside brackets, then add.	multiplication	$a(b + c) = ab + ac$
identity property	Adding 0 or multiplying by 1 will not change the original value.	addition multiplication	$a + 0 = a$ $a \times 1 = a$
zero property	Multiplying any value by 0 yields a result of 0.	multiplication	$a \times 0 = 0$

When solving a multistep equation, the order of operations must be used to get the correct answer. Generally speaking, the problem should be worked in the following order: 1) parentheses and brackets; 2) exponents and square roots; 3) multiplication and division; 4) addition and subtraction. The acronym PEMDAS can be used to remember the order of operations.

Please **E**xcuse (**M**y **D**ear) (**A**unt **S**ally)

P – Parentheses

E – Exponents

M – Multiply

D – Divide

A – Add

S – Subtract

> **STUDY TIP**
>
> To multiply binomials, use FOIL: First – Outer – Inner – Last. For example, $(a + b)(c + d) = ac + ad + bc + bd$.

The steps "Multiply-Divide" and "Add-Subtract" go in order from left to right. In other words, divide before multiplying if the division problem is on the left. For example, the expression $(3^2 - 2)^2 + (4)5^3$ is simplified using the following steps:

1. Parentheses: Because the parentheses in this problem contain two operations (exponents and subtraction) use the order of operations within the parentheses. Exponents come before subtraction.

   $(3^2 - 2)^2 + (4)5^3 = (9 - 2)^2 + (4)5^3 = (7)^2 + (4)5^3$

2. Exponents:

   $(7)^2 + (4)5^3 = 49 + (4)125$

3. Multiplication and division:

   $49 + (4)125 = 49 + 500$

4. Addition and subtraction:

   $49 + 500 = 549$

OPERATIONS WITH FRACTIONS AND DECIMALS

Fractions use two numbers separated by a horizontal bar to show as parts of a whole. Fractions include a **numerator**, the number on top of a fraction, and a **denominator**, the bottom number of a fraction. The denominator is the "whole," and the numerator is the "part." For example, if there are twelve students on the chess team, and five of students are selected to represent the school in a tournament, the fraction of the chess team going to the tournament is $\frac{5}{12}$.

If the numerator of a fraction is 1, it is called a **unit fraction**. In the chess team example, $\frac{1}{12}$ is the unit fraction. Five $\frac{1}{12}$ units represent the part of the team that is going to the tournament. As the "whole" gets larger, one "part" becomes smaller and smaller. Think of cutting a cake: cutting 8 slices creates smaller slices than cutting the same cake into 4 slices. So, as the denominator of unit fractions increases, the value of the fraction itself decreases.

The same basic operations that can be performed with whole numbers can also be performed on fractions, with a few modifications. When adding and subtracting fractions, each fraction must have a **common denominator**. The operation is performed in the numerator, and the denominator remains the same. For example, if $\frac{3}{12}$ of the chess team described above is eliminated in the second round of the tournament, the total fraction of the team remaining will be $\frac{5}{12} - \frac{3}{12} = \frac{5-3}{12} = \frac{2}{12}$.

In $\frac{2}{12}$, both the numerator and the denominator are divisible by 2, meaning the fraction is not in its simplest form. To simplify the fraction, reduce the numerator and denominator by dividing both by the same value: $\frac{2}{12} = \frac{2 \div 2}{12 \div 2} = \frac{1}{6}$.

If the fractions to be added or subtracted do not have a common denominator, the least common multiple of the denominators must be found. In the operation $\frac{2}{3} - \frac{1}{2}$, the common denominator will be a multiple of both 3 and 2. Multiples are found by multiplying the denominator by whole numbers until a common multiple is found:

- multiples of 3 are **3** (3 × 1), **6** (3 × 2), **9** (3 × 3) …
- multiples of 2 are **2** (2 × 1), **4** (2 × 2), **6** (2 × 3) …

Since 6 is the smallest multiple of both 3 and 2, it is the least common multiple and can be used as the common denominator. Both the numerator and denominator of each fraction should be multiplied by the appropriate whole number: $\frac{2}{3}\left(\frac{2}{2}\right) - \frac{1}{2}\left(\frac{3}{3}\right) = \frac{4}{6} - \frac{3}{6} = \frac{1}{6}$.

When multiplying fractions, simply multiply each numerator together and each denominator together. To divide two fractions, invert the second fraction (swap the numerator and denominator) then multiply normally. Note that multiplying fractions creates a value smaller than either original value.

> **STUDY TIP**
>
> **SMURF** is an acronym for dividing fractions. It stands for **S**ame – **M**ultiply – **U**pside down – **R**ename – **F**raction.

- $\frac{5}{6} \times \frac{2}{3} = \frac{10}{18} = \frac{5}{9}$
- $\frac{5}{6} \div \frac{2}{3} = \frac{5}{6} \times \frac{3}{2} = \frac{15}{12} = \frac{5}{4}$

Another way to represent parts of a whole is by using decimals. A **decimal** is any real number in the base-10 system, but it often refers to numbers with digits to the right of the decimal point.

5	4	.	3	2
$5 \times 10^1 =$ $5 \times 10 =$ 50	$4 \times 10^0 =$ $4 \times 1 =$ 4		$3 \times 10^{-1} =$ $3 \times \frac{1}{10} =$ 0.3	$2 \times 10^{-2} =$ $2 \times \frac{1}{100} =$ 0.02
tens	ones	decimal	tenths	hundredths
\multicolumn{5}{c}{$50 + 4 + 0.3 + 0.02 = 54.32$}

Figure 6.6. Decimals and Place Value

Fractions can be converted to decimals by simply dividing the numerator by the denominator. To convert a decimal to a fraction, place the numbers to the right of the decimal over the appropriate base-10 power and simplify the fraction.

- $\frac{1}{2} = 1 \div 2 = 0.5$
- $0.375 = \frac{375}{1000} = \frac{3}{8}$

Proportional Relationships

Ratios compare two things. For example, if Jaimie has 6 pairs of jeans and 8 t-shirts, then the ratio of jeans to t-shirts is 6:8. Like fractions, ratios can be reduced when both values are multiples of the same number. For example, the ratio 6:8 can be reduced by dividing both parts by 2: 6:8 = 3:4. The value of the ratio doesn't change because a ratio only describes a relationship. Whether Jaimie has 3 jeans and 4 shirts; 6 jeans and 8 shirts; or 12 jeans and 16 shirts, the ratio remains the same. In other words, for every 3 pairs of jeans Jaimie has, she has 4 t-shirts.

Problems involving ratios can often be solved by setting up a proportion, which is an equation stating that two ratios are equal. For example, if Jaimie wants to buy 9 pairs of jeans and maintain the ratio described above, a proportion can be used to find the number of shirts she'll need to purchase: $\frac{jeans}{t\text{-}shirts} = \frac{3}{4} = \frac{9}{x}$.

The two fractions can then be **cross-multiplied** to give the equation $3x = 36$, and the variable isolated: $x = 12$ shirts.

Unit rates are the ratio of two measurements in which the second term is 1. For example, if Patrick earns \$240 in 12 hours, he earns \$20 in 1 hour: $\frac{dollars}{hours} = \frac{240}{12} = \frac{x}{1}$, so $x = \$20$.

Percentages are another way to represent parts of a whole. In a percentage, the whole is always 100: $\frac{part}{whole} = \frac{percent}{100}$

In the example above, Jaimie bought 9 jeans and 12 shirts, for a total of 21 items of clothing. To find the percentage of her purchase representing shirts, a proportion can be set up where the shirts are the "part" and the total number of items are the "whole": $\frac{9}{12} = \frac{x}{100}$. By cross-multiplying, the equation can be solved to give a percentage: 0.75. Note that when using this equation, the percent is given as a decimal value. To find the percent, simply multiply by 100: $0.75 \times 100 = 75\%$.

> **STUDY TIP**
>
> cross-multiplication:
> $\frac{a}{b} = \frac{c}{d} \rightarrow ad = bc$

Reasonableness

Since minor mistakes can lead to major errors, mathematicians need quick and easy ways to assess the **reasonableness**, or common sense, of their answers. **Rounding**, or simplifying a number to any predetermined place value, enables a student to make an estimation. An **estimation** is a close prediction that involves minor calculations.

When rounding to a specific place value, the number in that place is rounded up if the digit immediately to the right is 5 or higher, and it remains the same if the number is less than 5. For example, the operation 22×8 is difficult to do quickly. However, rounding 22 to 20 and 8 to 10 allows for a quick and easy calculation: 20×10. This estimate will provide a product close enough to check for reasonableness of exact calculations. Math that can be done in the student's head without the use of tools is called mental math.

SAMPLE QUESTIONS:

1) Which expression is equivalent to dividing 400 by 16?

   A. $2(200 - 8)$
   B. $(400 \div 4) \div 12$
   C. $(216 \div 8) + (184 \div 8)$
   D. $(216 \div 16) + (184 \div 16)$

   Answers:

   A. Incorrect. $400 \div 16 = 25$. Order of operations says to solve the parentheses first; $200 - 8 = 192$. Then, multiply by 2; $192 \times 2 = 384$.

   B. Incorrect. $400 \div 16 = 25$. Order of operations says to solve the parentheses first; $(400 \div 4) = 100$. Then, $100 \div 12 = 8.333…$

   C. Incorrect. $400 \div 16 = 25$. Order of operations says to solve the parentheses first; $(216 \div 8) + (184 \div 8) = 27 + 23 = 50$.

   D. **Correct.** $400 \div 16 = 25$. Order of operations says to solve the parentheses first; $(216 \div 16) + (184 \div 16) = 13.5 + 11.5 = 25$.

2) What number is equal to $(5^2 + 1)^2 + 3^3$?

   A. 703
   B. 694
   C. 30
   D. 53

   Answers:

   A. **Correct.** $(5^2 + 1)^2 + 3^3 = (25 + 1)^2 + 3^3 = (26)^2 + 3^3 = 676 + 27 = 703$.

   B. Incorrect. This answer is the result of incorrectly solving for the exponent 3^3. Remember that $3^3 = 3 \times 3 \times 3$.

   C. Incorrect. Here, the exponents were solved incorrectly. $5^2 = 5 \times 5 = 25$, $3^3 = 3 \times 3 \times 3 = 27$.

   D. Incorrect. This answer reflects failure to use order of operations; the parentheses must be solved first.

3) A vending machine contains 12 types of snacks: some snacks are salty and some snacks are sweet. The ratio of sweet snacks to salty snacks is 1:3. How many types of sweet snacks are in the vending machine?

   A. 1
   B. 3
   C. 4
   D. 12

Go on

Answers:

A. Incorrect. There is only 1 sweet snack if there are only 4 snacks in total. Since there are 3 times as many snacks, both sides of the ratio must be multiplied by 3.

B. **Correct.** If there are 12 snacks total, the numbers on both sides of the ratio = 12. If both sides of the ratio are multiplied by 3, the number of salty to sweet would be 3:9. 3 sweet snacks plus 9 salty snacks equals 12 snacks in all.

C. Incorrect. If there are 4 sweet snacks, there would be 3 times as many, or 12, salty snacks. That would be 16 snacks in all. The problem states that there are only 12 snacks.

D. Incorrect. There are 12 snacks in total.

Algebraic Thinking

ALGEBRAIC EXPRESSIONS AND EQUATIONS

Algebraic expressions contain numbers, variables, and at least one mathematical operation. Each group of numbers and variables in an expression is called a term (e.g., $3x$ or $16y$). A binomial is an algebraic expression with two terms (e.g., $3x + 16y$), a trinomial has three terms, and a polynomial has more than three terms. Algebraic expressions can be evaluated for a specific value by plugging that value into the expression and simplifying.

> **STUDY TIP**
>
> A formula is an equation that uses variables to represent patterns between numbers. For example, the formula for the distributive property is $a(b + c) = ab + ac$.

In an equation, two expressions are joined by an equal sign, which indicates that the two expressions are equal to each other. The two sides of an equation act like a balanced scale: operations can be performed on equations as long as the same operation is performed on both sides to maintain the balance.

This property can be used to solve the equation by performing operations that isolate the variable on one side. For example, the equation $4x + 12 = 2x + 48$ can be solved for x using the following steps:

1. Subtract 12 from both sides of the equation:

    $(4x + 12) - 12 = (2x + 48) - 12 \rightarrow 4x = 2x + 36$

2. Subtract $2x$ from both sides of the equation:

    $(4x) - 2x = (2x + 36) - 2x \rightarrow 2x = 36$

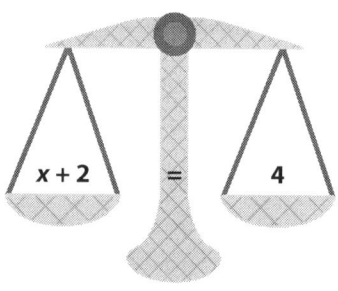

Figure 6.7. Equations

3. Divide both sides by 2:
$\frac{2x}{2} = \frac{36}{2} \rightarrow x = 18$

LINEAR EQUATIONS

Linear equations follow a specific pattern that results in a straight line when graphed. These equations have two variables, and the points on the graph can be determined using a function table. Functions demonstrate a relationship between input and output. The input is the independent variable, and the output is called the dependent variable because it depends on the input. Usually (but not always) x is the independent variable, and y is the dependent variable. The coordinates found in the function table can then be plotted on a set of axes to find the corresponding graph.

Table 6.3. Function Table

x	y	3x + y = 12
1	9	3(1) + y = 12 3 + y = 12 y = 9
2	6	3(2) + y = 12 6 + y = 12 y = 6
3	3	3(3) + y = 12 9 + y = 12 y = 3

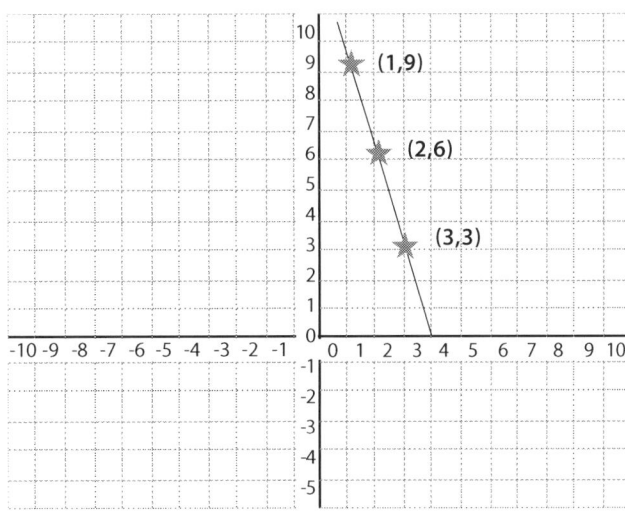

Figure 6.8. Dependent and Independent Variables

Inequalities

Inequalities are similar to equations, but both sides of the problem are not equal (≠). Inequalities may be represented as follows: greater than (>), greater than or equal to (≥), less than (<), or less than or equal to (≤).

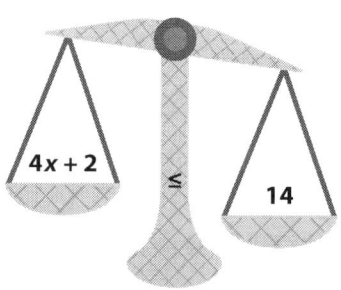

Figure 6.9 Inequality

Inequalities may be represented on a number line, as shown below. A circle is placed on the end point with a filled circle representing ≤ and ≥, and an empty circle representing < and >. An arrow is then drawn to show either all the values greater than or less than.

Inequalities can be solved by manipulating them much like equations. However, the solution to an inequality is a set of numbers, not a single value. For example, simplifying $4x + 2 \leq 14$ gives the inequality $x \leq 3$, meaning every number less than 3 would also be included in the set of correct answers.

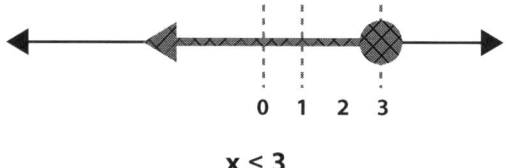

$x \leq 3$

Figure 6.10. Inequality Line Graph

SAMPLE QUESTIONS

4) Using the table, which equation demonstrates the linear relationship between x and y?

x	y
3	11
5	15
8	21

A. $y = 2x + 5$
B. $y = 5x + 5$
C. $y = 4x + 5$
D. $y = 3x + 5$

Answers:

A. **Correct.** $y = 2x + 5$ is a linear relationship because $11 = 2(3) + 5$. Substitute the *x* and *y* values into the equation.

B. Incorrect. $y = 5x + 5$ is not a linear equation because $11 \neq 5(3) + 5$.

C. Incorrect. $y = 4x + 5$ is not a linear equation because $11 \neq 4(3) + 5$.

D. Incorrect. $y = 3x + 5$ is not a linear equation because $11 \neq 3(3) + 5$.

5) If $x = 5$, what is the value of the algebraic expression $2x - x$?

A. 5
B. 10
C. 15
D. 20

Answers:

A. **Correct.** Substitute 5 for x; $2(5) - 5 = 10 - 5 = 5$.

B. Incorrect. Substitute 5 for x; $2(5) - 5 \neq 10$.

C. Incorrect. Substitute 5 for x; $2(5) - 5 \neq 15$.

D. Incorrect. Substitute 5 for x; $2(5) - 5 \neq 20$.

Geometry and Measurement

CLASSIFYING GEOMETRIC FIGURES

Geometric figures are shapes composed of points, lines, or planes. A **point** is simply a location in space; it does not have any dimensional properties like length, area, or volume. A collection of points that extend infinitely in both directions is a **line**, and one that extends infinitely in only one direction is a **ray**. A section of a line with a beginning and end point is a **line segment**. Lines, rays, and line segments are examples of **one-dimensional** objects because they can only be measured in one dimension (length).

Figure 6.11. One-Dimensional Object

Lines, rays, and line segments can intersect to create **angles**, which are measured in degrees or radians. Angles between 0 and 90 degrees are **acute**, and angles between 90 and 180 degrees are **obtuse**. An angle of exactly 90 degrees is a **right angle**, and two lines which form right angles are **perpendicular**. Lines that do not intersect are described as **parallel**.

line   ray

Figure 6.12. Lines and Angles

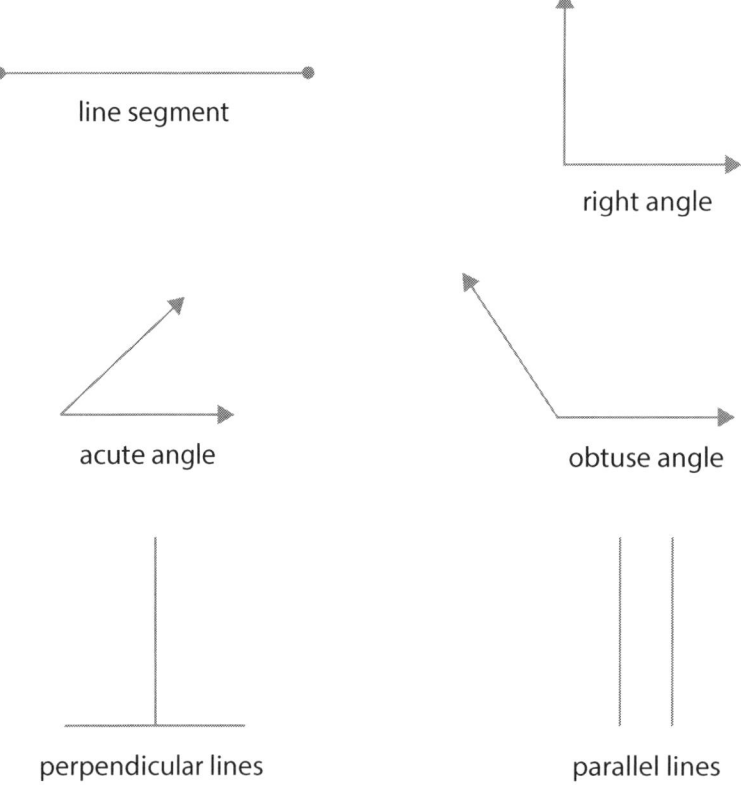

Figure 6.12. Lines and Angles (continued)

Two-dimensional objects can be measured in two dimensions (length and width). A **plane** is a two-dimensional object that extends infinitely in both dimensions. **Polygons** are two-dimensional shapes, such as triangles and squares, which have three or more straight sides. Regular polygons are polygons whose sides are all the same length.

Figure 6.13. Two-Dimensional Object

Figure 6.14. Polgygons

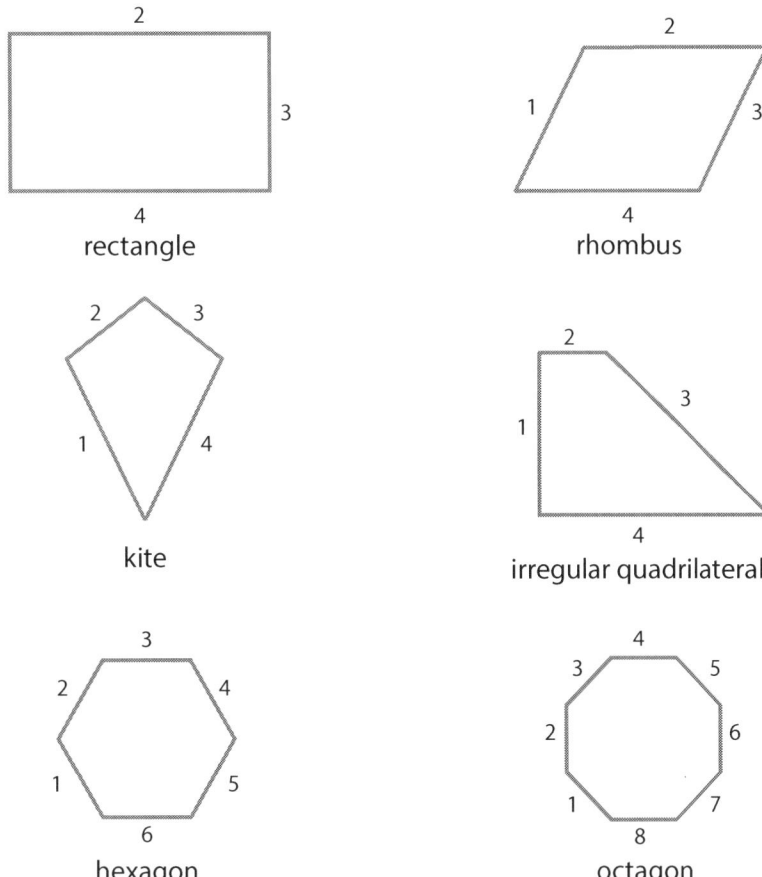

Figure 6.14. Polygons (continued)

Three-dimensional objects, such as cubes, can be measured in three dimensions (length, width, and height). Three-dimensional objects are also called **solids**, and the shape of a flattened solid is called a **net**.

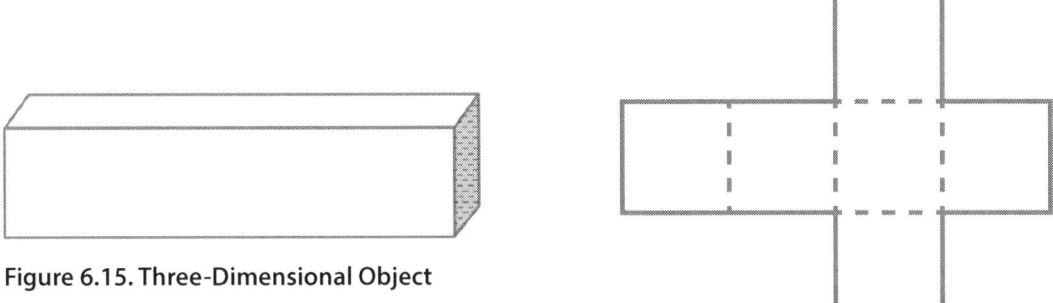

Figure 6.15. Three-Dimensional Object

Figure 6.16. Net

Go on

Solving Measurement Problems

The United States uses **customary units** of measure, such as inches or gallons. Metric units, like meters and grams, are the universal units of measure used in most of the world.

Table 6.4. Customary System

Length	Capacity and Weight
12 inches = 1 foot	2 tablespoons = 1 fluid ounce
36 inches = 1 yard	8 fluid ounces = 1 cup
3 feet = 1 yard	2 cups = 1 pint
5280 feet = 1 mile	2 pints = 1 quart
1760 yards = 1 mile	2 quarts = 1/2 gallon
	4 quarts = 1 gallon
	16 ounces = 1 pound
	2000 pounds = 1 ton
	4 cups = 1 quart
	16 cups = 1 gallon
	8 pints = 1 gallon

Table 6.5. Metric Units and Prefixes

Name	The Number	Prefix
billion	1,000,000,000	giga-
million	1,000,000	mega-
thousand	1000	kilo-
hundred	100	hecto-
ten	10	deca-
unit	1	
tenth	0.1	deci-
hundredth	0.01	centi-
thousandth	0.001	milli-
millionth	0.000 001	micro-
billionth	0.000 000 001	nano-

Prefixes affix to the following terms:

- meter (length); e.g., 10 centimeters would be 10 hundredths of a meter.
- gram (mass); e.g., 2 kilograms is 2000 grams of a substance.
- liter (volume); e.g., 1 deciliter is 1 tenth of a liter of a liquid.

The length, or distance from one point to another on an object, can be determined using a tape measure or a ruler. The size of the surface of a two-dimensional object is its area. The area of an object is its length times its width and is measured in square units. For example, if a cabinet is 3 feet long and 2 feet wide, its area would be 6 ft². The distance around a two-dimensional figure is its perimeter, which can be found by adding the lengths of all the sides.

Table 6.6. Area and Perimeter of Basic Shapes

Shape	Areas	Perimeter
Triangle	$A = \frac{1}{2}bh$	$A = s_1 + s_2 + s_3$
Square	$A = s^2$	$A = 4s$
Rectangle	$A = l \times w$	$A = 2l \times 2w$
Circle	$A = \pi r^2$	$A = 2\pi r$

For the rectangle below, the area would be 8 m² because 2 m × 4 m = 8 m². The perimeter of the rectangle would be 12 meters because the sum of the length of all sides is 2 m + 4 m + 2 m + 4 m = 12 m.

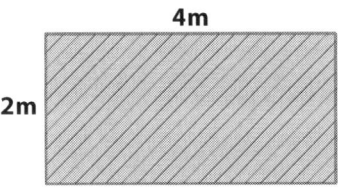

Figure 6.17. Fencing

The surface area of a three-dimensional object can be figured by adding the areas of all the sides. For example, the box below is 4 feet long, 3 feet wide, and 1 foot deep. The surface area is found by adding the areas of each face:

- top: 4 ft × 3 ft = 12 ft²
- bottom: 4 ft × 3 ft = 12 ft²
- front: 4 ft × 1 ft = 4 ft²
- back: 4 ft × 1 ft = 4 ft²
- right: 1 ft × 1 ft = 1 ft²
- left: 1 ft × 1 ft = 1 ft²

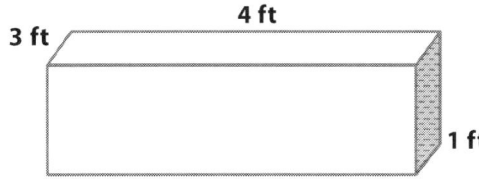

Figure 6.18. Surface Area

> **QUICK REVIEW**
>
> When would someone need to be able to calculate surface area of a three-dimensional object in the real world?

Volume is the amount of space that a three-dimensional object takes up. Volume is measured in cubic units (e.g., ft^3 or mm^3). The volume of a solid may be determined by multiplying length times width times height. In the rectangular prism below, the volume is $3 \text{ in} \times 1 \text{ in} \times 1 \text{ in} = 3 \text{ in}^3$.

The **mass** of an object is the amount of matter in the object. Mass is measured using a balance. Mass is different from weight because weight depends on the gravitational pull on the object, while mass stays the same whether on Earth, on the moon, or anywhere in the universe.

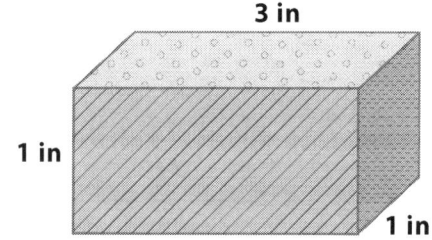

Figure 6.19. Volume

GRAPHING ON A COORDINATE PLANE

A coordinate plane is a plane containing the *x*- and *y*-axes. The *x*-axis is the horizontal line on a graph where $y = 0$. The *y*-axis is the vertical line on a graph where $x = 0$. The *x*- and *y*-axes intersect to create four quadrants. The first quadrant is in the upper right, and other quadrants are labeled counter-clockwise. Points, or locations, on the graph are written as ordered pairs, (*x*,*y*), with the point (0,0) called

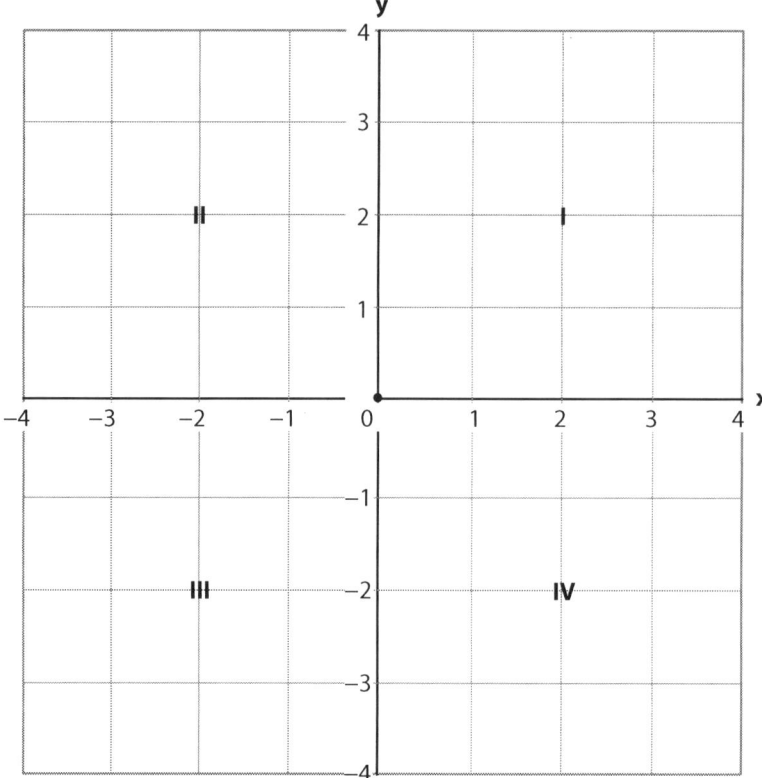

Figure 6.20. Four Quadrants

the origin. Points are plotted by counting over *x* places from the origin horizontally and *y* places from the origin vertically.

SAMPLE QUESTIONS

6) What is the perimeter of the regular polygon?

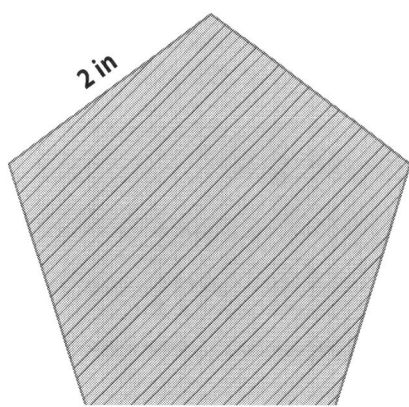

- A. 4 in
- B. 8 in
- C. 10 in
- D. 32 in

Answers:

- A. Incorrect. To find the perimeter, add the length of all sides.
- B. Incorrect. Add the length of all sides to find the perimeter.
- **C. Correct.** Adding the length of each side will determine the perimeter: 2 in + 2 in + 2 in + 2 in + 2 in = 10 in.
- D. Incorrect. This object only has 5 sides.

7) In which quadrant is the point (−5, 2) located in Figure 6.20 on the previous page?

- A. I
- B. II
- C. III
- D. IV

Answers:

- A. Incorrect. The negative five (−5) means that the point will be to the left of the origin.
- **B. Correct.** Starting at the origin, move 5 units to the left, and then up 2 units.

C. Incorrect. The positive two (2) means that the point will be above the origin.

D. Incorrect. The negative five (–5) and positive two (2) means that the point will be above and to the left of the origin.

Data, Statistics, and Probability

STATISTICS

Statistics is the study of data. Analyzing data requires using **measures of center** (mean, median, and mode) to identify trends or patterns.

The **mean** is the average; it is determined by adding all outcomes and then dividing by the total number of outcomes. For example, the average of the data set $\{16, 19, 19, 25, 27, 29, 75\}$ is equal to $\frac{16 + 19 + 19 + 25 + 27 + 29 + 75}{7} = \frac{210}{7} = 30$.

> **STUDY TIP**
>
> Mode is most common. Median is in the middle (like a median in the road). Mean is average.

The **median** is the number in the middle when the data set is arranged in order from least to greatest. For example, in the data set $\{16, 19, 19, 25, 27, 29, 75\}$, the median is 25. When a data set contains an even number of values, finding the median requires averaging the two middle values. In the data set $\{75, 80, 82, 100\}$, the two numbers in the middle are 80 and 82. Consequently, the median will be the average of these two values: $\frac{80 + 82}{2} = 81$.

Finally, the **mode** is the most frequent outcome in a data set. In the set $\{16, 19, 19, 25, 27, 29, 75\}$, the mode is 19 because it occurs twice, which is more than any of the other numbers. If several values appear an equal, and most frequent, number of times, both values are considered the mode.

Other useful indicators include range and outliers. The **range** is the difference between the highest and the lowest number in a data set. For example, the range of the set $\{16, 19, 19, 25, 27, 29, 75\}$ is $75 - 16 = 59$.

> **CONSIDER THIS**
>
> Why must teachers recognize the importance of outliers when looking at student data?

Outliers, or data points that are significantly different from other data points, should be noted as they can skew the central tendency. In the data set $\{16, 19, 19, 25, 27, 29, 75\}$, the value 75 is far outside the other values and raises the value of the mean. Without the outlier, the mean is much closer to the other data points.

▸ $\frac{16 + 19 + 19 + 25 + 27 + 29 + 75}{7} = \frac{210}{7} = 30$

▸ $\frac{16 + 19 + 19 + 25 + 27 + 29}{6} = \frac{135}{6} = 22.5$

Generally, the median is a better indicator of a central tendency if outliers are present to skew the mean.

Data Presentation

Data can be presented in a variety of ways. The most appropriate depends on the data being displayed. **Box plots** (also called box and whisker plots) show data using the median, range, and outliers of a data set. They provide a helpful visual guide, showing how data is distributed around the median. In the example below, 81 is the median and the range is 100 − 0, or 100.

Figure 6.21. Box Plots

Bar graphs use bars of different lengths to compare data. The independent variable on a bar graph is grouped into categories such as months, flavors, or locations, and the dependent variable will be a quantity. Thus, comparing the length of bars provides a visual guide to the relative amounts in each category. **Double bar graphs** show more than one data set on the same set of axes.

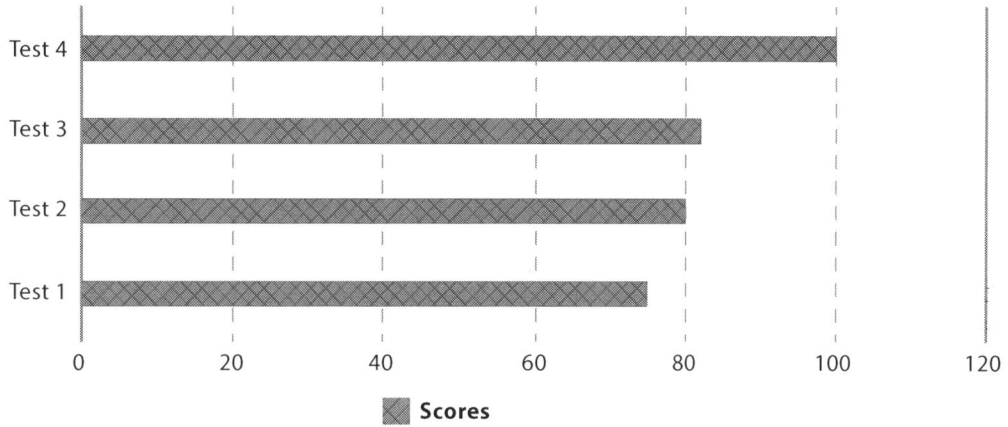

Figure 6.22. Bar Graph

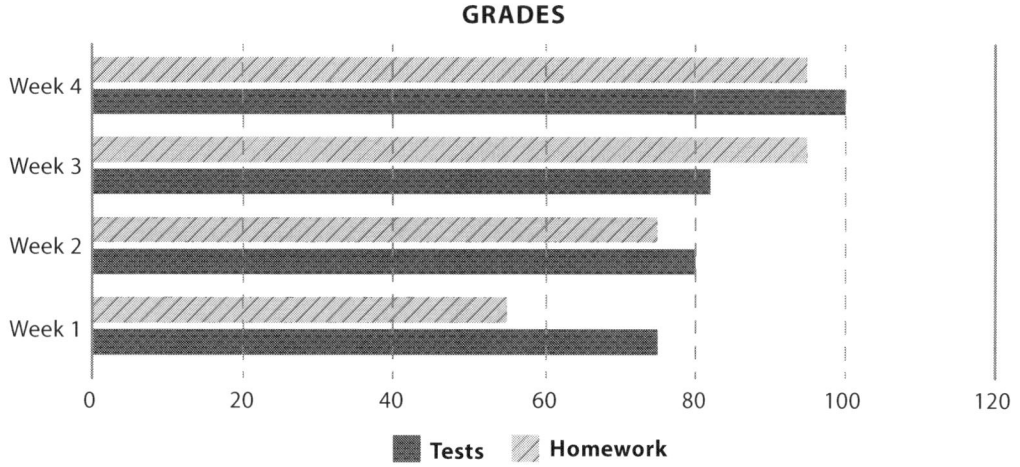

Figure 6.23. Double Bar Graph

Histograms similarly use bars to compare data, but the independent variable is a continuous variable that has been "binned" or divided into categories. For example, the time of day can be broken down into 8:00 a.m. to 12:00 p.m., 12:00 p.m. to 4:00 p.m., and so on. Usually (but not always), a gap is included between the bars of a bar graph but not a histogram.

Dot plots display the frequency of a value or event data graphically using dots, and thus can be used to observe the distribution of a data set. Typically, a value or category is listed on the *x*-axis, and the number of times that value appears in the data set is represented by a line of vertical dots. Dot plots make it easy to see which values occur most often.

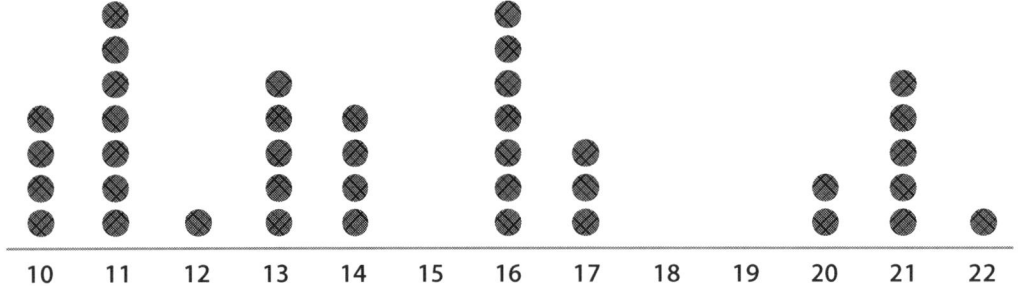

Figure 6.24. Dot Plot

Scatter plots use points to show relationships between two variables which can be plotted as coordinate points. One variable describes a position on the *x*-axis, and the other a point on the *y*-axis. Scatter plots can suggest relationships between variables. For example, both variables might increase, or one may increase when the other decreases.

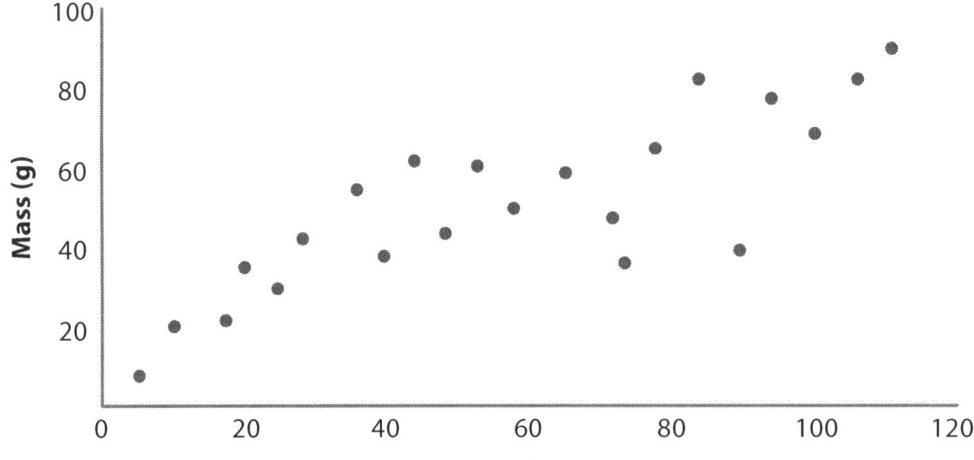

Figure 6.25. Scatter Plot

Line graphs show changes in data by connecting points on a scatter graph using a line. These graphs will often measure time on the *x*-axis and are used to show trends in the data, such as temperature changes over a day or school attendance throughout the year. Double line graphs present two sets of data on the same set of axes.

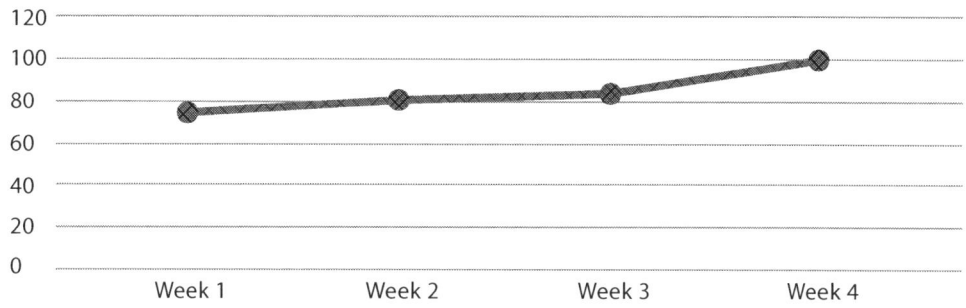

Figure 6.26. Line Graph

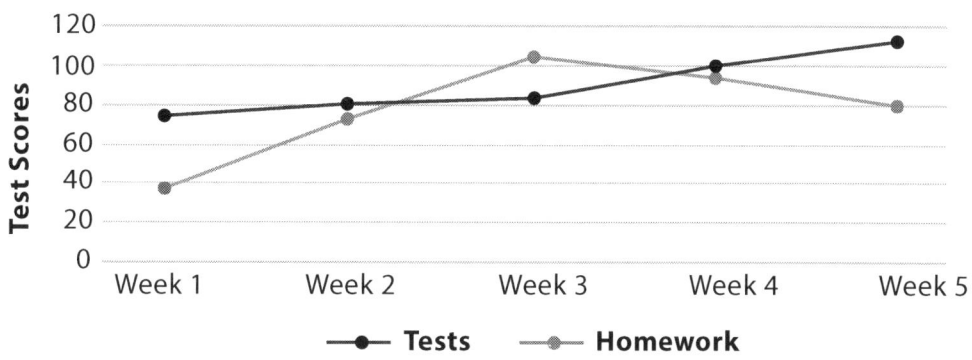

Figure 6.27. Double Line Graph

Circle graphs (also called pie charts) are used to show parts of a whole: the "pie" is the whole, and each "slice" represents a percentage or part of the whole.

Probability

Probability is the likelihood, or chance, that something will happen. Probability is expressed as a fraction with the numerator being the number of successful outcomes and the denominator being the total number of outcomes. For example, if there are 25 marbles in a bag and 4 marbles are red, the probability of randomly pulling a red marble out of the bag is $\frac{4}{25}$ (also written as 0.16 or 16%).

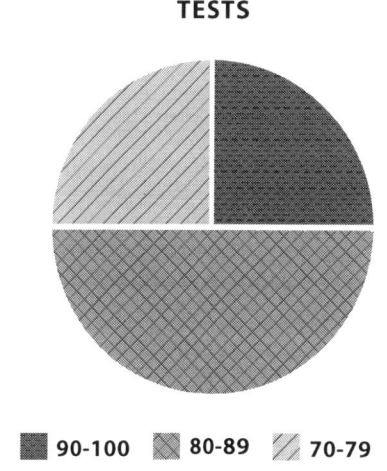

Figure 6.28. Circle Graph

SAMPLE QUESTION

8) Ken has 6 grades in English class. Each grade is worth 100 points. Ken has a 92% average in English. If Ken's first 5 grades are 90, 100, 95, 83, and 87, what did Ken make for the 6th grade?

- A. 80
- B. 92
- C. 97
- D. 100

Answers:

A. Incorrect. If Ken made an 80 on the 6th test, his average score would be 90 + 100 + 95 + 83 + 87 + 80 = 535; 535 ÷ 6 ≠ 92.

B. Incorrect. If Ken made a 92 on the 6th test, his average score would be 90 + 100 + 95 + 83 + 87 + 92 = 547; 547 ÷ 6 ≠ 92.

C. **Correct.** If Ken has 6 scores that average 92%, his total number of points earned is found by multiplying 92 × 6 = 552. To find how many points he scored on the 6th test, subtract the sum of the other scores from 552. 90 + 100 + 95 + 83 + 87 = 455; 552 − 455 = 97.

D. Incorrect. If Ken makes a 100 on the 6th test, his average score would be 90 + 100 + 95 + 83 + 87 + 100 = 555; 555 ÷ 6 ≠ 92.

Curriculum and Instruction

Elementary mathematics teachers should demonstrate an understanding of the Common Core State Standards and how they build upon each other throughout the elementary school years. Teachers should be familiar with best practices for teaching elementary school mathematics and implement them daily in the classroom.

Math lessons should be structured to provide students with whole group and small group lessons and activities based on students' needs, abilities, and developmental levels. **Whole group instruction** should consist of an introduction to the skill or concept and then include activities providing students with opportunities to practice that skill. **Small group instruction** should include activities that build on the whole group lesson. Instruction can be differentiated among the small groups to allow for remedial activities, on-level activities, and advanced activities to meet the needs of every student. While the teacher works with one small group of children, the other small groups should be playing games and completing activities on their own to develop and deepen their understanding of the content.

Elementary mathematics teachers should remember that children should be *doing* rather than *sitting* during math instruction. Students should be provided with activities and manipulatives and encouraged to develop their own strategies to solve problems. Mathematics teachers must offer students the opportunity to explain how they arrived at their answers and the reasoning behind their conclusions (the *how* and the *why*). Students learn a great deal from each other and so they must have the time to share their ideas.

> **TEACHING TIP**
>
> S-T-A-R is an acronym that helps students solve word problems. It stands for 1) Search the word problem. 2) Turn the words into an equation. 3) Answer. 4) Review.

With all mathematical concepts, instructions should be set up using **C-R-A order**. C-R-A stands for Concrete – Representational – Abstract. Abstract mathematical concepts use numeric representations and symbols rather than objects and pictures. When young students are learning about the number 3, the students should be able to count three objects, compare three items to other amounts of items, sort groups of three apart from other amounts, and order groups of more and less than three before moving on to similar activities with pictures. Finally introduce the numeral, or symbol: 3.

Numbers and Operations

Numeracy concepts provide children with the mathematical foundation they need so that they can use math in their everyday lives. Children must have a clear understanding of numeracy concepts before they can begin to understand and apply more difficult concepts such as place value, addition, and subtraction. Children must become familiar and comfortable with numbers, their roles, and their relationships. For example, they need to understand what the number 2 is, how to show that number using objects, and the role of the number 2 in other processes (such as describing quantities).

> **QUICK REVIEW**
>
> Why is it important for students to learn numeracy concepts?

The main key in teaching numeracy concepts is the use of **manipulatives**. Instruction should include a plethora of concrete activities using various manipulatives in order for children to gain a clear understanding of these concepts. Some examples of manipulatives that can be used include unifix cubes, Dienes blocks, beans, beads, popsicle sticks, coins, buttons, playing cards, sorting mats, number/coin stamps, dominoes, and five/ten frames (just to name a few).

Children need to engage in a variety of hands-on activities that allow the exploration of numbers. The objective of these activities is to make children comfortable with numbers, what they mean, and the role they play in the environment.

> **EXAMPLE QUESTIONS**
>
> 1) A kindergarten teacher puts students in pairs and gives each student a domino with dots on both ends. The teacher asks the students to count the number of dots and write the number on a whiteboard. The teacher then asks whose numbers are higher, whose are lower, and if any partners have equal numbers. The teacher is most likely helping the students understand
>
>   A. how to count the dots on a domino.
>   B. how to identify and compare numbers.
>   C. how to construct an addition sentence.
>   D. how to write numbers.

Answers:

- A. Incorrect. Counting the dots on the domino would have previously been assessed before teachers move on to this activity.
- **B. Correct.** The students will identify and write down the correct the number of dots. By discussing how many numbers of dots each student in the class has, the students are comparing numbers.
- C. Incorrect. Students at this early stage of learning are not yet ready to construct an addition sentence; they need more practice with numeracy concepts.
- D. Incorrect. Students will indeed get practice writing the numbers; however, this is not the objective of the activity. While it is good practice for students, number writing is not the main focus at this point in their development of numeracy concepts.

2) A first grade teacher provides students a part/part/whole mat and cubes. The teacher asks the students to find a way to make the number 7 using the cubes and mat. The teacher is most likely helping the students to understand

- A. the different number pairs that will equal the number 7.
- B. how to identify the number of items in a set.
- C. how to show conservation of numbers.
- D. how to compare numbers.

Answers:

- **A. Correct.** Students are using the cubes to find different ways to make the number 7. The different ways can be listed on chart paper as number pairs that equal 7.
- B. Incorrect. Students can subitize when they are able to quickly identify the number of items in a set without counting them.
- C. Incorrect. Students must master conservation of numbers before they begin breaking specific numbers down into parts.
- D. Incorrect. Students must master comparing numbers using the terms *greater*, *fewer*, *less*, and *more* before they begin breaking specific numbers into parts.

Algebraic Thinking

Algebraic concepts include patterning, identifying variables in equations, equivalency of numbers, and graphing. These concepts should be introduced to students gradually throughout their lower elementary school years. Teachers should use various manipulatives as described above to engage students in activities that will help them understand how to apply these concepts in the everyday world. Teaching these concepts early provides students with years of opportunities to understand these skills and practice using them.

Teachers can teach **patterns** with pattern blocks, buttons, shapes, and the daily calendar. Students learn to sort and classify according to the attributes of the item they are using, at which point they can then identify and make patterns. Using calendar pieces with different pictures also helps students strengthen their patterning skills. As students learn to recognize patterns using various manipulatives, they can then begin to make connections to the world around them. Students will notice that patterns are all around them: in nature, in poems, in songs, etc.

> **TEACHING TIP**
>
> Provide students with many opportunities to identify, extend, and create patterns using various manipulatives.

Teachers can use symbols such as the plus sign (+) and the minus sign (–) to teach **variables**. Using the plus and minus signs allows students to identify and describe a relationship between two quantities. Using the equal sign (=) allows students to understand **equivalency**, which means that quantities have the same value. Having students identify a missing number that will make one equation equivalent to another is a great way to help students strengthen this skill.

Graphing enables students to understand relationships between different groups of items. Asking questions such as "Which group has more candy?" or "How many more pieces of candy does one group have than another?" allows students to compare numbers and draw conclusions based on those numbers. Students can sort items such as jellybeans, shapes, or cereal and graph the results. Students can use the information in the graph to solve basic addition and subtraction sentences and make comparisons.

> **TEACHING TIP**
>
> Have students create **interactive math notebooks** to record the basic math skills and concepts being introduced throughout the year. These notebooks serve as a reference for the students and get them excited about what they are learning.

EXAMPLE QUESTIONS

3) A second grade teacher has given students manipulatives and whiteboards. The teacher writes the following equation on the board: 12 + 5 = 9 + ? and has students write and solve the problem. Which algebraic concept is the teacher assessing?

   A. patterning

   B. variables

   C. equivalency of numbers

   D. graphing

Answers:

A. Incorrect. The teacher has not assigned any identifying and sorting activities; students are not using shared attributes to create a repeating pattern in any way.

B. Incorrect. The students are not being asked to identify and describe the relationship between two quantities.

C. **Correct.** The students are being asked to find the number that will make a number sentence equivalent, or the same, as another number sentence.

D. Incorrect. The students are not being asked to identify and understand relationships between different groups of items.

4) When introducing equations to students, which step should Ms. Martin take first?

A. assign students to work with a partner to solve $3x + 5 = 20$ on whiteboards

B. assign students to work individually to solve $3x + 5 = 20$ on paper

C. assign students to work with a partner to draw a picture representing $3x + 5 = 20$

D. assign students to use mats and counters to demonstrate $3x + 5 = 20$

Answers:

A. Incorrect. Partner work is great, but this activity is abstract.

B. Incorrect. Solving problems is abstract and should come after the mathematical concept has been learned using concrete objects.

C. Incorrect. This lesson is a great way to incorporate partner work with representational materials, but begin teaching the concept with concrete objects.

D. **Correct.** Using concrete objects will help students obtain a conceptual understanding of the mathematical principles behind solving equations.

Geometry and Measurement

Geometry is the study of shapes and their properties and how the shapes relate to each other. Geometry is broken down into two categories: plane geometry and solid geometry. **Plane geometry** is the study of two dimensional, or flat, shapes that can be drawn on paper. Examples of plane geometry include lines, circles, triangles, squares, and rectangles. **Solid geometry** is the study of three-dimensional objects such as cubes, spheres, pyramids, cylinders, and prisms. Students should be engaged in hands-on activities using plane and solid shapes in order to develop a deep understanding of each shape, its attributes, and how these shapes are used in students' everyday environment. They should also be encouraged to use positional words such as *above, below, left, right*, etc. as they engage in shape activities.

> **CONSIDER THIS**
>
> How does creating simple patterns in kindergarten build a foundation for solving linear equations later?

Students must have a clear understanding of **plane shapes** before they can move on to working with three-dimensional shapes. Students should use attribute blocks and pattern blocks to begin their study of plane shapes. Sorting the shapes according to different attributes helps students gain a clear understanding of important terms, including *sides, edges, corners, vertices,* and *faces*; students will also learn that these terms can be interchanged because they have the same meaning. Teachers should construct a **plane shape anchor chart** identifying each shape, its number of sides, corners, and faces, and some real-world examples. Learning activities include identifying, naming, and describing the shapes; sorting shapes according to different attributes; comparing them by determining differences and similarities; examining symmetry; and creating pictures out of shapes.

> **QUICK REVIEW**
>
> Think of an activity to teach symmetry to second grade students.

Solid geometry further explores shapes and their properties. As with plane shapes, teachers should construct a **solid shape anchor chart** identifying each shape and its number of sides, corners, and faces; real world examples of each shape should be included as well. Students should engage in the same types of activities as used for learning about plane shapes. Other fun activities for students include stamping or tracing solid shapes to determine the face of each shape, sorting real-world examples of each shape into solid shape categories, using the attributes and properties of the shapes to create new shapes, and creating shapes using toothpicks and marshmallows. Students can construct these shapes digitally and print them out using a three-dimensional printer.

Measurement includes length, weight, capacity, and time. Before learning to use standard measurement tools such as rulers or scales, students should understand the basic concepts of measurement using nonstandard measurement tools like blocks, erasers, and even fingers. Basic concepts of measure, such as comparing lengths and weights, have more meaning to students when everyday objects are used. Once students have a basic understanding of measurement, conversions can be introduced using **nonstandard tools**. For example, measure the length of a desk using a thumb. Then measure the length of a desk using an unsharpened pencil. Will the student need more thumbs or more pencils to measure the desk? How many thumbs equal a pencil?

Discuss **vocabulary words** such as *measure, scale, balance, length, weight, capacity, short (–er, –est), long (–er, –est) more, less*, etc.; students will gain a clear understanding of these terms by engaging in various measurement activities. These activities include estimating and then determining the length of items such as pencils, crayons, scissors, books, desks, and even students themselves using standard and nonstandard units of measure and ordering objects from least to greatest and greatest to least. Students can also use scales and balances to weigh various objects and to explore relationships between different objects (which objects are heavier, lighter, heaviest, and lightest).

Students should identify basic vocabulary words such as *morning*, *afternoon*, *night*, *today*, *yesterday*, *tomorrow*, *minutes*, *hour*, *day*, *week*, *month*, and *year* when learning about **time**. Students should be able to compare two activities and determine which will take more or less time; understand and explore relationships between minutes, hours, days, months, and years; and tell time using analog and digital clocks. Students can identify activities and sort them according to the time of day when they occur and decide which activity will take more or less time by comparing them. They can also match digital and analog times to the correct clock and sequence activities and the times when they occur throughout the day. Materials that should be used for time activities include Judy clocks, paper clocks, pictures of analog and digital clocks and cards with times written on them, and picture cards of events throughout the day.

> **TEACHING TIP**
>
> Teachers should make sure anchor charts are easily accessible to students so they can have a point of reference during various activities.

EXAMPLE QUESTIONS

5) A kindergarten teacher gives students picture cards of various activities carried out throughout the day; she then asks the students to sort the pictures into groups and explain their reasoning. The teacher is most likely trying to assess

   A. whether the students can determine which activities will take more and less time during the day.

   B. whether the students can match digital time cards to each picture card.

   C. whether the students can match each picture card to an analog time card.

   D. whether the students can identify which activities are done during each time of the day (morning, afternoon, night).

   Answers:

   A. Incorrect. The students were not asked to determine which activities would take more or less time.

   B. Incorrect. The students were only given picture cards of activities; they do not have digital time cards.

   C. Incorrect. The students were not given analog time cards, so they cannot match the picture cards to them.

D. **Correct.** The students will sort the picture cards into morning, afternoon, and night groups; then they will explain why each card belongs in its group.

6) Which of the following could be used as an informal assessment for determining a student's understanding of solid shapes?

   A. a worksheet where students color each shape in a different color
   B. a teacher's observations and notes about each student during geometry work stations
   C. a multiple-choice test
   D. a group project about solid shapes

   Answers:
   A. Incorrect. A coloring worksheet permits students to practice shape identification but does not allow students to demonstrate a clear understanding of each shape and its attributes.
   B. **Correct.** Teacher observations would be a valuable informal assessment in a classroom where students discuss shapes and their attributes during hands-on activities, and use reasoning skills when explaining their creations.
   C. Incorrect. A multiple-choice test is a summative assessment that would assess student knowledge in comparison to the objectives of the geometry unit.
   D. Incorrect. A group project is a summative assessment that is usually used at the end of a unit to assess what students have learned.

Data, Statistics, and Probability

When teaching data and statistics in the elementary grades, teachers guide students through a four-step process: asking a question, collecting the data, analyzing the data, and interpreting the results. Teachers pose a question to the class such as "What's your favorite pizza topping?" or "What's your favorite color?" and have the students gather data from each other. The students can tally the answers to their question and then analyze class data by making a graph. Bar and picture graphs are most commonly used in the lower elementary grades.

Once the data has been recorded on a graph, students can make comparisons and draw conclusions from the information. Students in the upper elementary grades may conduct surveys or experiments, make observations, and record the data. They often use line graphs, bar graphs, and point plots to record, analyze, and interpret data in the upper elementary grades. A comparison of two or more sets of data is an extension of the skills students have already learned. They can create and analyze their own sets of data or use prerecorded data. These activities will prepare students for middle school work in statistics and probability.

Examples of opportunities for data collection in a classroom include:
- weather
- attendance
- lunch count
- grades (remember to maintain individual student confidentiality)
- outside reading (How many books have you read? How many pages long are they?)
- favorite recess activity

Teaching students about probability—the chance that an event may occur—should again involve hands-on activities and vocabulary development. A fun activity involves using different colored unifix cubes. Teachers pose a question such as "What are the chances of pulling a certain colored cube out of a bag?" The students can make predictions and talk about the chances of pulling out various colors. They pull a cube out of the bag a specific number of times and graph the results. After the results are graphed, students can interpret the data on the graph and see if their predictions were correct. Incorporating vocabulary words such as *probably*, *likely*, and *unlikely* into probability lessons and games will help students gain an understanding of these terms and allow them to make connections to real-world situations.

> **TEACHING TIP**
>
> Create an activity that will introduce students to probability.

EXAMPLE QUESTIONS

7) The students in Mrs. Mathis' class want to know the probability of pulling a yellow ball out of a jar that contains fifty balls. What information do the students need to know to find the answer?

   A. How many yellow balls are in the jar?
   B. How many different colors of balls are in the jar?
   C. How many purple balls are in the jar?
   D. How much do the balls cost?

   Answers:

   A. **Correct.** The students need to know how many of the fifty balls in the jar are yellow.
   B. Incorrect. It does not matter how many different colors of balls there are, only how many are yellow.
   C. Incorrect. This is extraneous information.
   D. Incorrect. The cost of the balls is irrelevant.

8) The students in Mr. Burd's class want to know if attendance affects math test scores. What information do the students need to know?

   A. What is the mean attendance rate?
   B. What did Daryl make on the math test?
   C. How many times has Kerry been absent?
   D. Who made the lowest grade on the math test?

Answers:

A. Correct. The students need to know the average attendance rate (and the average math score) for each attendance group.

B. Incorrect. When looking for trends, students must examine data reflecting the group of students, not individuals. Furthermore, obtaining information about individual scores is a breach in confidentiality.

C. Incorrect. This is also a breach in confidentiality and not relevant to the group.

D. Incorrect. This is another example of an irrelevant breach of confidentiality.

Terms

addition: the process of combining two or more numbers

algebraic expressions: contain numbers, variables, and a mathematical operation

algorithms: a set of steps to follow when solving a problem

angles: a shape formed by two rays that share a common point

area: the size of a surface measured in square units

area models (also called the box method): a nontraditional approach to multiplication that promotes understanding of place value

arrays: a pictorial representation of a multiplication problem

associative property: in multiplication and addition, the way numbers are grouped in parentheses does not matter, $(a + b) + c = a + (b + c)$

bar graphs: a graph that uses lengths of rectangles to show data

base-10: the numbering system where each digit is worth 10 times as much as the digit to the right of it

binomials: an algebraic expression with two different variables

box plots (also called box and whisker plots): data is shown using the median and range of a data set

circle graphs: a pie chart where each "piece" demonstrates a quantity

commutative property: in multiplication and addition, the order of the numbers on each side of the equation does not matter: $ab = ba$

composite numbers: a natural number greater than 1 that can be divided by at least one other number besides 1 and itself

coordinate plane: the plane containing the x-axis and y-axis

customary units: units of measure used in the United States

decimals: any real number in the base-10 system, but often refers to numbers with digits to the right of the decimal point

denominator: the number on the bottom of a fraction

dependent variables: variables whose value depends on other variables

digits: any number 0 – 9

distributive property: multiplication distributes over addition: $a(b + c) = ab + ac$

dividends: a number that is being divided by another number

division: splitting a number into equal parts

divisors: the number by which another number is divided

dot plots: a graphical display of data using dots

double bar graphs: bar graphs that present more than one type of data

double line graphs: a line graph that presents more than one type of data

equations: algebraic expressions that use an equal sign

estimation: a close prediction that involves minor calculations

expanded form: breaking up a number by the value of each digit

exponents: the number written to the upper right of another number that indicates how many times that number should be multiplied by itself

factors: numbers that are multiplied with each other

figures: geometric forms made up of points, lines, or planes

formulas: mathematical relationships expressed in symbols

fraction: a part of a whole

functions: a relationship between input and output

histograms: bar graph showing continuous data over time

inequalities: two mathematical quantities that are not equal to each other

independent variables: values that determine the value of other variables

integers: positive or negative whole numbers that are not fractions or decimals

inverse operations: an operation that reverses another operation

length: the measurement of something from end to end

linear equations: an equation that results in a straight line when graphed

line graphs: a graph that uses points connected by lines to show data

line segments: a part of a line that connects two points

lines: a one-dimensional geometric shape that is infinitely long

mass: the amount of matter in an object

mean: the average

measures of center: include mean, median, and mode

median: the number in the middle when the data set is arranged from least to greatest

mental math: math that can be done in the student's head without the use of tools

metric units: the universal units of measure

mode: the most frequent

models: a mathematical representation of the real world

multiples: the product of two whole numbers

multiplication: repeated addition of the same number to itself

natural numbers: numbers used when counting; do not include 0, fractions, or decimals

nets: the shape of a flattened three-dimensional object

numerator: the number on top of a fraction

one-dimensional: having only length

order of operations: work the problem in the order: 1) parentheses and brackets; 2) exponents and square roots; 3) multiplication and division; 4) addition and subtraction

ordered pairs: two numbers written to show the position of a point in a coordinate plane

origin: the point (0,0) on a graph

outlier: a data point that is vastly different from the other data points

parallel lines: lines that remain the same distance apart over their entire length and never cross

percentages: a part of a whole conveyed per 100

perimeter: distance around a two-dimensional shape

perpendicular lines: lines that cross at a 90 degree angle

place value: the value of the location of a digit within a number

points: location in a coordinate plane

polygons: two-dimensional shapes that have three or more straight sides

prime numbers: a natural number greater than 1 that can only be divided by 1 and itself

probability: the likelihood that something will happen

product: the result of multiplying two or more numbers

quadrants: the four areas created by the intersection of the x-axis and the y-axis

quotient: the result of dividing one number into another

range: the difference between the highest number and the lowest number in a data set

ratios: a comparison of two things

rational numbers: a number that can be made by dividing two integers; incudes fractions and terminating or repeating decimals

rays: a shape that starts at one point and goes infinitely in one direction

reasonableness: making common sense

remainder: the number that is left over when one number does not divide evenly into another

rounding: simplifying a number to any given place value

scatterplots: a graph of plotted points that compares two data sets

solids: three-dimensional objects

statistics: the study of data

subtraction: finding the difference between two numbers

surface area: the sum of the areas of all sides of a three-dimensional object

tessellations: creating patterns through the tiling of polygons

three-dimensional: having length, width, and height

trends: two sets of data that show a pattern

two-dimensional: having length and width

unit fractions: a fraction where the numerator is 1

unit rates: the ratio of two measurements in which the second term is 1

volume: the amount of space that an object occupies as measured in cubic units

whole numbers: counting numbers, including 0, that are not fractions or decimals

x-axis: horizontal position on a graph where $y = 0$

y-axis: vertical position on a graph where $x = 0$

Part IV: Social Studies

Content Knowledge

The social studies portion of the elementary education test covers content aligned with state and national standards. Questions focus on concepts appropriate to elementary-level anthropology, sociology, economics, geography, world history, United States history, United States government, civics, and social studies skills and processes. Not only do teachers need to understand these subjects individually, but they also need to understand the relationships among these subjects and why they are taught at the elementary level.

Geography, Anthropology, and Sociology

GEOGRAPHY

The study of geography is the study of spatial distribution. It stresses analyzing information based on the distribution, location, and interactions of different human and physical features of the earth. Geography is divided into two main areas. **Physical geography** explores the natural process of the earth, whereas **human geography** explores the impact of people on the physical world, such as how humans alter their environments. It also looks at **social structures** as they relate to geography, such as how social events relate to places. An example of that would be how immigration affected urban populations in the US during the nineteenth century.

Geography uses maps to determine spatial distributions, such as ethnic demographics in various **regions**, languages in a particular country, or even the number of volcanoes in a determined area. The main reason for creating a map or developing a geographic information system is to assess the **spatial relationships** between features. An example of a spatial relationship is the distance between residential areas and transportation stops.

All maps use **cardinal directions**: north, south, east, and west. Some maps also feature **intermediate directions** between each point. All of these are featured on a compass rose, which is used to determine locations and directions.

Absolute location describes a location identifiable by specific geographic coordinates. For example, latitude and longitude delineate specific coordinates, so the absolute location of New York City is 40°70'58" N, 74°11'81" W. Addresses are also absolute locations: for instance, the absolute location of the White House is 1600 Pennsylvania Avenue NW, Washington, DC 20500. **Relative location** describes where a place is situated in relation to another place or places. For example, the state of Illinois is located in the Midwest region of the United States; it borders Wisconsin to the north, Indiana to the east, Iowa and Missouri to the west, and Kentucky to the south.

> **DID YOU KNOW?**
>
> A thematic map shows more than just a physical map. It focuses on a theme, such as the US population in a certain year, or the size of rainforests from 1800 to 1900.

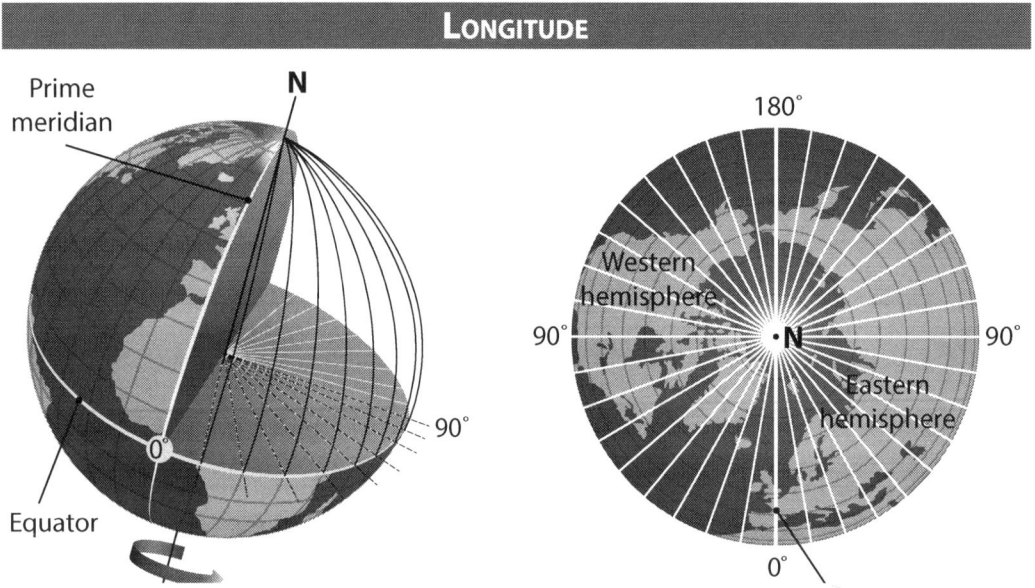

Figure 8.1. Latitude and Longitude

Maps display **geographic features**, physical features place like continents, bodies of water, plains, plateaus, mountains, and valleys. Raised elevations and bodies of water are indicated through shading or coloring; they are also labeled. In addition, maps show **political features** like towns and cities, and county, state, or national borders. They may also include significant bodies of water.

Despite their differences, physical and human geography are interconnected. For example, physical features can determine the feasibility of living in certain locations or practicing certain lifestyles. Physical features dictate the availability of **natural resources** such as fresh water, arable land, fuel, livestock, and game; they also affect climate patterns. Manmade resources also intersect with physical and human geography; for example, the Hoover Dam manages the Colorado River, a natural resource, in order to provide water and electricity to certain parts of the southwestern United States.

Physical regions of the world are broken down by distance from the equator. The **low latitudes**, from the equator to latitudes 23.5° north and south, have three distinct climates. **Tropical rainforests** can be found in the equatorial lowlands in Central Africa, Southeast Asia, and the Amazon basin. North and south of the rainforest is the **savannah**. The savannah is dry in the winter and wet in the summer, experiencing an average of 10 to 30 inches of rain. The **desert** lies beyond the savannah to the north and south. Deserts are the hottest and driest parts of the earth and receive less than 10 inches of rainfall a year. The best known deserts in the world are the Sahara Desert, the Australian Outback, and the Arabian Desert.

The **middle latitudes**, from latitudes 23.5° to 66.5° north and south, have a greater variety of climates, determined more by proximity to water than by the exact latitude. Three climates in the middle latitudes receive the most rain and therefore are the most fertile. The first is the **Mediterranean climate**, found in lands between latitudes 30° and 40° north and south that include land bordering the Mediterranean Sea, a small part of southwestern Africa, southern and southwestern Australia, a small part of the Ukraine near the Black Sea, central Chile, and southern California. The **humid subtropical climate** is located on coastal areas north and south of the tropics. This climate receives warm ocean currents and warm winds year round, leading to a climate that is warm and moist. This is also the climate that supports the greatest percentage of the world's population. Japan, southeastern China, northeastern India, southeastern South Africa, the southeastern United States, and parts of South America all have subtropical climates. Finally, several areas that are near or surrounded by water experience the **marine climate**. Marine climates are warm and rainy, resulting in part from the warm ocean winds. Western Europe, the British Isles, the US and Canadian Pacific Northwest, southern Chile, southern New Zealand, and southeastern Australia all have marine climates.

The climate best for farming is the **humid continental climate**, the true four-season climate. This climate can be found in the northern and central United States, south-central and southeastern Canada, northern China, and the western and southeastern parts of the former Soviet bloc. Those areas of continents far from the ocean are called **steppes**, or prairie. Flatlands with minimal rainfall, steppes can even become deserts if rainfall consistently dips below 10 inches per year.

The **high latitudes**, from latitudes 66.5° north and south to the poles, are home to two climates: **tundra** and **taiga**. The tundra features extremely cold and long winters; while the ground is frozen for most of the year, during the short summer the ground becomes mushy. With no arable land, it is home to few people. The taiga can be found south of the tundra in Northern Russia, Sweden, Norway, Finland, Canada, and Alaska. Home to the world's largest forestlands, the taiga also exhibits many swamps and marshes; importantly, it contains extreme mineral wealth. While there is a growing season, it is so short that meaningful agriculture is impossible; thus, the taiga is sparsely populated.

Students should understand that human activity, such as agriculture, ranching, logging, mining, and urban and suburban development impact the earth and the environment by interrupting ecosystems. Furthermore, they should also understand that **industrialization**, the process of manufacturing, creates byproducts that affect and can harm the environment. **Urbanization**, or the development of cities, became a feature of human development at the advent of the nineteenth-century Industrial Revolution, when unskilled jobs in factories offered higher wages for workers than an agricultural lifestyle did. Urbanization and **suburbanization** continue today as cities develop and as urban dwellers move to growing suburbs. Development necessarily results in the destruction of surrounding environment; however, new urban ecosystems result, and **urban planning** is itself a geographic specialty.

Another way to illustrate human and social behavior is by mapping **migration** patterns. This is the study of movement from one place to another, with the intention of settling permanently at the new location. As discussed above, urbanization is one type of migration. Some migration is internal—people moving from one place to another within the same region, like urbanization. Other migration involves people moving from one region of the world to another. Many immigrants have migrated to the United States from other countries. Push and pull factors cause people to migrate: economic, cultural, sociopolitical, or

> **DID YOU KNOW?**
>
> Migrants fleeing conflict or other dangers are called *refugees* if they cross an international border; if they flee to another part of their home country, they are called *internally displaced persons (IDPs)*.

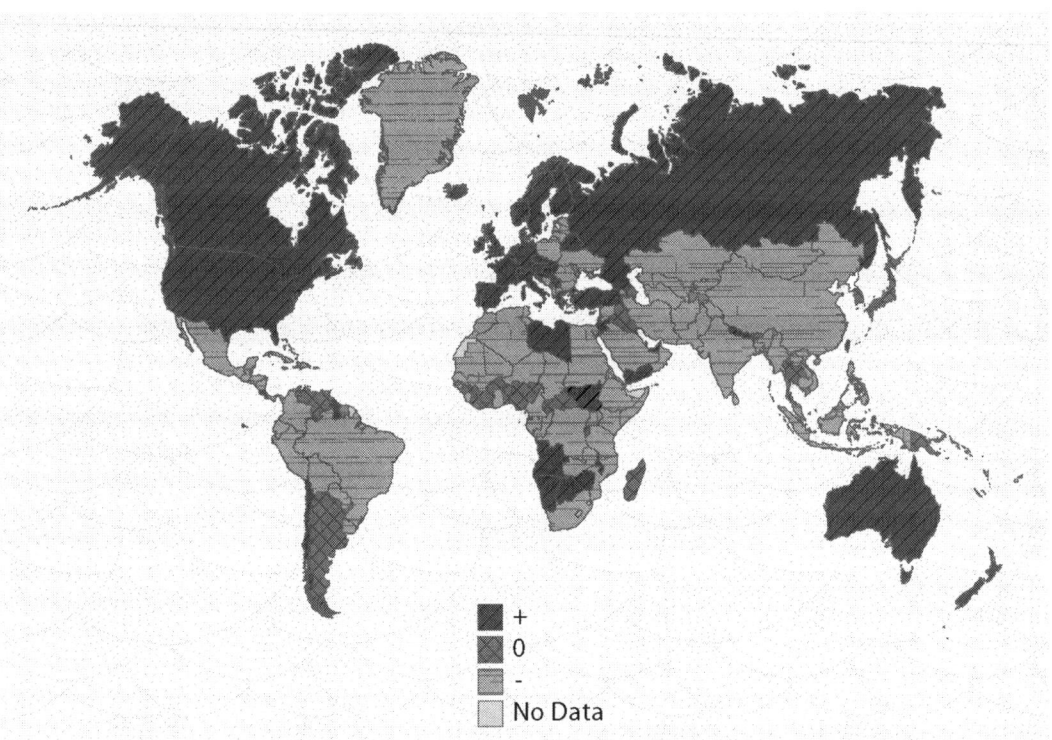

Figure 8.2. Human Migration Map

environmental reasons. Pull factors like job opportunities or better living standards attract people to new locations. Push factors like famine, drought, war, lack of economic opportunities, and political persecution drive people to leave their homes in search of relief.

ANTHROPOLOGY AND SOCIOLOGY

The elementary social studies curriculum also covers elements of **anthropology** and **sociology**. At the elementary level, these fields provide students insight into the behavior of individuals and groups relative to their location. Students should develop a knowledge of major world ethnic groups, organizations, and institutions, including understanding the major regions of the world and the general dominant cultures, religions, and languages therein. Students also begin developing their own personalities and learning the boundaries and limits of personal and social behavior.

Understanding personal identity in relation to peers, family, and institutions provides the tools for analyzing the reasons behind their behavior. Developing personal identity entails exploring and analyzing how individuals relate to others. **Socialization** is a process where individuals learn skills, beliefs, values, and behavior patterns of society and how these can influence their own norms and customs. For example, family roles differ depending on age and gender, and there are norms that dictate how certain family members should act.

Primary socialization occurs when children learn the values, actions, and attitudes that are appropriate for members of their particular culture. For example, if a family eats dinner together every night, that child will likely assume that he or she must regularly communicate with the closest and most important people in his or her life. **Secondary socialization** occurs when an individual learns the appropriate values, actions, attitudes, and behaviors as a member of a smaller group within a larger society. Secondary socialization generally occurs in adolescence or young adulthood, and influences will be teachers, employers, and other authority figures.

Examining **conflict**, **cooperation**, and **exchange** is a feature of social studies; students encounter these in history, economics, and geography. **Conflict** is the process of disagreement and is usually resolved when one of the two parties receives either the entirety or a satisfactory amount of their desired goal. **Cooperation**, on the other hand, is the process of working together to achieve similar goals; it often leads to positive outcomes. **Exchange** is the process of giving one thing and receiving another (usually with similar value) in return.

Students learn that **institutions** are extensions of core social values and are created in response to varying individual and group needs. Institutions are formally structured groups that comprise society. At the macro level they include government, private enterprise, religious institutions, and academic institutions. At the micro level, they include local communities and the family unit. They are composed of a usually formal, often top-down structure with a small governing body in charge (either the executives in a government or private company or the parents in the family unit). For example, labor unions fight for better conditions for workers; governments maintain social stability; businesses provide goods, services, and profit; and religious organizations fulfill social and personal needs.

The study of institutions also includes understanding how they are maintained and changed, as well as how they exert influence among individuals. Studying communities helps clarify how individuals, families, and institutions socialize and come together to form values, beliefs, and behavior patterns, and how they may differ from those of other communities.

More broadly, studying culture relates to understanding human and group behavior. Studying culture helps students understand that individuals develop culture and also adapt to it in changing circumstances (such as migration). Examining different belief systems and practices, such as celebrations, languages, and other norms, exposes students to multiple cultural perspectives on shared human experiences. Studies may also explore the similarities and differences among cultures and how they evolve in various regions.

The map above may be used as a general reference; however it is important for students to keep in mind that millions of people migrate temporarily or permanently throughout the world and that all regions have minority groups, so the map simply depicts dominant, not uniform, cultures.

SAMPLE QUESTIONS

1) Which of the following are major physical regions in the continental United States?

   A. humid continental, humid subtropical, Mediterranean, marine, desert
   B. humid continental, humid subtropical, taiga, tundra, Mediterranean
   C. humid continental, Mediterranean, marine, taiga, tropical rainforest
   D. the Sun Belt, the Bible Belt, and the Coasts

   Answers:
   A. **Correct.** These are all major physical regions in North America.
   B. Incorrect. While Alaska has taiga and tundra, it is not considered part of the continental United States.
   C. Incorrect. While Hawaii and US territories in the Caribbean and Pacific Ocean have tropical rainforest, they are not considered part of the continental United States.
   D. Incorrect. These terms may be used in human geography, anthropology, or history but not in physical geography.

2) Which of the following is NOT an example of human geography?

   A. studying the importance of trade among Central American countries
   B. examining regional differences in cuisine around the world
   C. studying the distribution of fauna and flora in North America
   D. deciding whether to build retail outlets based on local population

Answers:

   A. Incorrect. Studying international trade explores how the physical environment (differing countries) affects human behavior (trade agreements).
   B. Incorrect. Studying dishes from different regions relates to studying human behavior, consumption, and resource use in a geographical area.
   C. **Correct.** Studying only flora and fauna is physical geography; the geographer is not studying human interactions with or impact on the earth.
   D. Incorrect. Studying population and developing a commercial zone is an exercise in human geography and urban development.

World History

ANCIENT (CLASSICAL) CIVILIZATIONS

Classical civilizations have had a lasting influence on human history. Elementary-level students should be aware of the ancient civilizations in the Fertile Crescent (including ancient Egypt), ancient Greece and Rome, and ancient China.

Around 2500 BCE (or possibly earlier) the **Sumerians** emerged in the Near East (eventually expanding into parts of Mesopotamia). Developing irrigation and advanced agriculture, they also developed **cuneiform**, the earliest known example of writing to use characters to form words. Sumer featured city-states, the potter's wheel, early astronomy and mathematics, early education, literary and artistic developments, and religious thought. Cuneiform also allowed advanced governance and administration.

Later, **Assyria** and **Babylonia** developed as important empires in the region. The Assyrians had based much of their culture on Sumer, contributing unique sculpture and jewelry, establishing military dominance, and playing an important role in regional trade. Babylonia also inherited elements of Sumerian civilization and developed them further. In the eighteenth century BCE, King Hammurabi in Babylonia had developed courts and an early codified rule of law—**the Code of Hammurabi**—which meted out justice on an equal basis: "an eye for an eye, a tooth for a tooth."

Meanwhile, development had been under way in the **Nile Valley** in ancient **Egypt**. The fertile land on the banks of the Nile River allowed the early Egyptians to develop settled communities thanks to agriculture and irrigation. Known for their pyramids, art, use of papyrus as paper, and pictorial writing (**hieroglyphs**), the ancient Egyptians emerged as early as 5000 BCE and were united under one monarch, or **pharaoh**.

Around 2500 BCE, Egypt's civilizational institutions, administrative structure, written language, art, and architecture were becoming well developed. In addition, the religious framework of ancient Egypt had become established, with a complex mythology of various gods. The ancient Egyptians also developed astronomy and the twenty-four-hour system of measuring time. It was during this period that the famous **pyramids** were erected at Giza; these structures were actually burial tombs for pharaohs. Major pharaohs included Hatshepsut, Thutmose III, Akhenaten, and Ramesses II.

Egyptian architecture also influenced many civilizations in the Western world. The use of columns in Pharaoh Hatshepsut's temple in Luxor is an example. It influenced Greek architectural design, which was copied by the Romans and many civilizations since.

Figure 8.3. Hatshepsut's Temple in Luxor

In **China**, the Shang Dynasty, the first known dynasty, emerged around the second millennium BCE and developed the earliest known Chinese writing, which helped unite Chinese-speaking people throughout the region. Like other early civilizations, the Shang Dynasty featured the use of bronze technology, horses, wheeled technology, walled cities, and other advances. Later, under the Zhou dynasty, China developed the concept of the **Mandate of Heaven**, in which the emperor had a divine mandate to rule, based on an understanding that land was divinely inherited. **Confucius** lived toward the end of this dynasty (c. 551 – 479 BCE). His teachings would be the basis for Confucianism, the foundational Chinese philosophy emphasizing harmony and respect for hierarchy.

The Qin dynasty (221 – 206 BCE) was characterized by a centralized administration, expanded infrastructure, standardization in weights and measures, writing, currency, and strict imperial control. The administrative bureaucracy was established by the first emperor, **Qin Shihuangdi**, and it was the foundation of Chinese administration until the twentieth century. In addition, the emperor constructed the **Great Wall of China**; his tomb is guarded by the famous **terracotta figurines**.

Figure 8.4. Great Wall of China

Ancient Greece was composed of small **city-states** like **Athens**, the first known **democracy**, and the military state **Sparta**. Around 460 BCE, Athens became a revolutionary democracy controlled by the poor and working classes. In fact, the term *democracy* comes from the Greek word *demokratia*—"people power." It was participatory rather than representative; officials were chosen by groups rather than elected. Athenian ideals have influenced politics and governance throughout history.

Athens was the strongest of the many small political bodies (in fact, the word *political* comes from the Greek word *polis* meaning "city-state" or "community") and much of Greece became unified under Athens following the Peloponnesian war between Athens and Sparta. It was during this period, the **Golden Age** of Greek civilization, that much of the Hellenic art, architecture, and philosophy known today emerged, including the **Parthenon** and other masterpieces of ancient Greek sculpture and architecture. **Socrates** began teaching philosophy, influencing later philosophers like **Plato** and **Aristotle**, establishing the basis for modern Western philosophical and political thought. Mathematical advances included the Pythagorean Theorem, Euclidean geometry, and the calculation of the circumference of the earth. Playwrights like **Sophocles** and **Euripides** emerged; their work influenced later Western literature. The Greeks practiced the Olympic Games to honor their gods, a diverse panoply of deities with a detailed mythology.

> **DID YOU KNOW?**
>
> Despite its status as a democracy, Athens was not fully democratic: women did not have a place in politics, and Athenians practiced slavery.

The Greeks established numerous colonies across the Black Sea, southern Italy, Sicily, and the eastern Mediterranean, spreading Greek culture throughout the Mediterranean world; it was eventually conquered by the rising Mediterranean power, Rome.

Originally a kingdom, Rome became a republic in 509 BCE, and as such, Romans elected lawmakers (senators) to the **Senate**. The Romans developed highly advanced infrastructure, including aqueducts and roads, some still in use today. Economically powerful, Rome began conquering areas around the Mediterranean with its increasingly powerful military, including Greece, expanding westward to North Africa. With conquest of territory and expansion of trade came increased slavery, and working-class Romans were displaced; at the same time, the wealthy ruling class became more powerful and corrupt.

The people, or *Populare*, wanted a more democratic republic. As the Senate weakened due to its own corruption, **Julius Caesar**, a popular military leader widely supported by the *Populare*, emerged. Forcing the corrupt Senate to give him control, Caesar began to transition Rome from a republic to what would become an empire. Caesar was assassinated in 44 BCE; however, in that short time he had been able to consolidate and centralize imperial control. His nephew Octavian eventually gained control of Rome in 27 BCE, taking the name **Augustus Caesar** and becoming the first Roman emperor.

At this time, Rome reached the height of its power, and the Mediterranean region enjoyed a period of stability known as the *Pax Romana*. Rome controlled the entire Mediterranean region, Europe, and much of the Middle East and North Africa. Latin literature flourished, as did art, architecture, philosophy, mathematics, science, and international trade throughout Rome and beyond into Asia and Africa.

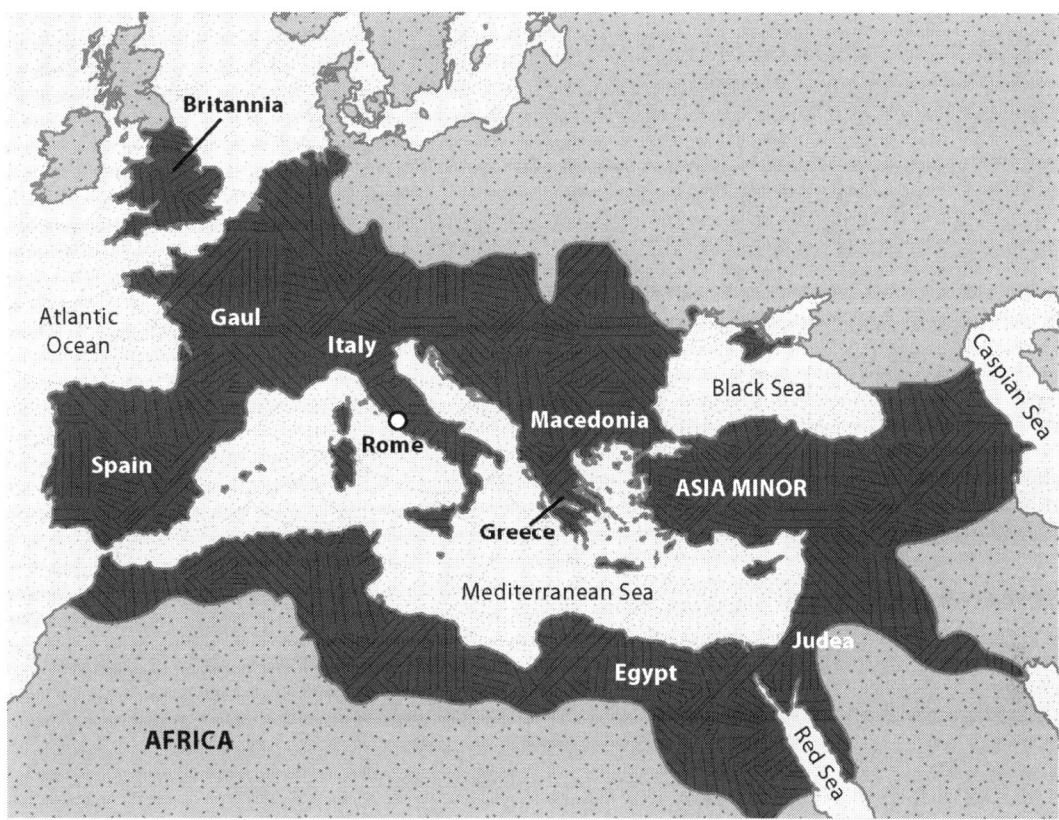

Figure 8.5. Roman Empire (200 AD)

TWENTIETH CENTURY

Elementary-level students should also be aware of major twentieth- and twenty-first-century developments such as the world wars, the Cold War, and globalization.

Instability and tensions in Europe culminated with the assassination of the Austro-Hungarian Archduke Franz Ferdinand in Sarajevo on June 28, 1914, igniting the **system of alliances** that had been in place among European powers.

Austria-Hungary declared war on Serbia, and Russia came to Serbia's aid. As an ally of Austria-Hungary as part of the **Triple Alliance**, Germany declared war on Russia. Russia's ally France prepared for war; as Germany traversed Belgium to invade France, Belgium pleaded for aid from other European countries, and so Britain declared war on Germany.

Germany had been emphasizing military growth since the consolidation and militarization of the empire under Bismarck in the mid-nineteenth century. Now, under **Kaiser Wilhelm II**, who sought expanded territories in Europe and overseas for Germany, Germany was a militarized state and important European power in its own right.

Figure 8.6. Europe during World War I

Britain's imperial power allowed it to call on troops from all over the globe—Indians, Canadians, Australians, South Africans, and New Zealanders all fought in Europe. France, too, imported colonial fighters from North Africa.

In Europe, the 1914 Battle of the Marne between Germany and French and British forces defending France resulted in **trench warfare** that would continue for years, marking the Western Front. At Gallipoli in 1915, Australian and New Zealander troops fought the Ottoman Empire, allies of Germany, near Istanbul. Later that year, a German submarine, or U-boat, sank the Lusitania, a passenger ship in the Atlantic, killing many American civilians. In 1916, the Battle of Verdun, the longest battle of the war, ended in the failure of the Germans to defeat the French army. On July 1, 1916, the Battle of the Somme became part of an allied effort to repel Germany using artillery to end the stalemate on the Western Front; after four months, however, the front moved only 5 miles.

DID YOU KNOW?

The first international war to use industrialized weaponry, WWI was called "the Great War" because battle on such a scale had never before been seen.

Finally, in 1917, the United States discovered that Germany secretly proposed an alliance with Mexico to attack the US. This finally spurred US intervention in the war; despite Russian withdrawal after the Bolshevik Revolution in October 1917, Germany was forced to surrender in the face of invasion by the US-supported allies.

According to the Schlieffen Plan, Germany had planned to fight a war on two fronts against both Russia and France. However, Russian forces stretched the

German army too thin on the Eastern Front, while it became bogged down in trench warfare on the Western Front against the British, the French, and later the Americans.

Germany lost the war and was punished with the harsh **Treaty of Versailles**, which held it accountable for the entirety of the war. The Treaty brought economic hardship on the country by forcing it to pay **reparations**. German military failure and consequent economic collapse due to the Treaty of Versailles and later worldwide economic depression set the stage for the rise of Adolf Hitler.

The Treaty also created the **League of Nations**, an international organization designed to prevent future outbreaks of international war; however, it was largely toothless, especially because the powerful United States did not join. However, it would be the model for the stronger United Nations.

Instability between the First and Second World Wars resulted from the worldwide **Great Depression**. Growing nationalism in Germany, Italy, and Japan added to political uncertainty.

In Asia, Japan invaded Manchuria, northern China, in 1931. It already controlled Korea, Taiwan, and other Asian territories and began expanding its control farther into Southeast Asia and throughout the Pacific.

In Germany, Hitler's popular platform—to cancel the Treaty of Versailles—allowed him to rise. In 1934 he became the *Führer*, or leader, of Germany, and took total control of the country. He and the Nazis set into motion their agenda of racism and genocide against "non-Aryan" (non-Germanic) or "racially impure" people.

Jewish people were especially targeted. Throughout the 1930s, the Nazis began restricting Jewish rights. In 1938, an organized series of attacks on Jewish businesses, homes, and places of worship called **Kristallnacht** took place, so called because the windows of these places were smashed. In 1939, Jews were forced from their homes into **ghettoes**, isolated and overcrowded urban neighborhoods; in 1941, they were forced to wear **yellow stars** identifying them as Jewish.

Millions of Jewish people were sent to **concentration camps**, where many were murdered through forced labor and systematic gassing. At least six million European Jews were murdered by the Nazis in the **Holocaust**, as were Roma, Slavic people, homosexuals, disabled people, people of color, prisoners of war, communists, and others not considered "Aryan."

> **DID YOU KNOW?**
>
> Killing people based on their ethnicity is called *genocide*.

Meanwhile, Hitler sought to restore Germany's power and expand its reach by annexing and invading various countries. Germany's 1939 invasion of Poland is commonly considered the beginning of the **Second World War**. In 1940, Germany took Paris. The Battle of Britain began in July of that year; however Germany suffered its first defeat and was unable to take Britain.

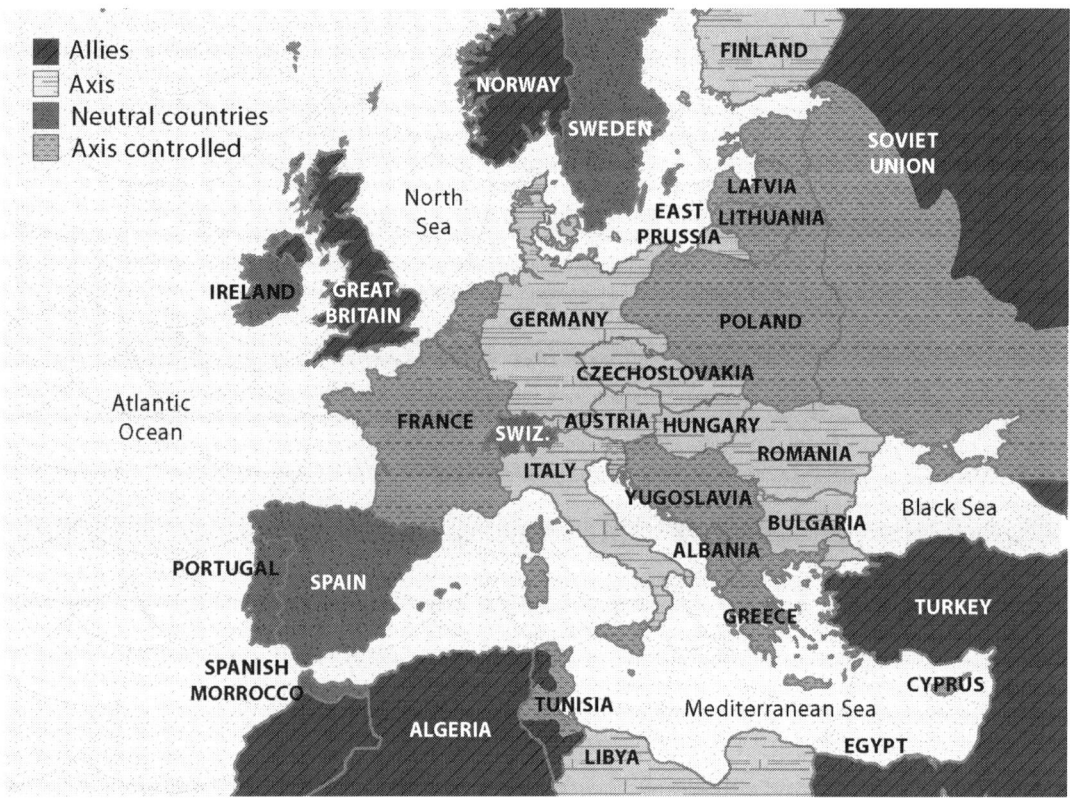

Figure 8.7. Europe during World War II

When Japan joined the **Axis** powers of Germany and Italy, the war officially spread to Asia, which was already in conflict. The **Chinese Civil War** was interrupted when Japan invaded China past Manchuria. In response, the Chinese factions joined forces against Japan; the communists became powerful. In December of 1941, Japan attacked the United States at **Pearl Harbor**. Consequently, the US joined the war in Europe and in the Pacific.

Back in Europe, having broken a promise made to the Soviet Union in 1939, Hitler invaded the USSR; however Germany was defeated at the Battle of Stalingrad, a turning point in the war. In 1944, the Allies invaded France on D-Day. While they liberated Paris in August, the costly Battle of the Bulge extended into 1945. Despite thousands of American casualties, Hitler's forces were pushed back. In the spring of 1945, the US crossed the Rhine while the USSR invaded Berlin; Hitler killed himself, and the Allies accepted German surrender.

The war in the Pacific would continue, however. Strategic battles were fought throughout the islands. **President Truman**, who had succeeded Roosevelt, elected to use the nuclear bomb on Japan to force its surrender rather than invade that country. In 1945, the war ended with Japanese surrender after the US bombed the Japanese cities Hiroshima and Nagasaki. That year in China, the Chinese Civil War recommenced; by 1949 the communists had emerged victorious.

Because of the widespread violence of the war and the millions of soldiers and civilians who died, especially those killed because of genocide, the **United Nations** was formed to prevent another world war. It was based on the League of Nations, and its mission is to champion human rights and uphold international security.

Allied forces took the lead in rebuilding efforts: the US occupied areas in East Asia and Germany, while the Soviet Union remained in Eastern Europe. The Allies had planned to rebuild Europe according to the Marshall Plan; however, the USSR occupied Eastern Europe. The **Cold War** had begun.

The US, Britain, and the USSR had originally agreed to divide Germany and to hold free elections in Eastern Europe, but by 1945, things had changed. The USSR felt betrayed by the US use of the nuclear bomb; likewise, the US and Britain felt betrayed by the Soviet Union, which had occupied Eastern Europe and prevented democratic elections in order to establish a buffer zone following its extraordinarily heavy casualties in WWII—around twenty million. An *iron curtain* had come down across Europe, dividing east from west.

The United States adopted a policy of containment, the idea that communism should be *contained*. Therefore, the United States became involved in the **Korean War** in 1950 and later the controversial **Vietnam War** throughout the 1960s and early 1970s.

Toward the end of the 1960s and into the 1970s, the Cold War began to thaw. The US and USSR signed a series of treaties to limit nuclear weapons. In 1972, President Richard Nixon visited China, establishing relations between the communist government and the United States.

> **QUICK REVIEW**
>
> Name three reasons for the eruption of the Cold War.

However, the climate would change again in the 1970s and 1980s. The **arms race** was underway. President Ronald Reagan pursued a militaristic policy, prioritizing weapons development with the goal of outspending the USSR on weapons technology.

In 1991, the Soviet Union fell thanks in part to reforms like *glasnost* and *perestroika* (or openness and transparency). After a coup overthrowing Premier Mikhail Gorbachev, the Soviet leader, the USSR was dissolved. A Soviet war in Afghanistan and military overspending in an effort to keep up with the United States had weakened the USSR to the point of collapse, and the Cold War ended.

GLOBALIZATION

Globalization is increasing economic, political, and cultural interdependence and interaction throughout the world. At its core, globalization is an economic trend; **multinational corporations (MNCs)** are the primary driving forces of globalization. However, globalization has significant cultural and political impacts as well. For example, the exportation of American fast food restaurants, like McDonald's (one example of an MNC), to other parts of the world reflects the capitalist drive to find new markets. Furthermore, the introduction of this type of food has a significant impact on one of the major distinguishing cultural traits of other countries—their cuisine.

Another example is language; English continues to spread throughout the world as the main language used in business and on the Internet. Spanish, French, Arabic, and Chinese are also widely spoken and used as second or third languages by millions of people in business, in pop culture, and to disseminate news. Looking at causes and events in history is another way to make **cross-cultural comparisons**. For example, students could analyze different holiday traditions from various countries.

In this era of globalization, international markets became increasingly open through free-trade agreements among countries, making doing international business easier. Technological advances like improvements in transportation and the Internet made international trade and communication faster, easier, and cheaper. Political cooperation like the formation of the European Union and other groups all make globalization possible.

The **European Union**, as it is known today, was formed in 1992 after the Cold War. Former communist countries became democratic societies and joined it; as of 2015, twenty-eight countries are members, with more on the path to membership. EU countries cooperate politically; many also share a common currency, the **euro**, and some EU countries even have open borders. In Africa, the **African Union**, similar to the EU, is a forum for African countries to organize and cooperate politically, militarily, and economically. The **G-20**, the world's twenty most important economic and political powers, includes many former colonies and non-European countries.

However, more open borders, reliable international transportation, and faster, easier worldwide communication brought risks, too. In the early twenty-first century, the United States was attacked by terrorists on **September 11, 2001**, resulting in thousands of civilian casualties. Consequently, the US launched a major land war in Afghanistan and another later in Iraq.

SAMPLE QUESTIONS

3) Which of the following is an example of a cross-cultural comparison?
   A. A chef studies variations in a recipe depending on the diner's preference for sweets.
   B. A Thai husband learns different holiday traditions from his wife, who is Chinese.
   C. Students compare the prices of groceries in different cities.
   D. A career coach helps clients determine their goals.

Answers:

A. Incorrect. Personal preferences are not an example of culture.

B. Correct. Reviewing different holiday celebrations exemplifies studying different cultures.

C. Incorrect. Studying different prices is economic, not cultural, study.

D. Incorrect. Determining career goals relates to personal preferences.

4) Which of the following happened to Jewish people under the Nazi regime?

   A. Their homes and businesses were attacked and destroyed.

   B. They were forced to live in ghettoes, overcrowded neighborhoods with poor living conditions.

   C. They were sent to concentration camps and murdered.

   D. all of the above

Answers:

A. Incorrect. While Jewish people suffered such attacks under the Nazis, they faced other consequences as well.

B. Incorrect. Jewish people were indeed forced to live in ghettoes; however, they were persecuted in other ways and so there is a better answer choice here.

C. Incorrect. Millions of Jews were sent to concentration camps, forced into slave labor, and murdered. However, there is a better answer choice here.

D. Correct. Under the Nazis, Jewish people were forced to live in ghettoes; their businesses and homes were destroyed; and they suffered other persecution. Jews, communists, Roma, homosexuals, and others were also forced into slave labor in concentration camps, and millions were murdered.

United States History

Elementary-level students should be aware of major Native American societies; reasons for colonization; the causes, events, and consequences of the American Revolution and its major figures; important developments like westward expansion, urbanization, and immigration; abolitionism, Southern Secession and reasons, events, and consequences of the Civil War; industrialization, the Great Depression, and the New Deal; the world wars and the Cold War; the Civil Rights Movement; and technology and the US today.

Native American Societies

Prior to European colonization, diverse Native American societies controlled the continent; they would later come into economic and diplomatic contact, and military conflict, with European colonizers and United States forces and settlers.

Major civilizations that would play an important and ongoing role in North American history included the **Iroquois** in the Northeast, known for longhouses and farming in the Three Sisters tradition; they consisted of a confederation of six tribes. The **Algonquin** were another important northeastern civilization; rivals of the Iroquois, the Algonquin were important in the fur trade. Algonquin languages were spoken throughout the Great Lakes region.

> **DID YOU KNOW?**
>
> In the Three Sisters tradition, farmers grow maize, beans, and squash together; these plants naturally complement each other by providing mutual protection from pests and the elements. They also enrich the soil.

Farther west, the **Shawnee** were an Algonquin-speaking people based in the Ohio Valley; however their presence extended as far south and east as the present-day Carolinas and Georgia. While socially organized under a matrilineal system, the Shawnee had male kings and only men could inherit property. Also matrilineal and Algonquin-speaking, the **Lenape** were considered by the Shawnee to be their "grandfathers" and thus accorded respect. Another Algonquin-speaking tribe, the **Kickapoo** were originally from the Great Lakes region and moved west. The Algonquin-speaking **Miami** moved from Wisconsin to the Ohio Valley region, forming settled societies and farming maize. They too took part in the fur trade as it developed during European colonial times. These tribes later formed the Northwest Confederacy to fight US westward expansion.

In the South, major tribes included the **Creek**, **Chickasaw**, and **Choctaw**, the descendants of the **Mississippi Mound Builders** or Mississippian cultures, societies which built mounds from around 2100 to 1800 years ago as burial tombs or the bases for temples. Sharing similar languages, all the tribes would later participate in an alliance—the Muscogee Confederacy—to engage the United States. The Chickasaw and Choctaw were matrilineal; the former also engaged in Three Sisters agriculture like the Iroquois.

Another major southern tribe, the **Cherokee** spoke (and speak) a language of the Iroquoian family. It is thought that they migrated south to their homeland in present-day Georgia sometime long before European contact, where they remained until they were forcibly removed in 1832. Organized into seven clans, the Cherokee were also hunters and farmers like other tribes in the region and would later come into contact—and conflict—with European colonizers and the United States of America.

The nomadic tribes of the Great Plains like the **Sioux**, **Cheyanne**, **Apache**, **Comanche**, and **Arapaho** lived farther west. These tribes depended on the **buffalo**

Figure 8.8. Mississippi Mounds

for food and materials to create clothing, tools, and domestic items; therefore they followed the herds. While widely known for their equestrian skill, horses were introduced by Europeans and so Native American tribes living on the Great Plains did not access them until after European contact. Horseback riding facilitated the hunt; previously, hunters surrounded buffalo or frightened them off of cliffs.

In the Southwest, the **Navajo** controlled territory in present-day Arizona, New Mexico, and Utah. Pastoralists, they had a less hierarchical structure than other Native American societies. The Navajo were descendants of the **Ancestral Pueblo** or **Anasazi** (pictured on the following page), who practiced Three Sisters agriculture and stone construction, building cliff dwellings.

In the Pacific Northwest, Native American peoples depended on fishing, using canoes. Totem poles depicted histories. The **Coast Salish**, whose language was widely spoken throughout the region, dominated the Puget Sound and Olympic Peninsula area. Farther south, the **Chinook** controlled the coast at the Columbia River.

Ultimately, through both violent conflict and political means, Native American civilizations lost control of most of their territories and were forced onto reservations by the United States. Negotiations continue today over rights to land and opportunities and reparations for past injustices.

Figure 8.9. Ancestral Pueblo Cliff Palace at Mesa Verde

THE AMERICAN REVOLUTION

European powers had begun colonizing North America in the sixteenth century to access fur and agricultural resources; by the eighteenth century, Britain controlled most of the east coast of the continent, including the Thirteen Colonies, which became the original United States. France and Britain battled for control of northeastern North America, and following the **French and Indian War**, Great Britain consolidated its control over much of the continent.

Despite British victory in the French and Indian War, it had gone greatly into debt. Furthermore, there were concerns that the colonies required a stronger military presence following Native American attacks and uprisings like **Pontiac's Rebellion** in 1763. Consequently, **King George III** signed the **Proclamation of 1763**, an agreement not to settle land west of the Appalachians, in an effort to make peace; however much settlement continued in practice.

King George III enforced heavy taxes and restrictive acts in the colonies to generate income for the Crown and eventually to punish disobedience. England expanded the **Molasses Act** of 1733, passing the **Sugar Act** in 1764 to raise revenue by taxing sugar and molasses, which were widely consumed in the colonies. In 1765, Britain enforced the **Quartering Act**, forcing colonists to provide shelter to British troops stationed in the region.

The 1765 **Stamp Act**, the first direct tax on the colonists, triggered more tensions. Any document required a costly stamp, the revenue reverting to the British government. Colonists felt the tax violated their rights, given that they did not have direct representation in British Parliament. As a result, they began boycotting British goods and engaging in violent protest. **Samuel Adams** led the **Sons and Daughters of Liberty** in violent acts against tax collectors and stirred up rebellion with his **Committees of Correspondence**, which distributed anti-British propaganda.

Protests against the Quartering Act in Boston led to the **Boston Massacre** in 1770, when British troops fired on a crowd of protestors. By 1773, in a climate of continued unrest driven by the Committees of Correspondence, colonists protested the latest taxes on tea levied by the **Tea Act** in the famous **Boston Tea Party** by dressing as Native Americans and tossing tea off a ship in Boston Harbor. In response, the government passed the **Intolerable Acts**, closing Boston Harbor and bringing Massachusetts back under direct royal control.

In response to the Intolerable Acts, colonial leaders met in Philadelphia at the **First Continental Congress** in 1774 and presented colonial concerns to the king, who ignored them. However, violent conflict began in 1775 at **Lexington and Concord**, when American militiamen (**minutemen**) gathered to resist British efforts to seize weapons and arrest rebels in Concord. On June 17, 1775, the Americans fought the British at the **Battle of Bunker Hill**; despite American losses, the number of casualties the rebels inflicted caused the king to declare that the colonies were in rebellion. Troops were deployed to the colonies; the Siege of Boston began.

> **DID YOU KNOW?**
>
> King George III also hired Hessian mercenaries from Germany to supplement British troops; adding foreign fighters only increased resentment in the colonies and created a stronger sense of independence from Britain.

In May 1775, the **Second Continental Congress** met at Philadelphia to debate the way forward. Debate among leaders like Benjamin Franklin, John Adams, Thomas Jefferson, and James Madison centered between the wisdom of continued efforts at compromise and negotiations, and declaring independence. Again, the king ignored them. By the summer of 1776, the Continental Congress agreed on the need to break from Britain; on July 4, 1776 it declared the independence of the United States of America and issued the **Declaration of Independence**.

> When in the Course of human events, it becomes necessary for one people to dissolve the political bands which have connected them with another, and to assume among the powers of the earth, the separate and equal station to which the Laws of Nature and of Nature's God entitle them, a decent respect to the opinions of mankind requires that they should declare the causes which impel them to the separation.
>
> We hold these truths to be self-evident, that all men are created equal, that they are endowed by their Creator with certain unalienable Rights, that among these are Life, Liberty and the pursuit of Happiness. That to secure these rights, Governments are instituted among Men, deriving their just powers from the consent of the governed, that whenever any Form of Government becomes destructive of these ends, it is the Right of the People to alter or to abolish it, and to institute new Government, laying its

> foundation on such principles and organizing its powers in such form, as to them shall seem most likely to effect their Safety and Happiness. Prudence, indeed, will dictate that Governments long established should not be changed for light and transient causes; and accordingly all experience hath shewn, that mankind are more disposed to suffer, while evils are sufferable, than to right themselves by abolishing the forms to which they are accustomed. But when a long train of abuses and usurpations, pursuing invariably the same Object evinces a design to reduce them under absolute Despotism, it is their right, it is their duty, to throw off such Government, and to provide new Guards for their future security.--Such has been the patient sufferance of these Colonies; and such is now the necessity which constrains them to alter their former Systems of Government. The history of the present King of Great Britain is a history of repeated injuries and usurpations, all having in direct object the establishment of an absolute Tyranny over these States. To prove this, let Facts be submitted to a candid world.
>
> Preamble to the Declaration of Independence

Americans were still divided over independence; **Patriots** favored independence while those still loyal to Britain were known as **Tories**. **George Washington** had been appointed head of the Continental Army and led a largely unpaid and unprofessional army; despite early losses, Washington gained ground due to strong leadership, superior knowledge of the land, and support from France.

Initially, the British seemed to have many advantages in the war, including more resources and troops. Britain won the **Battle of Brooklyn** (Battle of Long Island) in August 1776 and captured New York City. The tide turned in 1777 at **Valley Forge**, when Washington and his army survived the bitterly cold winter and managed to overcome British military forces.

A victory at **Saratoga** led the French to help the rebels in 1778. Now fighting shifted south. Britain captured Georgia and Charleston, South Carolina; however, British forces could not adequately control the country as they proceeded to Yorktown, Virginia in 1781. At the **Battle of Yorktown**, British forces were defeated by the Continental Army with support from France and were forced to surrender.

Meanwhile, the British people did not favor the war and voted the Tories out of Parliament; the incoming Whig party sought to end the war. After troops fought for two more years, the **Treaty of Paris** ended the revolution in September 1783. In 1787, the first draft of the Constitution was written, and George Washington became the first president of the United States two years later. The American Revolution would go on to inspire revolutions around the world.

Manifest Destiny

In the nineteenth century, the idea of **Manifest Destiny**, or the sense that it was the fate of the United States to expand westward and settle the continent, pervaded. In 1803 President Thomas Jefferson oversaw the **Louisiana Purchase**, which nearly doubled the size of the United States. **Meriwether Lewis** and **William Clark** were dispatched to explore the western frontier of the territory: Jefferson hoped to find an all-water route to the Pacific Ocean (via the Missouri River). While this route did not exist, Lewis and Clark returned with a deeper knowledge of the territory the US had come to control.

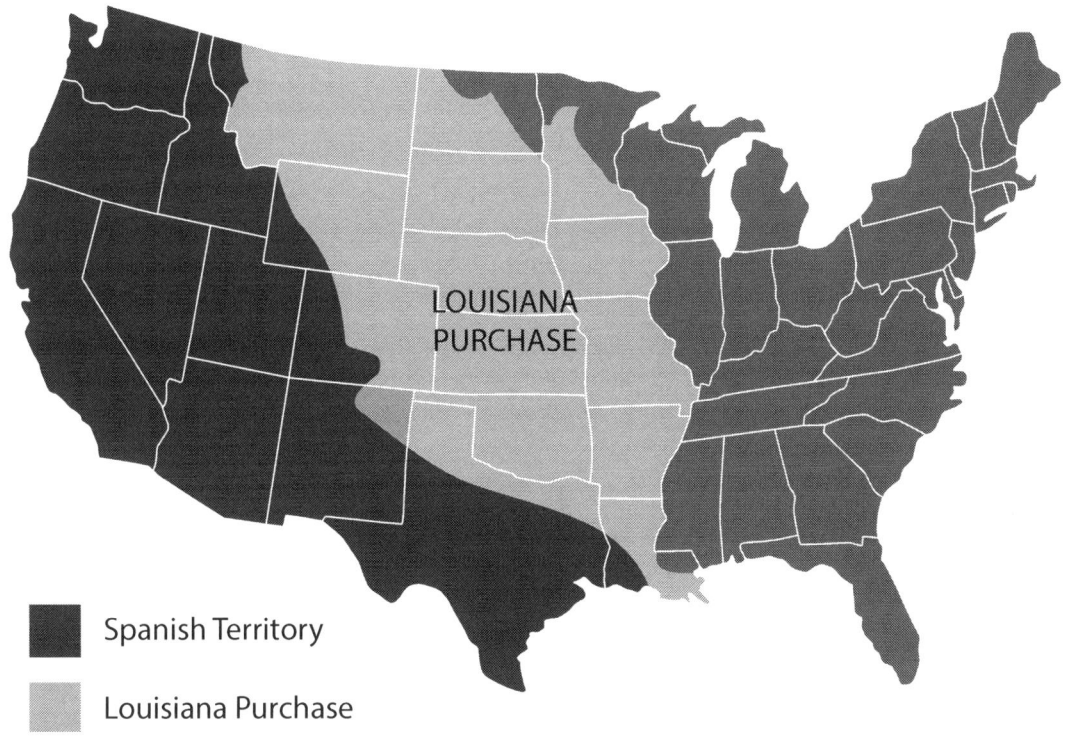

Figure 8.10. Louisiana Purchase

Later, British provocation at sea and in the northwest led to the **War of 1812** between the United States and Britain, which was allied with the Shawnee-led Northwest Confederacy. Growing nationalism in the United States pressured Madison into pushing for war; Congress declared war under President Madison with the intent to defend the United States, end unfair trade practices and poor treatment of Americans on the high seas, and penetrate British Canada. Despite the Confederacy's alliance with Britain, the United States prevailed.

The war resulted in no real gains or losses for either the Americans or the British, yet at the war's end, the United States had successfully defended itself as a country and reaffirmed its independence. Patriotism ran high, strengthening the idea of Manifest Destiny. In 1819, following the Seminole War the United States purchased Florida from Spain in the **Adams-Onis Treaty** (conflict with the Seminole would continue). The **Monroe Doctrine**, President James Monroe's policy that the Western Hemisphere was "closed" to any further European colonization or exploration, asserted US power in the region.

With westward expansion came questions over the expansion of slavery. In 1820, the **Missouri Compromise** allowed Missouri to join the union as a slave state but provided that any other states north of the thirty-sixth parallel (36°30') would be free. However, more tension and compromises over the nature of slavery in the West were to come.

With continental expansion came more conflict with Native Americans. Despite legal resistance by the Cherokee, President Andrew Jackson enforced the 1830 **Indian Removal Act**, forcing Cherokee, Creek, Chickasaw, Choctaw, and others from their lands in the Southeast. Thousands of people were forced to travel to Indian Territory (today, Oklahoma) on the infamous **Trail of Tears** to make way for white settlers.

> **DID YOU KNOW?**
>
> Hispanics who had lived in the region under Mexico lost their land and faced discrimination, even though they had been promised US citizenship and equal rights.

The United States continued to grow throughout the nineteenth century. In 1845, the United States annexed Texas, which contributed to the outbreak of the Mexican-American War the next year. As a result, it gained California and the Utah and New Mexico territories in the 1848 Treaty of Guadalupe Hidalgo. In 1846, the United States and Britain agreed on the Oregon Treaty, which established a border at the forty-ninth parallel.

Meanwhile, social change in the Northeast and growing Midwest continued. As the market economy and early industry developed, so did an early **middle class**. Women asserted their rights: activists like **Susan B. Anthony** and **Elizabeth Cady Stanton** worked for women's suffrage, culminating in the 1848 **Seneca Falls Convention**.

The country was increasingly divided over slavery; **sectionalism** grew, strengthening disunity between the North and the South. Reform movements continued to include **abolitionism**, the ending of slavery. The former slave **Frederick Douglass** advocated abolition. An activist leader and writer, Douglass publicized the movement along with the American Anti-Slavery Society and publications like Harriet Beecher Stowe's *Uncle Tom's Cabin*. He and other activists like **Harriet Tubman** helped free slaves using the **Underground Railroad**. An estimated 100,000 slaves escaped the South between 1810 and 1850 through a system of safe houses, even though these actions violated state laws. The radical abolitionist **John Brown** led violent protests against slavery. Abolitionism became a key social and political issue in the mid-nineteenth century; slavery was the main cause of the **Civil War**.

> **DID YOU KNOW?**
>
> *Sectionalism* is when a segment of a group is more loyal to itself than to the rest of the group. It can apply to regions of countries (such as the South of the United States before the Civil War).

Antislavery factions in Congress had attempted to halt the extension of slavery to the new territories obtained from Mexico, but they were unsuccessful; in the

Compromise of 1850, Congress decided that the voters in some new territories would be allowed to decide whether slavery should be legal or determined by popular sovereignty. In 1854, Congress passed the Kansas-Nebraska Act, effectively repealing the Missouri Compromise, allowing those territories to decide slavery by popular sovereignty as well. In response, the new **Republican Party** emerged. One of its members, **Abraham Lincoln**, was elected president in 1860 on an antislavery platform.

CIVIL WAR

Following Lincoln's election, South Carolina immediately seceded, followed by Mississippi, Alabama, Florida, Louisiana, Georgia, and Texas. They formed the Confederate States of America, or the **Confederacy**, on February 1, 1861, under the leadership of **Jefferson Davis**, a senator from Mississippi.

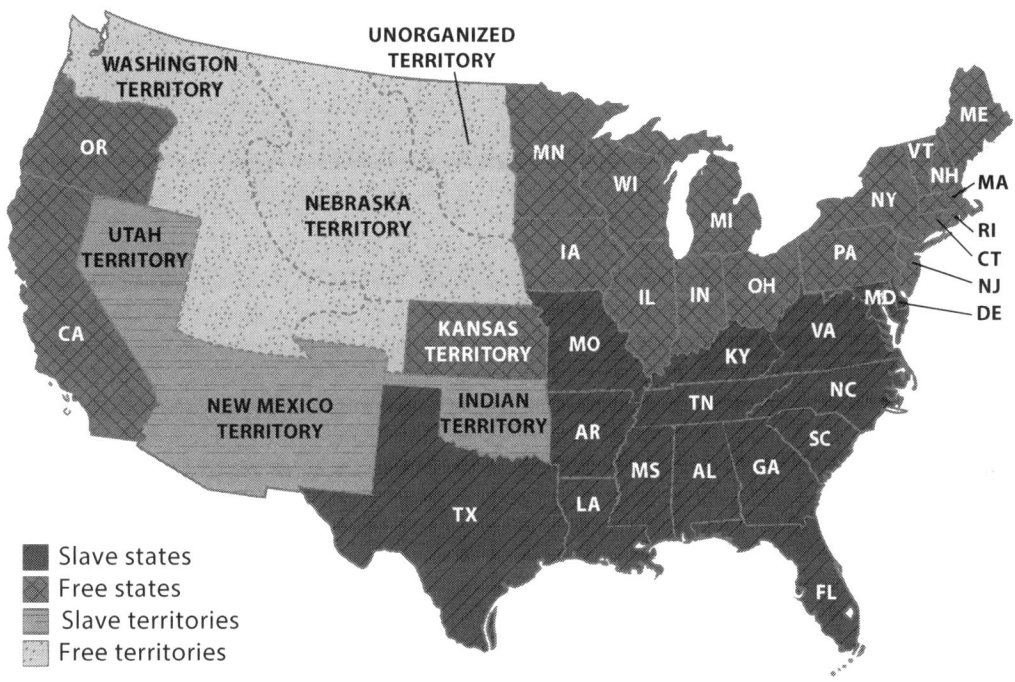

Figure 8.11. Civil War

Shortly after the South's secession, Confederate forces attacked Union troops in Sumter, South Carolina; the **Battle of Fort Sumter** sparked the Civil War. As a result, Virginia, Tennessee, North Carolina, and Arkansas seceded and joined the Confederacy. West Virginia was formed when the western part of Virginia refused to join the Confederacy.

Both sides believed the conflict would be short-lived; however, after the First Battle of Bull Run when the Union failed to route the Confederacy, it became clear that the war would not end quickly. Realizing how difficult it would be to defeat the Confederacy, the Union developed the **Anaconda Plan**, a plan to "squeeze" the Confederacy, including a naval blockade and taking control of the Mississippi River.

Since the South depended on international trade in cotton for much of its income, a naval blockade would have serious economic ramifications for the Confederacy.

However, the Second Battle of Bull Run was a tactical Confederate victory led by General Robert E. Lee and Stonewall Jackson. The Union army remained intact, but the loss was a heavy blow to morale. The Battle of Antietam was the first battle to be fought on Union soil. Union General George B. McClellan halted General Lee's invasion of Maryland but failed to defeat Confederate forces. Undaunted, on January 1, 1863, President Lincoln decreed the end of slavery in the rebel states with the **Emancipation Proclamation**. The Battle of Gettysburg was a major Union victory. It was the bloodiest battle in American history up to this point; the Confederate army would not recover.

> **DID YOU KNOW?**
>
> President Lincoln later delivered the Gettysburg Address onsite, in which he framed the Civil War as a battle for human rights and equality.

Meanwhile, following the Siege of Vicksburg, Mississippi, Union forces led by General Ulysses S. Grant gained control over the Mississippi River, completing the Anaconda Plan. The Battle of Atlanta was the final major battle of the Civil War; victorious, the Union proceeded into the South, and the Confederacy fell. In April 1865, General Lee surrendered to General Grant at Appomattox, Virginia, and the war ended.

Reconstruction and Industrialization

Reconstruction after the war would bring huge changes in the South and redefine how blacks fit into American society. The South was in economic ruins; many Southerners, especially newly freed slaves and other African Americans, sought better economic opportunities by moving to the North. Congress passed the Civil Rights Act in 1866 recognizing the rights of former slaves as US citizens; it also passed the Reconstruction Acts the next year, enforcing military occupation of the South. These acts laid out the process for readmission to the Union: among other requirements, states had to ratify the Thirteenth, Fourteenth, and Fifteenth Amendments. These made slavery illegal, recognized equal rights, and permitted African American males to vote, respectively.

Still, agriculture and infrastructure were ruined, and many were bitter over Northern occupation and involvement. Even though the South was forced to accept the end of slavery, Southern states created 'black codes' which restricted black Americans' rights. African Americans faced ongoing discrimination and violence in the South, including segregation and threats from hate groups.

The end of the Civil War also brought on an increase in **industrialization**. A British phenomenon, industrialization made its way to the United States. Machines replaced hand labor as the main way of manufacturing, exponentially increasing production capacities. Later in the nineteenth century, the US began developing heavy industry.

The **assembly line** developed by Henry Ford enabled **mass production**. Factors that contributed to this boom included the invention of new products (e.g., the automobile, the telephone, and the electric light), improvement of production methods, an abundance of natural resources and infrastructure (railways opened the West further and connected factories and markets to raw materials), and banking (more people wanted to invest in booming businesses, and banks were financing them).

New cities and towns became larger as people started to live and work in urban areas, attracted by employment opportunities. Unfortunately, lack of planning for this phenomenon—**urbanization**—led to inadequate sanitation (which contributed to cholera and typhoid epidemics), pollution, and crime. However, overall, the United States' economy was growing, the middle class was becoming larger, and industry and technology were developing.

> **DID YOU KNOW?**
>
> Social unrest was a consequence of urbanization; the poor living conditions faced by workers lead to strikes and riots.

WORLD WAR AND COLD WAR

While the United States became increasingly prosperous and stable, Europe was becoming increasingly unstable. Americans were divided over whether the US should intervene in international matters. This debate became more pronounced with the outbreak of **World War I** in Europe.

Inflammatory events like German submarine warfare (*U-boats*) in the Atlantic Ocean, the sinking of the *Lusitania*, which resulted in many American civilian deaths, the embarrassing Zimmerman Telegram (in which Germany promised to help Mexico in an attack on the US), and growing American nationalism, or pride in and identification with one's country, triggered US intervention in the war. On December 7, 1917, the US declared war. With victory in 1918, the US had proven itself a superior military and industrial power. Interventionist President **Woodrow Wilson** played an important role in negotiating the peace; his Fourteen Points laid out an idealistic international vision, including an international security organization.

However, European powers negotiated and won the harsh **Treaty of Versailles**, which placed the blame for the war entirely on Germany and demanded crippling reparations from it, one contributing factor to **World War II** later in the twentieth century. The League of Nations, a collective security organization, was formed, but a divided US Congress refused to ratify the Treaty, so the US did not join it. Consequently the League was weak and largely ineffective.

After the war ended, the US suffered from a slight recession. It wasn't until 1929 that the stock market crashed, which triggered the **Great Depression**. Millions of investors saw their fortunes disappear and consumer spending and investing continued to drop, which led to large unemployment rates. Approximately half the banks closed, and upward of 15 million people were unemployed.

Franklin Delano Roosevelt was elected to the presidency in 1932. FDR offered Americans a **New Deal**: a plan to bring the country out of the Depression. During the **First Hundred Days** of FDR's administration, he stabilized the economy through a series of emergency acts for the immediate repair of the banking system. FDR did not only address economic issues; a number of acts provided long-term relief to the poor and unemployed. The New Deal especially generated jobs through programs that developed infrastructure and provided construction jobs for the unemployed. The economy truly rebounded during the Second World War.

FDR was increasingly concerned about the rise of fascism in Europe, seeing it as a global threat. Thus the United States provided support to Great Britain before entering the war. FDR spoke publicly about the **Four Freedoms**: freedom of speech, freedom of religion, freedom from want, and freedom from fear.

However after the Japanese attack on **Pearl Harbor** on December 7, 1941, the US entered the war. While directly attacked by Japan, which was allied with the fascist Axis powers of Italy and Germany, the United States focused first on the European theater. On June 6, 1944, or **D-Day**, the US led the invasion of Normandy, invading Europe. After months of fighting, following the deadly and drawn-out Battle of the Bulge, the Allies were able to enter Germany and end the war in Europe.

The United States was then able to focus more effectively on the war in the Pacific. President **Harry Truman** had taken power following FDR's death in 1945. Rather than force a US invasion of Japan, which would have resulted in huge numbers of casualties, he authorized the bombing of Hiroshima and Nagasaki in Japan, the only times that **nuclear weapons** have been used in conflict. The war ended with Japanese surrender on September 2, 1945.

DID YOU KNOW?

Japanese Americans faced oppression and discrimination at home simply due to their race and were forced to live in internment camps.

With most of Europe destroyed, the victorious US and the Soviet Union emerged as the two global **superpowers**. Although the Soviet Union and the United States were allies during the war, the relationship between them grew tense as the war ended. When the Soviet Union occupied Eastern European countries, suppressing democracy there, the **Cold War** effectively began.

During the Cold War, the US and the USSR never came into direct conflict; rather, there were alternating periods of tension and relaxed relations, or détente. During the **Cuban Missile Crisis** (1962), Soviet missiles were discovered in Cuba, and military crisis was narrowly averted thanks to the diplomacy of the Soviet leader Nikita Khrushchev and the popular US president John F. Kennedy. The two countries also supported opposing sides in wars throughout the world—the Korean

War, the **Vietnam War**, the Soviet-Afghan War, and many more. Finally, the two superpowers both possessed **nuclear weapons**; thankfully, both sides developed a series of agreements placing limitations on those weapons, and they were never used.

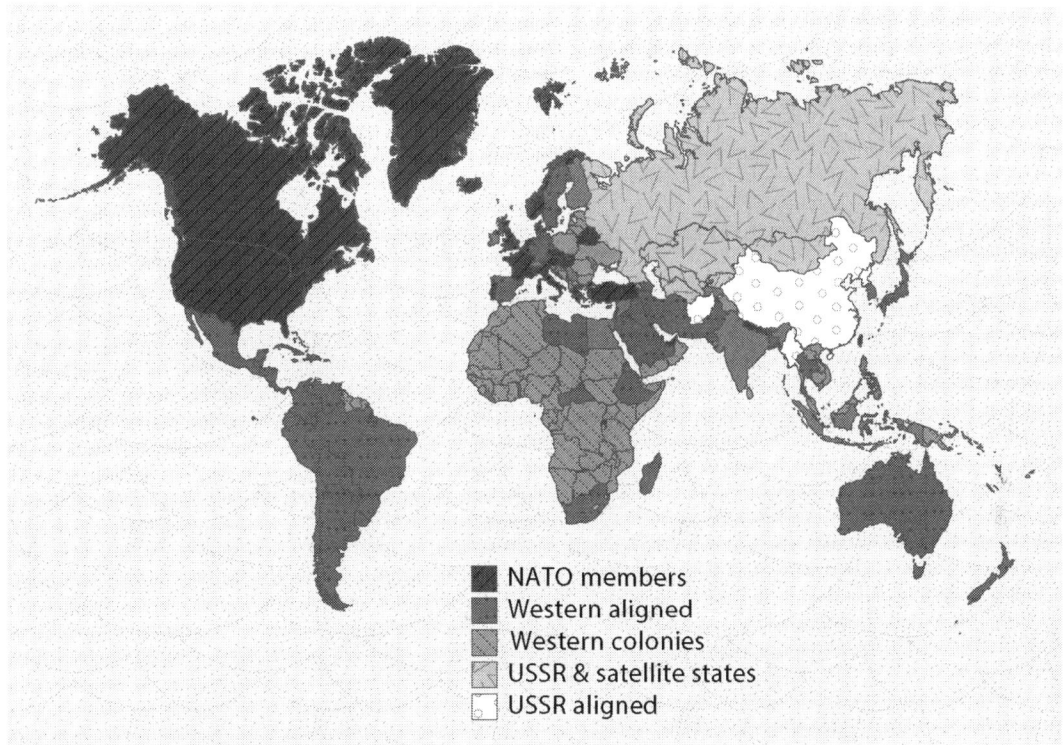

Figure 8.12. The Cold War (1953)

The Cold War extended to **space exploration**, also known as the space race. The Soviets launched the first artificial satellite on October 4, 1957, known as Sputnik. The US launched its own satellite called Explorer 1 the following year. While the US created the National Aeronautics and Space Administration (NASA) to further space exploration, on April 1961 the Soviets launched the first person, Yuri Gargarin, into space. However, the American Neil Armstrong was the first person to set foot on the moon during NASA's Apollo 11 mission on July 20, 1969.

The Cold War ended with the collapse of the Soviet Union in 1991; without two superpowers, the world entered a period of globalization (see the section on world history for details).

CIVIL RIGHTS

During the 1960s, the US experienced social and political change. The **Civil Rights Movement**, led by activists like the **Rev. Dr. Martin Luther King, Jr.** and **Malcolm X**, fought for African American rights in the South, including the abolition of segregation, and also for better living standards for blacks in northern cities. In Montgomery, Alabama, **Rosa Parks**, an African American woman, was arrested for refusing to give up her seat to a white man on a bus. Buses were segregated at the time, and leaders including Dr. King organized the Montgomery Bus Boycott to challenge segregation; the effort was ultimately successful. Building on their success, civil rights activists led peaceful protests and boycotts to protest segregation at lunch counters, in stores, at public pools, and in other public places.

The movement grew to include voter registration campaigns supported by students and other activists (both black and white) from around the country—the **Freedom Riders**, so-called because they rode buses from around the country to join the movement in the Deep South. Civil rights workers organized the March on Washington in 1963, when Dr. King delivered his famous *I Have a Dream* speech. In 1964, Congress passed the Civil Rights Act, which outlawed segregation.

Figure 8.13. March on Washington

The Civil Rights Movement extended beyond the Deep South. **Cesar Chavez** founded the **United Farm Workers**, which organized Hispanic migrant farm workers in California and the Southwest who faced racial discrimination, poor treatment, and low pay. The UFW used boycotts and nonviolent tactics similar to those used by civil rights activists in the South. The **American Indian Movement (AIM)** brought attention to injustices and discrimination suffered by Native Americans nationwide. **Feminist** activists fought for fairer treatment of women in the workplace and for women's reproductive rights. Finally, activists in New York and San Francisco began openly fighting for the civil rights of gays and lesbians.

THE TWENTY-FIRST CENTURY

By the end of the twentieth century, the United States had established itself as the dominant global economic, military, and political power. It had established military bases and a military presence worldwide, in Europe, Asia, the Pacific, and the Middle East. However, its global power did not prevent conflict. After the terrorist attacks on September 11, 2001, the United States began a war in Afghanistan, and later one in Iraq.

Still, the US dominated global trade: American corporations established themselves globally. American culture was widely popular: since the early twentieth century, American pop culture like music, movies, television shows, and fashion was enjoyed by millions of people around the world. Domestically, society became increasingly liberal. In 2008, the country elected the first African American president, **Barack Obama**. Technology like the **Internet** facilitated national and global communication, media, and business; minority groups like the LGBT community engaged in more advocacy; and environmental issues became more visible. The country continues to evolve.

SAMPLE QUESTIONS

5) How did Martin Luther King and other activists achieve civil rights for black Americans?

   A. through violent uprisings

   B. using nonviolence

   C. with the help of the Soviet Union

   D. by lobbying Congress only

Answers:

   A. Incorrect. For the most part, civil rights activists took a nonviolent approach in their work.

   B. Correct. Nonviolence was a defining characteristic of the mainstream Civil Rights Movement.

   C. Incorrect. The Civil Rights Movement was a domestic phenomenon.

   D. Incorrect. Civil rights activists did eventually succeed in getting civil rights legislation passed by working with the government; however, the movement was based in grassroots activism and protest.

6) Controversy over the Kansas-Nebraska Act of 1854 illustrated which of the following?

   A. immigration
   B. Reconstruction
   C. westward expansion
   D. sectionalism

   Answers:

   A. Incorrect. The Kansas-Nebraska Act did not address population movements into the country from overseas.
   B. Incorrect. Reconstruction happened when the Civil War was over in 1865.
   C. Incorrect. The United States had already controlled this territory since the Louisiana Purchase.
   D. **Correct.** The Kansas-Nebraska Act further divided the nation over slavery.

United States Government, Civics, and Democracy

Students should understand and be aware of the purpose of US government and its major principles; the three branches of government; federalism; major speeches and key documents; and the rights and responsibilities of US citizens.

In 1776, colonial leaders including John Adams and Thomas Jefferson began drafting a formal statement of the colonies' intentions for independence from the British government. The Continental Congress adopted the **Declaration of Independence** on the fourth of July of that year, now celebrated as Independence Day in the United States. According to the document, independence from Britain was necessary: it outlined grievances against the British Crown, and it asserted that "all men are created equal; that they are endowed by their Creator with certain unalienable rights; that among these are Life, Liberty and the pursuit of Happiness."

Dominating American political thought since the American Revolution, **republicanism** stresses liberties and rights as central values, opposes corruption, rejects inherited political power, and encourages citizens to be civic minded and independent. It is based on **popular sovereignty**, that is, the concept that the people are the source of political power. These ideas helped to form not only the Declaration of Independence but also the Constitution.

The colonies had broken away from Britain because of what they viewed as an oppressive, overbearing central government. As a result, the first government they created, whose framework was called the **Articles of Confederation**, was an intentionally weak, democratic government. Called a "firm league of friendship," it was designed to create a loose confederation between the colonies (now states) while allowing them to retain much of their individual sovereignty.

As a result, the Articles established a weak government with extremely limited authority: it did not have the power to levy taxes or raise an army. The legislature was intentionally and clearly subordinate to the states. Representatives were selected and paid by state legislatures.

It quickly became clear that this government was too weak to be effective, and by 1787, the new government of the United States was already in crisis. Without the power to levy taxes, the federal government had no way to alleviate its debt burden from the war. In addition, without an organizing authority, states began issuing their own currencies and crafting their own, competing trade agreements with foreign nations, halting trade and sending inflation through the roof. Without a national judicial system, there was no mechanism to solve the inevitable economic disputes. Furthermore, there were uprisings in the country.

A convention of the states was called to address problems in the young United States. At the **Constitutional Convention** in 1787, a decision was made to completely throw out the old Articles and write a new governing document from scratch.

The states did not want a central government that was so strong that it would oppress the states or the people, so they decided to prevent the concentration of power by dividing it. **Separation of powers** limited the powers within the federal government, dividing power among three branches: the executive, the legislative, and the judicial. In addition, each branch was given powers that would limit the power of the other branches in a system called **checks and balances**.

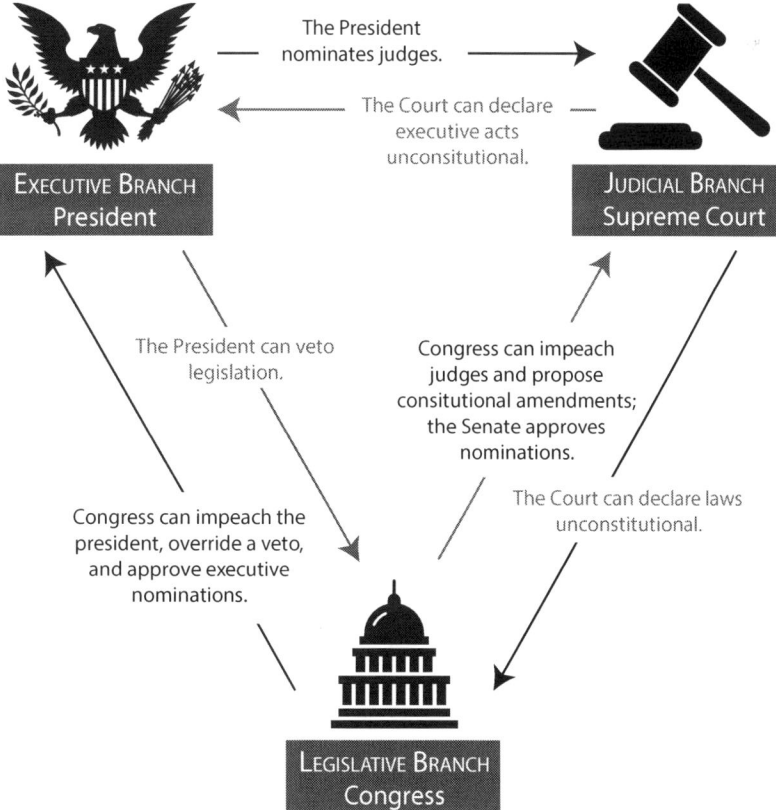

Figure 8.14. Checks and Balances

The executive branch—via the role of president—has the power to veto (reject) laws passed by the legislature. The legislative branch, consisting of Congress, can override the president's veto (with a two-thirds vote) and pass the law anyway. Finally, the judicial branch, consisting of the Supreme Court and other courts, can determine the constitutionality of laws (**judicial review**).

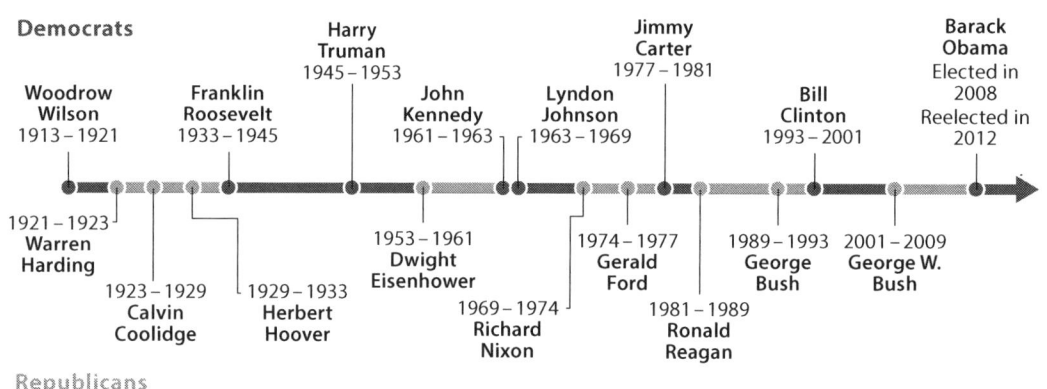

Figure 8.15. Presidential Timeline

At the writing of the Constitution, the branch of the federal government endowed with the most power was the legislative branch, which makes laws. Simply called **Congress**, this branch is composed of a bicameral legislature (two houses). While this structure was not originally adopted under the Articles of Confederation, the framers chose it when reorganizing the government, mainly due to a dispute at the convention over the structure of the legislative body—specifically the voting power of each state.

Small states advocated equal representation, with each state having the same number of representatives, each with one vote. However, the more populous states argued for a plan based on **proportional representation**. Each state would be assigned a number of representatives based on its population (enslaved people deprived of their rights would even be counted among the population, benefiting those states with large slave populations). In the end, the **Great Compromise** was reached. There would be two houses: the **House of Representatives** (the lower house) would have proportional representation, and the **Senate** (the upper house) would have equal representation.

> **DID YOU KNOW?**
>
> According to the Three-Fifths Compromise, enslaved persons were counted as three-fifths of a person in order to determine the population of a state. Slaves could not vote at all.

This system had two other advantages. The House of Representatives would also be directly elected by the people, and the Senate by the state legislatures. This supported the federal structure of the government: one house would serve the needs of the people directly, and the other would serve the needs of the states. Also, it curbed federal power by fragmenting it and slowing down the legislative process. Today, senators are also directly elected by the people.

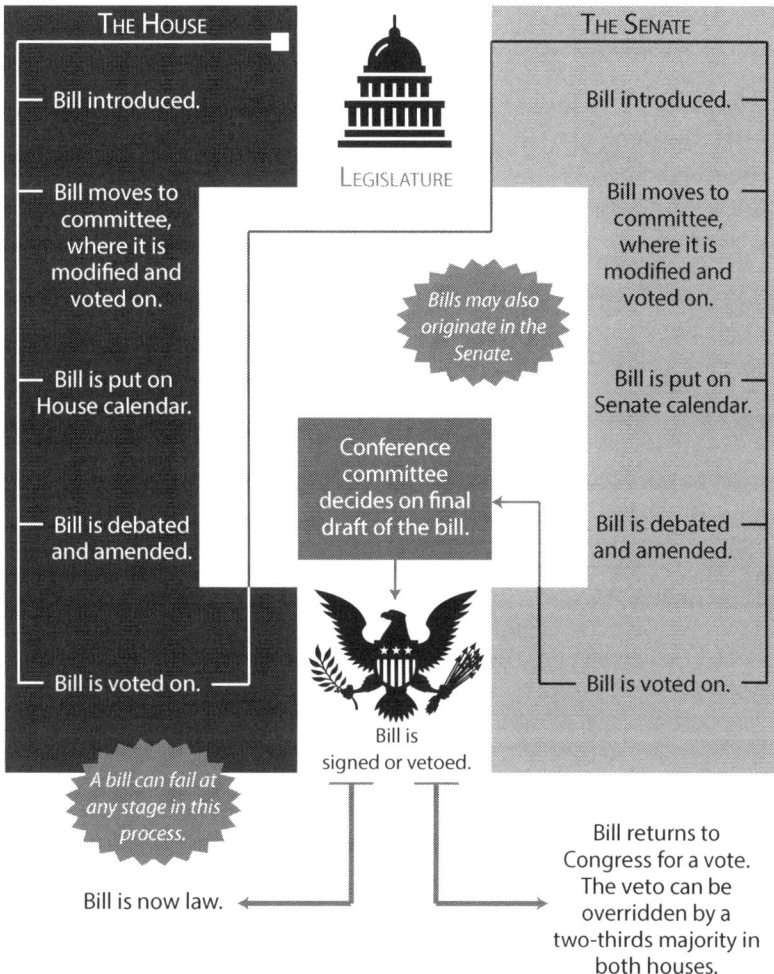

Figure 8.16. Bill to Law

Under the Constitution, the federal government is charged with matters that concern the population at large, such as managing federal lands, coining money, and maintaining an army and navy. It also handles conflicts between the states via the federal judiciary and by regulating interstate trade. Matters of regional or local concern are handled by state or local governments. This relationship is best codified in the Tenth Amendment, which states that any powers not explicitly given to the federal government are reserved for the states. The written Constitution can only be amended by a super majority.

State governments are generally modeled after these three branches, with the executive branch headed by the governor, the legislative branch headed by elected representatives, and the judicial branch headed by the state supreme court. **Local governments** have elected officials and generally follow charters that state constitutions have adopted. As they do with the federal government, the people vote for their state and local government representatives.

> **QUICK REVIEW**
>
> Describe how the legislative branch checks the power of the executive branch.

It took three years for all states to ratify the Constitution, with Rhode Island being the last to ratify on May 29, 1790. Much of the debate was over the lack of guarantees of basic civil rights in the Constitution. As a solution, James Madison in 1789 introduced twelve amendments to the Constitution. Ten of these twelve are known as the Bill of Rights.

The First Amendment protects **freedom of speech**. Congress may not pass laws that prohibit people from exercising freedom of religion, the press, assembly, or the right to petition against the government.

The Second Amendment allows citizens to bear arms.

The Third Amendment stops the government from quartering troops in private homes.

The Fourth Amendment protects citizens from searches and seizures without a warrant.

The Fifth Amendment ensures that citizens cannot be punished or subject to criminal prosecution without due process. Citizens also have the power of eminent domain, which means that private property cannot be seized for public use without proper compensation.

The Sixth Amendment gives citizens a right to a fair and fast trial by jury, the right to know the crimes for which they are charged, and the right to confront witnesses. Citizens also have the right to legal representation and to gather testimonies from witnesses.

The Seventh Amendment allows civil cases to be tried by jury (in the Articles of Confederation, only criminal trials could be tried by jury).

The Eighth Amendment disallows excessive bail or fines; it also prohibits cruel and unusual punishment.

The Ninth Amendment gives all rights not specifically enumerated in the Constitution to the people; it provides that the list of rights is not exhaustive.

The Tenth Amendment provides that all other powers not provided to the federal government in the Constitution belong to the states.

In the **Gettysburg Address**, Abraham Lincoln referred to the Constitution and the Declaration of Independence, asserting that the Civil War was a test of the survival of the Union as established in 1776. Declaring that the people must ensure that the "government of the people, by the people, for the people, shall not perish from the earth," he claimed that the Declaration of Independence was the ultimate expression of the original democratic intentions for the United States. Using the founding document as a basis for his speech, he pointed out that the Civil War was a "new birth of freedom," bringing equality to US citizens.

With citizenship comes responsibility. Today, US citizens maintain their government by **voting** for public officials at the local, state, and national levels. They also must pay **taxes** in order to provide the revenue the government requires to carry out its functions. The federal, state, and local governments all levy taxes of different kinds: income taxes, sales taxes, property taxes, and others. This money supports everything from installing stop signs to maintaining military aircraft.

US citizens are free to join **civic groups** that lobby government for legislation that works in their interest or that carry out public service in their communities. Some of these groups include the ACLU, which defends individual liberties, the NAACP, which works for African American rights, and the AARP, which supports the interests of the elderly. Citizens can also join groups that carry out **community service** such as the Boy Scouts and the Girl Scouts, or they may do such work through their church, mosque, synagogue, or other place of worship. Some students may already be doing community service themselves.

> **DID YOU KNOW?**
>
> Remind students that if they have purchased items, they have already likely paid taxes themselves.

SAMPLE QUESTIONS

7) Which of the following is NOT one of the amendments in the Bill of Rights?

   A. Citizens have the right to bear arms.

   B. The Senate must have equal representation.

   C. Citizens have the power of eminent domain.

   D. The government cannot quarter troops in private homes.

Answers:

A. Incorrect. According to the Second Amendment, US citizens have the right to bear arms.

B. Correct. The Bill of Rights does not determine representation in Congress.

C. Incorrect. The Fifth Amendment states that private property cannot be seized for public use without proper compensation.

D. Incorrect. The Third Amendment prohibits the government from quartering troops in private homes.

8) Which of the following is an example of a representative democracy?

   A. Citizens vote on legislation.

   B. Citizens vote on constitutional amendments.

   C. Citizens can directly vote for policies.

   D. The House must have proportional representation in order to adequately reflect population size.

Answers:

   A. Incorrect. In a representative democracy, citizens vote for representatives who vote on legislation.

   B. Incorrect. Citizens amend a constitution in a direct democracy.

   C. Incorrect. This is an example of direct democracy, where the people do not elect representatives to vote on policy for them.

   D. **Correct.** Representatives are elected to the House to represent the people; they vote on legislation on their behalf.

Economics

Elementary-level students should understand the basic concepts of supply and demand, scarcity, opportunity cost, how and why people generate wealth, how technology affects the economy, and the government's role in the economy.

The study of economics is the study of the production and consumption of products as well as how people produce and obtain these goods. It explains how people interact with the market; studying economics usually explains the behavior of people or the government.

One of the most important concepts in economics is **supply and demand**. Supply refers to how much the market can actually offer, and demand is how much desire there is for a product or service. The demand is the relationship between price and quantity, which is how much people are willing to pay for the product. The supply simply means how much product producers are willing to supply at a certain price. This relationship between price and how much product is offered to the market is known as the supply relationship.

Price is used to show the relationship between supply and demand. When the demand is high for a product, the price generally goes up. When the demand is low, price falls. However, if the price is considered too high by the public, there may be excess supply because people will purchase less. Causes of excess supply include other price changes, including the price of alternative goods, and public preferences. Likewise, there might be excess demand if the price is set too low and many people want the product, but there may not be enough supply. This might happen if there is a government ban on the product, the government imposes a price ceiling, or suppliers decide to not raise prices.

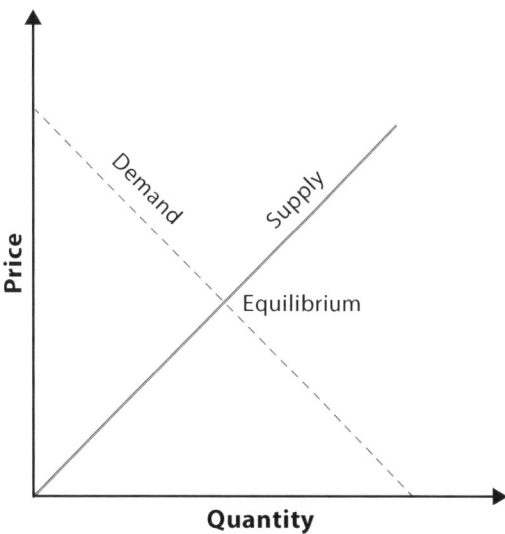

Figure 8.17. Supply and Demand

For example, before Halloween, prices of Halloween candy are high because consumers are willing to pay high prices. They want to purchase enough candy to celebrate the holiday at parties and to distribute to trick-or-treaters, even if it is expensive. However, after Halloween, leftover candy is usually on sale. This is because demand for candy is low: the holiday is over and so people do not need it. That leftover candy represents excess supply. In order to get rid of it, suppliers drop prices to entice consumers with a sweet tooth to buy it even though Halloween is past.

> **DID YOU KNOW?**
>
> An important idea in economics is wants and needs. *Wants* are the goods or services that people desire (like candy or manicures), whereas *needs* are the goods or services required to live and function (like water or medicine).

When supply and demand are equal, the economy is at equilibrium. However, that is not always the case. When there is insufficient supply to meet demand, the result is **scarcity**. People need to choose which want to satisfy. For example, if there is a low supply of chocolate, chocolate prices will be high. Consequently, a consumer must decide whether to spend more money than usual on chocolate or not to buy any at all.

Every choice has a value. **Opportunity cost** is when a consumer makes a choice at the cost of another choice or the value of an opportunity. For example, imagine that someone must choose between eating chocolate cake or apple pie. If that person chose the chocolate cake, he or she gave up the opportunity to eat the apple pie. The opportunity cost is the apple pie. Decisions made by an individual or the government based on opportunity cost are driven by needs, wants, income, and time.

When making economic choices both parts of the value (costs and benefits) should be considered. The ideal choice will have the greatest benefits at the lowest cost. For example, there are two stores that sell chocolate, but the first store sells it at $35 a box and the second store sells it at $40 a box. However, it takes an hour to drive to the first store and it will cost about $10 in gas to get there and back, while it takes 15 minutes and $2.50 in gas to reach the second store. Economically speaking, it is not worthwhile to drive to the first store. Choosing to pay more for the chocolate at the second store is the cost, and the benefit is the time and cost of gas saved by rejecting the first store.

People use resources in order to create **wealth** and enhance their lives. These resources are either goods or services people provide in exchange for money. People provide labor, creating goods and services available for purchase. Labor refers to people who work in almost any job: on farms, in factories, as computer programmers, etc. The goods and services produced enhance people's lives. For example, not everyone owns a farm or can grow a variety of produce, so consumers depend on farmers around the world to grow various agricultural products in order to obtain them. Those farmers use resources such as water and land in order to generate wealth. Likewise, not everyone can fix a computer, so a consumer can bring his or her computer to an expert to be repaired. The owner of a computer repair service would be compensated with cash, and he or she similarly builds wealth by using that cash to invest in the business, buy property, invest in the stock market, or for other purposes.

Technological innovation is also driven by the economy (and vice versa). For example, more efficient transportation has increased trade and the exchange of wealth. Railroads enabled US businesses to transport raw materials to their production facilities, thereby increasing production of goods. These areas then will need more people to provide labor, helping companies and individuals generate more wealth and providing jobs and salaries to workers, who themselves were thus able to generate more wealth in cash. More recently, computers and the Internet have sped up communication and commerce, opening new ways of doing business.

When population increases, people consume more resources, generating more demand for products to meet their needs. In addition, as companies generate more wealth, they can invest in innovation and even more new technology.

The federal government helps to regulate the economy. **Government regulation** falls into either economic regulation or social regulation. Economic regulation controls prices directly or indirectly. The government works to prevent monopolies: the control of a market for a good or service by one company or group. For example, the government may prohibit utility companies from raising their prices beyond a certain point. Antitrust law is another type of economic regulation. It strengthens market forces to protect consumers from businesses and to eliminate or minimize the need for direct regulation. These laws are intended to ensure fair competition in the US economy.

Social regulation encourages businesses to behave responsibly and prohibits harmful behavior. For example, the US Occupational Safety and Health Administration enforces workplace regulations to protect worker safety, and the Environmental Protection Agency regulates industry by upholding environmental standards for emissions and waste.

Finally, the government collects **taxes** not only to cover its expenses but also to help fuel the economy. Federal taxes pay for costs like federal employee salaries and retirement programs, government programs, and the military. Other government programs that are financed through taxes include veterans' benefits and NASA. Payroll taxes help **finance** the Medicare and Social Security programs which provide assistance for the elderly and those with low incomes. Government spending helps to increase the wealth of businesses and individuals. For example, if the government spends money to build bridges and highways, construction businesses generate more income. If an individual is retired or cannot work for health reasons, Social Security will provide assistance.

> **DID YOU KNOW?**
>
> There are currently seven ways the US people pay taxes. They are income, excise, sales, payroll, estate, property, and gift taxes.

SAMPLE QUESTIONS

9) Which of the following terms best describes a situation in which the federal government prevents the only Internet service company in a local community from raising its prices?

    A. economic regulation

    B. social regulation

    C. opportunity cost

    D. scarcity

    Answers:

    A. **Correct.** In this instance of economic regulation, the government is controlling prices by preventing a monopoly.

    B. Incorrect. Social regulation works to ensure ethical business practices. In this example, the government is only concerned with prices.

    C. Incorrect. Opportunity cost describes making one choice at the expense of another; it does not apply to this situation.

    D. Incorrect. If the supply of a product cannot meet demand for it, the result is scarcity; that concept does not apply in this situation.

10) During Easter, chocolate eggs are sold at three for $3, while caramel eggs are two for $3. A consumer prefers caramel, but is very hungry, so he purchases the chocolate eggs to have one extra egg. Which of the following terms best describes this situation?

A. needs
B. opportunity cost
C. supply
D. demand

Answers:

A. Incorrect. *Needs* refers to goods and services that a consumer requires to live and function. Candy eggs are not necessary for survival; they are *wants*.

B. **Correct.** The customer enjoyed one extra egg at the expense of his preferred flavor, caramel. In this case, the caramel eggs were the opportunity cost: the loss he suffered at the expense of his choice to have an extra chocolate egg at the same price.

C. Incorrect. The question does not provide any information about the supply of either type of egg.

D. Incorrect. The question does not provide any information about the demand for either type of egg.

Social Studies Skills and Processes

Social studies encourages students to investigate questions about people, their values, and the choices they make. In other words, students engage in **inquiry**: they seek information, knowledge, or the truth. Inquiry-based learning in social studies is a process in which students gather information by identifying relevant questions and uncovering sources in order to interpret information and report their findings.

Teachers can help students develop critical thinking skills by encouraging **questioning**. The more questions students ask, the more carefully they evaluate sources and actively research information that helps them to draw conclusions.

Using research and resource materials is a critical component in social studies processes. There are two main types of sources: primary and secondary. **Primary sources** are original records and have information from a person who experienced the event firsthand. Primary sources include original documents like the US Constitution and Declaration of Independence, journals, speeches, physical artifacts, and some first-person accounts in places such as newspapers or historical documents.

Secondary sources are texts created by people who did not personally experience or witness the event. They are based on primary sources. Examples of secondary sources include books, research papers and analyses, and some reports or features in newspapers and magazines written by journalists and other writers.

Using a variety of sources is essential when conducting research. Analyzing the relationship between primary and secondary sources relating to the same subject matter gives students a deeper understanding of the topic being studied. Understanding the advantages and disadvantages of each source also helps students understand and actively engage in **data interpretation**: assessing whether their sources are valid or appropriate.

Using primary sources permits students to draw **conclusions** based on their own interpretations of those sources, rather than relying on secondary interpretations. Primary sources also allow students to more directly address the topic and usually provide information found nowhere else. However, certain primary sources may not have any objective information or accurate facts. Moreover, these types of sources can be difficult to find and analyze.

Secondary sources enrich study by providing different perspectives and expert conclusions. Furthermore, using reputable sources may be more efficient; they may be more accessible or easier to understand. However, secondary sources may focus on issues beyond the topic under study; they may be outdated; or they may be tainted by the author's bias.

Students must think critically when reading or using any source. They should understand how to distinguish between **fact** and **opinion**. Facts are statements that can be proven, and opinions are statements that reflect someone's view; they cannot be proven. Understanding these differences helps students evaluate sources. If students can distinguish between fact and opinion, then they can determine the validity of the source in question.

When interpreting information, students should be aware of variables involved. A **variable** is anything that can take on a different value. For example, age is considered a variable; so is place of origin. There are many kinds of variables, but they mainly fall into dependent and independent variables. Independent variables are manipulated or controlled by the researcher; they are not changed by any other factors. Dependent variables rely on the independent variable; they may be changed by other factors.

Understanding variables helps students interpret information and draw conclusions. For example, a student writing an essay arguing that westward expansion had a positive effect on the US would need to gather sources such as first-hand accounts of people who moved to the West for opportunities, charts demonstrating population growth, and information about the types of jobs available during those times.

> **DID YOU KNOW?**
>
> There are qualitative and quantitative data in variables. Qualitative data is based on human interpretation and quantitative data is based on statistical analysis.

When drawing conclusions, students should demonstrate an ability to address arguments and provide explanations. When constructing their conclusions, they should provide relevant information. They may even offer new perspectives on the research problem. For example, students can find ways to address local community problems. No matter what, they should all demonstrate an understanding of the problem being researched and thoughtful use of the tools available in social studies.

SAMPLE QUESTIONS

11) Which of the following best describes an independent variable?

    A. the amount of paint a painter needs to paint a room
    B. the number of errors an student gets on a test
    C. the dosage and timing of an anti-inflammatory drug to test its impact
    D. how much time it will take to drive between Houston and San Antonio

    Answers:

    A. Incorrect. The amount of paint required for a room is a dependent variable; it is determined not by the painter but by the room size.
    B. Incorrect. Test scores depend on a number of factors, such as the time the student devoted to studying or the student's confidence level.
    C. Correct. The doctor or scientist who carries out the experiment controls the timing and dose.
    D. Incorrect. While it is possible to estimate how long a trip between the two cities will take, factors like traffic and weather can change and will affect timing. Here, length of time is a dependent variable.

12) Which of the following are examples of primary sources?

    A. original photographs, first-hand newspaper reports, textbooks, and interviews
    B. memoirs, original photographs, first-hand newspaper reports, and diary entries
    C. speeches, newspaper reports, essays, and reviews
    D. essays, reviews, textbooks, and analytical papers

    Answers:

    A. Incorrect. Textbooks are not primary resources.
    B. Correct. All of these are examples of primary resources.
    C. Incorrect. While speeches are primary sources, only first-hand newspaper reports count as primary resources. If they are reported, then they are considered secondary resources. Essays and reviews are secondary sources.
    D. Incorrect. These are all examples of secondary resources.

9

Curriculum and Instruction

In designing instruction to meet the needs of students, teachers must understand the purpose of teaching social studies and be able to transfer knowledge effectively. To support student learning, teachers must select strategies and resources that address all social studies concepts and content areas.

Geography, Anthropology, and Sociology

Geography teaches students about global cultural and physical phenomena, providing them with the knowledge and skills to better understand their relationship to the earth and other people around the world. Geography in the elementary grades stresses the physical attributes of the earth, such as place names, locations, recognition of physical landforms, and map skills. When designing instruction, teachers should develop student understanding of map and globe skills like the cardinal directions and use of symbols.

Students begin by using small-scale political maps of the US, learning about the **states**; this will prepare them to work with more complex maps of **countries** and **continents**. As students progress to higher grades, they should gain exposure to physical and cultural maps. Understanding physical attributes helps students develop an awareness of relationships between physical and human geography, or how people interact in physical space: conceptual examples include **communities** and the usage of **transportation**.

> **TEACHING TIP**
>
> Current events like natural or human-made disasters are great topics for class discussion in explaining why masses of people would move to or from a certain geographic area.

When teaching how humans and geography impact each other, create lessons that address migration. Students should understand why people choose where they live, such as language, social structures, pull factors like economic opportunity, and push factors like droughts or conflict. Students should understand how **technology** facilitates global interaction and movement; they should have a grasp of the concept of **globalization**.

When introducing anthropology and sociology concepts, teachers should focus on developing students' understanding of their relationships with the world around them. Since many of these concepts revolve around current events, a wide variety of sources should be used, including primary sources and reported works (such as TV news or newspapers).

Lessons should also help students develop an understanding of how individuals and society impact each other. Teaching about communities enriches student understanding of the different roles people play in society and the services society offers to individuals. Exploring different types of communities—for instance, looking at the differences between urban, suburban, and rural ones—helps students understand how different communities interact and impact one another.

Teachers should also design instruction around the concept of **social structures**, or how people behave in social relationships. Students need to understand that such interactions have guidelines: people who choose to be part of these social structures are expected to behave in a certain way. Concrete concepts such as explaining the rules of a classroom or traffic laws can demonstrate what social structures are before scaffolding into more complex ideas.

Content for lessons can include information about different cultural backgrounds, the contributions of different cultures, and cultural value systems. For example, students can study differences and similarities in school between locally born and immigrant students. How many languages are spoken by students in the school, and which ones? What holidays and foods do all students have in common, and which ones have the students from other countries introduced to the school community?

To further develop student understanding, teachers can create lessons addressing social institutions that meet basic social needs and organize social behavior. Students can gain a better perspective on social institutions by exploring different types of families, neighborhoods, and communities. Lessons on prejudice and stereotypes would also fall under this category. Students learn how individual styles of **communication** impact others by studying social class, inequality, and bullying.

Teachers can present transportation and **technology** through discussions about industrialization and its effects. Specific lessons on the Industrial Revolution help students understand the impact of technology and transportation on society and social organization. (Also see *Economics*, later in the chapter.) Finally, students must be aware of the impact of computer technology and the Internet.

EXAMPLE QUESTIONS

1) A third grade teacher shows students a physical map of the state in which they live. The teacher highlights the location of agricultural resources, natural water sources, major roads, and areas with dense population. The teacher is most likely teaching the students

   A. that people tend to build major roads to agricultural resources.
   B. the relationship between human settlement and physical features.
   C. the reason for the state's high agricultural output.
   D. that there are many ecosystems in the state, and they must be preserved.

   Answers:

   A. Incorrect. This explanation does not address why the teacher highlighted natural water sources.
   B. **Correct.** The teacher is showing the influence of geographical features on human and physical systems. People will go to places that can sustain life, such as sources of food and water.
   C. Incorrect. This explanation does not address all the factors that the teacher discusses.
   D. Incorrect. The information in the question does not address ecosystem preservation.

2) Which of the following would be the best example to use in a lesson discussing push factors in migration?

   A. political stability
   B. war
   C. more employment opportunities
   D. less crime

   Answers:

   A. Incorrect. Political stability would not force a population to leave a particular area.
   B. **Correct.** The danger posed by a war clearly illustrates why an individual or group would leave an area or country.
   C. Incorrect. Employment opportunities are pull factors; migrants and immigrants often move in search of work.
   D. Incorrect. Less crime would not push a population from a location.

History

Understanding **chronology** is essential to student understanding of history at the elementary level. Teachers must cover classical civilizations, US history from

founding to the twenty-first century, and twentieth century developments and transformations worldwide. To help students understand these events, teachers should select a variety of sources to supplement textbooks, including historical maps, historical photographs, architecture, and political cartoons, to help students deepen their understanding.

Developing chronological thinking is one of the first steps in teaching history; chronologies help students examine relationships between the past and present, the causes and effects of historical events. Teachers help students identify the temporal structure of a historical narrative (e.g. the beginning, middle, and end) so that they can construct their own historical narratives. Students should practice explaining the origins of an event and how it developed over time.

To help students develop chronological thinking, assignments may include creating and interpreting timelines illustrating the differences among the past, present, and future. Teachers should select well-written historical narratives such as biographies and historical literature to supplement class work. These resources enable students to analyze patterns of historical duration (like the legacy of a notable historical document, such as the US Constitution) and historical succession (such as the evolution of broad systems over time, like trade and communication networks).

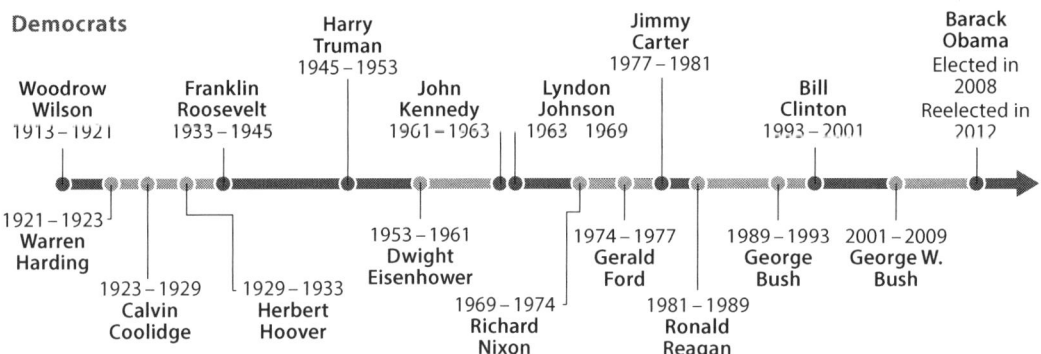

Figure 9.1. Presidential Timeline

For students to develop a deeper understanding of history, they cannot simply view it as a series of facts. Students should develop an understanding of **historical analysis,** the interpretation of historical processes, documents, and events. The goal is for students to understand not only what happened, but also how and why it did.

Historical analysis requires evaluating sources and developing reasonable conclusions based on the evidence gathered. Students need to address multiple perspectives so they can assess whether a source is credible. Teaching students to use primary and secondary sources is integral for them to develop a deeper understanding of the topic being studied.

Students who successfully grasp historical analysis will be able to **analyze** the causes and effects of events. To do so, students can look at both immediate and underlying causes. Immediate causes are what trigger the main event. For example, Japan's surrender in the Second World War was an immediate cause for the war's end. Underlying causes are more likely to be trends that emerged long before the event in question; for instance, sectionalism was an underlying cause of the US Civil War.

> **TEACHING TIP**
>
> Adding pictures to timelines can be helpful for students to visualize events in history.

Students must learn to compare events from different times and regions and hypothesize how the past influences the present. These comparisons can be as simple as comparing and contrasting Greek inventions with Roman ones, or discussing how Egyptian papyrus influenced how people communicate today.

EXAMPLE QUESTIONS

3) Which of the following is NOT an appropriate example to use in describing a cause or effect of the US Civil War?

   A. Inflation grew as more money was printed in both the North and the South.

   B. European immigrants were attracted to the South because of its booming economy, exacerbating tensions that led to the Civil War.

   C. Cotton exports to England stopped because the Union enforced a naval blockade of the South.

   D. Several states seceded from the Union when Abraham Lincoln became president.

   Answers:

   A. Incorrect. Both the Union and the Confederacy did indeed print money to generate revenue, which caused inflation.

   B. Correct. Immigrants from Europe actually preferred the North because there were more job opportunities there.

   C. Incorrect. The Confederacy was unable to export cotton for revenue or import supplies as a result of the successful naval blockade.

   D. Incorrect. Several Southern states did indeed secede from the Union upon Lincoln's election; President Lincoln opposed slavery.

4) A teacher asks students to compare different songs and poems about the War of 1812. In small groups, they must explain how these sources help people understand significant historical events and other people's perspectives on them. This assignment is an example of

A. questioning.

B. chronology.

C. interpreting timelines.

D. historical analysis.

Answers:

A. Incorrect. Questioning is only a part of the assignment. The teacher also asks students to develop conclusions.

B. Incorrect. Students must consider the events of a specific historical time period, but not necessarily in order.

C. Incorrect. The teacher asks students to interpret poetry and songs, not timelines.

D. **Correct.** This assignment requires students to understand the events of the War of 1812, analyzing primary resources, and then to develop their own conclusions.

Government, Civics, and Democracy

In civics, students learn about **politics** and the rights and responsibilities that accompany citizenship. Learning about government systems helps students understand their duties and rights as citizens. It also helps students to become active, engaged, and informed citizens.

Teachers should develop these concepts by helping students deepen their understanding of **democracy**. Lessons should emphasize the choices and opportunities that allow US citizens and residents to improve their country and each other's lives. To effectively teach these principles, teachers should model democracy in the classroom. For example, teachers can have students vote on class issues (like what to name a class pet) to show how democracy works.

Citizens must select people to fill positions of authority, like local and state representatives. In order to choose someone who best represents the interests of the people, citizens need to be informed. Teachers should emphasize that voting occurs at the federal, state, and local levels and that it is the voter's responsibility to learn about electoral candidates.

Students should also understand the role of the US Constitution in the federal government. To help students understand how and why the Constitution was formed, lessons may address the separation of powers. Students should understand that the federal legislative, judicial, and executive branches all check each other's powers to maintain a balance, and that similar processes occur at the state and local levels throughout the country. Examples might include studying the roles and actions of political entities, departments, or administrators in the local community.

Teaching **citizenship** is another integral part of civics education. Students should learn how a person becomes a citizen and the attitudes and actions that reflect responsible citizenship; the Bill of Rights is a strong discussion point in explaining how US citizens are granted certain freedoms. Well-known national symbols like the flag, the Statue of Liberty, and the Liberty Bell are just some examples that may be used as discussion points in teaching students about US values.

Exploring themes like responsibility, compassion, respect, and courage teaches students the value of participating in their own communities to maintain a strong democracy and protect their civil rights. Lessons present students with situations contrasting responsible citizenship with poor citizenship, conflict resolution, and the importance of democratic participation. Holidays like Presidents' Day, Veterans' Day, and Independence Day are a few examples of traditions students can study to explore themes like governance, civil liberties, and military and civil service.

> **QUICK REVIEW**
>
> What is one example of a lesson that teaches citizenship?

EXAMPLE QUESTIONS

5) Which of the following activities would be the best way for a teacher to address the theme of courage in a civics class?

   A. taking a class trip to help clean up the local park

   B. discussing the activism of Dr. Martin Luther King, Jr.

   C. establishing a classroom lost-and-found

   D. holding a mock trial to explain the concept of jury duty

Answers:

   A. Incorrect. Such a class trip would help teach students about respect—here, respect for public property—not courage.

   B. Correct. Dr. Martin Luther King, Jr. fought for the civil rights of people of color even though it was dangerous to do so. His story is a clear example of courageously doing the right thing, even when it might be unpopular or dangerous.

   C. Incorrect. A lost-and-found teaches students that lost property must still be returned to its rightful owner; it is dishonest for students to keep property that does not belong to them. This activity will help students learn the importance of honesty, not courage.

   D. Incorrect. Jury duty is just that—a duty. A mock trial would be a more appropriate activity for teaching civic responsibility.

6) Which of the following would NOT be a good lesson to teach the principles of democracy in the United States?

   A. having all students vote publicly for class officers
   B. engaging students in a class discussion on evaluating the powers, duties, and limitations of state government offices
   C. taking students through a mock process that mimics how laws are passed in Congress
   D. presenting the system of checks and balances

Answers:

   A. **Correct.** US citizens vote anonymously, in part to reduce the risk of political pressure, retribution, and discrimination during and after elections. Students should also vote for class officers using a secret ballot in order to understand the importance of avoiding the peer pressure, bullying, and retribution that could otherwise influence the voting process, whether in the classroom or in Congress.
   B. Incorrect. This lesson would demonstrate important factors to consider when voting in elections for such positions.
   C. Incorrect. This lesson would be an appropriate way for students to experience firsthand how laws are really passed.
   D. Incorrect. Studying checks and balances would clearly demonstrate how decisions are actually made in the government.

Economics

Teaching economics at the elementary level should emphasize basic economic concepts and how consumers, **employers**, and **employees** make economic decisions. Students should develop an understanding of the **market economy**. Teachers can create lessons that deal with how buyers and sellers interact to create markets, and how those interactions affect prices and scarcity of goods. Students should understand the concept of supply and demand, and that when either variable changes, the markets adjust accordingly. Further, the concept of competition should be introduced. For example, competition among producers helps to lower costs and prices for consumers, but competition among **consumers** leads to increases in price. Students can then apply their knowledge of supply and demand to analyze markets in which they personally participate, how buyers and sellers can influence prices, and predict if there will be a scarcity or surplus in goods. Examples might include seasonal demand for holiday greeting cards, holiday candy, Christmas trees, and other items, or availability and demand for sports paraphernalia before major sporting events like the Superbowl or World Series.

Teachers should also create instructional strategies to teach students that economic decision-making is based on weighing the **costs** and **benefits** of each choice. Demonstrating the **opportunity cost** associated with an individual's every economic decision can help students understand how to make better decisions as consumers. Lessons can include creating a class economy to show that individuals and communities have limited resources, and they need to make responsible decisions about their use.

Students will also benefit from lessons on how wealth is generated. Instruction should address how people generate income and the role of the market therein. For example, education and market demand for job skills can affect an individual's potential salary. Students can also study entrepreneurship in the higher grades to gain an understanding of how pooling resources together also increases wealth. Students will learn that their current decisions (e.g. education, training, etc.) may affect how much money they will make in the future. They can also use their knowledge of income to understand what opportunity cost is from a personal standpoint. Practical activities such as creating a budget help reinforce these concepts.

> **QUICK REVIEW**
>
> List two ways teachers can develop students' understanding of the concept of a market economy.

In addition to studying basic economic concepts, students should study the impact of economics on society and the role of government in the economy. Instruction should address socioeconomic institutions like labor unions, banks, legal organizations, and charity organizations; lessons can include studying actual such organizations in the local community and their impact on students' lives.

As students progress through the elementary grades, they should be taught how the government stimulates economic growth. For example, they can predict what might happen when the government invests in businesses, education, and public health. In addition, teachers should introduce the concept of taxes and how they help the government, and in turn, its people. Students may even consider how taxes and government programs impact the school and student activities.

Helping students develop an understanding of the **global marketplace** is also integral to the study of economics. Instruction should address concepts like trade and the exchange of wealth among countries. For example, students can track where the products they use originate and discover the sources of raw materials. Who makes their clothes, and where do the materials come from? Where do the minerals for their cell phones come from, and who assembles them? How do they get to the local stores? Students can also apply their knowledge of supply and demand on a global scale. They should investigate the way global interdependence impacts the local economy and how globalization affects decision-making in production and consumption of goods.

Finally, teachers must address the impact of **industrialization**. Students can study how new technologies have allowed more efficient trade opportunities; they should also examine the role of industry and technology in supply and demand. For example, students may investigate production methods: the assembly line increased economic output and thus the wealth of both workers and companies. Lessons can also revolve around how technology has influenced competition, increased standards of living, and offered more career choices.

EXAMPLE QUESTIONS

7) Which of the following is a primary reason to discuss needs and wants with students?

    A. Students must understand how to budget for their wants.

    B. Students can use this concept to understand opportunity cost.

    C. Needs and wants impact supply and demand.

    D. Understanding needs and wants is essential to understanding all other elements of economics.

    Answers:

    A. Incorrect. Learning to budget may be a result of learning about needs and wants, but this is not necessarily the most important part of an economics class.

    B. Incorrect. It is not necessary to understand needs and wants to understand opportunity cost.

    C. Correct. The concept of supply and demand is fundamental in understanding the free market economy.

    D. Incorrect. Ultimately all economics students should understand the concept of needs and wants, but it is not the most essential concept for the beginner student.

8) A lesson on job trends and average salaries of people who graduate college communicates which of the following concepts to students?

    A. the global marketplace

    B. generating wealth

    C. market economy

    D. supply and demand

    Answers:

    A. Incorrect. Employees are part of the global marketplace, but this term is too broad when referring specifically to the amount of money people can earn with certain credentials.

    B. Correct. This lesson can show students all the variables to consider as they contemplate earning money in the future.

    C. Incorrect. The term *market economy* is too broad; this lesson is specifically geared toward wealth generation.

    D. Incorrect. Supply and demand refers to the availability of and demand for goods and services; while there may be demand for certain job skills, this term does not adequately address the wealth generation concepts specifically taught in this lesson.

Social Studies Skills and Processes

Teaching social studies is not complete without giving students an understanding of the skills and processes they need to be informed and engaged with people in the world around them. Students must be aware that their world is continuously changing; the skills they learn in social studies enable them to cope with social change and thrive in society. Teachers must deliver social studies content in a way that students can understand; furthermore, teachers must help students develop their written and oral abilities to communicate their interpretations of current and historical events. Instructional strategies should address economic reasoning, chronological and spatial thinking, and historical interpretation by having students evaluate primary and secondary sources.

To do so, teachers should help students understand **information analysis**. Students consider an issue at hand and gather information to help them approach the issue. Lessons should address how students can find information, including appropriate materials, **text resources**, and technology to use in the inquiry process. Students should also learn the difference between primary and secondary resources, their advantages and disadvantages, and when it is appropriate to use them. For example, students should understand that **photographs** are considered a primary resource; they depict an original perspective on an event (see below). The overall

Figure 9.2. Primary Resource: Photograph Taken During the Great Depression

message should be that students need a variety of sources to best understand the topic being discussed.

Teachers should also help students determine the credibility of sources. For example, the Internet provides a wealth of information, but not everything that a student finds may be relevant or true. Students should understand that determining online credible resources requires knowledge of the author and his or her reputation, whether the domain name is linked to a reputable organization, and whether other references are cited (e.g. peer-reviewed articles and other appropriate authoritative sources).

The next step is learning to organize research to ensure it is relevant. Students should gain exposure to different kinds of social science resources and develop the skills needed to interpret and understand various types of information. For example, if students are studying deforestation, they might need to gather **maps**, **datasets**, or **images** that show how many trees have been cut down over a certain amount of time. Such projects can be used in lessons to illustrate the value of specific resources and how to find them.

From there, students should learn how to organize and **synthesize** information: social science students must process and interact with information rather than just regurgitating it. Here, strong reading comprehension skills are essential; furthermore, students should learn to closely examine data for repeating patterns and trends. Teachers help students to apply new knowledge to gain new insights.

Graphic organizers like **diagrams**, **tables**, and **graphs** help visually impart information, allowing students to identify variables or values affecting relevant data and determine the pros and cons of issues.

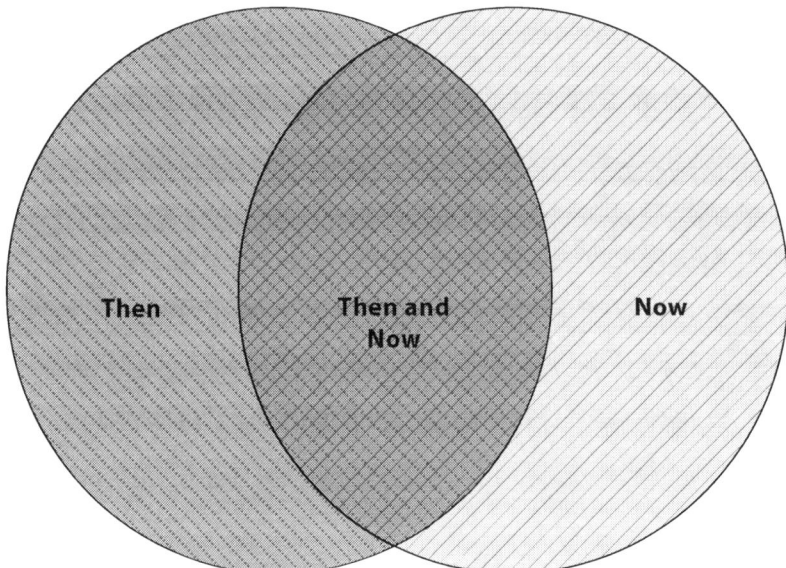

Figure 9.3. Venn Diagram

Popular types of graphic organizers include Venn diagrams (comparing and contrasting issues), semantic webs (to help students brainstorm ideas), mind maps, KWL charts (where students write down what they know, want to know, and want to learn about a given topic), and concept circles (in which students categorize words related to a certain topic). Graphic organizers also help students develop decision-making skills: students learn to take into account values, different courses of action, and potential consequences. As a result, teachers guide students toward better decision-making in their own lives.

EXAMPLE QUESTIONS

9) Which of the following would be the most appropriate graphic organizer for a student who is asked to organize a series of significant events?

   A. KWL chart

   B. timelines

   C. Venn diagram

   D. semantic web

   Answers:

   A. Incorrect. A KWL chart depicts what students already know, want to know, and (later) have learned about a topic.

   B. Correct. Timelines allow students to sequence events, organizing their thoughts.

   C. Incorrect. Venn diagrams are best suited for comparing and contrasting events, not organizing a series sequentially.

   D. Incorrect. Semantic webs are useful in making connections between concepts, but not necessarily used to depict the order of a series of events.

10) Which of the following is NOT a method teachers should encourage students to use when conducting online research?

    A. selecting appropriate keywords

    B. looking through a website for relevant information

    C. checking the validity of the source by researching its author or publisher

    D. choosing the first search result as a valid source

    Answers:

    A. Incorrect. Selecting appropriate keywords helps students narrow down their searches.

    B. Incorrect. Skimming for relevant information is appropriate both on- and offline, and students will be more efficient in their research if teachers show them how to spot relevant resources.

C. Incorrect. Checking the validity of sources is one of the most important lessons teachers can teach.

D. Correct. Not all search results are relevant or have correct information. Students should be encouraged to search until they can verify the validity of a source and determine if that source provides relevant information.

Terms

abolitionism: the ending of slavery

Abraham Lincoln: first Republican president, an abolitionist elected in 1860; his election triggered Southern secession. He led the country through the Civil War, but he was assassinated in 1865 before Reconstruction truly began

absolute location: a location identifiable by specific geographic coordinates

Algonquin: northeastern Native American civilization in the Great Lakes region

ancient Egyptians: emerged as early as 5000 BCE in the Nile Valley; known for their pyramids, art, use of papyrus as paper, and pictorial writing (hieroglyphs); united under one monarch, or pharaoh

anthropology: the study of humans and their cultures

arms race: competitive weapons development between the US and the USSR during the 1980s; the US intended to outspend the USSR, thereby weakening it

Articles of Confederation: the original framework of the US government, designed to create a loose confederation between the colonies (now states) while allowing them to retain much of their individual sovereignty; created an intentionally weak, democratic government

assembly line: a labor-intensive method of production developed by Henry Ford in which workers repetitively execute separate key tasks in production, expediting the product's completion

Assyria: Sumerian-based civilization in the Near East; established military dominance and played an important role in regional trade

Athens: ancient Greek city-state that became a revolutionary democracy controlled by the poor and working classes around 460 BCE; the first known democracy

Augustus Caesar: Julius Caesar's nephew Octavian who gained control of Rome in 27 BCE and became the first Roman emperor

Axis: the alliance of Germany, Italy, and Japan during WWII

Babylonia: Sumerian-based civilization in Mesopotamia; developed courts and an early codified rule of law—the Code of Hammurabi—"an eye for an eye, a tooth for a tooth"

Barack Obama: first African American president, elected in 2008; ended wars in Afghanistan and Iraq; halted the Great Recession; developed programs to provide healthcare to uninsured Americans

Battle of Bunker Hill: took place on June 17, 1775; caused King George III to declare that the colonies were in rebellion

Battle of Fort Sumter: 1861 attack on Union troops in Sumter, South Carolina, by Confederate forces shortly after South Carolina seceded from the Union; this battle sparked the Civil War

Battle of Lexington and Concord: beginning of violent conflict between American rebel militiamen (minutemen) and the British in 1775

Battle of Yorktown: 1781 defeat of British forces by the Continental Army with support from France, ending the Revolutionary War

Bill of Rights: the first ten amendments to the US Constitution; a set of guarantees of certain rights enjoyed by Americans

Boston Massacre: 1770 event in which British troops fired on a crowd of American protestors

Boston Tea Party: 1773 protest of the Tea Act in which American colonial protestors disguised as Native Americans tossed tea off a ship in Boston Harbor

cardinal directions: north, south, east, and west

Cesar Chavez: civil rights activist; led the United Farm Workers, who advocated for Hispanic farm workers who faced racial discrimination, poor treatment, and low pay

checks and balances: each branch of government has certain powers that limit the power of the other branches

Cherokee: Southeastern Native American civilization thought to be descended from the Iroquois; emerged in present-day Georgia; forced during the Trail of Tears to leave their land and migrate to Indian Territory (Oklahoma)

Civil Rights Movement: social and political movement for the rights of African Americans and other disenfranchised people in the 1960s

Cold War: period of ongoing tension and conflict between the US and the USSR, the post-WWII global superpowers; remained "cold" because the two countries never engaged in direct military confrontation

Committees of Correspondence: colonial rebel protest group that distributed anti-British propaganda

concentration camps: forced labor and death camps where the Nazis imprisoned and killed Jews, Roma, Slavic people, homosexuals, disabled people, people of color, prisoners of war, communists, and others as part of the Holocaust

Congress: the branch of the federal government that makes laws (the legislative branch); technically, it has the most power in government

Constitution: the document that provides the framework for the US government

Constitutional Convention: 1787 meeting of the states to resolve problems arising from limitations on federal power. A decision was made to completely throw out the old Articles and write a new governing document from scratch—the Constitution

Creek, **Chickasaw**, and **Choctaw**: major Muskogean-speaking southeastern Native American civilizations; descendants of the Mississippi Mound Builders

cuneiform: a Sumerian development; the earliest known example of writing using characters to form words (not pictographs)

conflict: the process of disagreement, usually resolved when one of the parties receives either the entirety or a satisfactory amount of the desired goal

cooperation: the process of working together to achieve similar goals; often leads to positive outcomes

D-Day: June 6, 1944, when the US led the invasion of Normandy, invading Europe during WWII

Declaration of Independence: issued on July 4, 1776, this document, written in great part by Thomas Jefferson and signed by the leaders of the Second Continental Congress, asserted US independence from Britain

demand: how much desire there is for a product or service

demokratia: ancient Greek word meaning "people power"

desert: a climate located in the low latitudes north and south of the savannah; the hottest and driest parts of the earth; receives less than 10 inches of rainfall a year

economic regulation: indirect or direct price control by the government

Elizabeth Cady Stanton: women's rights activist; founded the National Woman Suffrage Association and led the 1848 Seneca Falls Convention on women's rights

Emancipation Proclamation: January 1, 1863 declaration by President Lincoln that slavery was abolished in the rebel states

euro: a common currency shared by some European countries

European Union: a forum for European countries to organize and cooperate politically, militarily, and economically; formed after the Cold War to promote European unity

exchange: the process of giving one thing and receiving another (usually with similar value) in return

First Continental Congress: meeting of colonial leaders in Philadelphia in 1774, organized in response to the Intolerable Acts; colonial leaders later presented concerns to the king and were rebuffed

Four Freedoms: in the context of the rise of fascism, FDR defined these as freedom of speech, freedom of religion, freedom from want, and freedom from fear

Franklin Delano Roosevelt: elected to the presidency in 1932; developed the New Deal, rescuing the United States from the Great Depression, and led the country through WWII

genocide: killing people based on their ethnicity

geographic features: physical features of place like continents, bodies of water, plains, plateaus, mountains, and valleys

George Washington: colonial military leader, general of the Continental Army, first US president; his able military leadership helped the colonies eventually secure independence, and his political leadership helped keep the young country united

glasnost: Soviet reform meaning "openness"

government regulation: government involvement in the economy to effect an economic or social outcome

Great Depression: the global economic collapse that resulted in widespread poverty and unemployment in the United States and the world

hieroglyphs: ancient Egyptian writing (unlike cuneiform, pictographs, or pictorial writing)

high latitudes: latitudes from 66.5° north and south to the poles

Holocaust: the dispossession, imprisonment, and murder of at least six million Jews, Roma, Slavic people, homosexuals, disabled people, people of color, prisoners of war, communists, and others by the Nazis

House of Representatives (the lower house of Congress): the body of lawmakers in Congress with proportional representation reflecting the population of each state

human geography: the study of the impact of people on the physical world

humid continental climate: located in the middle latitudes, the agriculturally productive, true four-season climate

humid subtropical climate: located in the middle latitudes, a warm and moist climate on coastal areas north and south of the tropics that receive warm ocean currents and warm winds year round

Indian Removal Act: 1830 law that forced Cherokee, Creek, Chickasaw, Choctaw, and others from their lands in the Southeast to Indian Territory (Oklahoma)

industrialization: the process of manufacturing; the process of an economy transforming from dependence on agricultural to industrial production; replacement of hand labor by machines as the main way of manufacturing, exponentially increasing production capacities

institutions: extensions of core social values created in response to varying individual and group needs; include government, private enterprise, religious institutions, academic institutions, local communities, and the family unit

intermediate directions: the directions between the cardinal directions

Intolerable Acts: 1774 Acts enforced by Britain in response to tensions and violence in the colonies, including closing Boston Harbor and bringing Massachusetts back under direct royal control

iron curtain: a metaphor for the concept of a post-WWII Europe divided between east (with communist governments generally aligned with the USSR) and west (with democratic capitalist governments generally aligned with the US)

Iroquois: northeastern Native American civilization in New York and southern Ontario/Quebec; a confederation of six tribes

John Adams: colonial leader, member of the Continental Congress, federalist, second US president, brother to the radical Samuel Adams; Adams supported a strong federal government and expanded executive power

Julius Caesar: a popular Roman military leader who forced the corrupt Senate to give him control and who began transitioning Rome from a republic to what would become an empire; assassinated in 44 BCE

League of Nations: a largely toothless international organization established after WWI and designed to prevent future outbreaks of international war; the basis for the later United Nations

low latitudes: the region located from the equator to latitudes 23.5° north and south

Louisiana Purchase: 1803 purchase of French-controlled territory in North America by the United States, authorized, controversially, by President Jefferson; nearly doubled the size of the country

Manifest Destiny: the concept that it was the mission and fate of the United States to expand westward and settle the continent

marine climate: the warm and rainy climate located in the middle latitudes in areas that are near or surrounded by water

Martin Luther King, Jr.: civil rights leader who fought for equal rights for African Americans; embraced peaceful protest as a means to achieve legislative and social change to end segregation between black and white Americans

mass production: large-scale production of consumer products (enabled by the assembly line and factories)

Malcolm X: civil rights leader who championed better living standards for blacks in northern cities and the empowerment of African American communities

Mediterranean climate: a climate located in the middle latitudes between latitudes 30° and 40° north and south characterized by wet, mild winters and dry, warm summers

middle latitudes: the region located from latitudes 23.5° to 66.5° north and south

migration: patterns of movement from one place to another, with the intention of settling permanently at the new location

Missouri Compromise: 1820 legislation that allowed Missouri to join the union as a slave state but provided that any other states north of the thirty-sixth parallel (36°30') would be free

monopoly: the control of a market for a good or service by one company or group

multinational corporations (MNCs): companies based in one country with operations in one or more other countries; the primary driving forces of globalization

natural resources: fresh water, arable land, fuel, livestock, and game

Navajo: a pastoral people that controlled territory in present-day Arizona, New Mexico, and Utah; descendants of the Ancestral Pueblo or Anasazi, who built cliff dwellings

New Deal: plan presented by FDR to rescue the United States from the Great Depression; included emergency acts to save the banking system and long-term relief for the poor and unemployed

Nile Valley: the fertile land on the banks of the Nile River conducive to agriculture and irrigation

nuclear weapons: very powerful weapons that can destroy entire cities; possessed by only a few world powers; first developed by the United States and the Soviet Union

opportunity cost: when a consumer makes a choice at the cost of another choice or the value of an opportunity

Pax Romana: a period of stability in the Mediterranean region under the Roman Empire

Pearl Harbor: US military base in Hawaii; on December 7, 1941, Japan attacked Pearl Harbor, causing the US to enter WWII

perestroika: a term meaning "transparency" referring to Soviet reform

pharaoh: ancient Egyptian monarch

physical geography: the study of the natural processes of the earth

Plains tribes: included the Sioux, Cheyenne, Apache, Comanche, and Arapaho who lived in the Great Plains area; nomadic peoples; depended mainly on the buffalo for sustenance

polis: ancient Greek word meaning "city-state" or "community"

political features: towns and cities; county, state, or national borders

president: the head of state and head of the executive branch; has the power to appoint federal officials and judges, sign or veto laws (approve or deny them), and make foreign policy; he or she is also the commander-in-chief of the US armed forces

primary socialization: when a child learns the values, actions, and attitudes that are appropriate for members of his or her particular culture

pyramids: Egyptian burial tombs for pharaohs

Quartering Act: a 1765 law that forced American colonists to provide shelter, even in their homes, to British troops stationed in the region

regions: parts of the world with definable and identifiable characteristics

relative location: where a place is situated in relation to another place or places

reparations: costly financial compensation charged of Germany by the victors of WWI to cover the cost of the war

Samuel Adams: radical colonial American rebel; leader of the Sons and Daughters of Liberty and Committees of Correspondence

savannah: climate located in the low latitudes north and south of the rainforest; dry in the winter and wet in the summer, experiencing an average of 10 to 30 inches of rain

scarcity: insufficient supply to meet demand

Second Continental Congress: meeting of colonial leaders in Philadelphia in 1775 when colonial leaders agreed on declaring independence and forming the United States of America

secondary socialization: occurs when an individual learns the appropriate values, actions, attitudes, and behaviors as a member of a smaller group within a larger society

Senate: the body of lawmakers in Congress with equal representation—two senators are elected to represent each state (the upper house of Congress); governing body of republican ancient Rome as of 509 BCE

separation of powers: limits the powers within the federal government by dividing power among three branches: the executive, the legislative, and the judicial

September 11, 2001: the date that the United States was attacked by terrorists, resulting in thousands of civilian casualties and major land wars in Afghanistan and Iraq

Shawnee: an Algonquin-speaking people based in the Ohio Valley; Shawnee leader Tecumseh led the Northwest Confederacy against the United States in 1812

social regulation: government regulation that encourages businesses to behave responsibly and prohibits harmful behavior

social structures: (as relates to geography) the organization of a society and how social events relate to and affect places, etc.

socialization: a process whereby individuals learn skills, beliefs, values, and behavior patterns of society and how these can influence their own norms and customs

sociology: the study of groups, institutions, and society

Sons and Daughters of Liberty: colonial rebel protest group that carried out violent acts against tax collectors

Sparta: ancient Greek military city-state

spatial relationships: how one place is located in relation to another place

Stamp Act: controversial 1765 tax on all published documentation in the colonies; the first direct tax on the colonists

steppes or prairie: a climate located in the middle latitudes far from the ocean, characterized by flatlands and minimal rainfall

suburbanization: the movement of urban dwellers from cities to live in growing suburbs, semi-rural areas at the outskirts of cities

Sumerians: ancient Near Eastern people who emerged around 2500 BCE; developed irrigation, agriculture, education, math, astronomy, religion, art and literature, city-states, governance, and administration

supply: how much of a product the market can actually offer

Susan B. Anthony: women's rights activist and leader in women's suffrage movement; leader at 1848 Seneca Falls Convention

system of alliances: the complicated diplomatic and military alliances among European powers that led to the outbreak and magnitude of WWI

taiga: a cold climate located in the high latitudes south of the tundra; contains the world's largest forestlands, extreme mineral wealth, and many swamps and marshes

taxes: money paid by the people, organizations, and companies to the government. This money covers government expenses like federal employee salaries and retirement programs, government programs, and the military. It also helps fuel the economy

Tea Act: controversial 1773 tax on colonial tea that triggered the Boston Tea Party

Thomas Jefferson: colonial leader, architect of the Declaration of Independence; third US president; Jefferson was antifederalist and disapproved of a strong US Constitution

Trail of Tears: the forced migration of Cherokee and others from their land in the Southeast to Indian Territory (today, Oklahoma) to make way for white settlers following the Indian Removal Act; the term describes the suffering, poor conditions, and death suffered by many during the migration

Treaty of Versailles: the treaty that ended WWI, held Germany accountable for the entirety of the war, and brought economic hardship to the country by forcing it to pay reparations to the other powers

trench warfare: bloody, long-term fighting in fortified trenches on the Western Front during WWI

tropical rainforests: moist forests exhibiting high biodiversity, located mainly in the equatorial lowlands in Central Africa, Southeast Asia, and the Amazon basin

tundra: a cold climate located in the high latitudes north of the taiga; with extremely cold and long winters, the ground is frozen for most of the year and becomes mushy during the short summer

Underground Railroad: a secret network of safe houses and connections to help Southern slaves escape to the North and to Canada

United Nations: an international organization formed after WWII to prevent another world war, to champion human rights, and to uphold international security

urban planning: managing the development and use of cities

urbanization: the development of cities; became a feature of human development at the advent of the nineteenth-century Industrial Revolution, when unskilled jobs in factories attracted rural workers to cities, offering them higher wages than an agricultural lifestyle did

vice president: fulfills the duties of the president when he or she is unable; becomes president in the event of the president's death; also serves as president of the Senate

War of 1812: conflict between the US, Britain, and the British-allied Northwest Confederacy (led by the Shawnee leader Tecumseh). The US maintained its territorial integrity despite British incursions from Canada; meanwhile, the US gained power in the Northwest (present-day Ohio Valley region), facilitating westward expansion despite resistance from the Shawnee and other tribes allied with the Confederacy

Part V: Science

Content Knowledge

Earth and Space Science

ASTRONOMY

Astronomy is the study of space. Our **planet**, Earth, is just one out of a group of planets that orbit the **sun**, which is the star at the center of our **solar system**. Other planets in our solar system include Mercury, Venus, Mars, Jupiter, Saturn, Uranus, and Neptune. Every planet, except Mercury and Venus, has **moons**, or naturally occurring satellites that orbit a planet. Our solar system also includes **asteroids** and **comets**, small rocky or icy objects that orbit the Sun. Many of these are clustered in the asteroid belt, which is located between the orbits of Mars and Jupiter.

Figure 10.1. Solar System

Our solar system is a small part of a bigger star system called a galaxy. (Our galaxy is called the Milky Way.) **Galaxies** consist of stars, gas, and dust held together by gravity and contain millions of **stars**, which are hot balls of plasma and gasses. The universe includes many types of stars, including supergiant stars, white dwarfs, giant stars, and neutron stars. Stars form in nebulas, which are large clouds of dust and gas. When very large stars collapse, they create **black holes**, which have a gravitational force so strong that light cannot escape.

Earth, the moon, and the sun interact in a number of ways that impact life on our planet. When the positions of the three align, eclipses occur. A **lunar eclipse** occurs when Earth lines up between the moon and the sun; the moon moves into the shadow of Earth and appears dark in color. A **solar eclipse** occurs when the moon lines up between Earth and the sun; the moon covers the sun, blocking sunlight.

The cycle of day and night and the seasonal cycle are determined by the earth's motion. It takes approximately 365 days, or one year, for Earth to revolve around the sun. While Earth is revolving around the sun, it is also rotating on its axis, which takes approximately 24 hours, or one day. As the planet rotates, different areas alternately face toward the sun and away from the sun, creating night and day.

The earth's axis is not directly perpendicular to its orbit, meaning the planet tilts on its axis. The seasons are caused by this tilt. When the Northern Hemisphere is tilted toward the sun, it receives more sunlight and experiences summer. At the same time that the Northern Hemisphere experiences summer, the Southern Hemisphere, which receives less direct sunlight, experiences winter. As the earth revolves, the Northern Hemisphere will tilt away from the sun and move into winter, while the Southern Hemisphere tilts toward the sun and moves into summer.

> **STUDY TIP**
>
> The phrase *My Very Educated Mother Just Served Us Noodles* can help students remember the order of the planets: Mercury – Venus – Earth – Mars – Jupiter – Saturn – Uranus – Neptune.

GEOLOGY

Geology is the study of the minerals and rocks that make up the earth. A **mineral** is a naturally occurring, solid, inorganic substance with a crystalline structure. There are several properties that help identify a mineral, including color, luster, hardness, and density. Examples of minerals include talc, diamonds, and topaz.

Although a **rock** is also a naturally occurring solid, it can be either organic or inorganic and is composed of one or more minerals. Rocks are classified based on their method of formation. The three types of rocks are igneous, sedimentary, and metamorphic. **Igneous** rocks are the result of tectonic processes that bring **magma**, or melted rock, to the earth's surface; they can form either above or below the surface. **Sedimentary** rocks are formed from the compaction of rock fragments that results from weathering and erosion. Lastly, **metamorphic rocks** form when extreme temperature and pressure cause the structure of pre-existing rocks to change.

The rock cycle describes how rocks form and break down. Typically, the cooling and solidification of magma as it rises to the surface creates igneous rocks. These rocks are then subject to **weathering**, the mechanical and/or chemical processes by which rocks break down. During **erosion** the resulting sediment is deposited in a new location. As sediment is deposited, the resulting compaction creates new sedimentary rocks. As new layers are added, rocks and minerals are forced closer to the earth's core where they are subject to heat and pressure, resulting in metamorphic rock. Eventually, they will reach their melting point and return to magma, starting the cycle over again. This process takes place over hundreds of thousands or even millions of years.

> **DID YOU KNOW?**
>
> *Luster* describes how light reflects off the surface of a mineral. Terms to describe luster include dull, metallic, pearly, and waxy.

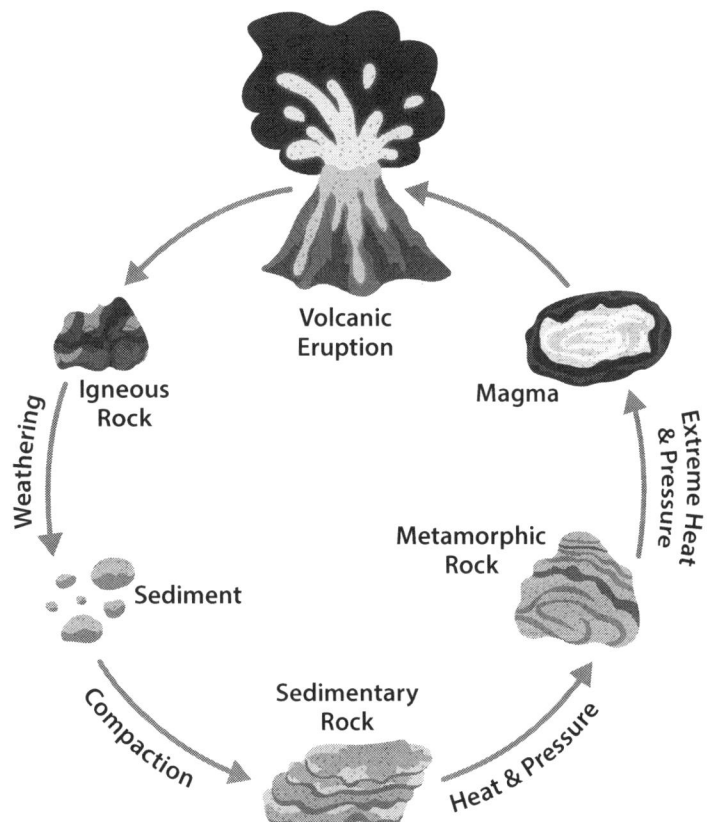

Figure 10.2. The Rock Cycle

Paleontology, the study of the history of life on Earth, is sometimes also considered part of geology. Paleontologists study the **rock record**, which retains biological history through **fossils**, the preserved remains and traces of ancient life. Fossils can be used to learn about the evolution of life on the planet, particularly bacteria, plants, and animals that have gone extinct. Throughout Earth's history, there have been five documented catastrophic events that caused major extinctions. For each mass extinction, there are several theories about the cause but no definitive answers. Theories about what triggered mass extinctions include climate change, ice ages, astcroid and comet impacts, and volcanic activity.

The surface of the earth is made of large plates that float on the less dense layer beneath them. These **tectonic plates** make up the lithosphere, the planet's surface layer. Over 200 million years ago, the continents were joined together in one giant landmass called Pangea. Due to continental drift, or the slow movement of tectonic plates, the continents gradually shifted to their current positions.

The boundaries where plates meet are the locations for many geologic features and events. Mountains are formed when plates collide and push land upward, and trenches form when one plate is pushed beneath another. In addition, the friction created by plates sliding past each other is responsible for most **earthquakes**.

Volcanoes, which are vents in the earth's crust that allow molten rock to reach the surface, frequently occur along the edges of tectonic plates. However, they can also occur at hotspots located far from plate boundaries.

The outermost layer of the earth, which includes tectonic plates, is called the **crust**. Beneath the crust is the **mantle**, and beneath that is the **core**. The core includes two parts: the outer core is a liquid layer, and the inner core is composed of solid iron. It is believed the inner core spins at a rate slightly different than the rest of the planet, which creates the earth's magnetic field.

HYDROLOGY

The earth's surface includes many bodies of water that together form the **hydrosphere**. The largest of these are the bodies of salt water called **oceans**. There are five oceans: the Arctic, Atlantic, Indian, Pacific, and Southern. Together, the oceans account for 71 percent of the earth's surface and 97 percent of the earth's water.

Oceans are subject to cyclic rising and falling water levels at shore lines called **tides**, which are the result of the gravitational pull of the moon and sun. The oceans also experience **waves**, which are caused by the movement of energy through the water.

Other bodies of water include **lakes**, which are usually freshwater, and **seas**, which are usually saltwater. **Rivers** and **streams** are moving bodies of water that flow into lakes, seas, and oceans. The earth also contains **groundwater**, or water that is stored underground in rock formations called aquifers.

Much of the earth's water is stored as ice. The North and South Poles are usually covered in large sheets of ice called **polar ice**. **Glaciers** are large masses of ice and snow that move. Over long periods of time, they scour Earth's surface, creating features such as lakes and valleys. Large chunks of ice that break off from glaciers are called **icebergs**.

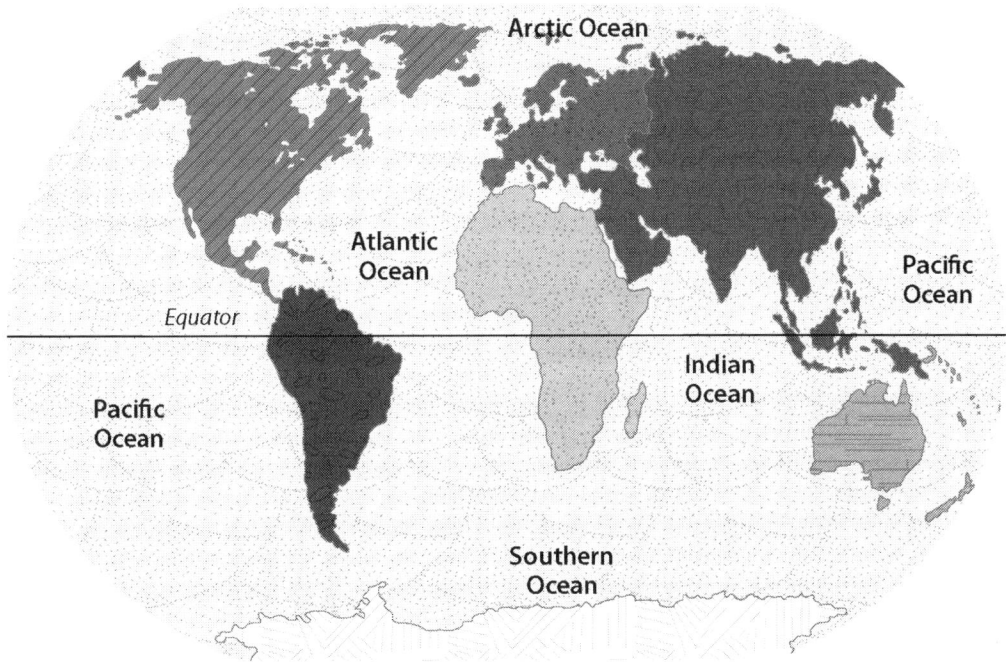

Figure 10.3. The Earth's Oceans

The **water cycle** is the circulation of water throughout the earth's surface, atmosphere, and hydrosphere. Water on the earth's surface **evaporates**, or changes

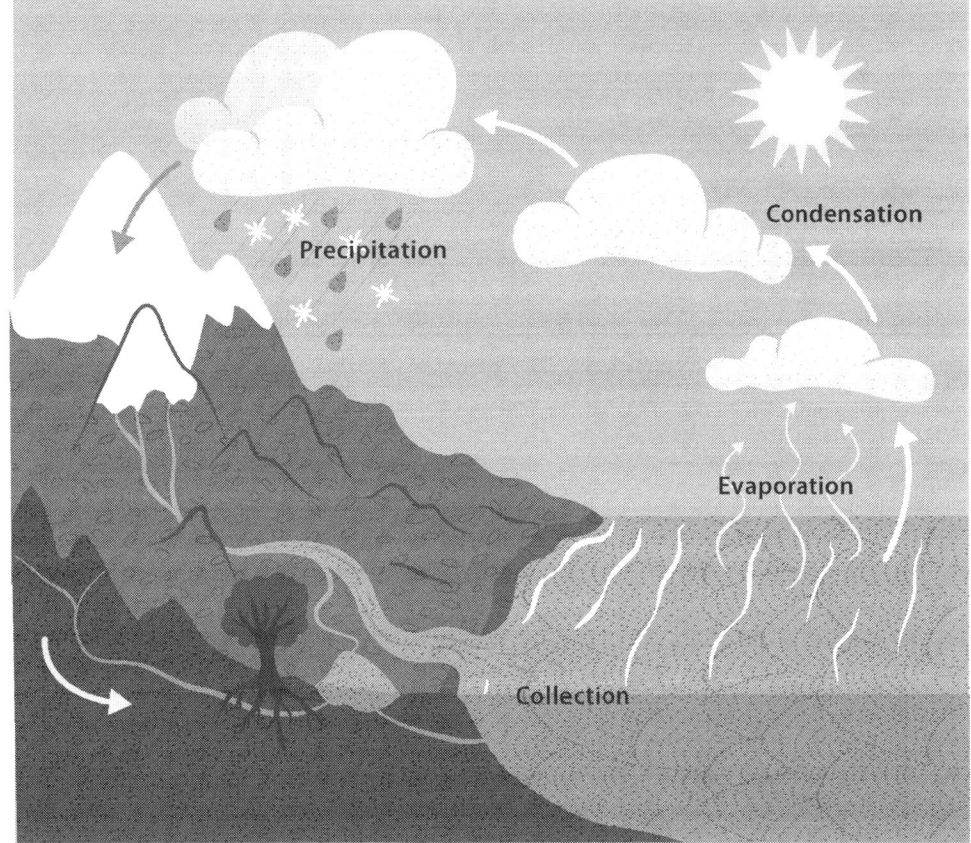

Figure 10.4. The Water Cycle

from a liquid to a gas, and becomes water vapor. Water vapor in the air then comes together to form **clouds**. When it cools, this water vapor condenses into a liquid and falls from the sky as **precipitation**, which includes rain, sleet, snow, and hail. Precipitation replenishes groundwater and the water found in features such as lakes and rivers, thus starting the cycle over again.

METEOROLOGY

Above the surface of Earth is the mass of gasses called the **atmosphere**. The atmosphere includes the troposphere, which is closest to the earth, followed by the stratosphere, mesosphere, and thermosphere. The outermost layer of the atmosphere is the exosphere, which is located 6200 miles above the surface. Generally, temperature in the atmosphere decreases with altitude. The **ozone layer**, which captures harmful radiation from the sun, is located in the stratosphere.

The humidity, or amount of water vapor in the air, and the temperature are two major atmospheric conditions that determine **weather**, the day-to-day changes in atmospheric conditions. A warm front occurs when warm air moves over a cold air mass, causing the air to feel warmer and more humid. A cold front occurs when cold air moves under a warm air mass, causing a drop in temperature.

> **DID YOU KNOW?**
>
> Between each layer, a boundary exists where conditions change. This boundary takes the first part of the name of the previous layer followed by "pause." For example, the boundary between the troposphere and stratosphere is called the tropopause.

Sometimes, weather turns violent. Tropical cyclones, or **hurricanes**, originate over warm ocean water. Hurricanes have destructive winds of more than 74 miles per hour and create large storm surges that can cause extensive damage along coastlines. Hurricanes, typhoons, and cyclones are all the same type of storm; they just have different names based on where the storm is located. Hurricanes originate in the Atlantic or Eastern Pacific Ocean, typhoons in the Western Pacific Ocean, and cyclones in the Indian Ocean. **Tornadoes** occur when unstable warm and cold air masses collide and a rotation is created by fast-moving winds.

The long-term weather conditions in a geographic location are called **climate**. A **climate zone** is a large area that experiences similar average temperature and precipitation. The three major climate zones, based on temperature, are the polar, temperate, and tropical zones. Each climate zone is subdivided into subclimates that have unique characteristics. The tropical climate zone (warm temperatures) can be subdivided into tropical wet, tropical wet and dry, semiarid, and arid. The temperate climate zones (moderate temperatures) include Mediterranean, humid subtropical, marine West Coast, humid continental, and subarctic. The polar climate zones (cold temperatures) include tundra, highlands, nonpermanent ice, and ice cap.

Polar climates are cold and experience prolonged, dark winters due to the tilt of Earth's axis.

SAMPLE QUESTIONS:

1) What term is used when the moon moves between the earth and the sun?
   A. aurora
   B. lunar eclipse
   C. black hole
   D. solar eclipse

   Answers:
   A. Incorrect. An aurora occurs when particles from the solar wind are trapped in the earth's magnetic field.
   B. Incorrect. A lunar eclipse is when the earth moves between the moon and the sun, blocking moonlight.
   C. Incorrect. A black hole is a massive star with a gravitational field so strong that light cannot escape.
   D. **Correct.** When the moon moves between the earth and the sun, a solar eclipse occurs, blocking sunlight from the planet.

2) Which planet does *not* have a moon?
   A. Mercury
   B. Earth
   C. Jupiter
   D. Saturn

   Answers:
   A. **Correct.** Only the first two planets, Mercury and Venus, lack moons.
   B. Incorrect. Earth has one moon.
   C. Incorrect. Jupiter has many moons.
   D. Incorrect. Saturn has many moons.

Life Science

STRUCTURE AND FUNCTION OF ORGANISMS

Life is made possible by a set of biological molecules that each serve a specific purpose. **Carbohydrates** are the sugars that act as a source of energy for all living things. **Lipids**, or fats, are a way for organisms to store energy, and also help with cell functioning. **Proteins** serve a wide variety of biological functions, and are composed of building blocks called amino acids. Lastly, **nucleic acids**, such as DNA and RNA, store an organism's genetic code, which is all the information needed for the organism to function. Both DNA and RNA are made of small molecules called nucleotides. Within the nucleus, DNA is packed into units called **chromosomes**.

> **STUDY TIP**
>
> Phases of mitosis can be remembered using the phrase *I Picked My Apples Today*. The order is Interphase – Prophase – Metaphase – Anaphase – Telophase.

Organisms are living things consisting of at least one **cell**, which is the smallest unit of life that can reproduce on its own. Unicellular organisms, such as amoebas, are made up of only one cell, while multicellular organisms are composed of many cells. In a multicellular organism, the cells are grouped together into **tissues**, and these tissues are grouped into **organs**, which perform a specific function. The heart, for example, is the organ that pumps blood throughout the body. Organs are further grouped into **organ systems**, such as the digestive or respiratory systems.

A cell consists of cytoplasm and genetic material (DNA) held within a **membrane**, or protective covering. Within the cytoplasm of eukaryotic cells are a number of **organelles** which perform specific functions. These include **mitochondria**, which produce energy; **ribosomes**, which produce proteins; and **vacuoles**, which store water and other molecules. Separate from the cytoplasm is the **nucleus**, which is the membrane-bound body that holds the cell's DNA.

Plant cells include a number of structures not found in animal cells. These include the **cell wall**, which provides the cell with a hard outer structure, and chlo-

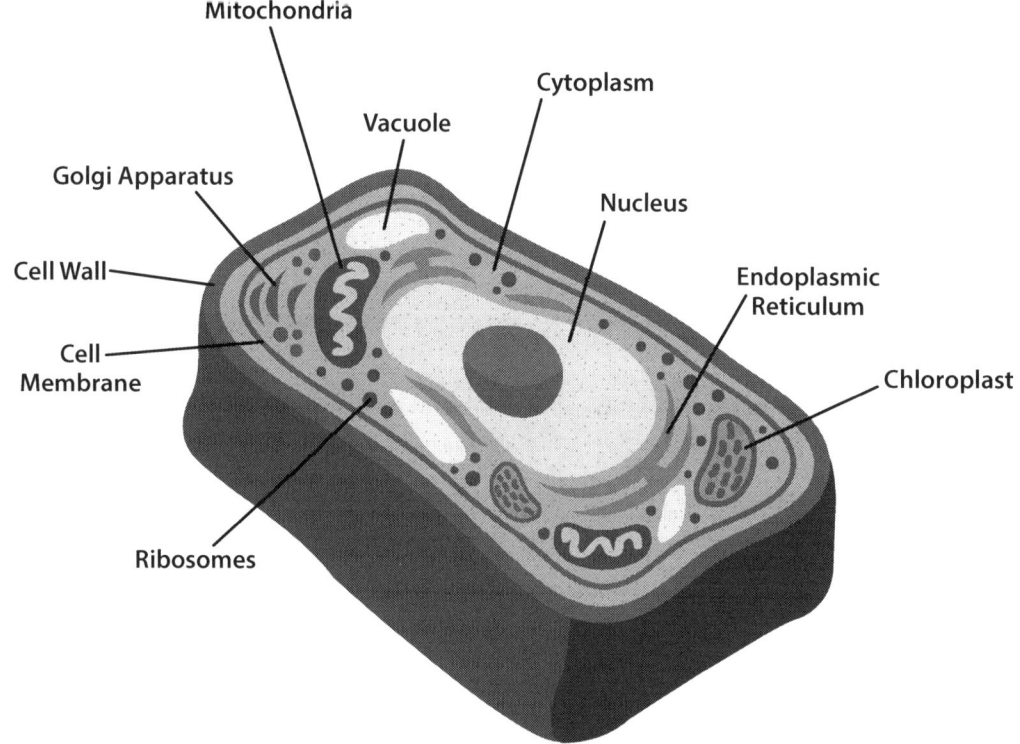

Figure 10.5. Plant Cell

roplasts, where **photosynthesis** occurs. During photosynthesis, plants store energy from sunlight as sugars, which serve as the main source of energy for cell functions.

Cell division, or **mitosis**, is the replication of cells and produces two cells with the same DNA as the original cell. **Meiosis** is the reproduction of sex cells (eggs and sperm). Sex cells are not exact copies of their parent cells and instead have only half the DNA of a somatic (body) cell. When an egg is fertilized by the sperm to form a zygote, half of the new organism's chromosomes come from the egg (mother) and half come from the sperm (father). In humans, sex cells have twenty-three chromosomes, and body cells have forty-six (one set of twenty-three from each parent).

> **DID YOU KNOW?**
>
> Many of the rules of genetics were discovered by Gregor Mendel, a nineteenth-century abbot who used pea plants to show how traits are passed down through generations.

GENETICS AND EVOLUTION

When organisms reproduce, **genetic** information is passed to the next generation through deoxyribonucleic acid, or DNA. Within DNA are blocks of nucleotides called **genes**, each of which contains the code needed to produce a specific protein. Genes are responsible for **traits**, or characteristics, in organisms such as eye color, height, and flower color. During sexual reproduction, the child receives two copies of each gene—one each from the mother and the father. Some of these genes will be dominant, meaning they are expressed, and some will be recessive, meaning they are not expressed. Thus, each child will have a mix of its parents' traits.

When a person's genetic code is damaged, that organism may have a **genetic disorder**. For example, cystic fibrosis, which causes difficulty with basic bodily functions such as breathing and eating, results from damage to the gene which codes for a protein called CFTR. Down Syndrome, which causes developmental delays, occurs when a person has three copies of chromosome twenty-one (meaning they received two copies from a parent as a result of an error in meiosis).

Genes are not static. Over time, **mutations**, or changes in the genetic code, occur that can affect an organism's ability to survive. Harmful mutations will appear less often in a population or be removed entirely because those organisms will be less likely to reproduce (and thus will not pass on that trait). Beneficial mutations may help an organism reproduce, and thus that trait will appear more often. Over time, this process, called **natural selection**, results in the evolution of new species. The theory of evolution was developed by naturalist Charles Darwin when he observed how finches on the Galapagos Islands had a variety of beak shapes and sizes that allowed them to coexist by using different food sources.

> **CONSIDER THIS**
>
> Why might a harmful mutation continue to exist in a population?

Classification of Organisms

Scientists use the characteristics of organisms to sort them into a variety of **classifications** using a system called taxonomy. The highest level of taxonomic classification is the **kingdom**, and each kingdom is then broken down into smaller categories. The smallest level of classification is a **species**, which includes individuals with similar genetics that are capable of breeding. The entire system is given below:

- Kingdom
- Phylum
- Class
- Order
- Family
- Genus
- Species

All organisms are sorted into one of five kingdoms: Monera, Protista, Fungi, Plantae, and Animalia. The kingdom **Monera** includes bacteria, which are unicellular organisms that have no nucleus. **Protists** are also unicellular organisms, but they have a nucleus. Both Monera and Protists reproduce asexually by cellular division.

Fungi are a group of unicellular and multicellular organisms that have unique cell walls and reproduction strategies. This kingdom includes common organisms like mushrooms and molds. Fungi can reproduce both asexually by cellular division and sexually through spores. Many species of fungi are decomposers and attain energy by breaking down organic matter in the environment.

Plants are a kingdom of organisms that use the energy from sunlight to make food (the sugar glucose) through the process of photosynthesis. A plant has **roots** that anchor the plant to the ground and absorb water and nutrients from the soil. The **stem** transports nutrients and water from the roots to other parts of the plant, including the **leaves**, where photosynthesis occurs.

Plants can reproduce asexually when a part of the plant (e.g., a cut branch) buds to create a new, identical plant. Plants can also reproduce sexually. Seed plants produce **pollen** (male sex cells) and eggs (female sex cells). When the pollen fertilizes the egg, an embryo is formed. This embryo is protected and nourished by the **seed**. In angiosperms (flowering plants), seeds are contained within fruit. In gymnosperms, such as spruce and pines, seeds are contained within cones.

> **STUDY TIP**
>
> *LAWN* represents the requirements for plants: Light – Air – Water – Nutrients.

The kingdom Animalia contains multicellular organisms that can move around and must consume other organisms for energy. The kingdom includes several notable classes that divide organisms based on a number of important features. These include whether the organism has a backbone or spine: **vertebrates** do, while **invertebrates** do not. Animals are also classified based on whether they are **exothermic**, meaning their source of body heat comes from the environment, or **endothermic**, meaning their body heat is derived from metabolic processes within the body. Exothermic animals are sometimes known as cold-blooded, and endothermic animals as warm-blooded. Animal classification also looks at animal reproduction: some animals lay eggs, while others give birth to live young.

Amphibians are exothermic vertebrate animals that have gills when they hatch from eggs but develop lungs as adults. Examples of amphibians include frogs, toads, newts, and salamanders. **Reptiles**, such as snakes, lizards, crocodiles, turtles, and tortoises, are cold-blooded vertebrates that have scales and lay eggs on land. **Mammals** are endothermic vertebrate animals that have hair, give live birth, and produce milk for the nourishment of their young.

> **STUDY TIP**
>
> The phrase *King Phillip Came Over From Great Spain* is a way to remember the order of taxonomic classification of organisms: Kingdom – Phylum – Class – Order – Family – Genus – Species.

All organisms have a **life cycle**, the stages of life for that organism. For example, when a frog lays eggs in water, the eggs hatch to become tadpoles with gills. The tadpoles eventually grow legs and develop lungs, and the tail is absorbed into the body. At this point, a tadpole has become an adult frog.

Body Systems

Anatomy is the study of the structure of organisms, and **physiology** is the study of how the structures of an organism function. Both disciplines study the systems that allow organisms to perform a number of crucial functions, including the exchange of energy, nutrients, and waste products with the environment. This exchange allows organisms to maintain **homeostasis**, or the stabilization of internal conditions.

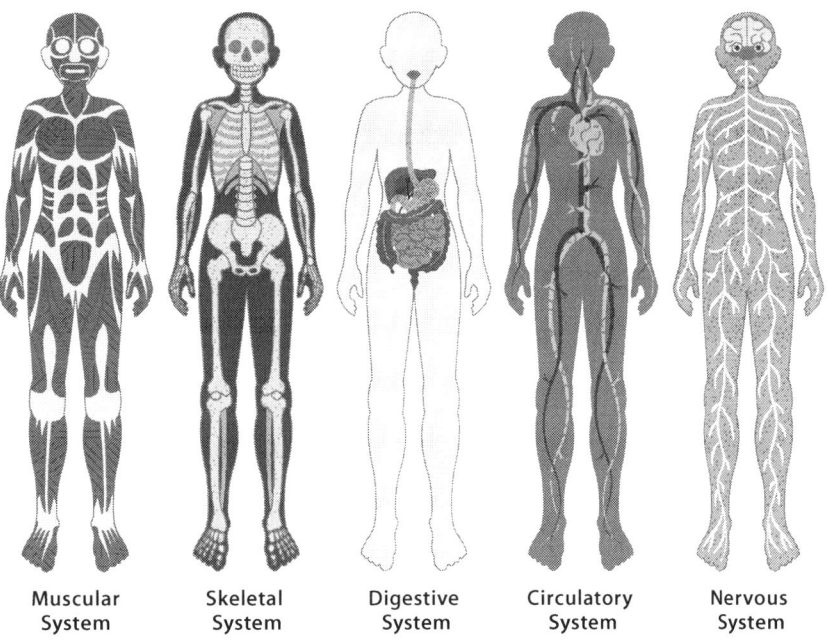

Figure 10.6. Body Systems

Humans have a number of body systems that allow us to perform these vital functions, including the digestive, excretory, respiratory, circulatory, skeletal, muscular, immune, nervous, endocrine, and reproductive systems.

The **digestive system** breaks down food into nutrients for use by the body's cells. Food enters through the **mouth** and moves through the **esophagus** to the **stomach**, where it is physically and chemically broken down. The food particles then move into the **small intestine**, where the majority of nutrients are absorbed. Finally, the remaining particles enter the **large intestine**, which mostly absorbs water, and waste exits through the **rectum** and **anus**. This system also includes other organs, including the **liver**, **gallbladder**, and **pancreas**, that manufacture substances needed for digestion.

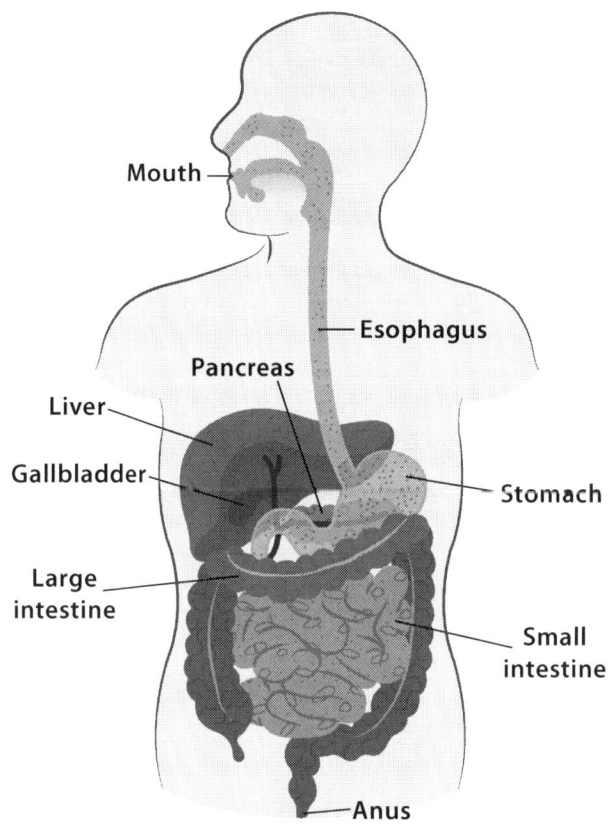

Figure 10.7. Digestive System

The **excretory system** removes waste products from the body. Its organs include the liver, which breaks down harmful substances, and the **kidneys**, which filter waste from the bloodstream. The excretory system also includes the **bladder** and **urinary tract**, which expel the waste filtered by the kidneys; the lungs, which expel the carbon dioxide created by cellular metabolism; and the skin, which secretes salt in the form of perspiration.

The **respiratory system** takes in oxygen (which is needed for cellular functioning) and expels carbon dioxide. Humans take in air primarily through the nose but also through the mouth. This air travels down the **trachea** and **bronchi** into the **lungs**, which are composed of millions of small structures called alveoli that allow for the exchange of gases between the blood and the air.

The circulatory system carries oxygen, nutrients, and waste products in the blood to and from all the cells of the body. The **heart** is a four-chambered muscle that pumps blood throughout the body. Deoxygenated blood (blood from which all the oxygen has been extracted and used) enters the heart in the right side and then is sent by the heart to the lungs, where it collects oxygen. The oxygen-rich blood then returns to the left side of the heart and is pumped out to the rest of the body.

Blood travels through a system of vessels. The largest of these are the **arteries**, which branch directly off the heart. The vessels then branch into smaller and smaller vessels until they become **capillaries**, which are the smallest vessels and the site where gas exchange occurs. Deoxygenated blood travels back to the heart in **veins**.

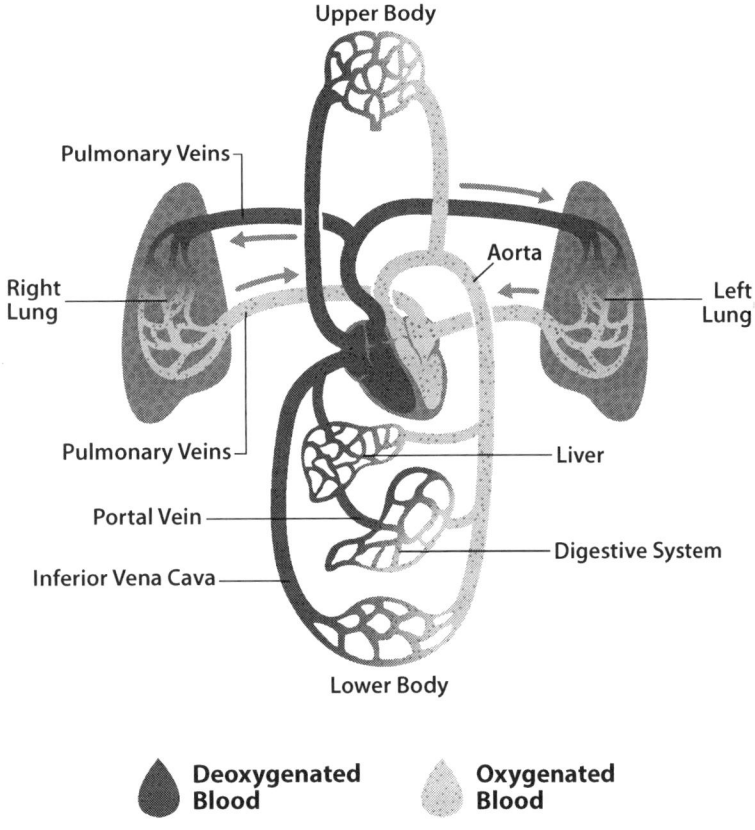

Figure 10.8. Circulatory System

The **skeletal system**, which is composed of the body's **bones** and **joints**, provides support for the body and helps with movement. Bones also store some of the body's nutrients and produce specific types of cells. Humans are born with 237 bones.

However, many of these bones fuse during childhood, and adults will have only 206 bones.

The **muscular system** allows the body to move and also moves blood and other substances through the body. The human body has three types of muscles. Skeletal muscles are voluntary muscles (meaning they can be controlled) that are attached to bones and move the body. Smooth muscles are involuntary muscles (meaning they cannot be controlled) that create movement in parts of the digestive tract, blood vessels, and reproduction system. Finally, cardiac muscle is the involuntary muscle that contracts the heart, allowing it to pump blood throughout the body.

The **immune system** protects the body from infection by foreign particles and organisms. It includes the **skin** and mucous membranes, which act as physical barriers, and a number of specialized cells that destroy foreign substances in the body. The human body has an adaptive immune system, meaning it can recognize and respond to foreign substances once it has been exposed to them. (This is the underlying mechanism behind vaccines.)

The **nervous system** processes external stimuli and sends signals throughout the body. It is made up of two parts. The central nervous system (CNS) includes the brain and spinal cord and is where information is processed and stored. The peripheral nervous system (PNS) includes small cells called neurons that transmit information throughout the body using electrical signals.

> **DID YOU KNOW?**
>
> In science, a **system** is a collection of interconnected parts that make up a complex whole with defined boundaries. Systems may be closed, meaning nothing passes in or out of them, or open, meaning they have inputs and outputs.

The **endocrine system** is a collection of organs that produce **hormones**, which are chemicals that regulate bodily processes. These organs include the pituitary gland, hypothalamus, pineal gland, thyroid gland, parathyroid glands, adrenal glands, testes (in males), ovaries (in females), and the placenta (in pregnant females). Together, the hormones produced by these organs regulate a wide variety of bodily functions, including hunger, sleep, mood, reproduction, and body temperature. Some organs that are part of other systems can also act as endocrine organs, including the pancreas and liver.

The reproductive system includes the organs necessary for sexual reproduction. In males, these include the **testes**, where sperm is produced, and the **urethra**, which carries sperm through the **penis**. In the female reproductive system, eggs are produced in the **ovaries** and released roughly once a month to move through the **fallopian tubes** to the **uterus**. Once fertilized, the new embryo implants in the lining of the uterus and develops over the course of roughly nine months. At the end of **gestation**, the baby exits the uterus through the **vagina**. If the egg is not fertilized, the uterus will shed its lining roughly once a month.

ECOLOGY

Ecology is the study of organisms' interactions with each other and the environment. As with the study of organisms, ecology includes a classification hierarchy. Groups of organisms of the same species living in the same geographic area are called **populations**. These organisms will compete with each other for resources and mates and will display characteristic patterns in growth related to their interactions with the environment. For example, many populations exhibit a **carrying capacity**, which is the highest number of individuals the resources in a given environment can support. Populations that outgrow their carrying capacity are likely to experience increased death rates until the population reaches a stable level again.

Populations of different species living together in the same geographic region are called **communities**. Within a community many different interactions among species occur. **Predators** consume **prey** for food, and some species are in **competition** for the same limited pool of resources. Two species may also have a **parasitic** relationship in which one organism benefits to the detriment of the other, such as ticks feeding off a dog.

> **STUDY TIP**
>
> The five levels of ecology from smallest to largest (Organisms – Populations – Communities – Ecosystems – Biosphere) can be remembered using the phrase *Old People Catch Easy Breaks*.

Within a community, a species exists in a **food web**: every species either consumes or is consumed by another (or others). The lowest trophic level in the web is occupied by **producers**, which include plants and algae that produce energy directly from the sun. The next level are **primary consumers** (herbivores), which consume plant matter. The next trophic level includes **secondary consumers** (carnivores), which consume herbivores. A food web may also contain another level of **tertiary consumers** (carnivores that consume other carnivores). In a real community, these webs can be extremely complex, with species existing on multiple trophic levels. Communities also include **decomposers**, which are organisms that break down dead matter.

The collection of biotic (living) and abiotic (nonliving) features in a geographic area is called an **ecosystem**. For example, in a forest, the ecosystem consists of all the organisms (animals, plants, fungi, bacteria, etc.) in addition to the soil, groundwater, rocks, and other abiotic features.

> **CONSIDER THIS**
>
> What would happen if all of the decomposers disappeared from an ecosystem?

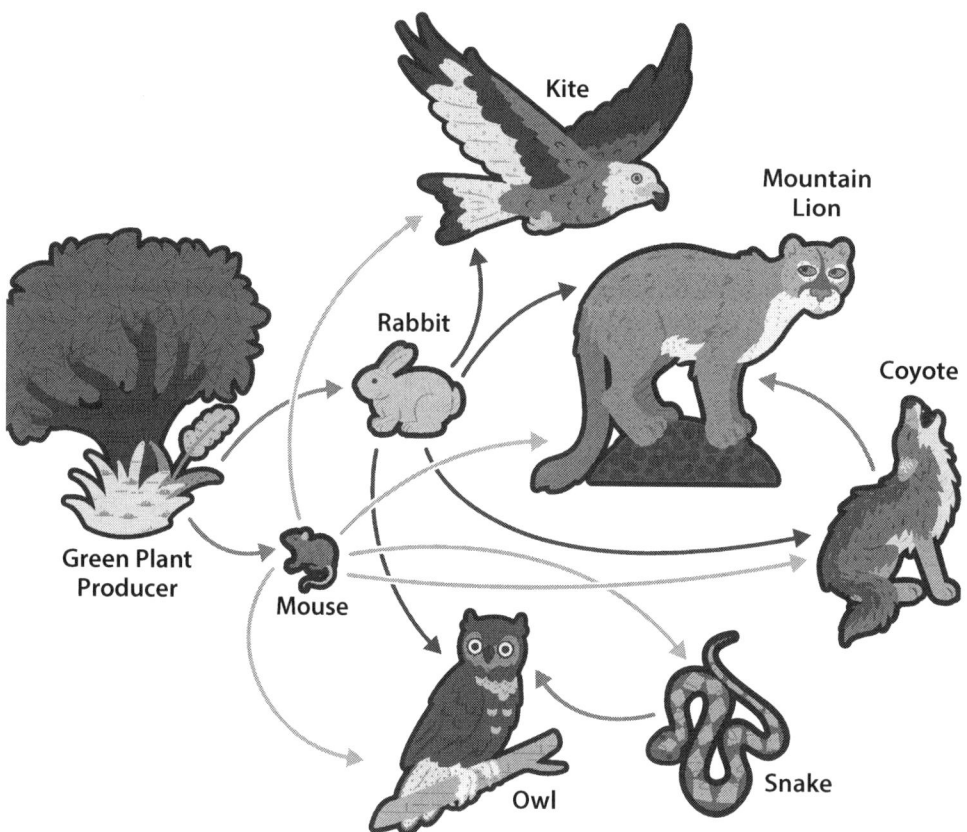

Figure 10.9. Food Web

Biomes are collections of plant and animal communities that exist within specific climates. They are similar to ecosystems, but they do not include abiotic components and can exist within and across continents. For example, the Amazon rainforest is a specific ecosystem, while tropical rainforests in general are considered a biome that includes a set of similar communities across the world. Together, all the living and nonliving parts of the earth are known as the **biosphere**.

Terrestrial biomes are usually defined by distinctive patterns in temperature and rainfall, and aquatic biomes are defined by the type of water and organisms found there. Examples of biomes include:

- **deserts**: extreme temperatures and very low rainfall with specialized vegetation and small mammals
- **tropical rainforests**: hot and wet with an extremely high diversity of species
- **temperate grasslands**: moderate precipitation and distinct seasons with grasses and shrubs dominating
- **temperate broadleaf forests**: moderate precipitation and temperatures with deciduous trees dominating
- **tundra**: extremely low temperatures and short growing seasons with little or no tree growth

- **coral reefs**: a marine (saltwater) system with high levels of diversity
- **lake**: an enclosed body of fresh water

If the delicate balance of an ecosystem is disrupted, the system may not function properly. For example, if all the secondary consumers disappear, the population of primary consumers would increase, causing the primary consumers to overeat the producers and eventually starve. Species called **keystone species** are especially important in a particular community, and removing them decreases the overall diversity of the ecosystem.

> **DID YOU KNOW?**
>
> Deciduous trees lose their leaves in the winter. Evergreen trees keep their leaves year round.

SAMPLE QUESTIONS:

3) Which organism is a primary consumer?

   A. mushroom
   B. corn
   C. cow
   D. lion

   Answers:

   A. Incorrect. Mushrooms are fungi, which are decomposers.
   B. Incorrect. Corn is a plant, which is a producer.
   C. **Correct.** Cows eat plants but do not eat other animals; therefore cows are primary consumers.
   D. Incorrect. Lions eat other consumers, which make lions a secondary or tertiary consumer.

4) Which organism is an amphibian?

   A. snake
   B. frog
   C. dolphin
   D. pelican

   Answers:

   A. Incorrect. Snakes are reptiles.
   B. **Correct.** Frogs are amphibians; they are born with gills but develop lungs as an adult.
   C. Incorrect. Dolphins are mammals.
   D. Incorrect. Pelicans are birds.

Physical Science

PROPERTIES OF MATTER

The basic unit of all matter is the **atom**. Atoms are composed of three subatomic particles: protons, electrons, and neutrons. **Protons** have a positive charge and are found in the nucleus, or center, of the atom. **Neutrons**, which have no charge, are also located in the nucleus. Negatively charged **electrons** orbit the nucleus. If an atom has the same number of protons and electrons, it will have no net charge. If it has more protons than electrons, it will be positively charged, and if it has more electrons it will be negative. Charged atoms are called **ions**.

> **STUDY TIP**
>
> The parts of an atom can be remembered using *PEN*: Protons – Electrons – Neutrons.

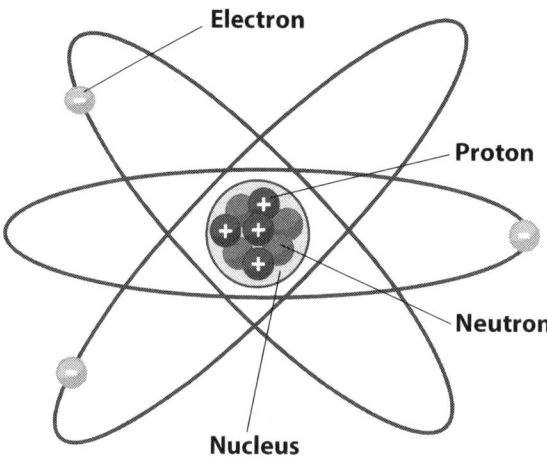

Figure 10.10. Atomic Structure

The mass of an atom is determined by adding the number of protons, neutrons, and electrons. However, electrons have very little mass, so the **atomic mass** is determined by adding just the mass of protons and neutrons.

Elements, such as hydrogen and oxygen, are substances in their simplest form that retain their unique characteristics. Each element has a distinct **atomic number** based on the number of protons in the nucleus. For example, hydrogen has one proton in its nucleus, and oxygen has six. A table of chemical elements arranged by atomic number is called **the periodic table**.

When two or more atoms join together they form a **molecule**. For example, O_3 (ozone) contains three oxygen atoms bound together, and H_2O (water) contains two hydrogen atoms and one oxygen. Water is considered a **compound** because it is made by combining two or more different elements. Atoms can be joined together by different types of bonds. In a **covalent bond**, the atoms share electrons. In an **ionic bond**, two ions with opposite charges are attracted to each other and bind together.

1 H 1.0079																		2 He 4.0026
3 Li 6.9411	4 Be 9.0122												5 B 10.811	6 C 12.011	7 N 14.007	8 O 15.999	9 F 18.998	10 Ne 20.180
11 Na 22.990	12 Mg 24.305												13 Al 26.982	14 Si 28.086	15 P 30.974	16 S 32.065	17 Cl 35.453	18 Ar 39.948
19 K 39.098	20 Ca 40.078		21 Sc 44.956	22 Ti 47.867	23 V 50.942	24 Cr 51.996	25 Mn 54.938	26 Fe 55.845	27 Co 58.933	28 Ni 58.693	29 Cu 63.546	30 Zn 65.39	31 Ga 69.723	32 Ge 72.61	33 As 74.922	34 Se 78.96	35 Br 79.904	36 Kr 83.80
37 Rb 85.468	38 Sr 87.62		39 Y 88.906	40 Zr 91.224	41 Nb 92.906	42 Mo 95.94	43 Tc [98]	44 Ru 101.07	45 Rh 102.91	46 Pd 106.42	47 Ag 107.87	48 Cd 112.41	49 In 114.82	50 Sn 118.71	51 Sb 121.76	52 Te 127.60	53 I 126.90	54 Xe 131.29
55 Cs 132.91	56 Ba 137.33	57-70 *	71 Lu 174.97	72 Hf 178.49	73 Ta 180.95	74 W 183.84	75 Re 186.21	76 Os 190.23	77 Ir 192.22	78 Pt 195.08	79 Au 196.97	80 Hg 200.59	81 Tl 204.38	82 Pb 207.2	83 Bi 208.98	84 Po [209]	85 At [210]	86 Rn [222]
87 Fr [223]	88 Ra [226]	89-102 **	103 Lr [262]	104 Rf [261]	105 Db [262]	106 Sg [266]	107 Bh [264]	108 Hs [269]	109 Mt [268]	110 Uun [271]	111 Uuu [272]	112 Uub [277]		114 Uuq [289]				

* Lanthanide Series	57 La 138.91	58 Ce 140.12	59 Pr 140.91	60 Nd 144.24	61 Pm [145]	62 Sm 150.36	63 Eu 151.96	64 Gd 157.25	65 Tb 158.93	66 Dy 162.50	67 Ho 164.93	68 Er 167.26	69 Tm 168.93	70 Yb 173.04
** Actinide Series	89 Ac [227]	90 Th 232.04	91 Pa 231.04	92 U 238.03	93 Np [237]	94 Pu [244]	95 Am [243]	96 Cm [247]	97 Bk [247]	98 Cf [251]	99 Es [252]	100 Fm [257]	101 Md [258]	102 No [259]

Figure 10.11. Periodic Table

All matter exists in one of four **states**: solid, liquid, gas, or plasma. **Solid** matter has densely packed molecules and does not change volume or shape. **Liquids** have more loosely packed molecules and can change shape but not volume. **Gas** molecules are widely dispersed, and gasses can change both shape and volume. **Plasma** is similar to a gas but contains free moving charged particles (although its overall charge is neutral).

Changes in temperature and pressure can cause matter to change states. Generally, adding energy (in the form of heat) changes a substance to a higher energy state (e.g., solid to liquid). Transitions from a high to lower energy state (e.g., liquid to solid) release energy. Each of these changes has a specific name:

- solid to liquid: melting
- liquid to solid: freezing
- liquid to gas: evaporation
- gas to liquid: condensation
- solid to gas: sublimation
- gas to solid: deposition

Matter changing state is an example of a **physical change**, which is a change in matter that does not alter the chemical composition of a substance. The state of matter changes, but the underlying chemical nature of the substance itself does not change. Other examples of physical changes include cutting, heating, or changing the shape of a substance.

When substances are combined without a chemical reaction to bond them, the resulting substance is called a **mixture**. In a mixture, the components can be unevenly distributed, such as in trail mix or soil. Alternatively, the components can be uniformly distributed, as in salt water. When the distribution is uniform, the mixture is called a **solution**. The substance being dissolved is the **solute**, and the substance being dissolved in is the **solvent**. Physical changes can be used to separate mixtures. For example, heating salt water until the water evaporates, leaving the salt behind, will separate a salt water solution.

> **DID YOU KNOW?**
>
> In both physical and chemical changes, matter is always conserved, meaning it can never be created or destroyed.

In contrast to a physical change, a **chemical change** occurs when bonds between atoms are made or broken, resulting in a new substance or substances. Chemical changes are also called **chemical reactions**. Chemical reactions are either **exothermic**, meaning energy (heat) is released, or **endothermic**, meaning energy is required for the reaction to take place.

Common reactions include:

- **oxidation**: a chemical change in which a substance loses electrons, as when iron rusts when exposed to oxygen, forming iron oxide
- **combustion**: a chemical reaction that produces heat, carbon dioxide, and water, usually by burning a fuel
- **synthesis**: a chemical reaction in which two substances combine to form a single substance
- **decomposition**: a chemical reaction in which a single substance is broken down into two or more substances
- **neutralization**: a chemical reaction that occurs when an acid and a base react to produce a salt and water

> **DID YOU KNOW?**
>
> A molecule is two or more atoms bound together. A compound is two or more atoms of *different elements* bound together. A compound is always a molecule, but a molecule is not always a compound.

Matter is classified by its **properties**, or characteristics. These properties include mass, weight, density, solubility, conductivity, and pH. **Mass** refers to the amount of matter in an object. Although the terms are often used interchangeably, mass is distinct from **weight**, which is the force of the gravitational pull on an object. Unlike weight, mass stays the same no matter where an object is located. When two objects of the same mass are on the earth and on the moon, the object on the moon will weigh less because the force of gravity on the moon is less than it is on the earth.

Density is the mass of the object divided by its volume, or the amount of space the object occupies. A denser object will contain the same amount of mass in a smaller space than a less dense object. This is why a dense object, such as a bowling ball, will feel heavier than a less dense object, like a soccer ball. The density of an object determines whether an object will sink or float in a fluid. For example, the bowling ball will sink because it is denser than water, while the soccer ball will float.

Solubility refers to the amount of a solute that will dissolve in a solvent. **Conductivity** describes how well a material conducts heat or electricity. Silver, copper, aluminum, and iron are good conductors, while rubber, glass, and wood are poor conductors. Poor conductors are also called **insulators**.

Finally, the pH scale is used to describe the acidity of a substance. **Acids** are compounds that contribute a hydrogen ion (H+) when in solution, and bases are compounds that contribute a hydroxide ion (OH–) in solution. The pH scale goes from 1 – 14, with 7 considered neutral. Acids (such as lemon juice) have a pH lower than 7; bases (such as soap) have a pH greater than 7. Water is neutral with a pH of 7.

FORCE AND MOTION

The motion of objects can be measured using a number of different variables, including speed, velocity, and acceleration. **Speed** describes how quickly something moves, while **velocity** is the rate at which an object changes position. Velocity is different from speed in that it includes a direction. Speed is found by examining how far an object travels; velocity is found by studying how far an object ends up from its starting point. An object that travels a certain distance and then returns to its starting point has a velocity of zero because its final position did not change. Its speed, however, can be found by dividing the total distance it traveled by the time it took to make the trip. **Acceleration** is how quickly an object changes velocity.

A push or pull that causes an object to move or change direction is called a **force**. Forces can arise from a number of different sources. **Gravity** is the attraction of one mass to another mass. For example, the earth's gravitational field pulls objects toward it, and the sun's gravitational field keeps planets in motion around it. Electrically charged objects will also create a field that will cause other charged objects in that field to move. Other forces include **tension**, which is found in ropes pulling or holding up an object; **friction**, which is created by two objects moving against each other; and the **normal force**, which occurs when an object is resting on another object.

> **DID YOU KNOW?**
>
> The normal force balances out gravity in resting objects. When a book rests on a table, gravity pulls down on it and the normal force pushes up, cancelling each other out and holding the book still.

An object that is at rest or moving with a constant speed has a net force of zero, meaning all the forces acting on it cancel each other out. Such an object is said to be at **equilibrium**. Isaac Newton proposed three **Laws of Motion** that govern forces:

- ▶ **Newton's First Law**: An object at rest stays at rest, and an object in motion stays in motion, unless acted on by a force.

▸ **Newton's Second Law:** Force is equal to the mass of an object multiplied by its acceleration ($F = ma$).

▸ **Newton's Third Law:** For every action, there is an equal and opposite reaction.

The laws of motion have made it possible to build **simple machines**, which take advantage of the rules of motion to make work easier to perform. Simple machines include the inclined plane, wheel and axle, pulley, screw, wedge, and lever.

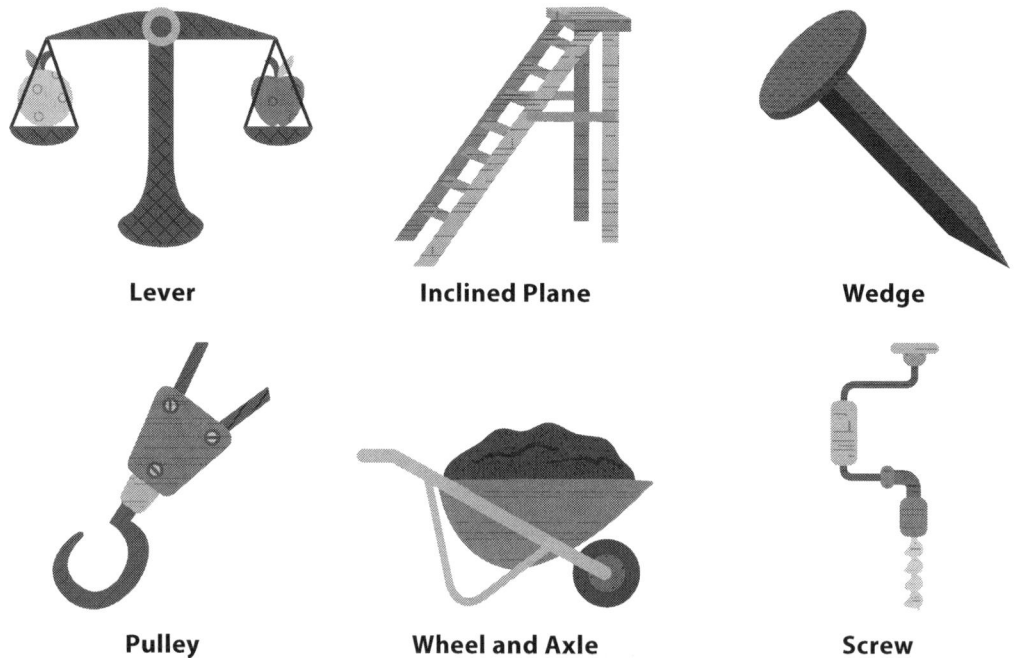

Figure 10.12. Simple Machines

Energy and Matter

Energy is the capacity of an object to do work. In other words, it is the capacity of an object to cause some sort of movement or change. There are two kinds of energy: kinetic and potential. **Kinetic energy** is the energy possessed by objects in motion, and **potential energy** is possessed by objects that have the potential to be in motion due to their position. Potential energy is defined in relation to a specific point. For example, a book held 10 feet off the ground has more potential energy than a book held 5 feet off the ground, because it has the potential to fall farther (i.e., to do more work).

> **DID YOU KNOW?**
>
> Like matter, energy is always conserved. It can be changed from one form to another, but never created or destroyed.

Kinetic energy can be turned into potential energy, and vice versa. In the example above, dropping one of the books turns potential energy into kinetic energy. Conversely, picking up a book and placing it on a table turns kinetic energy into potential energy.

There are several types of potential energy. The energy stored in a book placed on a table is **gravitational potential energy**; it is derived from the pull of the earth's gravity on the book. **Electric potential energy** is derived from the interaction between positive and negative charges. Because opposite charges attract each other, and like charges repel, energy can be stored when opposite charges are moved apart or when like charges are pushed together. Similarly, compressing a spring stores **elastic potential energy**. Energy is also stored in chemical bonds as **chemical potential energy**.

Temperature is the special name given to the kinetic energy of all the atoms or molecules in a substance. While it might look like a substance is not in motion, in fact, its atoms are constantly spinning and vibrating. The more energy the atoms have, the higher the substance's temperature. **Heat** is the movement of energy from one substance to another. Energy will spontaneously move from high energy (high temperature) substances to low energy (low temperature) substances.

This energy can be transferred by radiation, convection, or conduction. **Radiation** does not need a medium; the sun radiates energy to Earth through the vacuum of space. **Conduction** occurs when two substances are in contact with each other. When a pan is placed on a hot stove, the heat energy is conducted from the stove to the pan and then to the food in the pan. **Convection** transfers energy through circular movement of air or liquids. For example, a convection oven transfers heat through circular movement caused by hot air rising and cold air sinking.

WAVES

Energy can also be transferred through **waves**, which are repeating pulses of energy. Waves that travel through a medium, like ripples on a pond or compressions in a slinky, are called **mechanical waves**. Waves that vibrate up and down (like the ripples on the pond) are **transverse waves**, and those that travel through compression (like the slinky) are **longitudinal waves**. Mechanical waves will travel faster through denser mediums; for example, sound waves will move faster through water than air.

Sound is a special type of longitudinal wave created by vibrations. Our ears are able to interpret these waves as particular sounds. The frequency, or rate, of the vibration determines the sound's **pitch**. **Loudness** depends on the amplitude, or height, of a sound wave.

The **Doppler Effect** is the difference in perceived pitch caused by the motion of the object creating the wave. For example, as an ambulance approaches, the siren's pitch will appear to increase to the observer and then to decrease as the ambulance moves away. This occurs because sound waves are compressed as the ambulance

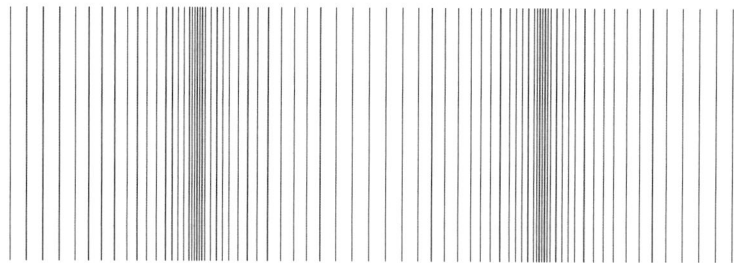

Longitudinal Wave

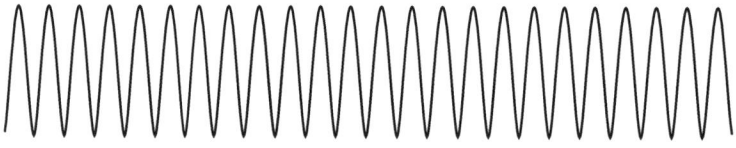

Transverse Wave

Figure 10.13. Types of Waves

approaches an observer and spread out as the ambulance moves away from the observer.

> **QUICK REVIEW**
>
> What are some other ways to demonstrate refraction?

Electromagnetic waves are composed of oscillating electric and magnetic fields and thus do not require a medium to travel through. The electromagnetic spectrum classifies the types of electromagnetic waves based on their frequency. These include radio waves, microwaves, x-rays, and visible light.

The study of light is called **optics**. Because visible light is a wave, it will display similar properties to other waves. It will **reflect**, or bounce off surfaces, which can be observed by shining a flashlight on a mirror. Light will also **refract**, or bend when it travels between substances. This effect can be seen by placing a pencil in water and observing the apparent bend in the pencil.

> **STUDY TIP**
>
> The order of the colors in the spectrum of light can be remembered using *ROY G. BIV*; Red – Orange – Yellow – Green – Blue – Indigo – Violet.

Curved pieces of glass called **lenses** can be used to bend light in a way that affects how an image is perceived. Some microscopes, for example, make objects appear larger through the use of specific types of lenses. Eye glasses also use lenses to correct poor vision.

The frequency of a light wave is responsible for its **color**, with red/orange colors having a lower frequency than blue/violet colors. White light is a blend of all the frequencies of visible light. Passing white light through a prism will bend each frequency at a slightly different angle, separating the colors and creating a **rainbow**. Sunlight passing through raindrops can undergo this effect, creating large rainbows in the sky.

ELECTRICITY AND MAGNETISM

Electric charge is created by a difference in the balance of protons and electrons, which creates a positively or negatively charged object. Charged objects create an electric field that spreads outward from the object. Other charged objects in that field will experience a force: objects that have opposite charges will be **attracted** to each other, and objects with the same charge will be **repelled**, or pushed away, from each other.

Because protons cannot leave the nucleus, charge is created by the movement of electrons. Static electricity, or **electrostatic** charge, occurs when a surface has a buildup of charges. For example, if a student rubs a balloon on her head, the friction will cause electrons to move from her hair to the balloon. This creates a negative charge on the balloon and positive charge on her hair; the resulting attraction will cause her hair to move toward the balloon.

Electricity is the movement of electrons through a conductor, and an electric circuit is a closed loop through which electricity moves. Circuits include a **voltage** source, which powers the movement of electrons known as **current**. Sources of voltage include batteries, generators, and wall outlets (which are in turn powered by electric power stations). Other elements, such as lights, computers, and microwaves, can then be connected to the circuit to be powered by its electricity.

Magnets are created by the alignment of spinning electrons within a substance. This alignment will occur naturally in some substances, including iron, nickel, and cobalt, all of which can be used to produce **permanent magnets**. The alignment of electrons creates a **magnetic field** which, like an electric or gravitational field, can act on other objects. Magnetic fields have a north and a south pole which act similar to electric charges: opposite poles will attract, and same poles will repel each other. However, unlike electric charge, which can be either positive or negative, a magnetic field ALWAYS has two poles. If a magnet is cut in half, the result is two magnets, each with a north and south pole.

Electricity and magnetism are closely related. A moving magnet creates an electric field, and a moving charged particle will create a magnetic field. A specific kind of **temporary magnet** known as an electromagnet can be made by coiling a wire around a metal object and running electricity through it. A magnetic field will be created when the wire contains a current but will disappear when the flow of electricity is stopped.

> **SAMPLE QUESTIONS:**

5) Which type of chemical reaction takes place when kerosene reacts with oxygen to light a lamp?

    A. oxidation
    B. neutralization
    C. combustion
    D. convection

    Answers:

    A. Incorrect. Oxidation is a chemical change in which a substance loses electrons, as happens when iron is exposed to oxygen and rusts.
    B. Incorrect. Neutralization is a chemical reaction that occurs when an acid and a base react to form a salt and water.
    C. **Correct.** Combustion is a chemical reaction that produces carbon dioxide and water. Burning lamp oil (fuel) is combustion.
    D. Incorrect. Convection is the transfer of heat caused by heat rising and cold sinking.

6) Which substance is a good insulator?

    A. glass
    B. water
    C. silver
    D. aluminum

    Answers:

    A. **Correct.** Glass is a good insulator.
    B. Incorrect. Water is a good conductor.
    C. Incorrect. Silver is a good conductor.
    D. Incorrect. Aluminum is a good conductor.

Science and Technology

MEDICAL TECHNOLOGY

Scientists have made great strides in developing **medical technology**, including technology designed to diagnose, prevent, and treat many medical conditions. Diagnostic equipment, which is used to identify medical conditions, includes such technology as **Magnetic Resonance Imaging** (**MRI**) machines, **x-rays**, and **electrocardiograms** (**EKGs**), all of which are used to observe organs and internal structures. Recent developments have also made it possible for doctors to identify some specific genetic disorders by testing a patient's DNA.

Many new or improved treatment options are also available to patients. **Defibrillators**, which reestablish heart rhythms, have become more common and portable. Patients also have reliable options for surgical interventions to treat heart disease, back pain, and damaged joints. Treatments for cancer, including chemotherapy (anticancer drugs) and radiation therapy, continue to improve.

New medicines are being discovered to treat diseases in better ways than ever before. These include **pharmaceuticals** that target conditions like heart disease, mental illness, and seizures as well as bacterial and viral infections. Researchers are also developing new **vaccines** to prevent common infections such as the flu and shingles and also emerging diseases like the Ebola and Zika viruses.

Technology has also changed our relationship with food and nutrition. Processes like pasteurization and refrigeration reduce the risk of food-borne illnesses and allow food to be kept fresh longer. Similarly, water treatment facilities prevent the spread of previously common water-borne bacteria and parasites. Scientists are also constantly revising the **food pyramid**, which is designed to help people understand which types of food make up a healthy diet.

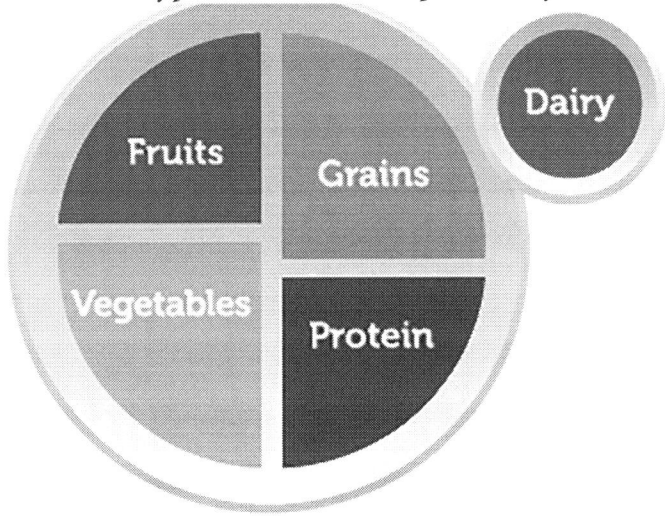

Figure 10.14. USDA Food Recommendations

Technology and the Environment

Fossil fuels, such as oil, natural gas, and coal, are nonrenewable resources, meaning the earth contains a finite amount of those substances. These carbon-based fuels were produced over millions of years by the decomposition and compression of organisms that lived long ago. When burned, fossil fuels emit pollutants that damage the environment. Some of these pollutants include greenhouse gases such as carbon dioxide and methane, which when emitted into the atmosphere, trap heat and contribute to **global warming**.

As **nonrenewable resources** become depleted, scientists are working toward advancements in using **renewable resources** as replacements. Other possible sources of energy include nuclear, hydropower, wind, solar, biomass, and geothermal power. These all have less of an impact on the environment than fossil fuels, but many need to be more thoroughly researched and developed before they can supply the energy the world needs.

Nuclear power is created by releasing the energy stored in large atoms by breaking them into smaller atoms. Nuclear power does not release emissions into the atmosphere like burning fossil fuels does, but nuclear power produces dangerous radioactive waste that has the potential to cause other environmental problems.

Through the use of dams, **hydropower** converts the energy in moving water into mechanical energy, which can then be transformed into electricity. Dams do not release harmful emissions like fossil fuels do, but they can be disruptive to natural environments and waterways.

> **CONSIDER THIS**
>
> What would be the pros and cons of using wind, solar, nuclear, and hydropower in your area?

Energy from the **wind** is harnessed using turbines (also called windmills), transforming mechanical energy into electricity. Wind turbines are becoming more common in areas where windy conditions are common, including plains regions and coastlines. **Solar energy** transforms energy from the sun into electricity using solar panels. These panels can be laid out in giant arrays called solar farms in order to provide energy to a large area, but they can also be installed on individual homes or buildings.

Biofuels are biological matter that can be burned to produce heat, steam, or electricity. While biofuels such as ethanol are renewable, they can create many of the same environmental concerns as fossil fuels. Finally, **geothermal** energy converts heat from below Earth's surface into steam. This type of energy has been used since ancient times to heat water and homes and has recently been harnessed to produce electricity.

While commercial agriculture is able to provide food for an extraordinary number of people, many agricultural practices can be damaging to the environment. For example, fertilizers and pesticides may run off fields and pollute nearby lands and waterways. The large swaths of land required for farming can also damage the diversity and stability of ecosystems. Recently, **genetically modified organisms (GMOs)**, which contain genes inserted in their DNA by scientists, have come under scrutiny. While some believe that these GMOs, which include corn, soybean, and potatoes, can create a safer, more plentiful food supply, others question whether the new plants will have detrimental effects on natural environments.

Scientists urge people to protect the environment and Earth's natural resources through **conservation**. One main aspect of conservation is the attempt to limit the number of natural resources that are used to manufacture and dispose of consumer products. By **recycling**, or reusing, common materials like glass, steel, and paper, we limit the resources needed to produce new products. Recycling also reduces the amount of waste put into landfills.

Another important part of conservation is setting aside dedicated tracts of land for protection. National, state, and local parks are important ways to preserve species and ecosystem diversity. Similarly, many **endangered species**, which are at risk for extinction, are protected by national and international governments.

> **QUICK REVIEW**
>
> How can students conserve resources and reduce waste in schools?

SAMPLE QUESTIONS:

7) Which natural resource is a fossil fuel?

   A. water
   B. wind
   C. coal
   D. sun

   Answers:

   A. Incorrect. Water is a renewable resource.
   B. Incorrect. Wind is a renewable resource.
   C. **Correct.** Coal is a nonrenewable resource that comes from the remains of plants that lived in swamps millions of years ago.
   D. Incorrect. Solar power is a renewable resource.

8) Which medical technology can be used to detect cancerous tumors?

   A. MRI
   B. defibrillator
   C. EKG
   D. patient monitor

   Answers:

   A. **Correct.** MRI stands for Magnetic Resonance Imaging and is used to observe organs and internal structures.
   B. Incorrect. A defibrillator is used to reestablish heart rhythms.
   C. Incorrect. An EKG, or electrocardiogram, is used to observe the rhythms of the heart.
   D. Incorrect. A patient monitor measures and records vital signs.

Science Skills and Processes

SCIENTIFIC INQUIRY

Investigation, or **inquiry** science, provides the strongest foundation for scientific thinking. Inquiry science is guided by the scientific method, which provides a framework for observing, measuring, and drawing conclusions about the world.

The first step in the scientific method is **observation**. From these observations, scientists develop questions and do research on current available information about a particular topic. This research helps them formulate a reasonable and testable explanation for their observations, a statement known as a **hypothesis**. Scientists then design and conduct an **experiment** in which they collect data that will demonstrate whether their hypothesis is false or not. It is important to note that a hypothesis can never be proven true—it can be confirmed as false, or enough data can be collected to *infer* that it is true. In order for data to support a hypothesis, it must be consistent and reproducible.

When scientists have repeatedly tested a hypothesis, and that hypothesis has become widely accepted, it becomes known as a **theory**. Theories provide an explanation for a natural phenomenon that is widely accepted by scientists. The theory of evolution, for example, states that natural selection is the mechanism that led to the current diversity of species found on Earth. A scientific **law** is a description of a natural phenomenon. However, unlike a theory, it does not explain how something happens. For example, Newton's law of universal gravitation states the gravitational force between two objects depends on their distance and mass.

> **STUDY TIP**
>
> The phrase *Queen Rachel Hopes Every Coward Gains Courage* can help students remember the scientific method: question – research – hypothesis – experiment – collect data – graph/analyze data – conclusion.

Science, while grounded in observation and data, is not perfect, and scientific knowledge is always growing and changing. Scientists must be able to react to new observations and adjust their hypotheses as needed to address new evidence. By constantly observing, asking questions, and rigorously testing hypotheses, scientists are able to slowly build on the collective pool of scientific knowledge.

EXPERIMENTAL DESIGN

Scientists use a rigorous set of rules to design experiments. The protocols of experimental design are meant to ensure that scientists are actually testing what they set out to test. A well-designed experiment will measure the impact of a single factor on a system, thus allowing the experimenter to draw conclusions about that factor.

Every experiment includes variables, which are the factors or treatments that may impact the outcome of the experiment. **Independent variables** are controlled by the experimenter. They are usually the factors that the experimenter has hypothesized will have an effect on the system. Often, a design will include a treatment group and a **control group** (which does not receive the treatment). The **dependent variables** are factors that are influenced by the independent variable.

For example, in an experiment investigating which type of fertilizer has the greatest effect on plant growth, the independent variable is the type of fertilizer used. The scientist is controlling, or manipulating, the type of fertilizer. The dependent variable is plant growth because the amount of plant growth depends on the type of fertilizer. The type of plant, the amount of water, and the amount of sunlight the plants receive are controls because those variables of the experiment are kept the same for each plant.

When designing an experiment, scientists must identify possible sources of error. These can be **confounding variables**, which are factors that act much like the independent variable and thus can make it appear that the independent variable has a greater effect than it actually does. The design may also include unknown variables that are not controlled by the scientists. Finally, scientists must be aware of human error, particularly in collecting data and making observations, and of possible equipment errors.

> **CONSIDER THIS**
>
> What are the limitations of adhering rigidly to the scientific method?

During the experiment, scientists collect data, which must then be analyzed and presented appropriately. This may mean running a statistical analysis on the data (e.g., finding the mean) or putting the data in graph form. Such an analysis allows scientists to see trends in the data and determine if those trends are statistically significant. From that data, scientists can draw a **conclusion** about the experiment.

Scientists often use **models** in their research. These models are a simplified representation of a system. For example, a mathematical equation that describes fluctuations in a population might be used to test how a certain variable is likely to affect that population. Or, a scientist might use a greenhouse to model a particular ecosystem so she can more closely control the variables in the environment.

> **FOR REFERENCE**
>
> See page 51 – 53 for more information about using charts and graphs.

SAFETY PROCEDURES

When choosing and setting up a lab, teachers need to remember that they are liable for any accidents or hazardous incidents that occur under their supervision. For an elementary classroom, **standard laboratory equipment** includes flat top tables with stools so students can view experiments from several angles. Safety gear, microscopes, beakers, measurement tools, test tubes, eyedroppers, weights, magnets, and timers should be some of the available tools. Measurement tools for length include metric rulers and tape measures. Beakers and graduated cylinders are used to measure volume. Balance scales measure mass.

Standard safety equipment like safety goggles, aprons, protective gloves, and a fire extinguisher must be available. In addition to using standard safety equipment, students should be instructed on wearing appropriate **apparel**. For example, long hair should be tied back and loose clothing and jewelry should be secured. Closed-toed shoes should be worn.

Student **behavior** guidelines are important, but they take on even more significance when students are working in potentially dangerous situations. Adults should model safety practices, such as wearing goggles. Science safety procedures should be outlined for parents and students on a document requiring signatures. Students should be warned about potential dangers in new situations as they arise in each experiment. Students must be diligently supervised; those students who do not meet safety standards should be removed immediately. At the end of an experiment, students must know how to properly clean up equipment and dispose of waste.

Emergency procedures should include proactively monitoring students and equipment and wearing safety gear. Predetermined plans for emergency first aid, electric shock, poisoning, burns, fire, evacuations, spills, and animal bites should be established.

SAMPLE QUESTIONS:

9) Which tool measures the volume of an object?
    A. thermometer
    B. graduated cylinder
    C. balance
    D. barometer

   Answers:
    A. Incorrect. A thermometer measures temperature.
    B. Correct. A graduated cylinder measures volume.
    C. Incorrect. A balance measures mass.
    D. Incorrect. A barometer measures atmospheric pressure.

10) Which step should students take before making a hypothesis in a scientific experiment?
    A. interpret data
    B. make a graph
    C. research
    D. do the experiment

Answers:

A. Incorrect. Interpreting data comes after an experiment; the hypothesis comes before.

B. Incorrect. Displaying data comes after an experiment; the hypothesis comes before.

C. Correct. Students need to conduct research before making a reasonable and testable hypothesis.

D. Incorrect. The hypothesis comes before an experiment and guides the experimental process.

11

Curriculum and Instruction

Today, science instruction engages students in hands-on activities and investigations that promote critical thinking and reasoning skills in order to align with the Next Generation Science Standards (NGSS). These research-based standards lay out expectations for student knowledge and capabilities. They also allow teachers to create learning experiences that generate interest and excitement in students about learning science.

The STEM fields (Science, Technology, Engineering, and Math) are at the forefront of instruction. This curriculum is embedded into the NGSS; the four areas are integrated rather than taught separately. These new standards involve incorporating real-world applications into the classroom. Students are encouraged to explore, design, create, and solve problems in the classroom as preparation for applying these skills in daily life. The standards also incorporate math and literacy skills, addressing consistency between the NGSS and Common Core State Standards.

Earth and Space Science

Earth and space science is the study of Earth and its place in the universe. This discipline is broken down into four categories: geology, oceanography, astronomy, and meteorology. There are many dangers (both natural and manufactured) facing the earth and the environment. Earth Day is a useful opportunity to promote awareness among elementary students of these dangers and how to prevent them.

Geology is the study of the earth, its structure, and the processes that led to its composition. It also deals with the organisms found on the earth and how they have changed over time. At the elementary level, geology includes learning about natural resources and minerals,

> **QUICK REVIEW**
>
> Why is it important to make students aware of the dangers facing the earth and environment?

natural hazards, and protecting the earth's environment. The study of volcanoes and earthquakes is also included in geology. Scientists work to determine their causes and predict when they may occur.

Teachers should provide students with activities that allow them to explore the many aspects of geology. Creating interactive **science notebooks** and providing ample investigation opportunities are great ways to enhance students' understanding of the discipline. Students can **model** the different layers of the earth using play dough; make their own rocks using sand; create volcanoes using clay, vinegar, baking soda, and dishwashing liquid; and sort and classify rocks to learn about geological processes. Gelatin, toothpicks, and mini marshmallows can be used to simulate earthquakes.

Oceanography is the study of the earth's oceans. Oceans cover over 71 percent of the earth and provide food and other assets. By studying the composition of oceans, the organisms that live there, and how they move, students discover their resources and learn the importance of protecting them from dangers posed by humans. Furthermore, oceans affect climate and change in weather. Students can create the ocean zones in a jar using food coloring, corn syrup, oil, dishwashing liquid, rubbing alcohol, and water.

> **QUICK REVIEW**
>
> How is space science relevant to students' daily lives?

Astronomy is the study of the solar system and how it affects the earth; likewise, astronomy considers how the earth itself affects the solar system. Students should especially understand the importance of astronomy, given the role of the moon in controlling ocean tides and the effect of the sun on weather and climate. To help them understand astronomy, students can use cookies to create the phases of the moon, create a model of the sun, earth, and moon to show how the earth orbits the sun and how the moon orbits the earth, and make moon craters.

Meteorology is the study of the earth's weather. By studying the atmosphere, students develop an understanding of the earth's weather and climate. Shaving cream, water, food coloring, and microwaving a bar of soap help students understand clouds. Students can create a tornado using a two-liter soda bottle, water, and food coloring. They can also create the water cycle in a bag and make an anemometer to measure wind.

> **CONSIDER THIS**
>
> How would you explain to students what causes rain?

SCIENCE: CURRICULUM AND INSTRUCTION 245

EXAMPLE QUESTIONS

1) Which of the following could be used as a culminating activity for a unit on weather to allow the students to use what they have learned?

   A. Assign students group projects on different types of storms. Students should provide an example of the storm and describe the characteristics and effects of the storm.
   B. Give an essay test on the types of clouds. Students list all of the types of clouds and describe their characteristics.
   C. Give students a multiple-choice test on all of the elements of meteorology.
   D. Assign students an end-of-chapter test in their science workbooks.

   Answers:

   A. Correct. This activity would allow students to pair what they have learned with critical thinking and reasoning skills to complete their projects. Students can demonstrate their deep understanding of the material.
   B. Incorrect. Students may be able to name the clouds and their characteristics, but they are only demonstrating their ability to memorize rather than their actual understanding of the material.
   C. Incorrect. Multiple-choice tests only prove rote memorization about material. Students learn the information for the test but do not necessarily retain that information upon the test's completion.
   D. Incorrect. Completing a generic end-of-chapter test only tests the information presented in that particular chapter and does not permit students to use their critical thinking and reasoning skills.

2) Which of the following would be a good introduction to a unit on astronomy?

   A. to read the overview of the chapter on astronomy in the science textbook
   B. to take a pretest about astronomy
   C. to show students videos about the solar system
   D. to have students draw what they think the solar system looks like

   Answers:

   A. Incorrect. Reading a chapter overview will not necessarily engage students.
   B. Incorrect. A pretest is a way for teacher's to assess students' prior knowledge about the subject but does not necessarily engage the students.
   C. Correct. Showing videos about a subject is a great hook to capture students' attention and create a level of excitement and enthusiasm.

D. Incorrect. While drawing the solar system may be a fun activity for the students, it would not necessarily generate excitement about the subject.

Life Science

Life science is the study of all living things: plants, animals, and human beings. Life science in elementary school encompasses ecosystems, information processing, and inherited traits.

> **CONSIDER THIS**
>
> What skills can students gain by learning about life science?

As with all science disciplines, **inquiry**, **experimentation**, and **studying patterns** play big roles in instruction. Students should be given the opportunity to observe, interact, and record data on the life cycles of plants and animals in real time. **Classroom gardens** or single **plants** provide opportunities for students to explore life science. Interest in plants can lead to careers in ecology, pharmaceuticals, or agriculture. Bean plants are easy to grow in a classroom setting: using a wet paper towel and a dried bean seed in a plastic bag, students can observe the life cycle of a bean plant.

Classroom pets contribute to student understanding of the life cycle and classification of animals. Each school has its own rules governing the use of classroom pets, but some common classroom pets and habitats include ant farms, butterfly gardens, goldfish, hamsters, and guinea pigs. When choosing a pet, consider the amount of care needed during weekends and school holidays, potential disruptions, upkeep and cost, and how the experience aligns with curriculum objectives. Learning about animal life may spark students' interest in future careers in veterinary medicine, ecology, and marine biology.

When possible, **vocabulary** should be taught using a hands-on approach through manipulating objects, drawing pictures, and role-playing. In addition to learning how plants and animals develop, students should gain an understanding of the environment in which different animals thrive and the role that each organism plays in the food chain.

When studying ecosystems, students will learn about the needs of human beings, plants, and animals, how they depend on each other, and what roles they play in the environment. Information processing relates to the different body parts and senses that animals use to grow, survive, and guide their actions. Inherited traits refer to what humans, plants, and animals inherit from their parents. The environment also affects the traits a living thing develops.

> **QUICK REVIEW**
>
> Why are interactive notebooks so useful when teaching science?

Once again, interactive notebooks are extremely helpful when teaching science. Students can use the notebooks to record the basic concepts of each category of life science and as a reference for later activities. Students should become scientists, engaging in hands-on learning experiences and investigations that allow them to explore the world around them. These learning experiences enable students to classify, observe, and record their findings.

EXAMPLE QUESTIONS

3) Which of the following would be a good activity for teaching students about life cycles and the four stages of metamorphosis?

    A. Have students create a food chain.

    B. Use mealworms and follow their development. Have students observe and record the process.

    C. Have students draw an animal cell.

    D. Have students grow a bean.

    Answers:

    A. Incorrect. Creating a food chain only shows students how each living thing obtains nourishment; it does not address life cycles or metamorphosis.

    B. Correct. Students can follow the life cycle of the mealworms and witness the process of metamorphosis in real time.

    C. Incorrect. Having students draw an animal cell will only assess whether the students can identify and label the parts of a cell.

    D. Incorrect. Growing a bean only demonstrates the life cycle of this plant, not the four stages of metamorphosis.

4) Which activity would be LEAST effective for teaching students about amphibians?

    A. looking up and copying definitions in the dictionary

    B. sorting animal cards based on characteristics

    C. dissecting a frog

    D. making a word map that represents the habitats of amphibians

    Answers:

    A. Correct. There is no evidence supporting the effectiveness of copying definitions of terms to learn new vocabulary. An active, hands-on approach to learning vocabulary using objects, role play, drawing, or other activities is more effective.

    B. Incorrect. Amphibians have distinct characteristics; sorting cards based on their unique characteristics would indeed be a good learning activity for students.

C. Incorrect. Depending on school policy, dissecting frogs may be an effective activity for teaching older students about amphibians. Computer-based dissection tools may also be used.

D. Incorrect. Word maps are an effective, research-based approach for learning.

Physical Science

Physical science involves force and motion, matter, and light and sound. When students learn about force and motion, they can compare the effects of pushes and pulls; furthermore, they can determine how to change speed or direction with pushes and pulls. Students can act as engineers as they conduct experiments. Fun activities include pretending to ride a roller coaster and determining the effect of the force on the riders; students can take turns pushing and pulling each other in a box, they can blow bubbles, spin tops, throw balls, and even create ramps to roll balls off of. These activities will allow the students to gain a clear understanding of force and motion.

> **QUICK REVIEW**
>
> Why do students need to learn about pushes and pulls?

The three states of matter are solid, liquid, and gas. Students will learn about the physical and chemical properties of different substances. Teachers should provide **anchor charts** of the three states of matter for students to use as a point of reference when completing activities. Again, hands-on activities are the key to helping students develop a clear understanding of matter. To help students understand solids teachers can simply show various objects around the room and have students name some examples of their own. When teaching about liquids, teachers can **provide examples** and indicate how liquids take the form of the vessel in which they are held by pouring them into different containers. To teach about gases, teachers may inflate a balloon with helium. While this gas is invisible, students can still see the effects of the gas going into the balloon. Other engaging activities include freezing water, making ice cream, and melting chocolate chips. Students enjoy these types of activities because they can eat the food at the conclusion of the experiment.

> **TEACHING TIP**
>
> A solid has a firm shape and form. A liquid is a substance that flows easily and takes the shape of its container. A gas is a substance that is fluid and has no shape or volume.

Students will again **predict**, **observe**, **explore**, **discuss**, and **investigate** when studying light and sound. Students should be able to demonstrate how vibrating materials generate sound and how sound can make materials vibrate, understand how light reveals objects, and understand the variety of devices used to communicate. Students will learn how light and sound travel. Light travels as a wave, but it can also act like a particle that reflects off of a mirror. When light is blocked, it creates a shadow. Vocabulary words such as *absorption*, *circuit*, *echo*, *frequency*, *opaque*, *translucent*, *perception*, *photon*, *pitch*, *ultrasonic*, *ultraviolet*, *vibrate*, *volume*, and *wavelength* should be introduced and discussed throughout experiments and investigations.

> **DID YOU KNOW?**
>
> Rainbows form in the sky when sunlight bends as it passes through raindrops.

EXAMPLE QUESTIONS

5) Which of the following activities would help students learn and understand how sound travels from one end to the other?

   A. making a flute out of straws
   B. putting a balloon over a plastic cup, pouring salt on it, and playing music
   C. using spoons to tap on jars filled with varying amounts of water
   D. making a string phone

   Answers:

   A. Incorrect. Making a flute out of straws only helps students determine how high or low a note is.
   B. Incorrect. This technique is called salt vibrations. When the music is played, the salt "dances" due to the vibrations caused by the sound; however, this activity does not explain how sound moves across space.
   C. Incorrect. Using spoons to tap on jars filled with varying amounts of water only teaches students about pitch.
   D. **Correct.** When students speak into the cups, they create sound waves that turn into vibrations. These vibrations travel along the string and are turned back into sound waves when they reach the other cup.

6) Which of the following would be a good activity to teach students about the three states of matter?

   A. making root beer floats
   B. making homemade butter
   C. making ice cream in a bag
   D. blowing up a balloon

   Answers:

   A. **Correct.** Making root beer floats demonstrates the three states of matter: liquid, solid, and gas.

B. Incorrect. This activity helps students learn how cream and water (both liquids), and salt (a solid) make butter. However, it does not address gases.

C. Incorrect. In this activity, students use solids (ice cubes, salt, and sugar) and liquids (milk and vanilla) to make ice cream. However, the activity does not address gases.

D. Incorrect. This activity only addresses gases.

Science Skills and Processes

There are six science process skills. They are observing, classifying, measuring, communicating, inferring, and predicting.

Observation is the most basic science skill. Observation uses all five senses. All of the other science process skills require strong observation skills. Observations can be broken down into two types: qualitative and quantitative. A **qualitative observation** only uses the five senses. For example, the observation *a kitten's fur is fluffy and brown* acknowledges sight and touch. A **quantitative observation** uses a quantity or number as well as the five senses. For example, the observation *three fluffy kittens weigh two pounds each* accounts for touch and quantity (of both kittens and pounds). Students often write or draw their observations; teachers need to guide students in making detailed observations. Detailed observations will help students better understand the concepts they are learning about.

A good activity to help students use their observation skills is growing a seed in a clear plastic sandwich bag. Students wet a paper towel and wrap two or three lima bean seeds in it. They place the paper towel in a sandwich bag and tape it to a window. The students will now observe what takes place and record their observations daily. When the seeds sprout and start to grow, students should write and draw detailed descriptions and pictures. Students can say, "the seed has sprouted and the stem has appeared. It's about half an inch tall, it's skinny, and it's green. There's a tiny green leaf on the left side of the stem." Teaching students how to make detailed observations will make them more aware of changes when they are doing experiments and investigations.

Classifying is the next science process skill. Students need to learn how to identify similarities and differences among things and be able to put objects into groups according to their similarities and differences. When students classify and group objects, they gain a sense of order. There are several different ways to classify objects. The first way is to order objects based on a **property** (such as shortest to longest or lightest to heaviest). **Binary classification** occurs when a group of objects is divided into two smaller groups according to a certain property. A group of animals can be further divided into two groups: for instance, those that have fur and those that do not. **Multi-stage classification** involves taking groups from a binary classification and dividing them even further. Each object will be placed into a category by itself. Students could use marine animals to create multi-stage classification.

Measurement is important when collecting, comparing, and interpreting data. Measuring is usually done first with **nonstandard units of measure** followed by **standard units of measure**. Teachers usually have students measure length, weight, or distance first because these are the easiest for students to understand. They can begin by measuring objects in the classroom and even each other, moving on to more difficult measurements such as the mass and volume of various liquids or the distance an object can travel.

> **QUICK REVIEW**
>
> Why is measurement taught with nonstandard units of measure first?

Communication is extremely important because students must be able to share their observations with others. This can be done through maps, pictures, diagrams, graphs, power point presentations, slideshows, and oral presentations.

Students can use their observations to make **inferences**, explanations based on their observations. Students make inferences in everyday life without even realizing it. Once students have made their observations, teachers should ask questions, forcing the students to consider what their observations mean. Inferences can change as students' observations change; it is important that students know and understand this. Sometimes students reject their original inferences based on their new observations.

When students make a **prediction**, they are making an educated guess about a future event. They can relate predictions to weather forecasts, using the information they have gathered to "forecast" future events. Observations and inferences are crucial when making predictions.

Students must understand that science is not exact and that they learn by doing. Using science process skills when completing experiments and investigations will make students become more engaged and interested in science content, resulting in better understanding of the content. It is important to note that students use these skills—observation, measuring, communication, and making inferences and predictions—in their everyday lives.

> **CONSIDER THIS**
>
> Think about the science process skills and how they can be applied in other subject areas.

EXAMPLE QUESTIONS

7) Which activity would be helpful in teaching science process skills?

   A. a vocabulary worksheet on which students match each science process to its meaning
   B. having a classroom pet that the students care for
   C. a science workbook page about an experiment
   D. writing an essay describing science process skills

   Answers:

   A. Incorrect. This activity would assess whether the students know what each process skill means. They would not be actively engaged in any activities that would help them learn the processes.

   B. Correct. Keeping a classroom pet would help students develop science process skills.

   C. Incorrect. This activity would allow students to read about an experiment performed by someone else. The students would not be engaged in the experiment themselves.

   D. Incorrect. This activity would assess whether students knew what each science process meant but would not give the students an opportunity to use them in the classroom.

8) A teacher plays a game with students called *Mystery Bags*. The students must feel an object in a bag and try to determine what it is without looking at it. Which science process skills would the students be using during this activity?

   A. measurement and classification
   B. communication and classification
   C. predicting and measurement
   D. observation and inferring

   Answers:

   A. Incorrect. The students are not measuring the object in the bag; in addition, they are not classifying the object according to specific attributes.

   B. Incorrect. The students may be talking, but they are not classifying the object according to specific attributes.

   C. Incorrect. The students make predictions after they have made observations; furthermore, they are not measuring the object.

   D. Correct. The students are making observations about the object based on what they feel inside the bag. Using these observations, the students can infer what the object is.

Terms

acceleration: how quickly an object changes velocity

acid: a compound that is able to contribute a hydrogen ion and has a pH lower than 7

adaptations: adjustments to the environment

agrology: the study of the relationship between soil and agriculture

amphibians: a class of cold-blooded vertebrate animals that have gills when they hatch but develop lungs in adulthood

anatomy: the study of the structure of living organisms

asexual: does not require the union of sex cells to reproduce

asteroid: a large rocky body, smaller than a planet, that orbits the sun

atmosphere: the mass of gases that surround Earth

atom: the smallest particle of a chemical element that retains the properties of the element

atomic mass: the mass of an atom calculated by adding the number of protons and neutrons

atomic number: the number of protons in the nucleus of an atom

attraction: a force that draws objects closer

base: a compound that is able to contribute a hydroxide ion and has a pH greater than 7

biomass: plant-based fuel, usually burned, for generating heat, steam, or electricity

biomes: large geographic areas that provide the environmental conditions in which certain organisms live

black holes: a massive star that has collapsed and has a gravitational force so strong that light cannot escape

cell: the smallest living part of an organism

cell division: the separation of a cell into two cells with identical genes

cell membrane: the outer covering of a cell

chemical change: making or breaking chemical bonds between atoms in a chemical reaction

classification: sorting according to characteristics

climate: an area's weather conditions over time

combustion: a chemical reaction that produces carbon dioxide and water, usually from the burning of fuels

comet: a small object made of ice and dust that orbits the sun

communities: interdependent organisms living together in a habitat

compound: a combination of two or more elements

conclusions: inferences based on data collected in an experiment

condensation: the process when water vapor in the air comes in contact with a cold surface and turns into liquid water

conduction: the transfer of heat through physical contact

conductivity: a property that determines how well a material conducts electricity and heat

connections: linking prior knowledge with new information

conservation: protecting the environment and natural resources

controls: the parts of an experiment that stay the same

convection: transfer of heat that occurs in a circular motion caused by heat rising and cold sinking

core: the layer at the center of the earth

covalent bonding: a chemical bond in which electrons are shared

data presentation: an organized display of data

density: a property of matter that can be determined by dividing mass by volume

dependent variable: part of an experiment that responds to, or depends on, the independent variable

deposition: the laying down of sediment in a new location

disciplines: areas of science

DNA: deoxyribonucleic acid (carries genetic information)

Doppler Effect: the change in wavelength when waves are compressed as an object approaches an observer and spread out as the object moves away from the observer

Earth system: the interaction of all physical, chemical, and biological components

earthquake: breaking of rock below the surface that releases energy

eclipse: when Earth, the moon, and the sun align so that light from one object is blocked

ecosystem: a community of organisms and their interaction with each other and the environment

edaphology: the study of how soils affect living things, especially plants

electricity: energy of moving electrons

electron: subatomic particle with a negative charge found outside the nucleus of an atom

elements: substances made of one type of atom

energy conservation: controlling energy consumption

equilibrium: a state of balance

erosion: the movement of sediments from one place to another

evaporation: the process of changing from a liquid to a gas

evolution: the progressive changes of living things throughout Earth's history

experimental design: an experiment that includes an objective, standard protocols, a control group, and independent and dependent variables

experimental error: mistakes made during an experiment caused by limitations of the equipment or external influences

food chain: producers, consumers, predators, and decomposers that live interdependently in an ecosystem

force: any push or pull on an object

fossil fuels: nonrenewable fuels made from organisms that lived millions of years ago

friction: the force of one object resisting another

function: the activity of a part of an organism

geology: the study of Earth

geothermal: converting heat from below the earth's surface to make steam

galaxy: a large system of stars, gas, and dust held together by gravity

generator: a device that transforms mechanical energy into electrical energy

genetic: hereditary

genetic disorder: a hereditary abnormality that creates a health condition

genus: the level of taxonomic classification that ranks above species

glacier: a large mass of slowly moving ice and snow

gravity: the attraction of one mass to another mass

greenhouse gases: gases that trap heat in the atmosphere

groundwater: water that is stored underground in rock layers called aquifers

homeostasis: regulation and stabilization of internal conditions

hurricane: a large, violent storm with winds greater than 74 mph

hydrology: the study of water

hydropower: transforms the energy of moving water into mechanical energy and then electricity

hydrosphere: the water found on and below Earth's surface and in the atmosphere

hypothesis: an educated guess

icebergs: a large chunk of ice that has broken off from a continental glacier and is floating in the ocean

independent variables: part of an experiment that is manipulated to test the effect on the dependent variable

inheritance: a feature passed down from one generation to the next

inquiry: questioning

interdependence: two or more things that rely on each other

ionic bonding: a chemical bond that involves the attraction between two ions with unlike charges

kinetic energy: the energy of motion

kingdom: the highest level of taxonomic classification

laws: descriptions of scientific phenomenon

leaves: the part of a plant where photosynthesis takes place

life cycles: the stages of life in an organism

loudness: the amplitude of a sound wave

mammals: a class of warm-blooded vertebrate animals that have hair, give birth to live young, and produce milk

mantle: the layer of Earth below the crust

mass: the amount of matter in an object

matter: any substance that takes up space and has mass

measurement tools: equipment used to collect data

mechanics: the science of energy and force

medical technology: research and development for improving patient care

medicine: pharmaceuticals used to treat or prevent medical conditions

meteorology: the study of the atmosphere and weather

mixtures: two or more substances combined without a chemical reaction to bond them

models: representations of the real world

molecules: two or more atoms bonded together

moon: a large body that orbits a planet

mutation: a change in genetic information that may be passed on to future generations

natural selection: Darwin's theory that living things that adapt to their environment have a higher survival rate and produce more offspring

neutralization: a chemical reaction that occurs when an acid and a base react to form a salt and water

neutron: subatomic particle with no charge found within the nucleus of an atom

Newton's First Law of Motion: an object at rest stays at rest, and an object in motion stays in motion, unless a force acts on it

Newton's Second Law of Motion: force equals mass multiplied by acceleration; $F = ma$

Newton's Third Law of Motion: for every action, there is an equal and opposite reaction

nonrenewable resources: resources that take millions of years to replenish

nuclear power: energy stored in large atoms that is released when large atoms are broken into smaller atoms

nucleus: the center of a cell that contains DNA

oceanography: the study of oceans

optics: the study of light

organ: a body part that serves an important function in a system

organ systems: groups of organs that work together to perform one or more functions

organism: a living thing

oxidation: a chemical change in which a substance loses electrons

paleontology: the study of the history of life through fossils

parasitism: a relationship between two organisms when one organism benefits to the detriment of the other

pedology: the study of soils in their natural environment

the periodic table: a table of chemical elements listed in order by atomic number

pH scale: a standard measure of acidity or alkalinity where 7 is neutral

photosynthesis: the process by which energy from sunlight is used to make food (glucose) from carbon dioxide and water

physical change: change in a substance that does not change the composition of the substance

physiology: the study of the functions of living organisms

pitch: the frequency of vibrations

planet: a large body in space that orbits a star

plants: a kingdom of organisms that make food using photosynthesis

plate tectonics: a theory that Earth is made of large crustal plates that move over its surface

polar ice: regions at the North and South Poles covered in ice

poles: the ends of a magnet

populations: a group of organisms of the same species

potential energy: the amount of energy of an object due to its position

precipitation: any form of water that falls from the sky

predators: animals that kill other animals for food

prey: an organism that is hunted and killed for food

property: a characteristic

protons: subatomic particle with a positive electric charge found within the nucleus of an atom

radiation: transfer of heat without a medium

reflection: to change the direction of a wave by bouncing the wave off a surface

refraction: the bending of a wave as the wave travels through different media

reliability: the extent to which the results remain the same if an experiment is repeated

renewable resources: resources that replenish quickly

reproduction: the process of making a copy

reptiles: a class of cold-blooded vertebrates that have scales and lay eggs on land

repulsion: a force that pushes objects away

results: outcomes

rock record: a biological history of Earth recorded in rocks

roots: the part of a plant that absorbs water and nutrients from the soil

sexual: requires the union of gametes (sex cells) to reproduce

solar energy: converts energy from the sun into electricity

solar system: a system that includes a star or stars, along with planets, moons, asteroids, meteoroids, and comets, that is held together by gravity

solubility: the amount of a solute that will dissolve in a solvent

solution: the answer to a problem

solutions: a mixture that is evenly distributed and thoroughly dissolved

species: the most specific level of taxonomic classification in which organisms with similar genetics can breed

speed: distance divided by time

stars: large masses of gas

stem: the main stalk of a plant that carries the nutrients and water from the roots to other parts of the plant

structure: the organization of a part of an organism

sun: the star in our solar system

territoriality: animal behavior of defending a specific area

theories: principles explained by science

tides: the movement of large bodies of water caused by the gravitational pull of the moon and the sun

tissue: groups of cells that have a similar function

traits: characteristics

units of measurement: nonstandard, metric, and US customary are systems of measurement; science uses the metric system

velocity: the rate at which an object changes position; change of distance divided by change of time

volcanoes: vents in Earth's crust that allow molten rock to reach the surface

water cycle: the circulation of water throughout Earth's surface, atmosphere, and hydrosphere

wave: a pulse of energy

weather: daily atmospheric conditions

weathering: the mechanical and/or chemical process by which rocks break down

weight: the force of the gravitational pull on an object

wind energy: energy from the wind is transformed into mechanical energy and then electricity

Part VI: Art, Music, and Physical Education

12

Curriculum and Instruction

The elementary art curriculum helps students gain an understanding of artwork creation by drawing upon various types of media, techniques, and processes. Students learn that historical and cultural contexts, including symbols and individual and collective expression, create meaning in art. Instruction is geared towards helping students identify and analyze various elements and principles of art and select them for use in their own works. The ultimate goal is for students not only to be able to assess their own work, but that of others as well.

The music curriculum focuses on listening and responding to music others have created. Students learn the basic elements of music and have an opportunity to engage in musical history studies and participate in music ensembles.

The physical education curriculum concentrates on teaching students simple movements and skills and refining them into specific activities and games. These skills can include perceptual movement, manipulatives, locomotor and non-locomotor movements.

Art

Art is a tool for elementary students to learn about themselves and the world around them. Elementary-level art teachers present art as a lens through which to understand the world. To create a well-rounded art class, teachers provide students ample opportunities to create and reflect on their own creations, respond critically to other people's works and their contributions to the human experience, and to critique art in relation to its cultural and historical context.

Teachers can also use art to make connections between other subjects. For example, by completing written assignments about art criticism and art history, students connect art and literacy. Art history also lends itself well to social studies, as students learn about artists in historical and cultural contexts. Critical thinking skills exercised in art apply to all academic work.

Planning an art curriculum includes several objectives. One is to ensure that students learn the importance of **visual communication**. Then students can better communicate using images. This in turn will help them understand why people create art. In essence, instruction should ensure that students can produce images to inform, entertain, or persuade their desired audience.

Teachers can use universal symbols like flags, money, or even cave paintings to show students that images themselves communicate. Embedding symbols in their cultural and historical contexts is important to help students gain an understanding of the purpose of each art piece they are looking at. They can apply this knowledge to create more purposeful work and understand the significance and value of art in their own lives.

> **QUICK REVIEW**
>
> Consider three common universal symbols like the examples provided in the text.

A good understanding of the **elements and principles of art** is one of the most important ways to create quality art pieces and analyze the artwork of others. Teachers should show students that artists use these elements and principles to make decisions when creating their own art, and that students should apply this knowledge to their own works.

Creating visual work is based on the **elements of art**, and artists must be able to intelligently use them. The elements of art are line, shape, form, value, texture, space, and color. **Line** in art is called a moving dot: it can control the viewer's eye, indicate form and movement, describe edges, and indicate a light source in a drawing. Artists use different line qualities and contours to suggest form. To indicate value or a light source, artists use cross hatching lines in varying degrees.

A closed contour is what creates **shape**, which is two dimensional. It can create balance and affect the composition, creating positive and negative spaces. Different types of shapes include regular or geometric and organic or freeform shapes. When students understand the basics of shapes, they can create complex forms by combining simple organic and regular shapes.

Form, then, is like shape except it is three dimensional. Creating form requires an understanding of how light reflects upon an object, or its **value**. Teachers should help students understand where the highlight, reflect light, midtone, core shadow, and the cast shadows are in order to create an illusion of form. Helping students create a value scale and how it applies to objects they see is also helpful. Value also helps to create texture, which refers to how an object would feel if someone were to touch it. Students can develop their sense of **texture** through exposure to a wide variety of objects and understanding how light reflects off rough, smooth, matte, and shiny surfaces.

Creating an illusion of **space** can help students in creating artwork on a two dimensional surface. Students should experiment with different techniques such as overlapping shapes, shape placement, sizes of shapes, and perspective to see how objects can appear closer or farther away.

The color wheel is primarily used to teach students the theories of **color**. Students in the lower grades learn about the types of colors (primary, secondary, and tertiary), move on to values (tints and shades) and then color schemes (monochromatic, warm, cool, complementary, and analogous).

The **principles of art** refer to the composition of the elements of art within a piece of work. These are balance, unity, contrast, movement, emphasis, pattern, and proportion. In order to create balance in an artwork, colors, forms, shapes, or textures need to be combined in harmony. Harmony also helps to create unity in a piece of work, particularly when it creates a sense of wholeness.

STUDY TIP

Use the acronym *ROY G. BIV* to remember the order of the color wheel.

Artists generate contrast by using various elements of art like shapes, form, colors, or lines in order to capture the viewer's attention and draw it toward a certain part of the work. Movement guides the viewer's eye through a composition usually in order to highlight areas of contrast or emphasis. Repeating occurrences of a design element, such as shapes, forms, or textures in an art piece, are called patterns. Finally, proportion describes the way the sizes of objects appear. For example, objects that are farther away appear smaller and have less detail.

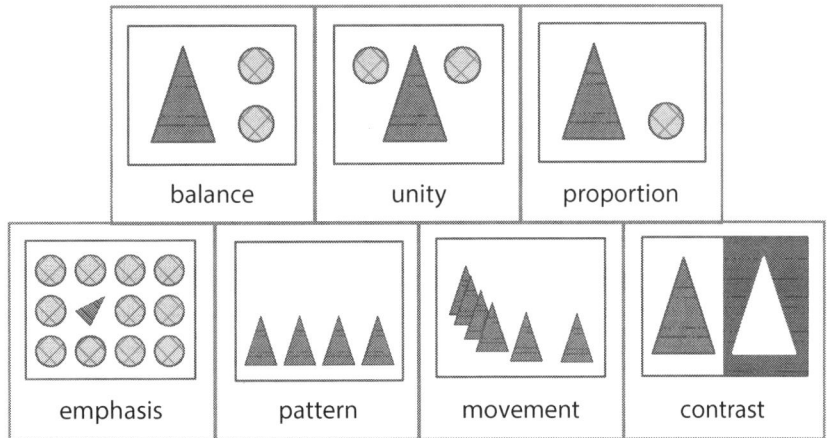

Figure 12.1. Principles of Art

As students progress through the elementary grades, their use of the elements and principles of art will improve. They will learn to choose which elements and principles to use in their works. Students need as much exposure as possible to the elements of art; furthermore, they need extensive practice in order to purposefully create artwork that imparts their intended meaning.

ART CRITICISM

The terminology associated with the elements and principles of art allows teachers and students to speak in a common language about art. They use this language to make judgments about their own artwork and that of others—to engage in **art criticism**. In the elementary grades, critique can be written or conducted through discussion; it helps students gather information and use their justification skills to analyze and interpret works of art.

The four major areas of art criticism are description, analysis, interpretation, and judgment. Depending on the number and type of art piece, the quantity and specifics of the questions will vary.

In describing a work of art, make sure students avoid using expressive words like *beautiful* or *ugly*. Instead, help them describe the piece as objectively as possible. Examples include using the title of the piece, observing technical qualities (e.g. tools), noting recognizable symbols or images, and addressing the elements of art present.

An analysis of the artwork entails discerning and describing how the piece is organized. Students should investigate the principles of art, such as emphasis, repetition, or contrast. Students can also consider the relationships between or among subjects, if applicable; they may also consider the relationship between the piece and the viewer, including how it affects the viewer when it is perceived from different angles. In addition, analysis may involve comparing the piece with other works of art.

When students are ready to interpret the artwork in question, they should discuss how the work impacts them and also discuss its unique qualities. For example, students may use expressive language (e.g. descriptors like *funny*, *sad*, and *beautiful*). They could also discuss how the work reminds them of personal experiences, world events, or issues they have encountered in their studies.

Finally, students should discuss and justify their opinion of the artwork. Whenever possible, students may compare the artwork with other pieces they have studied. They may even explain whether they think the work is original and justify their explanation.

> **QUICK REVIEW**
>
> List the four components of art criticism.

When getting responses from students during class discussions, ensure that students have enough time to gather their thoughts before starting the discussion. Ways to do so include letting individual students write down their thoughts, giving students a list of questions encouraging them to make judgments in a specific way, or even using a simple think-pair-share method. Students should always be able to defend their answers with supporting evidence. Remind students that there are no right or wrong answers in art criticism. Allow lots of opportunities for students to conduct art critiques, whether in formal or informal settings. The more they do so, the easier it will be for them to express their feelings about art.

AESTHETICS

Studying **aesthetics** is another avenue for students to talk about art. The study of aesthetics explores the definitions and meaning of art and beauty; it also helps students identify the types of art and design that please people. In situating art in historical and cultural context, students develop critical thinking skills that allow them to discuss judgments of an artwork. At the same time, they generate their own ideas about artwork; their ability to justify their own judgments matures.

Teachers help students develop their own sense of aesthetics. In the younger grades, the focus should be on the student's personal experiences and cultural contexts. By the third grade, students will have more vocabulary to discuss art, and teachers can introduce aesthetic theories which are realistic, hedonist, formalist, and expressive. It is helpful to start with a few and add more as students gain more experience. Teachers should emphasize that there are many conceptions of art and that none of these views are better than another.

ART HISTORY

Art history should also be taught in elementary school so students can gain an understanding of how artists and art made contributions to culture and society. In studying art history, students learn how artists interact with their contemporaneous cultures, respond to historical events and social change, and address other artistic movements. Art history lessons should encourage students to ask why an artist created a certain piece of art, how it was used, and what its purpose was.

In the elementary grades, students should be exposed to significant artists throughout history. Aim to expose students to many art pieces. If possible, take students on field trips to art fairs, galleries, and museums so they can gain an appreciation of art. As students study individual artists and their bodies of work, encourage them to consider the mind of the artist as he or she created the work, and how the artwork relates to its time period. Teachers should provide as much relevant background as possible so students can use that knowledge to view and discuss the artwork. Using the elements and principles of art is useful here to talk about these works, as well as reviewing the concepts of aesthetics. Teachers can also use art history lessons as an opportunity to apply **techniques** artists use so students can gain hands-on experience and create their own works.

TOOLS AND MEDIA

When creating lessons for students to produce their own art, all grade levels need time to explore and experiment with **tools** and **media**. Students in the younger grades, especially those in grade two or younger, need time to manipulate tools and media; many may be new to them and may not have the motor skills to handle tools with great control. Teachers should select short, simple arts and crafts projects with clear instructions. In two-dimensional works, teachers should help students explore tools such as charcoal, pastels, crayons, watercolor, and tempera paints. Tools, such as pastels with the names of colors written on them, can help students to develop their art vocabulary. Students should learn different techniques such as color blending and experience different kinds of painting including using brushes, sponges, paint splattering, and even their own fingers. Students at this age benefit from creating three-dimensional works through cutting and pasting paper and other two-dimensional materials. Popular projects include mask-making, puppet-making, and weaving.

In the middle elementary grades, students are better able to handle tools. Teachers can then select materials such as clay, giving students the opportunity to use materials that require more manipulation. Teachers can also introduce group activities like murals to help students practice communicating with each other using art terminology. They can also encourage students to create works from their own imagination to make personal connections and to develop the value of art in their lives. Students usually continue to refine two-dimensional skills and may use mixed media or more complex types of painting techniques. Students at this age are also ready to begin to learn simple skills to represent three dimensions, such as single-point perspectives. They might also learn how to manipulate clay in a more purposeful way.

Upper elementary students have the capabilities to create more in-depth works of art. At this stage, teachers should create lessons where students have multiple opportunities to communicate their process. Multi-step art projects ensure a more rounded artistic experience; aspects of these may include learning new techniques and materials, taking field trips, and conducting research. Students at this stage should be ready to learn more advanced drawing techniques such as contour, shading (e.g. hatching, smudging, cross-hatching, stippling), creating three-dimensional spaces using one- and two-point perspectives, shadowing, scale, and light sources. When assigning work with three-dimensional materials, teachers should ensure that students follow the design process; have students create plans or blueprints and even models before finishing their final work. Finally, no matter what techniques or media are used, encourage students to find new applications for tools.

SAMPLE QUESTIONS

1) Which of the following are considered the elements of art?
    A. line, shape, color, and proportion
    B. line, shape, color, and form
    C. balance, unity, proportion, and texture
    D. line, texture, unity, and aesthetics

Answers:

A. Incorrect. Proportion is considered a principle of art.

B. Correct. All of these are the elements of art.

C. Incorrect. All of these are considered principles of art.

D. Incorrect. Aesthetics is not an element of art; it is a way to discuss art.

2) Making a judgment about a piece of artwork is called

A. visual communication.

B. aesthetics.

C. debate.

D. art criticism.

Answers:

A. Incorrect. Visual communication is a way for artists to purposefully arrange elements in an artwork.

B. Incorrect. Aesthetics is not a form of art criticism; it is simply a way to understand conceptions of art and beauty. Art criticism usually discusses artwork in the context of aesthetics, but aesthetics alone is not criticism.

C. Incorrect. A debate can be about any topic, not just making judgments about a piece of artwork.

D. Correct. Art criticism includes the evaluation of a piece of art following its analysis. It is usually in the context of the theory of beauty or aesthetics.

Music

Teaching music in the elementary grades is important to help students enhance skills that they can transfer to other subject areas. Students who are exposed to music education tend to do better in language development (such as reading tests) than students who are not. Music education helps to develop the left side of the brain, which is critical to processing language. Music also engages numerous parts of the brain, including the cognitive, hedonic, planning, and sensory systems. Furthermore, research has shown links between spatial intelligence and music studies, which means that students learn to visualize different elements working together and recognize patterns, corresponding with the problem-solving skills needed in mathematics.

As a music teacher, it is also important to help students make connections between music across other disciplines and the real world. To do so, teachers must vary lessons. For example, listening to music can teach students about different musical genres and expose students to its history. Music can also be connected with literature: students may learn to conduct research for a music-related project, and in the process draw upon knowledge learned in different classes. Lessons on music culture may also tie in to social studies.

To make real-world connections, teachers help students recognize the impact of music in their everyday lives. Teachers expose students to music from popular culture, such as commercials, movies, and television shows. Teachers can also help students understand the emotional aspects of music—by using songs to remember significant events, for instance. Providing and studying informational texts is another way for students to understand music in real-world contexts.

Musical Notation

Teaching music requires that the teacher has a sound knowledge of music notation, music-making, and **music terminology**. Students should understand that music **notation** is a method of writing down music so that anyone can play it. It helps composers create music by clearly indicating how they want it to sound; anyone who can read music will be able to play or sing the song accurately. Teachers can start helping students understand music notation by presenting it and breaking down the different elements of the modern system of notation.

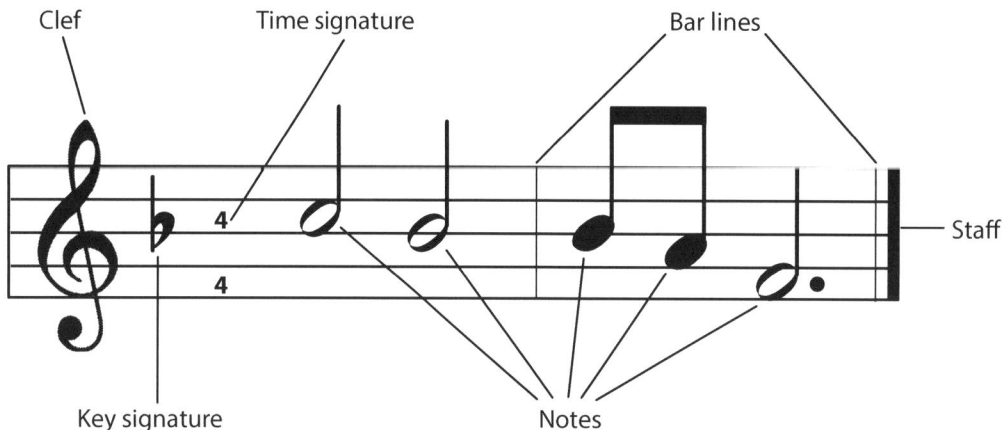

Figure 12.2. Musical Notation

The main system of notation currently used is writing musical notes on a stave, which is composed of a five-line staff with four spaces between. The music is read from left to right, and there is usually a clef in front of a staff of written music. This helps to show exactly which notes are played, such as the treble clef or the bass clef. The location of the note on the staff indicates the **pitch**; and sharps or flats may be in front of the note. Notes that are very high or low can be placed on ledger lines above or below the stave.

The key signature is found after the clef, which indicates which sharps or flats will be used regularly. The time signature, placed afterwards, divides the music into regular groupings of beats using bars or measures. There are usually words that show the tempo, or the speed of music. There may also be dynamic marks to indicate how loud or soft to play the music at certain points.

Understanding music terminology can help students better develop an understanding of the elements of music. Teachers must explain what pitch, rhythm, melody, texture, timbre, and dynamics are and how they apply to music. Teachers should help students develop these concepts by reading musical notation, listening to music, and carrying out practical exercises.

Aspects of Music

Pitch can be high or low; scales are created by organizing patterns of pitches with intervals in between. Types of **scales** include chromatic, gapped, pentatonic, and major/minor. Having students listen to many pitches and practice the different types of scales offers them a more practical approach to learning. Usually teachers start by using a number system to help younger students learn the notes, then move onto *solfeggio* (*do, re, mi, fa, so, la, ti, do*) as they progress.

Rhythm governs time in music. It is a specific pattern in time—a tempo—much like a steady pulse. These are organized into meter, which arranges these pulses into groups. These then can be further divided, into two, three, or four smaller units. To help students develop an understanding of rhythm, teachers begin by using familiar songs or nursery rhymes and have the students clap along. The students feel and count the beats in a song, learning to distinguish when notes should start and end. Then students can understand the rhythmic patterns of the song. Students can progress to recognizing rhythm just by listening to a song, or creating one by playing a musical instrument.

A combination of pitch and rhythm is called a melody. **Melody** describes the size of the intervals of the contour (rising or falling)—the tune of a song. As such, it is the main focus of a song and a way for a composer to communicate with his or her audience. **Harmony** relies on the melody, and is the use of pitches or chords simultaneously: the notes that support melodies. To develop the concept of melody, teachers should have students listen to and consider how a melody rises and falls, or compare melodic contours. These actions develop melodic personality. Teachers can also introduce the names and sounds of notes first to help children develop a sense of melody, as well as helping them understand how to read music. Having students learn a five-note scale and the different clefs can teach them how different pitches affect the melody. As students progress through the grades, teachers can even create lessons that help students see how different melodies can imply different emotions.

The **timbre**, or **tone**, is the musical characteristic that distinguishes between different instruments. When discussing timbre, expose students to as many sounds as possible. Students can describe the sound by naming the instrument (once they have learned it), or using different terms. Words can include brassy, bright, raspy, shrill, dark, or buzzy. As students become more advanced, they can group different timbres according to instrument type, whether it be woodwind, brass, string, or percussion. Help students understand that the timbre is the same even if the same instrument is played at different pitches and volumes.

Dynamics refers to the loud or soft parts of a piece of music. They can change gradually or suddenly (crescendo or decrescendo), or have a large dynamic range if there are very soft and incredibly loud passages in the composition.

Combining melody, rhythm, and harmony is what makes up the **texture** in a composition, as these all determine the overall quality of the sound. Texture includes the number of layers and how these relate to one another. There are different types of musical textures. Monophonic is made of one voice or line with no accompaniment. Polyphonic includes many musical voices that imitate or counter one another, including the rhythm or melody. An example of this would be songs popular during the Renaissance or the Baroque period. Homophonic consists of a main melody which is accompanied by harmonic chords. An example of this would be a singer with a piano accompaniment. The texture would be considered homorhythmic if all parts have a similar rhythm. Teachers should introduce one texture at a time so students have time to listen to and develop their understanding of how to accurately identify textures. Students can also preform different songs to get a feel for how different textures work.

> **DID YOU KNOW?**
>
> Each instrument differs in high and low pitches. The instruments with the highest pitch tend to be in the woodwind family, with the piccolo being the highest. The lowest-pitched instruments tend to be in the brass or string family, with the double bass being the lowest.

Teaching Music

When teaching music, it is important for teachers not only to select and use manipulatives, but also to choose developmentally appropriate materials in the classroom. At the elementary level, students learn to play simple instruments as they develop their understanding of the elements of music. At the early elementary level (up to the third grade), students may not have developed the fine muscle control that would allow them to play more complicated instruments. Teachers should select items such as Orff instruments and other simple percussion instruments; these are easier to play and help students visualize pitch and rhythm while they develop their motor skills. Later, recorders are introduced when students are able to physically play them. This simple instrument helps students develop the skills necessary for more advanced instruments, such as breathing techniques; students also gain experience reading sheet music, which is simplified with recorders as they need only concern themselves with one tone. Teachers can also use the recorder to teach a wide variety of songs and ensembles using one instrument.

In the upper elementary grades, students should have developed the motor skills to play the types of instruments used in band programs. Since students should have learned how to read basic sheet music and utilize the breathing techniques appropriate for woodwind instruments, teachers can help students advance by applying their knowledge of other elements of music such as harmony and timbre.

When choosing appropriate music for students to sing, teachers should select simple pieces, such as nursery rhymes for younger students. As students progress through the elementary grades, more complex pieces should be selected. These musical works should include the elements of music students need to master at that grade level, as well as a wide variety of musical styles. Choosing different contemporary and historical pieces of music helps students to compare music based on the historical context and the intent of the composer.

> **QUICK REVIEW**
>
> How does the recorder help students develop the skills to play more difficult instruments?

Teachers also must consider the different aspects of a musical piece when selecting one that is developmentally appropriate. Vocal demands should be considered to ensure that a song is not too difficult for students to master. Rather than singing scale patterns, students find it easier to sing skips, particularly descending skips. Teachers should also consider the level of rhythm patterns and the tempo. It is more difficult for younger students to sing fast songs and to move the voice quickly with difficult rhythm patterns; complex rhythm patterns are only appropriate for older classes. Furthermore, most elementary school students struggle with singing multiple notes on one syllable and repeating the same note; this should be avoided. A song's length should also be considered. The younger the student, the shorter the song. Generally speaking, songs with four beats of four phrases are usually appropriate.

> **STUDY TIP**
>
> Call-and-response songs are popular and appropriate for elementary-level choruses.

Selecting songs with lots of repetition is beneficial for younger students. Teachers should look for songs that have repeating melodies, rhythms, and words. However, elementary students frequently struggle with songs that have repeating words but changing melodies. When reviewing lyrics, teachers must choose texts relevant to student experiences and that use appropriate vocabulary.

SAMPLE QUESTIONS

3) What are some factors teachers should consider when selecting songs for students at the elementary level? Select all that apply.

   A. a manageable rhythmic pace

   B. repeating lyrics and melodies

   C. few vocal demands

   D. all of the above

Answers:

A. Incorrect. A manageable rhythmic pace is important; however, there are other important factors.

B. Incorrect. Elementary-level students should indeed work with repeating lyrics and melodies; however, this is not the best answer choice.

C. Incorrect. While few vocal demands should be made on students at the elementary level, teachers should consider other factors as well.

D. **Correct.** Rhythmic pace, repetition, and vocal demands are all equally important factors in choosing appropriate songs for elementary-level students.

4) Which of the following instruments has the lowest pitch?

A. piccolo
B. double bass
C. trumpet
D. trombone

Answers:

A. Incorrect. The piccolo is a woodwind instrument and is the highest pitched.

B. **Correct.** The double bass is part of the string family and is the lowest pitched instrument in an orchestra.

C. Incorrect. The trumpet is a moderately pitched woodwind instrument.

D. Incorrect. The trombone is a moderately pitched woodwind instrument.

Physical Education and Health

Teaching physical education and health aims to give students the skills and confidence to become physically active and remain so throughout their lives. A good quality physical education and health program incorporates lessons that identify student development and their changing movement abilities. Teachers must also consider the maturity level of students, their fitness level, and their motor skills.

TEACHING PHYSICAL EDUCATION

Physical education teachers should expose students to a wide variety of health- and skill-related fitness activities. Health-related fitness includes flexibility, body composition, cardiovascular fitness, muscular strength, and endurance. Skill-related components include balance, power, speed, coordination, and agility.

When designing lessons, teachers should keep in mind the FITT (frequency, intensity, time, type) principle. This acronym is one way to recall general guidelines for a fitness plan, and it can be applied to the whole class or simply to individual students if necessary. Each class and grade level's fitness goal will be different; modifications should be taken into consideration based on current fitness level and available resources.

Frequency refers to how often students should exercise. For example, lifestyle exercises may be scheduled more often than endurance ones. The **intensity** of the activity describes how hard students need to work during each class. **Time** refers to how long students should participate in the activity. Students should participate in at least thirty to sixty minutes of age-appropriate physical activity on a daily basis, ten minutes of which should be moderate to vigorous activity. The **type** of activity describes the kinds of activities students practice or play. Teachers should create different lessons incorporating a wide variety of lifestyle and recreational activities, active aerobics, flexibility, sports activities, and strength and muscular endurance exercises.

At the elementary level, learning movement fundamentals requires movement concepts and fundamental motor skills. Teaching movement concepts helps children increase their understanding of **body awareness and management**, including spatial awareness, qualities of movement, and relationships.

The objective of body awareness is for students to explore the body's capabilities. At the elementary level, students learn to identify and understand the locations of different body parts. They also practice the many shapes and positions they can form with their bodies. Teachers should help students gain an awareness of body movements and how the body can be used to communicate.

Spatial awareness is understanding where the body can move. Teachers should provide ample opportunities for students to explore the spatial qualities of movement. Examples include self-space, general space, pathways, range, and the direction of movement. Students should not only recognize these examples, but also respect the space of others, travel through space in a purposeful manner, and adjust their range of movement depending on the task.

> **STUDY TIP**
>
> Developing body management skills means integrating agility, coordination, balance, and flexibility to create effective movement.

The goal in teaching the qualities of movement is for students to understand how balance affects movement and the qualities of static and dynamic balance. Teachers should also help students generate and modify force to accomplish assigned tasks as well as differentiate among speeds so they can move more quickly or slowly. As students progress through the elementary grades, teachers should encourage them to accomplish movements within a certain amount of time and space.

Managing relationships in movements helps students understand how the body and its parts work together and with objects. Ultimately, students should move more effectively around individuals or with a group of people.

Developing student understanding and execution of fundamental motor skills should include a wide variety of **exercise** and games. Skill development should be emphasized, especially the importance of mastering basic skills to build more sophisticated ones. At the elementary level, teachers should emphasize student locomotor, non-locomotor, and manipulative skills in order to develop their motor skills.

Locomotor Skills

Locomotor skills are the numerous ways the body can move through space. They include walking, skipping, running, jumping, sliding, galloping, and leaping. Students should be given ample time to practice skills repeatedly after observing a proper demonstration.

When teaching students walking skills, teachers should demonstrate that each foot alternates and that there is always one foot touching the floor. Instruct students to point toes straight head, keep their eyes forward with their heads up, transfer weight from the heel to the ball of the foot. Students can also practice walking at different speeds, on their toes, or with bent legs.

Sliding involves students moving sideways with a leading foot. Students should focus on keeping the weight on the balls of their feet, eyes focused on the direction of travel with hips and shoulders pointing to the front. This **locomotor pattern** is commonly used in **sports** such as softball, basketball, and racquet sports. In the younger grades, the focus should be on introducing the basic movements so students develop proficiency in different sports as they get older.

Students must understand that galloping is similar to sliding, but it is done forwards and emphasizes an upward motion. Ensure that students make high gallops and that one foot is always in front of another.

Jumping and hopping are both rhythmic locomotor skills and used in activities such as dance and common games. Jumping entails pushing off the ground with both feet, whereas hopping involves pushing off with one foot. Teachers should help students develop these skills by teaching them how to jump by pushing off and landing with bent knees on their toes. Hopping is different in that students use one supporting leg that is bent in order to push off with the balls of the feet. Have students practice their hopping and jumping skills by moving in different directions and with their arms out, high to the side. Leaping is a similar airborne action; students move over an object leading with one foot and landing on another.

Finally, teachers should help students learn skipping by introducing the basic components in the younger grades. They should have been taught how to slide and hop before learning to skip. Students should practice marching with one knee high while hopping on the opposite foot at the same time. This is a rhythmical movement, and the focus should not be on speed but rather on mastering the rhythm of stepping and hopping. As students develop more proficiency in skipping, they should master it by the middle elementary grades.

NON-LOCOMOTOR SKILLS

Non-locomotor skills are movements that do not require moving through space. These include bending, stretching, twisting, turning, pushing, and pulling. As students develop their movement skills, teachers should give children ample opportunities to explore them, as well as combine them with locomotor skills so these can be applied to all physical education activities.

> **QUICK REVIEW**
>
> Consider the difference between locomotor and non-locomotor skills.

MANIPULATIVE SKILLS

Manipulative skills differ from locomotor and non-locomotor skills in that they involve students using objects like jump ropes and balls. Many of these skills are taught through sports or standalone lessons such as drills. These skills include throwing, catching, striking, and kicking. Manipulative skills tend to be more challenging for children and should only be introduced when children are more proficient with locomotor and non-locomotor skills. Teachers should understand that focusing on how the body can move through space is more important in the younger grades than their ability to manipulate an object.

> **DID YOU KNOW?**
>
> Since hand-eye coordination is more difficult at farther distances, striking is one of the last skills students develop. The length of the object that children use to strike further complicates learning the skill. Teachers need to modify equipment so that lower elementary students can more easily develop this skill.

GAME SKILLS

Although it is important to teach motor skills to students, teaching them **game skills** allows them to connect motor skill development and games they play. It also gives them an opportunity to practice skills in a team setting. This can include making decisions together and accepting individual differences in a group setting. Teaching game skills also helps students develop large muscle groups; finally, game skills allow students to experience success and a sense of accomplishment.

To master a game skill, teachers need to help students develop insights into the techniques of the skill and provide consistent feedback on their performance. One of the best ways to develop a game skill is through observation in a controlled setting. As students gain more experience, they can observe skills in games, giving them more context. Students should also experiment with performing the skill in different ways, moving in different ranges and directions. Students will learn that certain techniques or skills do not apply to all games, or even all parts of a game.

Mini games or drills provide the necessary structure for students to further develop game skills. These skills should to be used repeatedly, mimicking the teacher's demonstration.

Health and Safety

During physical education lessons, **safety** for teachers and students must be taken into consideration. Teachers should check the area before any activity or game begins to ensure there are no dangerous objects or hazards. Ensure that participants understand that a signal from the teacher indicates the beginning and end of play. Teach students that it is important to respect others and the equipment; students must follow commands and avoid grabbing or pushing. A warm-up period before starting any activity will prevent injuries, as will omitting skills that might put students in harm's way.

Teachers must consult with a school nurse or a health professional regarding the needs of students with health conditions like asthma or diabetes; teachers should also be aware of the effects of medication students take and symptoms of health emergencies. Lessons and physical activities may be modified to accommodate physical and social needs.

Teaching Health

Lessons on healthy living are integral to a well-rounded physical education and health curriculum. While it is important for students to practice motor development skills, a good physical education and health curriculum also shows students the benefits of a healthy lifestyle. Improved **physical fitness** and knowledge of proper **nutrition** helps students in other areas of life, including self-discipline, cooperation, stress reduction, goal setting, and better relationships with peers.

At the elementary level, lessons on health help students learn about wellness and unhealthy behaviors. They gain the ability to explain the importance of physical activity, what contributes to **disease** in the body, and how nutrition, stress, and **substance abuse** affect their **growth** and well-being.

Teaching students about the physical systems in the body is a great introduction to the theories of health and gives them the fundamental knowledge to better understand nutrition and fitness. In the early elementary grades, the focus should be on the elements of a balanced diet. Looking at the healthy eating plate and identifying nutrients helps students learn how their choices affect their bodies. As students progress to the mid-elementary level, lessons revolve around how to make healthy changes by examining food labels, monitoring caloric intake, and getting adequate rest and exercise.

Teachers can also address disease prevention and control. Students learn about practical ways to prevent disease, such as practicing personal hygiene, identifying symptoms of diseases and how they affect the body, and how to prevent diseases. Students may also learn about injury prevention and safety. Topics would include basic safety rules, reacting to emergencies, and understanding strategies for self-protection.

Beyond the physical body, students also need to understand that their mental well-being contributes to social and emotional health. Students should learn different strategies and skills to improve their relationships with others and themselves. Topics can include friends and family, effective communication, appropriate emotional responses, and assuming responsibility for their own decisions. Older students will learn about stress, its effects on the body, and identifying resources and constructive ways of dealing with it.

Learning about substance abuse helps students understand the impact drugs can have on their lives. Lessons should help students understand how alcohol and other types of drugs (including some types of medications) affect the body when abused; students should learn about decision-making. More specifically, lessons can examine media, peer pressure, and other external factors (such as laws) that impact decision-making. Equally important are lessons on internal factors like addiction.

EQUIPMENT

Choosing the right equipment for an elementary physical education class is essential for students to develop the skills at the right pace. Equipment should be matched to the confidence, size, and skill level of the student so that he or she is motivated to actively participate in class. For example, younger students who are not proficient in coordination might need equipment that is short and lightweight that can be more easily manipulated or handled.

Pedometers are useful tools; these devices reliably measure a student's physical activity levels. They enhance instruction by providing accountability, revealing students' activity levels and consequently providing feedback on the effectiveness of instruction. This feedback can then be used to create or modify lessons to ensure that students receive quality instruction.

Teachers should also ensure that there is enough equipment so that students are engaged at all times. Having enough equipment ensures that students have equal opportunities to practice and reinforce skills taught in class; sufficient equipment also prevents potential classroom management problems. In the case of equipment shortage, teachers should select a variety of activities that use different equipment so students are not left idle. Teachers can also create activities to engage some students in observing and giving feedback to others who are demonstrating skills they have learned.

SAMPLE QUESTIONS

5) **Which of the following is a feature of a hop?**

   A. Alternate legs move in front of one another.

   B. Using the ball of one foot, a person pushes off from the ground on one leg.

   C. The body uses one foot to push off the ground and lands on the other.

   D. Both legs are bent; the toes push off the ground at the same time.

   Answers:

   A. Incorrect. This is walking.

   B. Correct. Hopping also requires students to keep their heads forward and arms out. The leg that is not pushing off the ground is usually slightly bent.

   C. Incorrect. This is leaping.

   D. Incorrect. This is jumping.

6) **Which of the following is an appropriate topic in teaching students about decisions surrounding substance abuse?**

   A. understanding the physical consequences of substance abuse

   B. knowledge of alcohol, tobacco, and illegal drugs

   C. A and B

   D. none of the above

   Answers:

   A. Incorrect. While understanding the physical consequences of substance abuse is essential, it is not the only topic a teacher should focus on, given the other available choices here.

   B. Incorrect. While a knowledge of alcohol, tobacco, and illegal drugs is essential, it is not the only topic a teacher should focus on, given the other available choices here.

   C. Correct. Both A and B are equally important when teaching students about substance abuse so that they can make intelligent decisions.

   D. Incorrect. Both options are appropriate topics.

Assessment

Assessments in visual arts, music, and physical education guide students' progress and provide teachers with feedback to better create and implement curriculum. A wide variety of assessment strategies should be used, including formative assessments, summative assessments, anecdotal observations, and standardized tests; these all enable teachers to gain a holistic view of student skill and improve their learning. Authentic assessments may include constructed responses, rubrics, or traditional and non-traditional assessments; they allow the teacher to reflect on student skills and progress. A traditional assessment includes standardized tests, essays, and reports. Non-traditional assessments can include projects, performances, demonstrations, writing samples, and portfolios.

> **DID YOU KNOW?**
>
> A constructed response is a type of assessment in which students demonstrate in-depth understanding by completing assignments such as essay, short answer, and fill-in-the-blank questions.

Assessment in music and art has traditionally been based on assessing performance techniques; however, it really requires multiple assessment strategies that measure higher order ability and thinking to help teachers measure the product that is produced or performed. Furthermore, assessment accounts not only for the product that is created, but also the process a student used to create that work, like certain tools, techniques, and problem solving skills. Teachers should provide opportunities for students to showcase their abilities and skills in an authentic environment.

Although it may seem particularly difficult to assess art and music because they appear so subjective, if teachers set specific and clear criteria, then students understand what to expect. Teachers can also provide useful feedback to help students improve their learning.

Art Assessment

FORMATIVE ASSESSMENTS IN ART CLASSES

Formative assessments for art should be visual and hands-on. Moreover, they must be ongoing so that students have multiple opportunities for improvement. Providing immediate feedback helps students learn to better use tools to express creativity and refine their thought process as they create an artwork. Hence, feedback should occur during the art creation process. Assessments should offer feedback on art techniques and manipulating media using appropriate tools. Teachers may develop anecdotal observations to better recall individual progress and to determine when re-teaching may be necessary.

Informal assessment may take place during studio-based activities, promoting a highly interactive learning environment. Such an environment encourages frequent interaction between the teacher and student: the teacher is available to provide feedback often, sometimes at the student's request. Teachers can walk around the classroom as students practice techniques and skills and offer corrective feedback as needed. This immediate feedback is particularly helpful when students are beginning to practice manipulating tools. Offer ample time for students to practice the skill before offering feedback again.

Critiques give teachers the opportunity to view student work, whether completed or not. Students may conference with the teacher one-on-one and show a piece of art, using a checklist as a discussion point. Furthermore, groups of students or even the whole class may engage in constructive critique of a student artwork. This type of assessment is helpful when used meaningfully and when there is a good mixture of casual and informal critiques.

> **TEACHING TIP**
>
> While walking around the classroom and giving individual feedback is helpful for students, it can be challenging in a large class. Solutions include holding scheduled conferences or speaking with students in a group.

Portfolios take a more formal approach to formative assessments. They contain works that the student creates over a certain amount of time. Portfolios encourage students to practice higher-level thinking skills by reflecting about the processes of their work. Teachers should guide students as to what pieces they should choose for a portfolio, using a checklist or a rubric. Portfolios provide teachers with a tangible benchmark by which to better understand a student's strengths and weaknesses. When conferencing with students, teachers can review work with students and see how the variety of samples demonstrates whether they have achieved or mastered skills and processes in the curriculum. Students should keep conference notes to retain a record of what was discussed and how to improve. Along with the artworks in student portfolios, conference notes provide students with a wealth of ideas and the confidence to take more risks in their work.

SUMMATIVE ASSESSMENTS IN ART CLASSES

A summative assessment in art is an objective method to look at what students have learned at the end of a unit or course. It gives feedback on the types of topics and major areas in which students were struggling. These can include projects (which can be a combination of written theories and art creation), performance tasks, or tests that are then scored on a rubric.

Performance tasks evaluate students based on their mastery of a technique. Students are asked to perform a task that demonstrates learning based on knowledge of media techniques and theories. For example, if students are asked to draw a realistic street scene, suitable elements to evaluate would be the use of color, perspective, balance, depiction of light sources, and whether images are proportioned correctly. All of these elements must be explained in a rubric so that students understand what is expected of them.

Portfolios can also be used in summative assessments. Instead of processes, portfolios then become a way to assess a project. As a compilation of work samples and assignments, the portfolio can be used with a rubric to measure student achievement at the completion of a project. Criteria may include the ability to demonstrate original thinking, a sound understanding and application of the elements and principles of art, and the depth of work created. A portfolio provides an overview of the skills and knowledge demonstrated by the student in completing a work of art and whether it meets certain standards. Thus, students should include research notes, sketches, blueprints, and drafts in their portfolios. Feedback is not generally immediate for these types of portfolios; the teacher may offer written feedback and grade the portfolio.

A rubric should include ordered levels reflecting a full range of skills associated with the learning under scrutiny. Teachers should consider the purpose of the assessment and determine whether to use a developmental, task-specific, or relative rubric. Wording should not be negative; progression of levels should be clearly articulated. If possible, teachers should make every effort to include sample evidence for each level. For example, a rubric assessing a student's ability to create a realistic drawing should include precise language specifying the number of shading techniques used. Teachers may also create a similar rubric written in student-friendly language so that students have every opportunity to understand and implement the criteria.

Music Assessment

FORMATIVE ASSESSMENTS IN MUSIC CLASSES

Formative assessment in music reveals students' strengths and weaknesses regarding performance and the music learning process. It identifies a student's way of thinking, creating, and feeling about music. These types of assessments provide feedback to help students develop their musical skills in relation to their affective, psychomotor, and cognitive development.

> **DID YOU KNOW?**
>
> Affective development in music refers to how musical intelligence connects to intra- and interpersonal intelligences. Psychomotor development refers to how musical intelligence connects with spatial and bodily-kinesthetic intelligences. Cognitive development refers to how musical intelligence connects with logical-mathematical and linguistic intelligences.

As in art, portfolios help teachers assess student progress in music, revealing student progress in performance skills and knowledge of theory. Teachers should design a method for students to collect work, including planning forms or organizers, audio or video of practices and performances, practice records/logs, and drafts of research or creative work (such as music scores). Students should provide context for the works they choose, demonstrating previous reflection on each piece. Checklists, activity-specific rubrics, and analyses of evidence quality permit teachers to formatively evaluate a portfolio. For instance, if a teacher wants to review a student's progress on knowledge of rhythm, that teacher can use a checklist to look at all the instances the student was able to clap along successfully to music or create rhythms using percussion instruments.

Anecdotal Observations in Music Classes

Anecdotal observations are as effective in assessing music students as they are in art. Since making music is a hands-on activity, teachers need to frequently take notes on student action and behaviors in order to recall individual student progress. Such observations can be used in conjunction with student records in their portfolios during conferences to provide more specific feedback to students.

Summative Assessments in Music Classes

Summative assessments in music include projects and tests. Portfolios may be used, but students will need to provide more context for the teacher. For example, students should provide evidence of planning, research, preparatory work, or practice before demonstrating the final product. In these instances, teachers would use an age-appropriate scoring tool to evaluate student learning.

Music tests can be written or performance-based. If teachers use performance-based tests, they must provide clear instructions. Test lengths should be adjusted depending on the age of the students.

Physical Education Assessment

In physical education, both formative and summative assessments tend to be based on observation, though summative assessments may also include tests and projects.

Observation checklists allow teachers to record whether students are demonstrating proper technique; furthermore, they can be used to provide immediate feedback to students. Teachers should target only one specific skill at a time in order to provide more effective feedback to students. In addition, teachers can use skill checklists on an ongoing basis throughout a unit to document if and when a student has mastered specific skills. Students themselves can create exercise or practice logs to document how often they complete exercises and the type of exercises they do. If possible, teachers may record students demonstrating skills as further evidence they can use for feedback; this practice helps students better understand the teacher's perspective.

At the end of a unit, these checklists then can be complied to check for mastery of skills and be used as evidence in summative assessments. Teachers should look for patterns of performance to help score student achievement on a scoring rubric. Rubrics should break down the exact steps that lead to mastery of the skill being evaluated. They should also include whether students have actually demonstrated the skill. Moreover, physical education rubrics can include more specific numbers or occasions when students complete skills. For example, if a teacher is evaluating a student on locomotor skills, a rubric might specify that a student must keep his or her head up, arms out, and demonstrate a step-hop pattern to prove mastery of the skill. On the other hand, if the student can execute the step-hop pattern but cannot keep his or her arms stretched out, the student is only classified as proficient.

Re-teaching

A teacher might find that students have not understood certain concepts or techniques taught in class. In these cases, teachers must reflect on the elements of the lesson or series of lessons that may have caused this. Factors might include inappropriate equipment, lack of motor development, or a lack of connection between theory and practice.

In such cases, the teacher needs to determine whether to re-teach, modify equipment and tools, or allow more practice time. If a teacher determines that modifications are necessary, then modified equipment should be introduced—but re-teaching the technique would be unnecessary. For example, if a physical education teacher notices that students are unable to catch a ball after a few lessons, he or she may decide to use larger balls. During the next lesson, that teacher would observe if the same skill has improved among students using the modified equipment.

If a teacher determines re-teaching is necessary, he or she must identify where students lack understanding. If students have misunderstood application of techniques, then the teacher should demonstrate how to execute the technique again and can even show students examples of misuse. For example, in art, if a teacher finds that students are not able to understand how to create light sources, that teacher can demonstrate how to do so by drawing correctly him- or herself. The teacher then can also draw a non-example and ask students to compare the two.

If the lack of understanding is content or theory related, then teachers can demonstrate the content in a different or a completely new way. Students will find it helpful if teachers deconstruct the theory again and find more concrete or tangible ways of analyzing the theory. For instance, if students are confused about using emphasis in their artwork, the teacher should review the definition of emphasis. Outside artwork should then be presented to show students how a particular artist applied the theory. Finally, students should be given a series of small exercises to create images using emphasis.

Questioning should be incorporated for art, music, and physical education to help teachers gain an awareness of the degree and depth of student understanding. It helps to engage students in a way that allows them to demonstrate their learning. Questions can be as simple as asking whether students understood what was taught that day, or to recall a fact learned in class. Some common examples teachers use are *red/green* (stop/go) or *thumbs up/thumbs down* cards to elicit information about student learning, or *exit tickets* on which students record what they learned at the end of the lesson for submission before they leave the classroom. These examples offer immediate feedback so that teachers can either continue the lesson, or re-teach what was already introduced.

> **TEACHING TIP**
>
> Always allow time for students to answer questions after they are posed, since open-ended questions can be more challenging.

When asking questions, teachers should keep it as simple as possible and age-appropriate. Teachers should ask open-ended questions to provide more opportunities for students to demonstrate their understanding. Comprehension or knowledge questions that relate to new content material should be posed before asking questions of analysis and evaluation. This way, students consider questions at appropriate points in the unit or lesson and face appropriate cognitive demands.

Assessments provide teachers with a useful overview of student learning and the effectiveness of teacher instruction. A variety of assessment types helps to ensure that teachers and students both maximize their potential in class.

EXAMPLE QUESTIONS

1) Which of the following is an appropriate use of a portfolio for summative assessments?

   A. to use in student-teacher conferences throughout a unit

   B. to compile blueprints, sketches, and planning for a specific project in order to measure student achievement at the end of that project

   C. to collect examples of what students feel is their best work

   D. to include self-assessments throughout a unit

Answers:

A. Incorrect. Using a portfolio in student-teacher conferences is suitable for formative assessments.

B. Correct. Summative assessments evaluate a student on his or her knowledge of skills and content. Portfolios should include a wide variety of evidence to help a teacher grade student work.

C. Incorrect. While it is important for students to have control over what goes in their portfolios, in a summative assessment materials should demonstrate understanding of a specific area, not necessarily overall achievement.

D. Incorrect. Self-assessments can be a part of the evidence students provide for the progression of a project, but they also must include other works demonstrating evidence of skills.

2) Which of the following is NOT an example of how to create a rubric?

A. Teachers should avoid using negative language.

B. Some indication of progression in skill level is unnecessary.

C. Teachers should include specific examples demonstrating learning.

D. The purpose of the rubric must be clear.

Answers:

A. Incorrect. Teachers should always strive to avoid negative language when writing rubrics.

B. Correct. Showing a progression of levels is one of the most important aspects of a rubric.

C. Incorrect. Including samples of evidence of learning is useful in a rubric.

D. Incorrect. Choosing the purpose of a rubric is essential so that teachers and students understand what is being assessed.

Part VII: Practice

Reading and Language Arts Practice

Content Knowledge

1

A teacher asks, "What word am I trying to say, /p/ /i/ /n/?" and instructs students to say the word. Which strategy is the teacher using to build phoneme awareness?

A. phoneme blending
B. phoneme deletion
C. phoneme segmentation
D. phoneme substitution

2

An English-language learner who attempts to write simple sentences but uses a very limited vocabulary is functioning at which of the following language proficiency levels?

A. L1
B. L2
C. L3
D. L4

3

Which letter or word part forms the rime in the word *cake*?

A. c
B. e
C. cak
D. ake

4

How many phonemes are in the word *chick*?

A. 2
B. 3
C. 4
D. 5

5

The *cl* in the word *clap* is an example of

A. a syllable.
B. an onset.
C. a phoneme.
D. a rime.

6

Which of the following letters is most likely to be introduced first in progressive phonics instruction?

A. a
B. g
C. y
D. m

7

Which of the following best describes reading rate?

A. using appropriate vocal cues when reading aloud
B. decoding words correctly when reading aloud
C. having a significant inventory of known sight words
D. reading smoothly and steadily when reading aloud

8

Which part of the word *dream* is a phoneme?

A. *ea*
B. *dr*
C. *eam*
D. *re*

9

A student is able to orally substitute the initial consonant /g/ for /b/ in the word *boat* to make the word *goat*. What concept is the student demonstrating?

A. phonemic awareness
B. letter-sound correspondence
C. phonological awareness
D. manipulation of onsets and rimes

10

What is the purpose of sight word instruction?

A. to help students learn letter-sound correspondences to improve accuracy
B. to help students manipulate sounds in words to improve auditory skills
C. to help students recognize words automatically to improve fluency
D. to help students use word parts to improve reading comprehension

Questions 11 – 16 refer to the following text excerpt from *Black Beauty* by Anna Sewell.

The name of the coachman was John Manly; he had a wife and one little child, and they lived in the coachman's cottage, very near the stables.

The next morning he took me into the yard and gave me a good grooming, and just as I was going into my box, with my coat soft and bright, the squire came in to look at me, and seemed pleased. "John," he said, "I meant to have tried the new horse this morning, but I have other business. You may as well take him around after breakfast; go by the common and the Highwood, and back by the watermill and the river; that will show his paces."

"I will, sir," said John. After breakfast he came and fitted me with a bridle. He was very particular in letting out and taking in the straps, to fit my head comfortably; then he brought a saddle, but it was not broad enough for my back; he saw it in a minute and went for another, which fitted nicely. He rode me first slowly, then a trot, then a canter, and when we were on the common he gave me a light touch with his whip, and we had a splendid gallop.

11 Which inference can the reader make based on the text?

A. John Manly does not like his job.
B. John Manly has respect for horses.
C. John Manly is a coachman with a family.
D. John Manly has bought a new horse.

12 Which point of view is used by the author?

A. first-person
B. second-person
C. third-person objective
D. third-person omniscient

13 Who are the main characters in this excerpt?

A. John Manly, the squire, and the horse
B. John Manly and the horse
C. John Manly and the squire
D. John Manly and his family

14 Which is the best summary of the excerpt?

A. John Manly is a coachman who lives with his wife and a child in a cottage near a set of stables. He works in the stables grooming horses for the squire.
B. After he has breakfast, John Manly has a splendid gallop by the watermill and along the river with a new horse from the stables.
C. The horse is new to the stables, but the squire does not have time to check his paces, so he asks John Manly to do it, but John has to have breakfast first.
D. The coachman, John Manly, grooms the horse and fits him comfortably with a bridle and saddle. Then, he takes the horse for a ride to test the horse's paces for the squire.

15 What is the tone of this excerpt?

A. negative and foreboding
B. cheerful and positive
C. sad and depressing
D. elated and ecstatic

16

How can the reader best use the context of the excerpt to understand the meaning of the word *paces*?

A. The reader can find the definition of the word in the paragraph that follows.

B. The reader can figure out the word's meaning by analyzing its root and affix.

C. The reader can use the connotation of the word to determine its meaning.

D. The reader can analyze the setting for a hint to the meaning of the word.

Questions 17 – 19 refer to the following text and picture excerpt from *Frederick Francois Chopin: The Story of the Boy Who Made Beautiful Melodies*.

> During his boyhood Chopin played much in public, journeying to some of the great cities of Europe, among them Vienna, Berlin, and Munich.
>
> Therefore, when he played in Paris it was as an artist. Here, as at home, he charmed everyone by the beauty of his music and the loveliness of his touch.
>
> He possessed the true piano hand. It was somewhat narrow. The fingers were long and tapering. It seemed at once strong and vigorous, yet delicate and sensitive.

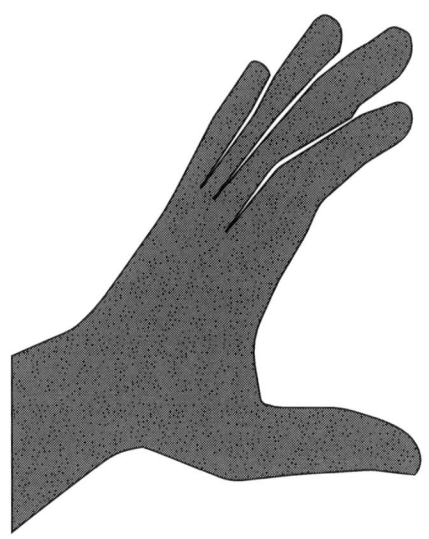

Figure 14.1. The True Piano Hand

17

This excerpt is an example of which type of text?

A. literary
B. informal
C. discipline-specific
D. informational

18

How does the picture of the "true piano hand" help a reader comprehend the excerpt?

A. It helps the reader better understand the tone of the text.
B. It helps the reader feel the beauty of Chopin's music.
C. It helps the reader better understand the word *tapering*.
D. It helps the reader recognize the hands of an artist.

19

Which text feature would best help the reader comprehend where Chopin played?

A. a chart
B. a map
C. a graph
D. a sidebar

20

Which is the root word of *loveliness*?

A. love
B. lovely
C. lov
D. loveli

Questions 21 – 25 refer to the following text excerpt from "King Midas and the Golden Touch" as told by Jean Lang.

The gods had indeed bestowed upon Gordias, the low-born peasant, a surprising gift, but he showed his gratitude by dedicating his wagon to the deity of the oracle and tying it up in its place with the wiliest knot that his simple wisdom knew, pulled as tight as his brawny arms and strong rough hands could pull. Nor could anyone untie the famous Gordian knot, and therefore become, as the oracle promised, lord of all Asia, until centuries had passed, and Alexander the Great came to Phrygia and sliced through the knot with his all-conquering sword.

In time Midas, the son of Gordias, came to inherit the throne and crown of Phrygia. Like many another not born and bred to the purple, his honours sat heavily upon him. From the day that his father's wain had entered the city amidst the acclamations of the people, he had learned the value of power, and therefore, from his boyhood onward, power, always more power, was what he coveted. Also his peasant father had taught him that gold could buy power, and so Midas ever longed for more gold, that could buy him a place in the world that no descendant of a long race of kings should be able to contest. And from Olympus the gods looked down and smiled, and vowed that Midas should have the chance of realising his heart's desire.

21
Which genre does this text excerpt represent?

A. myth
B. fairy tale
C. narrative poem
D. drama

22
What can the reader infer about Midas from reading the excerpt?

A. He is physically strong.
B. He is generous.
C. He is insecure.
D. He is angry.

23
Which stage of plot development best describes the excerpt?

A. rising action
B. exposition
C. climax
D. resolution

24
How best can a reader use the excerpt's context to decipher the meaning of the word *coveted*?

A. The reader can use the excerpt's register to determine the word's meaning.
B. The reader can use structural analysis to determine the word's meaning.
C. The reader can use the sentence's syntax to determine the word's meaning.
D. The reader can use the word's connotation to determine the word's meaning.

25
The phrase *born and bred to the purple* is an example of which of the following literary elements?

A. hyperbole
B. personification
C. simile
D. idiom

26
Which genre features animals and includes an explicit moral lesson?

A. myth
B. fable
C. legend
D. fairy tale

27
Which best describes the theme of a story?

A. the way the story is organized
B. the lesson the author wants to teach
C. the basic idea the author wants to convey
D. the point of view of the story

28
The sentence below is an example of a

> Despite the fact that the larger dog was ten times its size, the tiny dog continued to bark with ferocity.

A. simple sentence.
B. compound sentence.
C. complex sentence.
D. compound-complex sentence.

29

How do the two sentences below differ?

> The park naturalist visited the class to talk about the migration of Monarch butterflies.
>
> The naturalist visited the class to talk about the migration of Monarch butterflies from the park.

A. The word *park* acts as an adjective in the first sentence and is part of an adjective phrase in the second sentence.

B. The word *park* is the subject of the first sentence, and the word *naturalist* is the subject of the second sentence.

C. The word *park* is the subject of the first sentence and the predicate in the second sentence.

D. The word *park* acts as an adjective in the first sentence and is part of an adverb phrase in the second.

30

Which of the following statements about the sentence below is true?

> The trail is for advanced hikers because of it's steep incline.

A. The sentence is written correctly.

B. There should be a comma before *because*.

C. The word *it's* should be possessive.

D. The verb should be past tense.

31

Review the following sentence; then review the revision.

> *Original Sentence:*
> The scientist looked at the rocks to learn interesting things about the past.
>
> *Revision:*
> The geologist examined the rocks to discover evidence of historical events.

The revised sentence reflects an improvement in which of the following elements of writing?

A. conventions

B. organization

C. sentence fluency

D. word choice

32

What error has been made in the sentence below?

> Lucy thought the first movie was better then the second one.

A. The verbs are past tense.

B. *Then* indicates time, not comparison.

C. *One* is a dangling modifier.

D. The subject is misplaced.

33

Which of the following is considered an unreliable research source?

A. a self-published report

B. an edited book of essays

C. a newspaper article

D. a university study

Questions 34 – 37 refer to the poem below, "The Moon," from *A Child's Garden of Verses* by Robert Louis Stevenson.

> The moon has a face like the clock in the hall;
> She shines on thieves on the garden wall;
> On streets and fields and harbor quays,
> And birdies asleep in the forks of the trees.
>
> The squalling cat and the squeaking mouse,
> The howling dog by the door of the house,
> The bat that lies in bed at noon,
> All love to be out by the light of the moon.
>
> But all of the things that belong to the day
> Cuddle to sleep to be out of her way;
> And flowers and children close their eyes
> Till up in the morning the sun shall rise.

34

Which type of figurative language is used to describe the moon's face?

A. metaphor
B. assonance
C. alliteration
D. simile

35

How does the reader know that the word *quays* is pronounced using /ē/ as opposed to /ā/?

A. from the poet's use of simile
B. from the poet's use of rhyme scheme
C. from the poet's use of personification
D. from the poet's use of point of view

36

Which of the poet's word choices are examples of onomatopoeia?

A. *squalling, squeaking, howling*
B. *garden, streets, fields*
C. *asleep, bed, cuddle*
D. *shines, light, sun*

37

What type of writing does the poem represent?

A. expository
B. narrative
C. descriptive
D. persuasive

38

Which is the best writing style for a research paper?

A. expository
B. descriptive
C. narrative
D. persuasive

39

Which is the primary reason elementary students learn how to paraphrase and cite information from outside sources?

A. to learn the names of authors
B. to identify secondary sources
C. to avoid plagiarism
D. to condense writing

40

Which is an example of a secondary source?

A. a handwritten letter by a former president
B. a photograph from the turn of the century
C. an audio recording of a jazz composition
D. a book that discusses a historical time period

41

Which best states the purpose of the rewriting stage of the writing process?

A. presenting outcomes
B. organizing ideas
C. correcting errors
D. recording thoughts

42

Which of the following is NOT a positive nonverbal clue in active listening?

A. smiling at the speaker
B. leaning forward slightly
C. looking down at the floor
D. sitting up straight

43

What is the primary purpose of expository writing?

A. to entertain
B. to explain
C. to convince
D. to describe

44

Which of the following strategies is most beneficial for students who are at the beginning stage of writing a story?

A. revising the story's first paragraph
B. organizing ideas in a story element chart
C. drafting the exposition of the story
D. sharing the story with a classmate

45

Which of the following is Mr. Kahn modeling for students?

> Every morning, Mr. Kahn posts a morning message for students that contains errors in Standard English. Students read the message, identify the errors, and make suggestions for corrections.

A. paraphrasing
B. editing
C. decoding
D. inferring

Go on

46

Which best states the purpose of the drafting stage of the writing process?

A. revising the story's first paragraph

B. organizing ideas in a story element chart

C. drafting the exposition of the story

D. sharing the story with a classmate

47

A student is giving a speech on school start times. The following quote is included in his presentation:

> "Elementary school should start at 9 a.m. instead of 7:30 a.m. because children do their best thinking when they get enough sleep and have time to eat a healthy breakfast."

Which of the following is the best paraphrase of the speaker's message?

A. Later school start times are better for learning because children get more rest and eat properly.

B. School should start at 9 a.m. instead of 7:30 a.m. because children do their best thinking when they get enough sleep and have time to eat a healthy breakfast.

C. Elementary school should start earlier than it does now.

D. Many students are too tired during the school day to concentrate on learning.

48

Which behaviors best demonstrate focusing on a speaker during active listening?

A. moving around and eye contact

B. sitting up straight and interjecting questions

C. frowning and crossed arms

D. eye contact and leaning forward

49

What is finger spelling?

A. making crayon rubbings of sandpaper letters

B. using the hands to sign letters

C. counting letters in words using the fingers

D. writing letters in trays of colored sand

50

Which of the following can be classified as narrative writing?

A. an opinion piece on a political candidate

B. an essay on the causes and effects of erosion

C. a poem that evokes the feeling of a spring thunderstorm

D. a funny story about an adventure at the zoo

Curriculum, Instruction, and Assessment

1

How does the activity described below contribute to students' phonics proficiency?

> A teacher has her first grade students complete a journal page every day. They draw pictures and write descriptions of their pictures, spelling the words as well as they can.

A. Students actively connect letters to sounds.
B. Students actively improve drawing skills.
C. Students actively build fine motor skills.
D. Students actively write from left to right.

2

What is the primary purpose of repeated reading?

A. to build vocabulary
B. to build concepts of print
C. to build prediction skills
D. to build fluency

3

Which of the following is an effective strategy for strengthening decoding skills?

A. teaching character analysis
B. teaching word families
C. teaching active listening
D. teaching fact and opinion

4

Which strategy will best help students achieve understanding?

> A teacher notices that several students are having difficulty determining the text structure of an informational article.

A. repeated reading of the text
B. a mini-lesson on signal words
C. a Venn diagram graphic organizer
D. modeling thinking aloud

5

How best could a teacher model inferencing during reading?

A. by thinking aloud
B. by providing a graphic
C. by drawing a plot pyramid
D. by conducting a word investigation

6

A group of students has just finished reading an informational text about butterflies. How might the teacher extend learning on the topic?

A. by having students repeat read the text
B. by assigning each student a type of butterfly to research
C. by explaining difficult vocabulary in the text
D. by reviewing the text features

7

Which of the following describes systematic phonics instruction?

A. A series of lessons on sound-letter concepts that begins with the letter *a* and words that begin with *a*, then progresses sequentially through the alphabet to the letter *z* and words that begin with *z*.

B. A series of logically sequenced lessons on sound-letter concepts that begins with the simplest sound-letter correspondences and progresses to the more complex, from single letters to words.

C. A series of logically sequenced lessons that develop student understanding of how sounds, syllables, words, and word parts can be orally manipulated to break apart words, make new words, and create rhymes.

D. A series of lessons on roots and affixes derived from Greek or Latin, beginning with the most common prefixes and suffixes and progressing in a logical sequence to more complex word structures.

8

Which of the following are examples of figurative language?

A. metaphor and personification
B. rimes and onsets
C. roots and affixes
D. fact and opinion

9

Which best describes a reasoned judgment?

A. a truth that can be proven with hard evidence
B. a statement not supported by hard evidence
C. a point of view based on a strong belief system
D. a point of view supported by reasons and evidence

10

What is Mrs. Rogers' purpose for using a KWL chart before reading in the situation described below?

> Before reading a nonfiction text about sharks, Mrs. Rogers draws a KWL chart on a piece of chart paper and lists both what students already know about sharks, and what they want to know.

A. to introduce students to new vocabulary
B. to prepare students to sequence text events
C. to activate student background knowledge
D. to provide an overview of the text information

11

Which graphic organizer would be the best prewriting tool for a description of the steps in a process?

A. a sensory word chart
B. a sequencing map
C. a plot pyramid
D. an outline

12

Which of the following is the primary purpose for playing sight word games with a group of students?

A. to develop word recognition skills
B. to develop oral language skills
C. to develop social skills
D. to develop phonics skills

13

A teacher asks, "What word do we hear when we say *seat* without the /s/?" and instructs students to say the word. Which strategy is the teacher using to build phoneme awareness?

A. phoneme blending
B. phoneme deletion
C. phoneme segmentation
D. phoneme substitution

14

Mrs. Trent is preparing a peer-editing document for her students. What she should include?

A. a list of criteria for checking mechanics and a section for rewriting parts of the text under review
B. a section for compliments, a section for suggestions, and a section for criticisms
C. a list of criteria for checking mechanics, a section for helpful suggestions, and a section for compliments
D. a section for writing tips, a section for compliments, and a section for comments

15

Which poetry writing assignment would best reinforce syllable concepts?

A. a diamante poem
B. an acrostic poem
C. a haiku poem
D. a shape poem

16

Which of the following is the best strategy for improving the following student's fine motor skill development?

> A teacher notices that a student's writing progress is hindered due to difficulties with fine motor skills.

A. designing activities that require using tongs, tweezers, and/or melon ballers
B. adding more writing assignments to an instructional unit
C. having the student rewrite assignments until his or her penmanship is neat
D. asking the student to use a finger to point to words in the text while reading

17

A teacher asks students to identify the word formed when the /r/ at the beginning of the word *rug* is replaced by /b/. Which strategy is the teacher using to build phoneme awareness?

A. phoneme blending
B. phoneme deletion
C. phoneme segmentation
D. phoneme substitution

18

How can Mr. Dean best support student preparedness to meet the assignment's specific criteria?

> Each weekend, a different student in Mr. Dean's class takes home the classroom's stuffed animal mascot. On the following Monday, the student is required to give a short speech about the mascot's weekend adventures.

A. by administering a summative assessment of speaking ability

B. by including a speech rubric with the mascot when it is sent home

C. by issuing exit tickets with questions about oral presentations

D. by reserving the mascot for students with effective speaking skills

19

Which of the following is true of qualitative measures of text complexity?

A. They are readability scores based on word frequency and sentence length.

B. They are analytical measurements determined by knowledge demands.

C. They are statistical measurements determined by computer algorithms.

D. They are determinations of reading level based on professional judgment.

20

Which of the following is an example of a formative assessment?

A. a student portfolio

B. a final exam

C. a final research project

D. a standardized text

21

Which prewriting assignment would best prepare students for writing a quatrain poem?

A. an investigation of the word quatrain

B. listing pairs of rhyming words

C. a mini-lesson on syllabication

D. a concept map on the topic

22

Which formative assessment strategy will give the teacher described below a quick rundown of how well students understood the lesson?

> A teacher has just completed a lesson on similes, and her students are lining up to go to recess.

A. a rubric

B. exit tickets

C. a mini-lesson

D. anecdotal notes

23

Which of the following is an essential element of descriptive writing?

A. a plot arc

B. reasoned judgment

C. sensory words

D. a graphic

24

How are whiteboards useful as formative assessment tools?

A. They can be used by students to practice penmanship skills.

B. They can be used by students as exit tickets to show understanding of a concept.

C. They can be used by students to demonstrate understanding at a glance.

D. They can be used by students as self-assessment tools.

25

A student is able to write the word *cat* by sounding out each letter. What concept is the student demonstrating?

A. phonological awareness

B. phonics

C. syllabication

D. word analysis

Answer Key

Content Knowledge

1)
- **A. Correct.** The strategy of phoneme blending requires students to combine phonemes to make a word.
- B. Incorrect. The strategy of phoneme deletion requires students to remove phonemes in words to make new words.
- C. Incorrect. The strategy of phoneme segmentation requires students to separate the phonemes in a word.
- D. Incorrect. The strategy of phoneme substitution requires students to replace phonemes in words to make new words.

2)
- A. Incorrect. An English-language learner at the L1 level is not yet attempting to write simple sentences.
- **B. Correct.** An English-language learner at the L2 stage is at the very beginning stages of reading and writing and has a very limited vocabulary.
- C. Incorrect. An English-language learner at the L3 stage demonstrates an expanded vocabulary and an ability to speak in more complex sentences.
- D. Incorrect. An English-language learner at the L4 stage can function at the same level as his or her English-speaking peers.

3)
- A. Incorrect. The beginning consonant forms the onset of the word *cake*.
- B. Incorrect. The *e* is silent in the word *cake* and makes the *a* long.
- C. Incorrect. Dropping the *e* changes the word *cake* into a nonsense word.
- **D. Correct.** The rime in *cake* is formed by all of the letters that follow the beginning consonant.

4)
- A. Incorrect. The word *chick* is made up of three phonemes, or units of sound. They are the consonant diagraph /ch/, the short vowel /ĭ/, and the consonant diagraph /ck/.
- **B. Correct.** The word *chick* is made up of three phonemes, or units of sound: /ch/, /ĭ/, and /ck/.

C. Incorrect. The word *chick* is made up of three phonemes, or units of sound. Both /ch/ and /ck/ are letter combinations that work together to produce one sound.

D. Incorrect. The word *chick* is made up of five letters but only three phonemes, or units of sound. They are the consonant diagraph /ch/, the short vowel /ĭ/, and the consonant diagraph /ck/.

5)

A. Incorrect. The word *clap* is one syllable, and it contains both an onset and a rime.

B. **Correct.** The onset of a syllable is the beginning consonant or consonant blend.

C. Incorrect. The consonant blend *cl* contains two phonemes, /c/ and /l/.

D. Incorrect. The rime of a syllable includes the vowel and remaining consonants, in this case *ap*.

6)

A. Incorrect. The letter *a* is a vowel with both a short and long sound, which makes it less likely to be introduced during phonics instruction before the less complex consonant *m*.

B. Incorrect. While the letter *g* does contain its hard sound in its name, it also has a soft sound, so it a more complex letter than *m*, and thus, less likely to be introduced first.

C. Incorrect. The letter *y* does not contain its sound in its name and can change sounds depending on how it is placed in a word, so it is not likely to be introduced before the letter *m*.

D. **Correct.** The letter *m* is most likely to be introduced first because it contains its sound in its name and only forms one sound in words.

7)

A. Incorrect. Using appropriate vocal expressions when reading aloud demonstrates prosody.

B. Incorrect. Decoding words correctly when reading aloud demonstrates a reader's accuracy.

C. Incorrect. Having a significant inventory of known sight words relates to reading accuracy.

D. **Correct.** Reading smoothly and steadily when reading aloud is an example of reading rate.

8)

A. **Correct.** The diphthong *ea* produces one small unit of sound, /ē/, that cannot be reduced into a smaller unit.

B. Incorrect. The consonant blend *dr* can be separated into two smaller units of sound, /d/ and /r/, so it is not a phoneme. It is the onset of the word *dream*.

C. Incorrect. The word part *eam* contains two small units of sound, /ē/ and /m/. It is the rime of the word *dream*.

D. Incorrect. The word part *re* includes two sounds, /r/ and /ĕ/, and does not represent an appropriate way of breaking the word *dream* into parts.

9)

A. **Correct.** Phonemic awareness is an understanding of how phonemes can be orally manipulated to change the meanings of words.

B. Incorrect. When a student connects oral sounds to written letters, he or she is demonstrating an understanding of phonics.

C. Incorrect. Phonemic awareness is only one part of phonological awareness, which also includes creating rhyming words and breaking one-syllable words into onsets and rimes.

D. Incorrect. When students are able to orally manipulate onsets and rimes, they are demonstrating one aspect of phonological awareness.

10)

A. Incorrect. Phonics instruction is designed to help students learn letter-sound correspondences so they can decode accurately while reading.

B. Incorrect. Phonemic awareness instruction is designed to help students understand how language is formed by the manipulation of small units of sound.

C. **Correct.** Sight word instruction is designed to help students recognize high-frequency words automatically, without decoding, so they can read with fluency.

D. Incorrect. Word analysis instruction is designed to help students break words into meaningful parts in order to decipher their meanings in text.

11)

A. Incorrect. Nothing about John Manly's words or actions lead the reader to infer that he does not like his job.

B. **Correct.** The way that John Manly takes care to make the horse comfortable before riding leads the reader to infer that he has respect for horses.

C. Incorrect. This is information that is directly stated in the text; therefore, it does not need to be inferred.

D. Incorrect. The text leads the reader to understand that John Manly is an employee at a horse farm, not the owner of the horse.

12)

A. **Correct.** First-person point of view is written from the direct experience of one character—in this case, the horse—as indicated by the pronouns *I* and *my*.

B. Incorrect. Second-person point of view is written from the perspective of an external *you*, whether that be the reader or unknown other.

C. Incorrect. Third-person objective point of view is written from the perspective of a detached narrator.

D. Incorrect. Third-person omniscient point of view is written from the perspective of an all-knowing, detached narrator.

13)

A. Incorrect. The squire is a minor character in this excerpt. His presence simply moves the story along.

B. **Correct.** The excerpt is mainly about the interaction between John Manly and the horse. The focus is on the words and actions of both.

C. Incorrect. The squire is a minor character in the excerpt, while John Manly is a main character.

D. Incorrect. John Manly is one of the main characters, but his family does not play a role in the excerpt. They are mentioned only as a detail of John Manly's life.

14)

A. Incorrect. This is not an adequate summary of the excerpt because all it does is provide details about one of the main characters. It does not address the relationship between John Manly and the narrator.

B. Incorrect. This summary leaves out many important details a reader needs to know, such as who John Manly is and why he is riding the new horse.

C. Incorrect. This is a confusing summary because it contains irrelevant details and makes it seem as though the squire is one of the main characters instead of focusing on how John Manly interacts with the horse.

D. **Correct.** This is the best summary because it provides a brief explanation of the excerpt's main idea and key details. It only includes the most necessary information a reader needs to comprehend the story section.

15)

A. Incorrect. The horse describes a pleasant afternoon and does not suggest any negative events to come.

B. **Correct.** The horse describes an ordinary scene, expressing enjoyment at his grooming and ride with the attentive John Manly.

C. Incorrect. The horse expresses pleasure, not sadness.

D. Incorrect. The passage is positive, but not overwhelmingly euphoric.

16)

A. **Correct.** The author provides a definition of the word *paces* in the next paragraph when he lists them as trot, canter, and gallop.

B. Incorrect. In this instance, the Latin root could be deceptive and thus would not be helpful for determining the meaning of this word. *Pace* means *peace* in Latin; the English word *paces* comes from the Latin *passus* (to step or stretch).

C. Incorrect. The denotation of *paces* is used in this excerpt, so there is no connotation attached.

D. Incorrect. The setting does offer a limited hint as to the meaning of the word *paces*, in that it suggests that a large area is required, but the definition that the author provides within the third paragraph is clearer and more accessible.

17)

A. Incorrect. This excerpt is an example of informational text, or nonfiction text that provides information on a topic. Literary text is the fictional text of novels, stories, and poetry.

B. Incorrect. This excerpt uses academic language, or the language of school, as opposed to the informal language of conversation.

C. Incorrect. The informational text in this excerpt is accessible to the general public; thus it is not written with terms known specifically to music experts, or discipline-specific.

D. **Correct.** This text provides information about the composer Chopin in academic language that is accessible to the general public.

18)

A. Incorrect. The author's word choice, rather than the picture, determines the tone of the excerpt.

B. Incorrect. The picture does not help the reader feel the beauty of Chopin's music. This would be accomplished with an audio excerpt or more descriptive text.

C. **Correct.** The picture of the "true piano hand" allows the reader to see that the fingers become thinner at the tips, which is a clue to the meaning of the word *tapering*.

D. Incorrect. The picture shows a "true piano hand," not a "true artist's hand." Although Chopin is described as an artist, there are many different types of artists who require different types of hands, depending on their expertise.

19)

A. Incorrect. A chart listing the places Chopin played would just restate the text. It would not add to the reader's understanding.

B. Correct. A map would enable the reader to visualize the locations where Chopin played in relation to each other, thus giving the reader a clearer view of Chopin's area of impact.

C. Incorrect. A graph is not useful in this instance because there are no numbers to compare.

D. Incorrect. Places are best visualized on maps or in photographs, so a sidebar with additional text information would not be particularly helpful in this instance.

20)

A. Correct. *Love* is the smallest unit of the word *loveliness* to contain meaning; therefore, it is the root word. Some roots words like *love* can stand on their own and are sometimes referred to as base words.

B. Incorrect. *Lovely* contains both the root word *love* and the suffix *-ly* (meaning "the essence of something").

C. Incorrect. *Lov* is a combination of letters with no meaning; thus, it cannot be a root word.

D. Incorrect. *Loveli* is simply the word *lovely* with the *y* changed to an *i* before the second suffix (*-ness*, meaning "the state or condition of") is added.

21)

A. Correct. Myths typically include gods and goddesses with abilities that surpass those of humans. Myths describe an earlier version of the world and often attempt to explain how the world came to be as it is.

B. Incorrect. Fairy tales are make-believe stories that include magic, but not gods and goddesses. Fairy tales often include royal characters and standard beginnings and endings such as "once upon a time" and "they lived happily ever after."

C. Incorrect. Narrative poems are stories told with a poetic structure instead of in prose.

D. Incorrect. A drama includes stage directions and parts, or dialogue, for different characters; the story is acted out instead of read like a book.

22)

A. Incorrect. The excerpt describes Midas' father as physically strong, but it does not indicate that Midas is as well.

B. Incorrect. Midas' thoughts and actions in the excerpt do not suggest generosity. Instead, they reveal his insecurity at not descending from a long line of royalty.

C. Correct. The excerpt suggests that Midas' yearning for power comes from concern that he is judged negatively by those with a long lineage of royalty; therefore, the reader can conclude that Midas is insecure about his standing as king.

D. Incorrect. Midas' thoughts and actions in the excerpt do not suggest anger. Instead, they reveal his insecurity at not descending from a long line of royalty.

23)

A. Incorrect. This excerpt includes background information about the character of Midas, but no action, so it has not yet developed beyond the exposition phase of the story.

- B. **Correct.** This excerpt is introducing background information about the character of Midas, which is a characteristic of the exposition of a story.
- C. Incorrect. This excerpt has not yet developed beyond the exposition phase of the story, so the climax has not yet been revealed.
- D. Incorrect. So far, there is no action in the story, only background information about the character of Midas. Therefore, this excerpt comes from the story's exposition.

24)
- A. Incorrect. The excerpt does have a particular register that includes vocabulary and usage from the Edwardian era, but in this instance, the register does not aid the reader in determining the meaning of the word *coveted*.
- B. Incorrect. Structural analysis is not the optimal choice for determining the meaning of the word *coveted* because it is not a word that has an obvious or common Greek or Latin root.
- C. **Correct.** The repetition of the word *power* and the use of the words *always* and *more* in an additional phrase emphasize the idea that Midas desires power; thus, the syntax of the sentence, or the way it is constructed, provides significant clues to the meaning of *coveted*.
- D. Incorrect. While *coveted* tends to have a negative connotation, this connotation would not be understood apart from the meaning of the word, so in this instance, connotation is not the best choice for helping a reader to comprehend the word's meaning.

25)
- A. Incorrect. The expression *born and bred to the purple* does not use the overexaggeration characteristic of hyperbole.
- B. Incorrect. Personification is the attribution of human characteristics to a nonhuman thing or abstract idea; the expression *born and bred to the purple* does not feature personification.
- C. Incorrect. A simile is a comparison using *like* or *as*. The expression *born and bred to the purple* does not make such a comparison.
- D. **Correct.** The expression *born and bred to the purple* is an idiom, or an expression that means more than the sum of its parts. An idiom is commonly understood and used by a specific population; its connotations may not be understood beyond that population, even by people who speak the same language. Here, the expression connotes *royalty*.

26)
- A. Incorrect. Myths feature gods and goddesses and explain the origins of places, things, circumstances, etc.
- B. **Correct.** Fables feature animals and include explicit moral lessons for readers.
- C. Incorrect. Legends are unverified stories from long ago featuring heroes and heroines who overcome overwhelming obstacles.
- D. Incorrect. Fairy tales are imaginary, dream-like stories that feature royalty and magical creatures.

27)
- A. Incorrect. The way a story is organized may help convey the theme, but it is not the underlying idea that runs through the story.

B. Incorrect. The moral of a story is the lesson the author wants to teach, not the underlying idea that weaves in and out of the text from start to finish.

C. Correct. The theme runs throughout a story from start to finish and is the underlying idea that an author wants to convey.

D. Incorrect. Point of view describes the perspective from which a story is told, not the underlying idea that runs through it from start to finish.

28)

A. Incorrect. A simple sentence is constructed of only one independent clause.

B. Incorrect. A compound sentence is constructed of two or more independent clauses.

C. Correct. The sentence is an example of a complex sentence with one dependent clause and one independent clause.

D. Incorrect. A compound-complex sentence has two or more independent clauses and one or more dependent clauses.

29)

A. Correct. The word *park* acts as an adjective describing the noun *naturalist* in the first sentence, and is part of an adjective phrase *from the park*, which modifies the noun *migration* in the second sentence.

B. Incorrect. The word *naturalist* is the subject of both sentences. The word *park* acts as an adjective to describe the subject in the first sentence.

C. Incorrect. The word *park* is an adjective that describes the subject in the first sentence and part of an adjective phrase that describes the noun *migration* in the second sentence. The predicate of the second sentence includes the word *park* along with all of the other words following the subject (i.e., "visited the class to talk about the migration of Monarch butterflies from the park").

D. Incorrect. While the word *park* does act as an adjective to describe the noun *naturalist* in the first sentence, "from the park" is an adjective phrase that modifies the noun *migration*, not the verb *visited*.

30)

A. Incorrect. The use of the contraction *it's* is incorrect. The possessive *its*, without an apostrophe, should be used instead.

B. Incorrect. No comma is needed before *because* because the dependent clause follows the independent clause.

C. Correct. The word *it's* is a contraction meaning *it is*. The possessive form of *its* is written without an apostrophe.

D. Incorrect. The use of a present tense verb is correct because the steepness of the trail is a general truth.

31)

A. Incorrect. The conventions remain the same.

B. Incorrect. The sentences share similar organization.

C. Incorrect. Both sentences read naturally.

D. Correct. The revised sentence replaces vague and non-descriptive words with more specific words that provide the reader with a clearer idea of the author's message.

32)

A. Incorrect. The verb tenses are consistent and explain Lucy's thoughts after the movies have been viewed.

B. Correct. The word *than*, which is a conjunction used to make comparisons, should be used instead of *then*, which is an adverb that means *at that time*.

C. Incorrect. The word *one* refers back to a countable noun, in this instance, *movie*. It is not a dangling modifier, which is a word, phrase, or clause that modifies a subject misplaced in or missing from the sentence.

D. Incorrect. The subject of the sentence is *Lucy*, and it is correctly placed at the beginning of the sentence.

33)

A. **Correct.** Self-published materials are considered unreliable sources because expertise has not been established.

B. Incorrect. An edited book of essays is considered a reliable research source because expertise is authenticated by the editor selecting the essays.

C. Incorrect. A newspaper article is considered a reliable research source because expertise is authenticated by the publisher.

D. Incorrect. A university study is considered a reliable research source because expertise is authenticated by the reputation of the institution.

34)

A. Incorrect. A metaphor is a direct comparison made without the words *like* or *as*.

B. Incorrect. Assonance is the use of similar vowel sounds in a line of poetry.

C. Incorrect. Alliteration is the repetition of closely positioned words that begin with the same sound.

D. **Correct.** A simile is a comparison made using the words *like* or *as*.

35)

A. Incorrect. It is the poet's choice of rhyme scheme that leads the reader to the correct pronunciation of *quays*, not a comparison using *like* or *as*.

B. **Correct.** The poet uses an *aabb* rhyme scheme throughout the poem, which lets the reader know that the word *quays* should be pronounced to rhyme with *trees*.

C. Incorrect. It is the poet's choice of rhyme scheme that leads the reader to the correct pronunciation of *quays*, not the attribution of a human quality.

D. Incorrect. It is the poet's choice of rhyme scheme that leads the reader to the correct pronunciation of *quays*, not the point of view used to relate the poem.

36)

A. **Correct.** Onomatopoeia is the use of words that imitate or resemble sounds.

B. Incorrect. These words describe the poem's setting.

C. Incorrect. These words contribute to the calming tone of the poem.

D. Incorrect. These are sensory words that emphasize illumination.

37)

A. Incorrect. Expository writing is used to explain or inform a reader about a topic in a formal style.

B. Incorrect. Narrative writing is used to relate a highly structured fictional story or personal memoir.

C. **Correct.** Descriptive writing produces sensory imagery and vivid impressions and is often used in poetry.

D. Incorrect. Persuasive writing is used to convince a reader of an opinion or point of view.

38)

A. **Correct.** Expository writing is most appropriate for the formal and objective presentation of information required in a research paper.

B. Incorrect. A research paper needs to be written with a formal structure and an objective, straightforward tone, so writing that emphasizes imagery is not the best style choice.

C. Incorrect. Narrative writing is used to tell a personal or fictional story that entertains a reader, so it is not the best style choice for a research paper.

D. Incorrect. Persuasive writing is used to convince the reader of an opinion or point of view, but a research paper needs to be written with an objective tone.

39)

A. Incorrect. Learning the names of authors is secondary to avoiding plagiarism, which is a serious issue in the field of research.

B. Incorrect. Categorizing source material relies more on content knowledge than paraphrasing and citing information. It is also secondary to avoiding plagiarism, which is a serious issue in the field of research.

C. **Correct.** Learning the importance of avoiding plagiarism is a critical component of writing instruction for school and career success.

D. Incorrect. Learning how to condense writing for maximum impact relies more on content knowledge than paraphrasing and citing information.

40)

A. Incorrect. A handwritten letter by an established historical figure is an example of a primary source because it is significant original, first-hand material.

B. Incorrect. A photograph is an example of a primary source because it is original, first-hand material.

C. Incorrect. An audio recording is an example of a primary source because it is original, first-hand material.

D. **Correct.** A book that discusses a historical time period is an example of a secondary source because it's written by an author who synthesizes and analyzes primary sources to form conclusions.

41)

A. Incorrect. Presenting outcomes is the purpose of the final stage of the writing process.

B. Incorrect. Organizing ideas is the purpose of the first stage of the writing process.

C. **Correct.** Correcting errors is the purpose of the rewriting stage of the writing process.

D. Incorrect. Recording thoughts is the purpose of the drafting stage of the writing process.

42)

A. Incorrect. Smiling at the speaker demonstrates active listening because one's focus is on the speaker.

B. Incorrect. Leaning forward slightly demonstrates active listening because one's focus is on hearing the speaker's words.

C. **Correct.** Looking down at the floor does not demonstrate active listening because one's focus is not on the speaker.

D. Incorrect. Sitting up straight demonstrates active listening because it indicates alertness and concentration.

43)

A. Incorrect. The primary purpose of narrative writing is to entertain.

B. **Correct.** The primary purpose of expository writing to explain.

C. Incorrect. The primary purpose of persuasive writing is to convince.

D. Incorrect. The primary purpose of descriptive writing is to describe.

44)

A. Incorrect. Revising part of a story without an organizational framework is less beneficial.

B. **Correct.** It is most beneficial for students to use graphic organizers to shape their ideas before writing.

C. Incorrect. Drafting the beginning of a story without an organizational framework is less beneficial.

D. Incorrect. Sharing an original story with a classmate should come at the end of the writing process, when the writing has gone through all stages and is ready for an audience.

45)

A. Incorrect. Students are not restating the message in their own words; they are learning editing skills.

B. **Correct.** Mr. Kahn is modeling the editing process and reinforcing concepts related to the conventions of Standard English.

C. Incorrect. This lesson is designed for students who have advanced beyond the decoding stage of reading instruction.

D. Incorrect. Mr. Kahn is modeling the editing process, not the comprehension skill of inferencing.

46)

A. Incorrect. Revising part of a story without an organizational framework is less beneficial.

B. **Correct.** It is most beneficial for students to use graphic organizers to shape their ideas before writing.

C. Incorrect. Drafting the beginning of a story without an organizational framework is less beneficial.

D. Incorrect. Sharing an original story with a classmate should come at the end of the writing process, when the writing has gone through all stages and is ready for an audience.

47)

A. **Correct.** This sentence paraphrases the original sentence most accurately because it restates the speaker's main idea and reasoning in a revised and concise way.

B. Incorrect. This sentence is practically identical to the original statement, so it is not a proper example of paraphrasing.

C. Incorrect. This sentence restates the speaker's main idea, but it excludes his reasoning, so it is not a good example of paraphrasing.

D. Incorrect. This sentence alters the speaker's message because it excludes the speaker's main idea, which is that school start times should be later.

48)

A. Incorrect. Moving around demonstrates a lack of focus and is distracting to a speaker.

B. Incorrect. Interjecting questions does not demonstrate active listening because it interrupts the speaker.

C. Incorrect. Frowning and crossed arms do not demonstrate active listening because they are nonverbal cues that convey judgment.

D. **Correct.** Eye contact and leaning forward demonstrate that the listener is actively focusing on the speaker's message.

49)

A. Incorrect. Making crayon rubbings helps students internalize letter shapes, but it is not finger spelling.

- B. **Correct.** Finger spelling is a form of sign language that uses the hands to represent letters.
- C. Incorrect. Using the fingers to count the number of letters in words develops the concept of print, but it is not finger spelling.
- D. Incorrect. Writing letters in trays of sand helps students practice forming letters, but it is not finger spelling.

50)
- A. Incorrect. An opinion piece is an example of persuasive writing that aims to influence the reader to agree with what is stated and act accordingly.
- B. Incorrect. A cause-and-effect essay is an example of expository writing that explains and provides information.
- C. Incorrect. A poem that evokes feeling through imagery is an example of descriptive writing.
- D. **Correct.** A personal story with a plot arc is an example of narrative writing.

Curriculum, Instruction, and Assessment

1)

- **A. Correct.** Emergent writing activities such as journaling provide students with opportunities to connect the sounds they hear in words to the letters representing those sounds.
- B. Incorrect. Drawing is an important element of emergent storytelling, but it is not a strategy for connecting sounds to letters.
- C. Incorrect. Building fine motor skills contributes to handwriting proficiency, but it is not a strategy for connecting sounds to letters.
- D. Incorrect. Understanding that writing moves from left to right is an important print concept, but it is not a strategy for connecting sounds to letters.

2)

- A. Incorrect. The primary purpose of repeated reading is to build fluency.
- B. Incorrect. Building concepts of print is a pre-reading strategy, not a reading strategy.
- C. Incorrect. Prediction only applies to the first reading of a text or section of text, so it is not a skill built through repeated reading.
- **D. Correct.** Repeated reading helps students gain a feel for how fluent reading feels and sounds.

3)

- A. Incorrect. Character analysis instruction is a reading comprehension strategy.
- **B. Correct.** Word family instruction is a decoding strategy that reinforces student understanding of word patterns.
- C. Incorrect. Instruction in active listening is an oral comprehension strategy.
- D. Incorrect. Fact-and-opinion instruction is a reading comprehension strategy.

4)

- A. Incorrect. Repeated reading relates to text fluency, not text structure.
- **B. Correct.** A mini-lesson on signal words would best help students gain a better understanding of how to identify text structure.
- C. Incorrect. A Venn diagram helps students organize the similarities and differences between two texts.
- D. Incorrect. Thinking aloud is a less effective strategy than a mini-lesson on signal words because of the breadth of content requiring review.

5)

- **A. Correct.** Thinking aloud is when a teacher verbalizes thoughts and insights to model how to think logically and critically when applying a reading comprehension skill.
- B. Incorrect. Graphics can be used to illustrate a concept, but they are not the best choices for modeling inferencing.
- C. Incorrect. Plot pyramids can be used to help students understand the plot development in a story, but they are not the best choices for modeling inferencing.
- D. Incorrect. Word investigations can be used to build reading vocabulary, but they are not the best choices for modeling inferencing.

6)

A. **Incorrect.** Repeat reading is a tool for developing fluency, not an extension activity.

B. **Correct.** Assigning a related research project extends learning on the topic after reading.

C. **Incorrect.** Lessons on difficult text vocabulary happen before reading, not after.

D. **Incorrect.** Reviewing text features happens before reading, not after.

7)

A. **Incorrect.** Systematic phonics instruction does not follow an alphabetical sequence. Instead teachers begin instruction with letters that have names that are closely related to their sounds such as *m* and *s*. Lessons progress accordingly and whole words are added in a logical sequence that moves from simple word patterns and sound combinations to more complex ones.

B. **Correct.** Systematic phonics instruction is a series of logically sequenced lessons on sound-letter concepts that begins with the simplest sound-letter correspondences and progresses to the more complex, from single letters to words.

C. **Incorrect.** Lessons that develop student understanding of how sounds, syllables, words, and word parts can be orally manipulated to break apart words, make new words, and create rhymes demonstrate phonological awareness instruction, not phonics instruction.

D. **Incorrect.** Lessons on roots and affixes derived from Greek or Latin that progress in a logical sequence from the most common prefixes and suffixes to more complex word structures demonstrate word analysis instruction, not phonics instruction.

8)

A. **Correct.** Metaphor and personification are types of figurative language.

B. **Incorrect.** Rimes and onsets are the phonological units of spoken syllables.

C. **Incorrect.** Roots and affixes are structural word parts.

D. **Incorrect.** Fact and opinion define different types of statements.

9)

A. **Incorrect.** A truth that can be proven with hard evidence is a fact.

B. **Incorrect.** A statement not supported by hard evidence is an opinion.

C. **Incorrect.** A point of view based on a strong belief system is an opinion.

D. **Correct.** A reasoned judgment is neither fact nor opinion but a determination based on reasonable arguments and supporting evidence.

10)

A. **Incorrect.** A different strategy would be used to introduce students to new vocabulary before reading.

B. **Incorrect.** Sequencing instruction is more appropriate after reading.

C. **Correct.** A KWL chart activates student background knowledge about a topic before reading.

D. **Incorrect.** A KWL chart does not provide an overview of text information.

11)

A. **Incorrect.** A sensory word chart is a prewriting tool for creating imagery, which is not the focal point of a procedural text.

B. **Correct.** A sequencing map allows students to visualize and order the steps in a process before writing.

C. Incorrect. A plot pyramid is a prewriting tool for narrative fiction.

D. Incorrect. An outline is a prewriting tool for expository text and research projects.

12)

A. **Correct.** Sight word games are tools for developing word recognition skills in order to increase reading fluency.

B. Incorrect. Oral language skills in elementary school are best developed through group discussions, oral presentations, and oral reports.

C. Incorrect. Social skills in elementary school are best developed through cooperative learning activities, problem-solving strategies, and studies of good citizenship qualities.

D. Incorrect. Sight words are words that students need to be able to recognize automatically without the need for decoding via letter-sound correspondences.

13)

A. Incorrect. Phoneme blending requires students to combine phonemes to make a word.

B. **Correct.** Phoneme deletion requires students to remove phonemes from words to make new words.

C. Incorrect. Phoneme segmentation requires students to separate the phonemes in a word.

D. Incorrect. Phoneme substitution requires students to replace phonemes in words to make new words.

14)

A. Incorrect. Rewriting parts of someone else's text is not an appropriate editing practice.

B. Incorrect. Because elementary students are beginning writers, criticism by peers is to be avoided because it can interrupt writing development and progress.

C. **Correct.** This is a common three-part strategy used for peer editing.

D. Incorrect. Peer-editing criteria need to be clearly articulated and appropriate and inappropriate types of comments clarified in order to prevent writing reluctance. *Writing tips* and *Comments* are less positive in connotation than *Suggestions* and *Compliments*.

15)

A. Incorrect. A diamante poem is made up of seven lines with specific structure, but it does not depend on an understanding of syllables.

B. Incorrect. An acrostic poem has a structure based on the poem's topic, but it does not depend on an understanding of syllables.

C. **Correct.** An understanding of syllables is necessary for writing a haiku poem.

D. Incorrect. A shape poem is written in the shape of its topic, but it does not depend on an understanding of syllables.

16)

A. **Correct.** Engaging, playful activities that build smaller muscles in the hand outside of the context of writing are most likely to contribute to improved fine motor skills without increasing writing reluctance.

B. Incorrect. Increasing the workload of a struggling writer is more likely to increase stress levels related to writing than improve fine motor skills, which can be supported in other contexts.

C. Incorrect. Having students with weak fine motor skills rewrite assignments is more likely to produce negative associations with writing than improve fine motor skills.

D. Incorrect. Pointing to individual words while reading is a strategy for improving word recognition skills, not fine motor skills.

17)

A. Incorrect. Phoneme blending requires students to combine phonemes to make a word.

B. Incorrect. Phoneme deletion requires students to remove phonemes from words to make new words.

C. Incorrect. Phoneme segmentation requires students to separate the phonemes in a word.

D. **Correct.** Phoneme substitution requires students to replace phonemes in words to make new words.

18)

A. Incorrect. Summative assessments measure student growth at the end of a teaching unit. They are not the best choice for supporting student preparedness to meet an assignment's expectations.

B. **Correct.** A rubric provides students with specific criteria to consider and practice prior to their presentations.

C. Incorrect. An exit ticket provides a means of quickly assessing a single concept. It is not the most effective tool for supporting student preparedness for an oral presentation assignment.

D. Incorrect. The goal of classroom assignments is to provide all students with opportunities to grow academically. Reserving special assignments for children who already demonstrate proficiency with a skill defeats the purpose of a teaching strategy.

19)

A. Incorrect. Readability scores based on word frequency and sentence length are determined by computer algorithms and are therefore quantitative.

B. **Correct.** Analysis of the knowledge demands required by a text is a qualitative measure of text complexity.

C. Incorrect. Measures of text complexity based on objective statistics are quantitative.

D. Incorrect. Reading level determinations based on the reading needs of specific students are examples of reader and task considerations.

20)

A. **Correct.** A student portfolio is an example of a formative assessment that provides a perspective on a range of student work over time.

B. Incorrect. A final exam is an example of a summative assessment used to measure proficiency level at the end of an instructional unit.

C. Incorrect. A final research project is an example of a summative assessment used to measure academic ability.

D. Incorrect. A standardized test is a summative assessment that measures a student's subject area proficiency levels against predetermined benchmarks and/or criteria.

21)

A. Incorrect. A word investigation is a vocabulary development tool, not a prewriting tool.

B. **Correct.** A quatrain poem contains one or more four-line stanzas with a rhyme scheme, so a list of rhyming words is a helpful prewriting assignment.

C. Incorrect. A quatrain poem does not require specific syllable counts, so a mini-lesson on syllabication is not appropriate for this assignment.

D. Incorrect. A concept map is used for linking a main idea to supporting ideas, so it is not applicable to writing quatrain poems.

22)

A. Incorrect. A rubric is a self-assessment tool for students that is used as a guide during the completion of an activity.

B. Correct. Exit tickets can be turned in by students on their way out the door and quickly scanned for evidence of student understanding.

C. Incorrect. A mini-lesson is used to reteach a concept, not assess understanding of a concept.

D. Incorrect. Anecdotal notes are used to record observations of individual student learning during an activity, not at the end.

23)

A. Incorrect. A plot arc is essential to narrative writing.

B. Incorrect. Reasoned judgment is based on logic, not description.

C. Correct. Sensory words are essential to descriptive writing because they are necessary for creating imagery.

D. Incorrect. A graphic can be described, but it is not a description.

24)

A. Incorrect. Using whiteboards to practice penmanship skills is a learning strategy, not an assessment strategy.

B. Incorrect. Exit tickets are most effective when they are small pieces of paper as opposed to bulky boards.

C. Correct. Teachers can make at-a-glance assessments of understanding by having students simultaneously show answers to a question on whiteboards.

D. Incorrect. Rubrics and checklists are self-assessment tools; whiteboards are not.

25)

A. Incorrect. Phonological awareness is an oral skill that does not include letter-sound correspondence.

B. Correct. When a student connects oral sounds to written letters, he or she is demonstrating an understanding of phonics.

C. Incorrect. Syllabication is the ability to separate words into syllables.

D. Incorrect. Word analysis is the ability to separate words into meaningful parts.

Mathematics Practice

Content Knowledge

1

Which equation demonstrates the associative property of addition?

A. $2 + (1 + 5) = (2 + 1) + 5$
B. $2(1 \times 5) = (2 \times 1)5$
C. $1 \times 3 = 3 \times 1$
D. $2(7 + 4) = 2 \times 7 + 2 \times 4$

2

Using the information in the table, which equation demonstrates the linear relationship between x and y?

x	y
3	3
7	15
10	24

A. $y = 6x - 6$
B. $y = 5x - 6$
C. $y = 4x - 6$
D. $y = 3x - 6$

3

Using the table, which equation demonstrates the linear relationship between x and y?

x	y
3	−18
7	−34
10	−46

A. $y = -6x - 6$
B. $y = -5x - 6$
C. $y = -4x - 6$
D. $y = -3x - 6$

4

Students board a bus at 7:45 a.m. and arrive at school at 8:20 a.m. How long are the students on the bus?

A. 30 minutes
B. 35 minutes
C. 45 minutes
D. 60 minutes

5

Which expression has only prime factors of 3, 5, and 11?

A. 66 × 108
B. 15 × 99
C. 42 × 29
D. 28 × 350

6

Robbie has a bag of treats that contains 5 pieces of gum, 7 pieces of taffy, and 8 pieces of chocolate. If Robbie reaches into the bag and randomly pulls out a treat, what is the probability that Robbie will get a piece of taffy?

A. 1
B. $\frac{1}{7}$
C. $\frac{5}{8}$
D. $\frac{7}{20}$

7

Which figure is a concave polygon?

A.

B.

C.

D.

8

Micah invites 23 friends to his house and is having pizza for dinner. Each pizza feeds approximately four people. Micah does not want a lot of leftovers. How many pizzas should he order?

A. 4
B. 5
C. 6
D. 7

9

Kim and Chris are writing a book together. Kim writes twice as many pages as Chris. Altogether, there are 240 pages in the book. Which equation shows how many pages Chris writes?

A. $2 + 2p = 240$
B. $p + 2p = 240$
C. $2p - p = 240$
D. $p - 2p = 240$

10

An ice chest contains 24 sodas, some regular and some diet. The ratio of diet soda to regular soda is 1:3. How many regular sodas are there in the ice chest?

A. 1
B. 3
C. 18
D. 24

11

Which inequality is equivalent to $10 \leq k - 5$?

A. $k \leq 15$
B. $k \geq 15$
C. $k \leq 5$
D. $k \leq 10$

12

What is $\frac{5}{8}$ as a percent?

A. 16%
B. 62.5%
C. 1.6%
D. 0.625%

13

Simplify $(5^2 - 2)^2 + 3^3$.

A. 25
B. 30
C. 556
D. 538

14

Which statement describes the images?

	$\frac{1}{5}$
	$\frac{2}{5}$
	$\frac{3}{5}$
	$\frac{4}{5}$

A. When the numerator stays the same and the denominator increases, the fraction increases.
B. When the numerator increases and the denominator stays the same, the fraction increases.
C. When the numerator and the denominator increase, the fraction decreases.
D. When the numerator stays the same and the denominator decreases, the fraction decreases.

15

Danny collects coins. The table shows how many of each type of coin Danny collects for four days. Which statement is true?

Danny's Coin Collection

Coin	Day 1	Day 2	Day 3	Day 4
Pennies	1	4	5	1
Nickels	4	3	2	5
Dimes	3	2	2	3
Quarters	0	5	4	1

A. The mean number of nickels is greater than the mean number of quarters.
B. The mean number of quarters is greater than the mean number of pennies.
C. The range of dimes is greater than the range of quarters.
D. The median number of pennies is five.

16

Solve for x.

$x = 6(3^0)$

A. 0
B. 18
C. 180
D. 6

17

A table is 150 centimeters long. How many millimeters long is the table?

A. 1.5 mm
B. 15 mm
C. 150 mm
D. 1500 mm

18

Students are asked if they prefer vanilla, chocolate, or strawberry ice cream. The results are tallied on the table below.

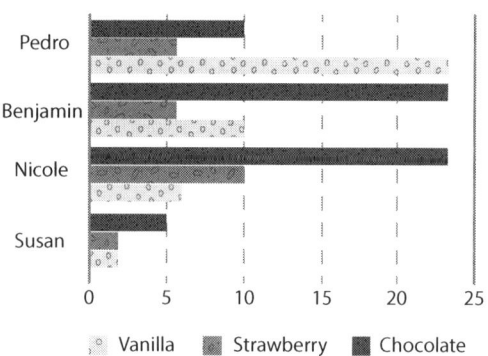

The students display the information from the table in a bar graph. Which student completes the bar graph correctly?

A. Pedro
B. Benjamin
C. Nicole
D. Susan

19

If the pattern continues, what is the next number?

{2, 5, 14, 41, 122, …}

A. 244
B. 264
C. 422
D. 365

20

What is the value of $3x + 7x$ if $x = 8$?

A. 10
B. 21
C. 31
D. 80

21

What is the value of the digit 4 in the number 654,123?

A. one thousand
B. four thousand
C. ten thousand
D. forty thousand

22

Which equation is described by the data in the table?

x	y
1	3
2	0
3	−5

A. $y = 4 - x^2$
B. $x^2 + y = 4$
C. $x^2 + y = 2^2$
D. all of the above

23

The formula for distance is $d = r \times t$. How long will it take a plane to fly 4,000 miles from Chicago to London if the plane flies at a constant rate of 500 mph?

A. 20 hours
B. 8 hours
C. 45 hours
D. 3.5 hours

24

Justin has a summer lawn care business. Justin earns $400 per week by taking care of ten lawns. Justin pays $35/week in business-related expenses. The money Justin saves after x weeks is represented by the expression $x(400 - 35)$. If y represents Justin's total earnings, which expression shows how many dollars Justin earns in a summer?

A. $y = 365x$
B. $35x = 400y$
C. $x + y = 365$
D. $x = 365y$

25

Which property is demonstrated by the equivalent expressions?

$7(3 + 5) = 7 \times 3 + 7 \times 5$

A. distributive
B. associative
C. commutative
D. multiplicative

26

Which expression can be solved using the following steps?

1. Subtract 5 from m.
2. Multiply the result by 2.
3. Cube the result.

A. $[2(m - 5)]^3$
B. $2m^3 - 5$
C. $2m - 5^3$
D. $2(m - 5)^3$

27

Using the function table, what is the value of $f(20)$?

x	f(x)
5	12
10	22
15	32
20	
25	52

A. 20
B. 25
C. 42
D. 50

28

Which number has a prime factorization of three odd numbers and one even number?

A. 9
B. 21
C. 45
D. 90

Go on

29

How much longer is line segment MN than line segment KL?

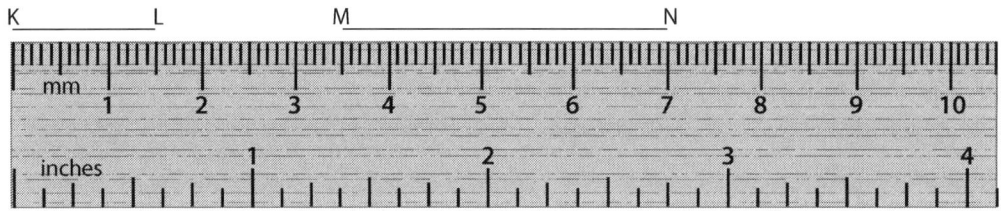

A. 15 mm
B. 20 mm
C. 2 mm
D. 55 mm

30

Which conclusion can be drawn from the graph?

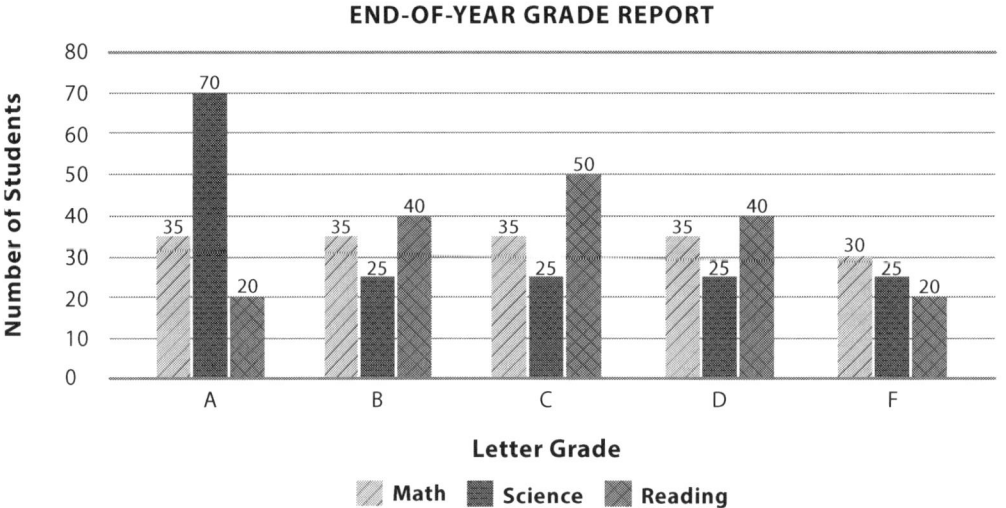

A. More than twice as many students score an "A" in science than score an "F" in science.
B. The majority of the students score a "C" in math.
C. The number of students who score a "B" in reading is equal to the number of students who score a "B" in math.
D. Next year's students do not need very much science instruction because students already know science.

31

In the fall, 425 students pass the math benchmark. In the spring, 680 students pass the same benchmark. What is the percent increase in passing scores from fall to spring?

A. 40%
B. 55%
C. 60%
D. 80%

32

Noah and Jennifer have a total of $10.00 to spend on lunch. If each buys his or her own order of french fries and a soda, how many orders of chicken strips can they share?

Menu	
Item	Price
Hamburger	$4.00
Chicken Strips	$4.00
Onion Rings	$3.00
French Fries	$2.00
Soda	$1.00
Shake	$1.00

A. zero
B. one
C. two
D. three

33

Lynn has 4 grades in science class. Each grade is worth 100 points. Lynn has an 85% average. If Lynn makes 100% on each of the first 3 grades, what does she earn on her 4th grade?

A. 40%
B. 55%
C. 85%
D. 100%

34

Which expression is equivalent to dividing 300 by 12?

A. $2(150 - 6)$
B. $(300 \div 4) \div 6$
C. $(120 \div 6) + (180 \div 6)$
D. $(120 \div 12) + (180 \div 12)$

35

Aprille has $50 to buy the items on her list. Assuming there is no sales tax, about how much change will Aprille receive after buying all the items on her list?

Aprille's List	
Item	Price
Hammer	$13.24
Screwdriver	$11.99
Nails	$4.27
Wrench	$5.60

A. $10
B. $15
C. $35
D. $50

Go on

36

Which number has the greatest value?

A. 9,299 ones
B. 903 tens
C. 93 hundreds
D. 9 thousands

37

Which number has the least value?

A. 0.305
B. 0.035
C. 0.35
D. 0.3

38

What is the perimeter of the shape?

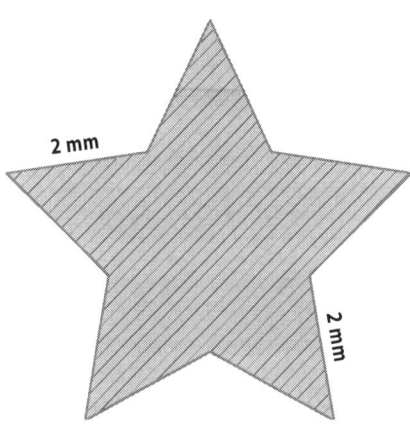

A. 2 mm
B. 4 mm
C. 10 mm
D. 20 mm

39

What is the area of the shape?

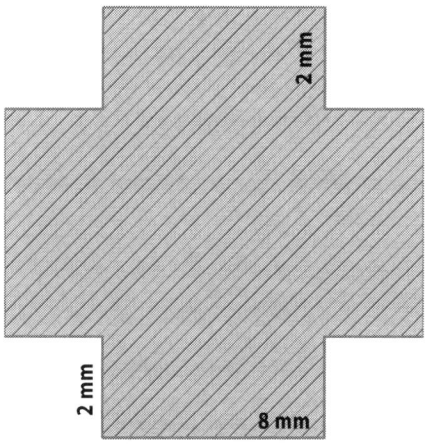

A. 64 mm²
B. 16 mm²
C. 128 mm²
D. 6 mm²

40

Which three-dimensional solid has 2 triangular faces and 3 rectangular faces?

A. pyramid
B. cube
C. rectangular prism
D. triangular prism

41

What are the coefficients and the degrees of the terms in the polynomial?

$4x^3 + 5x^2 + 1$

A. coefficients {4, 5}, degrees {3, 2}
B. coefficients {1, 4, 5}, degrees {3, 2}
C. coefficients {3, 2}, degrees {4, 5}
D. coefficients {3, 2}, degrees {1, 4, 5}

42

In which quadrant is the point (−3, −4) located?

A. I
B. II
C. III
D. IV

43

Which terms can be used to describe the polygon?

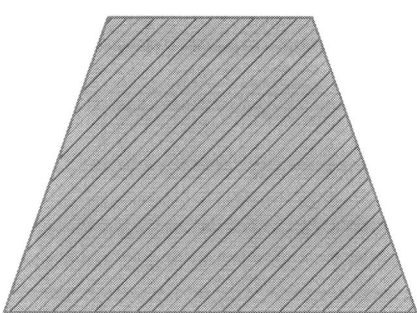

A. irregular and convex
B. irregular and concave
C. regular and convex
D. regular and concave

44

How many times larger is the digit 3 in the first number compared to the second number?

Number One: 846,307
Number Two: 209,023

A. 2
B. 4
C. 10
D. 100

45

A fruit stand sells apples, bananas, and oranges at a ratio of 3:2:1. If the fruit stand sells 20 bananas, how many total pieces of fruit does the fruit stand sell?

A. 10
B. 30
C. 40
D. 60

46

Which type of number is shown below?

3.65555555…

A. natural number
B. whole number
C. integer
D. rational number

47

Out of 1,560 students at Ward Middle School, 15% want to take French. Which equation can determine how many students want to take French?

A. $x = 1560 \div 15$
B. $x = 15 \div 1560$
C. $x = 1560 \times 0.15$
D. $x = 1560 \div 100$

48

What is the sixth term of the sequence if the pattern is to find the difference between the two preceding numbers and then multiply by −3?

{3, 0, −9, −36, ___, _?_ }

A. −81
B. −135
C. 135
D. 81

49

Kim drives 75 mph for *t* hours. If *t* = time and *d* = distance, the equation *d* = 75*t* describes Kim's drive. Which statement is true?

A. The dependent variable is *t* because time depends on the distance Kim travels.

B. The independent variable is *t* because the time is being multiplied by the independent rate of 75.

C. The dependent variable is *d* because the distance depends on the number of hours Kim drives.

D. The dependent and independent variable cannot be determined in the equation.

50

Which graph shows the solution to $y = 2x + 1$?

A.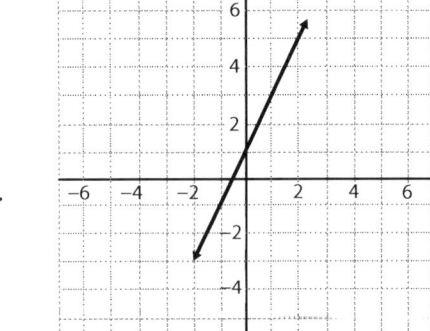

B.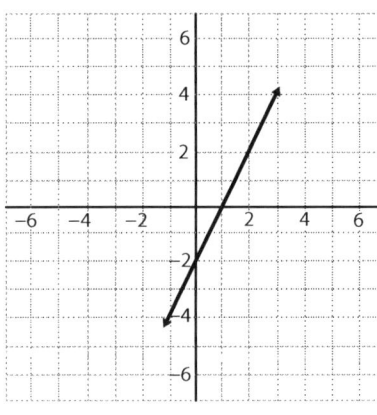

C.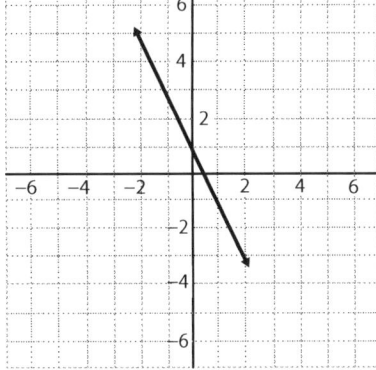

D.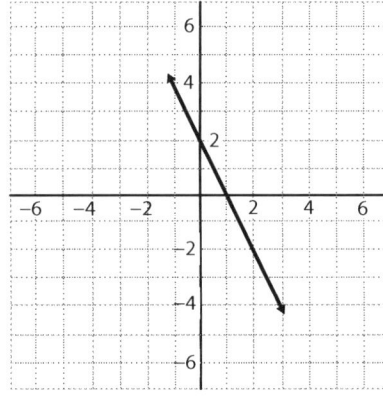

Curriculum, Instruction, and Assessment

1

Ms. Noyes teaches a lesson on order of operations. What information do the students need to know before the lesson begins?

A. how to simplify exponents
B. how to plot a function on a graph
C. how to write an equation in logarithmic form
D. how to expand binomials

2

Mrs. Omeira's class wants to find the probability of pulling a red gumball out of a jar that contains 50 gumballs. What information do the students need to know to find the answer?

A. How many green gumballs are in the jar?
B. How many different colors of gumballs are in the jar?
C. How many red gumballs are in the jar?
D. How long have the gumballs been in the jar?

3

Mrs. Brotherton provides students with pattern blocks and asks the students to tile their desks, leaving no gaps and no overlapping tiles. What concept are the students learning?

A. rotations
B. tessellations
C. reflections
D. symmetry

4

Which word problem is most appropriate when introducing percentages?

A. Saundra puts $2000 in a savings account. The interest rate is 4.2%. How much interest does Saundra earn in a year?
B. Ryan gets 35 questions correct on a test and scores 70%. How many questions are on the test?
C. Amanda earns $200,000 and pays 19% income tax. How many dollars does Amanda pay in taxes?
D. There are 20 students in the class. Five students have June birthdays. What percentage of students were born in June?

5

Mr. Pyle asks his students to answer a problem: There are 25 students in class. Ten are picked up from school by a parent. Ten ride the school bus. Five attend an after-school program in the library. What percentage of students will go to the library after school? Of the following, which student's response is correct?

A. Student A: 20%
B. Student B: 25%
C. Student C: 5%
D. Student D: 30%

6

Mrs. Klinck asks students to use base-ten blocks to represent the number 24. Which student has the best understanding of the concept of ten?

A. Student A

B. Student B

C. Student C

D. Student D

7

Which figure is a two-dimensional object?

A.

B.

C.

D.

8

Which model represents $2x = 4$?

A.

B.

C.

D.

9

Which graph shows $4x + 2 \geq 10$ on a number line?

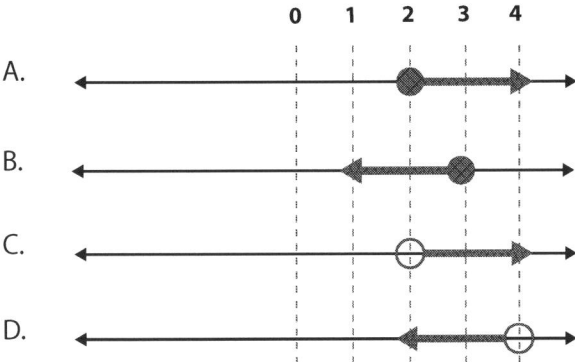

10

Amanda is having difficulty adding fractions with unlike denominators. With which of the following does Amanda need support?

A. how to simplify an exponent
B. how to multiply decimals
C. how to find the least common multiple
D. how to solve a multi-step equation

11

Each spring, the state gives a multiple choice test to every student in the first week of April using explicit instructions regarding security, time, and monitoring. Which type of test is described?

A. a formative assessment
B. an anecdotal record
C. a standardized test
D. remediation

12

A student in Miss Ward's class answers the questions as shown below. If the student's error pattern continues, what is the answer to question three?

1.	25 − 18 = 13
2.	87 − 58 = 31
3.	42 − 38 = ?

A. 4
B. 14
C. 16
D. 80

13

Which activity is most appropriate for a student who is learning to count to ten?

A. comparing integers on a number line
B. drawing pictures of combinations that equal ten
C. matching the numeral ten to cards with ten items on them
D. counting, comparing, and sorting ten plastic bears

14

When would students need to understand how to find the LCM (least common multiple)?

A. when adding fractions with unlike denominators
B. when adding fractions with unlike numerators
C. when multiplying fractions with unlike denominators
D. when dividing fractions with unlike numerators

15

Which mathematical principle will help students check the reasonableness of an answer to a two-digit multiplication problem?

A. estimation
B. associative property
C. ratios
D. probability

16

Which prerequisite skill should students master before learning the associative property?

A. order of operations
B. simplifying two-step equations
C. multiplication
D. adding fractions

17

Carla divides her pizza into 8 equal slices. If converted to a fraction, 8 would be _____.

A. the numerator
B. the denominator
C. a whole number
D. a natural number

18

Craig is learning to graph inequalities on a number line. Which skill should Craig understand first?

A. Cartesian coordinates
B. comparing integers
C. prime and composite numbers
D. converting decimals to percentages

19

Which skill must students master before learning the distributive property?

A. multiplying whole numbers
B. dividing integers
C. multiplying decimals
D. dividing fractions

20

Miss Meriwether asks her students to find the perimeter of the triangle below. Which student correctly finds the perimeter?

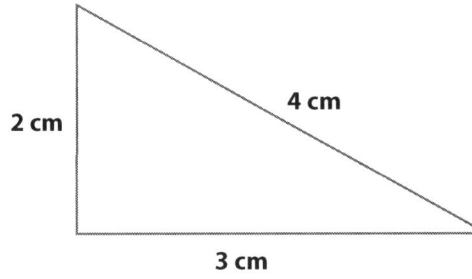

A. Jan multiplies $2 \times 3 \times 4$.
B. Jack multiplies 2×3, then divides by 2.
C. Molly adds $2 + 3 + 4$.
D. Matthew multiplies 4×3, then divides by 2.

21

Pounds per second is an example of which of the following?

A. a nonstandard unit of measure
B. a customary unit of measure
C. a metric unit of measure
D. elapsed time

22

The students in Mr. DeLuna's class investigate if there is a relationship between the weather and the number of bus riders. What data do the students need to collect?

A. the mean number of bus riders during the first week of the month
B. the number of rainy days this month
C. the number of students who walk home from school when it is sunny
D. the mean number of bus riders on rainy days this month

23

Which assessment is a type of formative assessment?

A. standardized test
B. benchmark test
C. ticket out the door
D. end-of-unit assessment

24

Which example is an abstract problem?

A. $4 + 3 = ?$
B. Abigail draws 5 plates. There are 3 apples on each plate. How many total apples are there?
C. Jacob has 12 marbles which he divides evenly among 3 friends. How many marbles will each friend receive?
D. Christi rolls 3 number cubes. What is the probability that one or more of the number cubes will land on 6?

25

According to anecdotal observations, six students have made the following error on guided practice. Which instructional technique would be most effective to remedy the error?

$$\frac{3 \times 15}{9} = 2$$

A. Reteach fractions to the entire class.

B. Reteach multiplication to the entire class.

C. Reteach multiplication to the group of struggling students.

D. Reteach fractions to the group of struggling students.

Answer Key

Content Knowledge

1)

A. **Correct.** When using the associative property, the answer will remain the same in an addition problem regardless of where the parentheses are placed.

B. Incorrect. This equation demonstrates the associative property of multiplication.

C. Incorrect. This equation demonstrates the commutative property of multiplication where the answer in a multiplication problem will remain the same regardless of the order of the numbers.

D. Incorrect. This equation demonstrates the distributive property, which says that multiplication can be distributed over addition.

2)

A. Incorrect. Solve for y by replacing x with 3.
$y = 6(3) - 6$
$y = 18 - 6$
$y = 12$
The table says that when $x = 3$, $y = 3$, not 12.

B. Incorrect. Solve for y by replacing x with 3.
$y = 5(3) - 6$
$y = 15 - 6$
$y = 9$
The table says that when $x = 3$, $y = 3$, not 9.

C. Incorrect. Solve for y by replacing x with 3.
$y = 4(3) - 6$
$y = 12 - 6$
$y = 6$
The table says that when $x = 3$, $y = 3$, not 6.

D. **Correct.** Solve for y by replacing x with 3.
$y = 3(3) - 6$
$y = 9 - 6$
$y = 3$
This is the correct answer because the table says that when $x = 3$, $y = 3$.

3)

A. Incorrect. Solve for y by replacing x with 3.
$y = -6(3) - 6$

$y = -18 - 6$

$y = -24$

The table says that when $x = 3$, $y = -18$, not -24.

B. Incorrect. Solve for y by replacing x with 3.

$y = -5(3) - 6$

$y = -15 - 6$

$y = -21$

The table says that when $x = 3$, $y = -18$, not -21.

C. Correct. Solve for y by replacing x with 3.

$y = -4(3) - 6$

$y = -12 - 6$

$y = -18$

The table says that when $x = 3$, $y = -18$.

D. Incorrect. Solve for y by replacing x with 3.

$y = -3(3) - 6$

$y = -9 - 6$

$y = -15$

The table says that when $x = 3$, $y = -18$, not -15.

4)

A. Incorrect. There are 15 minutes between 7:45 a.m. and 8:00 a.m. and 20 minutes from 8:00 a.m. until 8:20 a.m.; 15 minutes + 20 minutes = 35 minutes, not 30 minutes.

B. Correct. There are 15 minutes between 7:45 a.m. and 8:00 a.m. and 20 minutes from 8:00 a.m. until 8:20 a.m.; 15 minutes + 20 minutes = 35 minutes.

C. Incorrect. There are 15 minutes between 7:45 a.m. and 8:00 a.m. and 20 minutes from 8:00 a.m. until 8:20 a.m.; 15 minutes + 20 minutes = 35 minutes, not 45 minutes.

D. Incorrect. There are 15 minutes between 7:45 a.m. and 8:00 a.m. and 20 minutes from 8:00 a.m. until 8:20 a.m.; 15 minutes + 20 minutes = 35 minutes, not 60 minutes.

5)

A. Incorrect. Both numbers are even, so 2 is a factor of both numbers.

B. Correct. The factor trees show the factors for 15 and 99.

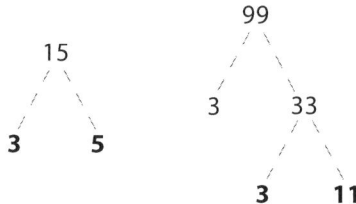

This answer choice has 3, 5, and 11 as the only prime factors.

C. Incorrect. 42 is an even number, so 2 is a factor.

D. Incorrect. Both numbers are even, so 2 is a factor of both numbers.

6)

A. Incorrect. $7 \div 20 \neq 1$.

B. Incorrect. $7 \div 20 \neq \frac{1}{7}$.

C. Incorrect. $7 \div 20 \neq \frac{5}{8}$.

D. Correct. Probability is the number of favorable events divided by the number of possible events. In this case, Robbie pulls out one treat from a bag that contains 7 pieces of taffy; therefore 7 is the number of favorable events. There are 20 total treats in the bag because $5 + 7 + 8 = 20$. $7 \div 20 = \frac{7}{20}$.

7)

A. Incorrect. A concave polygon must have an interior angle that measures greater than 180 degrees. A rectangle has four 90-degree angles.

B. Incorrect. A concave polygon must have an interior angle that measures greater than 180 degrees. The figure depicted is actually a convex polygon.

C. Incorrect. A concave polygon must have an interior angle that measures greater than 180 degrees. In contrast, the hexagon is a convex polygon.

D. **Correct.** The interior angle on the left side of the figure is greater than 180 degrees.

8)

A. Incorrect. 23 people ÷ 4 pizzas = 5.75 people/pizza. This would not be enough because each pizza feeds 4 people.

B. Incorrect. 23 people ÷ 5 pizzas = 4.6 people/pizza. This would not be enough because each pizza feeds 4 people.

C. **Correct.** 23 people ÷ 6 pizzas = 3.8 people/pizza. There would be some pizza left, but this is the closest Micah will be able to get to 4 people/pizza.

D. Incorrect. 23 people ÷ 7 pizzas = 3.3 people/pizza. Micah would have too much pizza left.

9)

A. Incorrect. If p is the number of pages Chris writes, the equation shows only the pages written by Kim ($2p$) and credits Chris with writing only 2 pages.

B. **Correct.** If p is the number of pages Chris writes, the equation shows that Kim writes $2p$, or twice as many pages as Chris writes. If the number of pages Chris writes is added to the number of pages Kim writes, the total is 240 pages.

C. Incorrect. Adding, not subtracting, will find the total number of pages.

D. Incorrect. Adding, not subtracting, will find the total number of pages.

10)

A. Incorrect. It represents the number of diet sodas for every 3 regular sodas.

B. Incorrect. It represents the number of regular sodas for every 1 diet soda.

C. **Correct.** One way to find the answer is to draw a picture.

Put 24 cans into groups of 4. One out of every 4 cans is diet (light gray) so there is 1 light gray can for every 3 dark gray cans. That leaves 18 dark gray cans (regular soda).

Another way to solve the problem is to use ratios. There is 1 diet soda for every 3 regular sodas, for a total of 4 sodas. Diet = 1, Regular = 3, and Total = 4.

$\frac{\text{Regular}}{\text{Total}} = \frac{3}{4} = \frac{x}{24}$

Cross multiply $4x = 72$ and $x = 18$.

D. Incorrect. It simply represents the total number of sodas.

11)

A. Incorrect. Use the steps to solve the inequality.

$10 \leq k - 5$

$5 + 10 \leq k - 5 + 5$

Add 5 to both sides to isolate the variable.

$15 \leq k$

15 is less than or equal to k. Notice that the answer choice is written as k is less than or equal to 15 ($k \leq 15$), which is backwards.

B. **Correct.** The sign is flipped from what is shown in the problem, but k is equal to or greater than 15.

C. Incorrect. Add 5 rather than subtract 5 from both sides of the inequality to isolate the variable.

D. Incorrect. Isolate the variable to solve the problem.

12)

A. Incorrect. To change a fraction to a percent, divide the numerator by the denominator and then multiply by 100. This answer results from dividing the denominator by the numerator.

B. **Correct.** $5 \div 8 = 0.625$ and $0.625 \times 100 = 62.5\%$.

C. Incorrect. This answer results from confusing the numerator (top number) and the denominator (bottom number), and forgetting to multiply by one hundred.

D. Incorrect. This answer results from correctly dividing the numerator by the denominator, but forgetting to multiply the answer by 100.

13)

A. Incorrect. Remember that 5^2 is equal to 5×5.

B. Incorrect. To solve the expression, use the order of operations. Step One: Solve the exponent in parenthesis. Step Two: Subtract the numbers in parenthesis. Step Three: Solve the exponents. Step Four: Add the numbers.

C. **Correct.** $529 + 27 = 556$

D. Incorrect. The answer resulted from the mistake of multiplying 3×3 rather than solving 3^3. Remember $3^3 = 3 \times 3 \times 3$.

14)

A. Incorrect. The images show the numerator increasing, not the denominator. If the denominator increases and the numerator remains constant $(\frac{1}{5}, \frac{1}{6}, \frac{1}{7}, \frac{1}{8})$, the fraction decreases.

B. **Correct.** The images show the numerator increasing while the denominator stays the same; meanwhile, the fraction is increasing.

C. Incorrect. When both the numerator and denominator increase, there are inconsistencies in the comparative size of the fraction.

D. Incorrect. If the numerator stays the same and the denominator decreases, the fraction will increase.

15)

A. **Correct.** To calculate the mean, add all the numbers in a set and divide by how many numbers are in the set. The mean number of nickels is $4 + 3 + 2 + 2 = 11$ divided by 4 (because there are 4 numbers in the set) $= 2.75$ nickels. The mean number of quarters is $0 + 5 + 4 + 1 = 10$ divided by $4 = 2.5$ quarters. $2.75 > 2.5$.

B. Incorrect. The mean of the pennies is $1 + 4 + 5 + 1 = 11$ divided by $4 = 2.75$. The mean number of quarters is $0 + 5 + 4 + 1 = 10$ divided by $4 = 2.5$. The mean number of pennies is equal to the mean number of quarters.

C. Incorrect. The range is the difference between the highest number and the lowest number in the set. For the dimes, the highest number is 3 and the lowest number is 2, so $3 - 2 = 1$. For the quarters, the highest number is 5 and the lowest number is 0. $5 - 0 = 5$, and $1 < 5$.

D. Incorrect. The mode for the set is 5; the median is a middle number in a set. The set of pennies in numerical order is {1, 1, 4, 5}. In this case, there are two numbers in the middle; therefore, averaging the one and the four will find the median. The median of the set of pennies is 2.5.

16)

A. Incorrect. The answer results from multiplying 3×0. Remember that $3^0 = 1$, not 0.

B. Incorrect. The first step in the equation is to solve the exponent.

C. Incorrect. The problem is not solved by multiplying 6×30.

D. **Correct.** Any number with a zero exponent equals one. Therefore, $6(3^0) = 6(1) = 6$.

17)

- A. Incorrect. One centimeter = 10 millimeters. The answer results from moving the decimal point two places and in the wrong direction.
- B. Incorrect. The answer results from moving the decimal point one place in the wrong direction.
- C. Incorrect. Millimeters are not equal to centimeters.
- D. **Correct.** One centimeter = 10 millimeters and $150 \times 10 = 1500$.

18)

- A. Incorrect. Pedro confuses the number of students who prefer vanilla with the number of students who prefer chocolate.
- B. **Correct.** Benjamin's bar graph indicates that 10 students prefer vanilla, 6 students prefer strawberry, and 23 students prefer chocolate ice cream.
- C. Incorrect. Nicole confuses the number of students who like vanilla with the number of students who like strawberry.
- D. Incorrect. Susan did not accurately count the tallies before making her bar graph.

19)

- A. Incorrect. The answer results from multiplying the last number in the set by two. Numbers in the set do not follow the pattern of multiplying by 2 because $2 \times 2 \neq 5$.
- B. Incorrect. Numbers in the set are not following a sequence that would match the answer.
- C. Incorrect. Numbers in the set are not following a sequence that would match the answer.
- D. **Correct.** The pattern follows the equation $3n - 1 = x$. $n =$ the last number in the set and $x =$ the next number in the set. Another pattern is adding by exponents of 3. Remember $3 \times 3 \times 3 \times 3 \times 3 = 3^5 = 243$. The pattern is $2 + 3^1 = 5$, $5 + 3^2 + 14$, $14 + 3^3 = 41$, $41 + 3^4 = 122$, $122 + 3^5 = 365$.

20)

- A. Incorrect. $3(8) + 7(8) = 24 + 56 \neq 10$.
- B. Incorrect. $3(8) + 7(8) = 24 + 56 \neq 21$.
- C. Incorrect. $3(8) + 7(8) = 24 + 56 \neq 31$.
- D. **Correct.** $3(8) + 7(8) = 24 + 56 = 80$. Or, put another way, $3x + 7x = 10x$ and $(10)(8) = 80$.

21)

- A. Incorrect. While 4 is in the thousands place, a 4 in that position is equal to four thousand.
- B. **Correct.** $654,123 = 600,000 + 50,000 + 4,000 + 100 + 20 + 3$.
- C. Incorrect. 5 is in the ten-thousands place.
- D. Incorrect. 4 is in the thousands place, not the ten-thousands place.

22)

- A. Incorrect. $y = 4 - x^2$ is a correct answer, but it's not the only correct answer. Substitute 1 for x and 3 for y.

  $3 = 4 - 1^2$

  $3 = 4 - 1$

  $3 = 3$

- B. Incorrect. $x^2 + y = 4$ is a correct answer, but it's not the only correct answer. Substitute 1 for x and 3 for y.

  $1^2 + 3 = 4$

  $1 + 3 = 4$

  $4 = 4$

- C. Incorrect. $x^2 + y = 2^2$ is a correct answer, but it's not the only correct answer. Substitute 1 for x and 3 for y.

  $1^2 + 3 = 2^2$

  $1 + 3 = 4$

  $4 = 4$

D. **Correct.** All of the above are correct. For each equation, replacing the variables with the numbers in the function table makes a true statement.

23)

A. Incorrect. Multiplying the rate by the distance does not find the time, so 20 hours cannot be the correct answer.

B. **Correct.** Time is distance divided by rate; 4000 mi/500 mph = 8 hours.

C. Incorrect. Adding the rate and the distance is not a way to find the time.

D. Incorrect. Subtracting the rate from the distance is a not a way to find the time.

24)

A. **Correct.** The total savings is equal to the number of weeks Justin works times $365/week profit.

B. Incorrect. The equation says that 400 times the total savings is equal to the business expenses times the number of weeks worked.

C. Incorrect. The weekly profit is not found by adding the number of weeks worked to the total savings.

D. Incorrect. The total number of weeks worked is not equal to the $365/week profit multiplied by the total savings.

25)

A. **Correct.** The equivalent expressions demonstrate the distributive property, which says that multiplication distributes over addition: $a(b + c) = ab + ac$.

B. Incorrect. The associative property states that multiplication or addition problems can be regrouped: $(ab)c = a(bc)$ or $(a + b) + c = a + (b + c)$.

C. Incorrect. The commutative property states that order does not matter when multiplying or adding: $ab = ba$ or $a + b = b + a$.

D. Incorrect. The multiplicative property states that both sides of the equation remain the same if they are multiplied by the same number; on the other hand, the distributive property says that multiplication distributes over addition.

26)

A. **Correct.** Using order of operations, the expression is solved using the steps.

B. Incorrect. In this expression, 5 is subtracted from $2m^3$.

C. Incorrect. In this expression, only 5 is cubed.

D. Incorrect. In this expression, only the parentheses are cubed.

27)

A. Incorrect. The relationship between x and $f(x)$ is $\neq$.

B. Incorrect. The relationship between x and $f(x)$ is $\neq +5$.

C. **Correct.** The relationship between x and $f(x)$ is $2x + 2$.

D. Incorrect. The relationship between x and $f(x)$ is $\neq 2x + 10$.

28)

A. Incorrect. The prime factorization of 9 is 3×3: there are no even factors.

B. Incorrect. The prime factorization of 21 is 3×7: there are no even numbers.

C. Incorrect. The prime factorization of 45 is $3 \times 3 \times 5$: there are no even numbers.

D. **Correct.** The prime factorization of 90 is $2 \times 3 \times 3 \times 5$. Ninety, as the only even number of the answer choices, has an even number (2) as a factor.

29)

A. Incorrect. 15 mm is the length of line segment $\overline{KL}$.

B. Correct. Line segment $\overline{MN}$ begins at 35 mm and ends at 70 mm, so 70 − 35 = 35 mm. Line segment $\overline{MN}$ is 35 mm. The length of line segment $\overline{KL}$ is 15 mm. To find out how much longer $\overline{MN}$ is than $\overline{KL}$, subtract, 35 mm − 15 mm = 20 mm.

C. Incorrect. 20 mm = 2 cm, not 2 mm.

D. Incorrect. 70 mm is where $\overline{MN}$ ends, 15 mm is the length of $\overline{KL}$, and 70 − 15 = 55; however the distance between L and M is ignored.

30)

A. Correct. 25 students score an "F" in science, and 70 students score an "A" in science; 2(25) < 70.

B. Incorrect. There are 170 students total with math grades. A majority would be more than half (85). Only 25 students score a "C" in math.

C. Incorrect. 40 students score a "B" in reading and 35 students score a "B" in math.

D. Incorrect. The graph does not include information about next year's students.

31)

A. Incorrect. 680 − 425 = 255, 255 ÷ 425 = .60, and .60 × 100 ≠ 40%.

B. Incorrect. 680 − 425 = 255, 255 ÷ 425 = .60, and .60 × 100 ≠ 55%.

C. Correct. To calculate the percent increase, find the difference between the ending number and the beginning number (680 − 425 = 255). Divide the difference by the beginning number (255 ÷ 425 = .60), and then multiply the decimal by 100 to change to a percentage (.60 × 100 = 60%).

D. Incorrect. 8680 − 425 = 255, 255 ÷ 425 = .60, and .60 × 100 ≠ 80%.

32)

A. Incorrect. $4.00 can buy 1 order of chicken strips.

B. Correct. To find out how many orders of chicken strips Jennifer and Noah can buy, use the equation:

$10 − 2($2.00 + $1.00) = x

$10 − 2($3.00) = x

$10 − $6.00 = $4.00

Four dollars is enough money to buy 1 order of chicken strips to share.

C. Incorrect. $4.00 is insufficient to buy 2 orders of chicken strips.

D. Incorrect. $4.00 is not enough money to buy 3 orders of chicken strips.

33)

A. Correct. To calculate the average, add all of the scores and divide by the total number of scores. Use the variable "x" in place of the missing score. (100 + 100 + 100 + x) ÷ 4 = 85

Isolate the variable. (300 + x) ÷ 4 = 85

Multiply both sides by 4. (300 + x) = 340

Subtract 300 from both sides. x = 40

B. Incorrect. If Lynn had scored 55%, her average would be 88.75% because 355 ÷ 4 = 88.75%.

C. Incorrect. If Lynn had scored 85%, her average would be 96.25% because 385 ÷ 4 = 96.25%.

D. Incorrect. If Lynn had scored 100%, her average would be 100% because 400 ÷ 4 = 100%.

34)

A. Incorrect. 2(150 − 6) ≠ 300 ÷ 12

2(144) ≠ 25

288 ≠ 25

B. Incorrect. (300 ÷ 4) ÷ 6 ≠ 300 ÷ 12

75 ÷ 6 ≠ 25

12.5 ≠ 25

C. Incorrect. (120 ÷ 6) + (180 ÷ 6) ≠ 300 ÷ 12

$20 + 30 \neq 300 \div 12$

$50 \neq 25$

D. **Correct.** $(120 \div 12) + (180 \div 12) = 300 \div 12$

$(10) + (15) = 25$

$25 = 25$

35)

A. Incorrect. $10 is insufficient change.

B. **Correct.** To estimate the amount of the change, round the price of each item to the nearest dollar amount and subtract from the total:

$50 − ($13 + $12 + $4 + $6)

$50 − $35 = $15

The correct answer is $15.

C. Incorrect. Adding the price of each item will equal approximately $35. To find out the amount of change, subtract $35 from $50.

D. Incorrect. $50 is the amount before any purchases are made.

36)

A. Incorrect. 9,299 ones = 9,299.

B. Incorrect. 903 tens = 9,030.

C. **Correct.** 93 hundreds = 9,300, and 9,300 is greater than the other answer choices.

D. Incorrect. because 9 thousands = 9,000.

37)

A. Incorrect. $0.305 = \frac{305}{1000}$.

B. **Correct.** $0.035 = \frac{35}{1000}$; notice the zero in the tenths place.

C. Incorrect. $0.35 = \frac{350}{1000}$.

D. Incorrect. $0.3 = \frac{300}{1000}$.

38)

A. Incorrect. One side is 2 mm long, but the shape has 10 sides.

B. Incorrect. Each of the 10 sides of this shape must be added to find the perimeter, not just the labeled sides.

C. Incorrect. There are 5 points to a star, but each point has 2 sides. While 5 × 2 mm = 10 mm, the lengths of all 10 sides must be added to get the perimeter.

D. **Correct.** There are 10 sides and each side is 2 mm in length. To find the perimeter, add the length of each side to find the total. P = 2 + 2 + 2 + 2 + 2 + 2 + 2 + 2 + 2 + 2 = 20 mm.

39)

A. Incorrect. 64 mm^2 is the area of the four small rectangles that protrudes on each side.

B. Incorrect. 16 mm^2 is the area of one of the small rectangles that protrudes on each side.

C. **Correct.** Find the area of the square as if it did not have cut-outs; each side would be 12 mm long. 12 mm × 12 mm = 144 mm^2. Next, subtract the area of the cut-outs from the total area of the square. The area of each cut-out is 2 mm × 2 mm = 4 mm^2. There are cut-outs in each of the 4 corners; therefore, multiply by 4; 4 × 4 = 16. Subtract the total area of the four cut-outs from the total area of the square without the cut-outs; 144 − 16 = 128 mm^2.

D. Incorrect. Subtracting 8 − 2 will not find the area of the shape.

40)

A. Incorrect. There are no rectangular faces on a pyramid.

B. Incorrect. There are no triangular faces on a cube.

C. Incorrect. There are no triangular faces on a rectangular prism.

D. **Correct.** A triangular prism has 2 triangular faces and 3 rectangular faces.

41)

A. Correct. The coefficients are the numbers before the exponent in a polynomial. The degrees are the exponents in a polynomial.

B. Incorrect. The number 1 is a constant in this polynomial; it is neither a coefficient nor a degree.

C. Incorrect. The degrees and coefficients are switched.

D. Incorrect. The degrees and coefficients are switched, and 1 is neither a coefficient nor a degree.

42)

A. Incorrect. Points in quadrant I have a positive x and a positive y coordinate.

B. Incorrect. Points in quadrant II have a negative x and a positive y coordinate.

C. Correct. Points in quadrant III have a negative x and a negative y coordinate.

D. Incorrect. Points in quadrant IV have a positive x and a negative y coordinate.

43)

A. Correct. The polygon is irregular and convex. A polygon is irregular if the sides and angles are not the same. In the trapezoid, the side on top is shorter than the bottom; therefore the trapezoid is irregular. Convex polygons have interior angles that are less than 180 degrees, which is true for this trapezoid.

B. Incorrect. This polygon is irregular, but it is not concave. Concave polygons have interior angles that are greater than 180 degrees. All interior angles in the trapezoid are less than 180 degrees.

C. Incorrect. The polygon is convex, but it is not regular. The trapezoid is not a regular polygon because all sides are not the same length.

D. Incorrect. The polygon is neither regular nor concave. Furthermore, all regular polygons are convex.

44)

A. Incorrect. The 3 has a difference of 2 place values and 2 place values are equal to 100.

B. Incorrect. The number 846,307 is about four times 209,023, but that is not what the question is asking. For this problem, only consider the digit 3 in each number.

C. Incorrect. If there is 1 place value difference between the digits, this would be the correct answer, but there are 2 place value differences between the digits.

D. Correct. In number one, the digit 3 represents 300. In number two, the digit 3 represents 3. $300 \div 3 = 100$.

45)

A. Incorrect. 10 oranges does not account for apples or bananas.

B. Incorrect. 30 apples does not account for oranges or bananas.

C. Incorrect. Bananas are not accounted for here.

D. Correct. 60 is the correct answer:
1. Assign variables.
   x = apples
   y = oranges
2. Write the ratios as fractions.
   apples/bananas = $\frac{3}{2} = \frac{x}{20}$.
   oranges/bananas = $\frac{1}{2} = \frac{y}{20}$.
3. Cross-multiply to solve.
   $60 = 2x$, $x = 30$ apples
   $2y = 20$, $y = 10$ oranges
4. To find the total, add the number of apples, oranges, and bananas together.
   $30 + 20 + 10 = 60$ pieces of fruit.

Go on

46)

A. Incorrect. Natural numbers used when counting. This number contains a repeating decimal.

B. Incorrect. Whole numbers are the set of natural numbers including zero.

C. Incorrect. Integers are positive or negative whole numbers and do not include repeating decimals.

D. **Correct.** This is a rational number. Rational numbers include fractions and repeating decimals.

47)

A. Incorrect. The total is never divided by the percent.

B. Incorrect. The percentage is never divided by the total.

C. **Correct.** To find a percentage, use a proportion: $15\%/100\% = x/1560$. Cross multiply: $100x = 1560 \times 15$. Isolate the variable by dividing both sides of the equation by 100: $x = 1560 \times 15/100$. $15/100$, expressed as a decimal, is 0.15.

D. Incorrect. This is part of the solution; do not forget to multiply by the percentage.

48)

A. Incorrect. -81 is the fifth term in the sequence. The question asks for the sixth term.

B. **Correct.** The difference between -9 and -36 is 27. $27 \times -3 = -81$. This is the fifth term in the set. To find the sixth term, find the difference between -81 and -36 (45). $45 \times -3 = -135$.

C. Incorrect. 135 is the opposite of the fifth term in the sequence.

D. Incorrect. 81 is the opposite sign of the correct answer. Remember that a positive number times a negative number gives a negative answer.

49)

A. Incorrect. t is not the dependent variable because the hours driven do not depend on the distance that is driven.

B. Incorrect. The rate of 75 mph is a constant and is neither a dependent nor an independent variable.

C. **Correct.** The distance that Kim travels depends on the number of hours Kim drives.

D. Incorrect. Distance is the dependent variable and can be calculated using the constant and the independent variable.

50)

A. **Correct.** To solve this problem, use a table to find some coordinates:

x	y
0	1
1	3
2	5

When plotting the coordinates on the graph, graph A is the only graph that has (0, 1), (1, 3), and (2, 5) as points on the line.

B. Incorrect. The line does not contain (0, 1), (1, 3), or (2, 5).

C. Incorrect. The line does not contain (0, 1), (1, 3), or (2, 5).

D. Incorrect. The line does not contain (0, 1), (1, 3), or (2, 5).

Curriculum, Instruction, and Assessment

1)

A. **Correct.** In order to solve order of operations expressions, students need an understanding of addition, subtraction, multiplication, division, and use of exponents.

B. Incorrect. Plotting functions on a graph relates to patterns and is not a prerequisite for order of operations.

C. Incorrect. Order of operations needs to be taught as a pre-algebra skill. Logarithms are taught in trigonometry.

D. Incorrect. Expanding binomials will be introduced in Algebra II, not pre-algebra.

2)

A. Incorrect. The number of green gumballs would only be relevant if there were no other colors besides green and red.

B. Incorrect. It does not matter how many colors there are if some are red and some are not.

C. **Correct.** It is important to know how many red gumballs there are since the class already knows how many gumballs there are in total.

D. Incorrect. This is irrelevant information.

3)

A. Incorrect. A rotation is a simple turn of objects in a plane.

B. **Correct.** Tessellations are patterns created through the tiling of polygons.

C. Incorrect. A reflection is a shape as it would be seen in a mirror.

D. Incorrect. Symmetry is equality in both shape and size on two sides of a plane.

4)

A. Incorrect. Before introducing problems with multiple steps, students require a basic understanding of how to calculate percentages.

B. Incorrect. This question is not appropriate as an introduction to percentages.

C. Incorrect. This question is not appropriate as an introduction to percentages.

D. **Correct.** This is a simple question about percentages that helps students understand the process of finding percentages without complicated calculations and multiple steps.

5)

A. **Correct.** Student A provides the correct response using the following steps:
1. Set up the problem: $\frac{5}{25} = \frac{x}{100}$
2. Cross multiply: $25x = 500$
3. Isolate the variable: $x = 20$

B. Incorrect. This answer is the number of total students.

C. Incorrect. This answer is the number of students attending the after-school program in the library.

D. Incorrect. This answer is the result of adding the total number of students (25) and to the number of students attending the after-school program (5).

6)

A. Incorrect. Student A reverses the tens and ones.

B. Incorrect. Student B does not understand that each bar represents ten.

C.	**Correct.** Student C understands that 24 is represented by two tens and four ones in the base-ten system.	B.	Incorrect. Multiplying decimals is not related to adding fractions.
D.	Incorrect. Student D needs to trade ten ones for a bar of tens to simplify the answer.	C.	**Correct.** Being able to find the least common multiple helps a student find an equivalent fraction with a common denominator.
		D.	Incorrect. Adding fractions is not a multi-step equation.

7)

A.	Incorrect. A line is a one-dimensional object.
B.	**Correct.** A triangle is a two-dimensional object.
C.	Incorrect. A cube is a three-dimensional object.
D.	Incorrect. A cylinder is a three-dimensional object.

11)

A.	Incorrect. Formative assessments are informal assessments used to guide instruction.
B.	Incorrect. Anecdotal records are informal observations.
C.	**Correct.** Standardized tests are formal assessments given to students in a specific way.
D.	Incorrect. Remediation is designed to fill gaps in learning through reteaching.

8)

A.	Incorrect. This model depicts an equation equal to 8.
B.	Incorrect. This model depicts an equation equal to 8.
C.	**Correct.** The 2 is represented by the squares, and the 4 represents the total number of stars. The variable x represents the number of stars per square when distributed evenly.
D.	Incorrect. This model depicts an equation equal to 16.

12)

A.	Incorrect. This would be the correct answer if the student was not making an error. The question asks for the incorrect answer that the student would get if the error pattern continues.
B.	Incorrect. This answer comes from the student adding ten to the ones column without reducing the tens column by one.
C.	**Correct.** This answer follows the error pattern. Rather than regrouping, the student is confusing the minuend and the subtrahend in the ones column.
D.	Incorrect. The answer adds instead of subtracts.

9)

A.	**Correct.** This graph shows that $x \geq 2$ by following the steps: $4x + 2 \geq 10$ $-2 -2$ $4x \geq 8$ $x \geq 2$
B.	Incorrect. This graph shows that $x \leq 3$.
C.	Incorrect. This graph shows that $x > 2$.
D.	Incorrect. This graph shows $x < 4$.

13)

A.	Incorrect. Students should grasp the concept of counting numbers before moving to negative numbers.
B.	Incorrect. Pictures are a representation. Students should

10)

A.	Incorrect. Simplifying exponents is not a step in adding fractions.

begin with concrete activities.

C. Incorrect. Numeral cards are abstract. Number cards are a representation.

D. **Correct.** Counters and toys are concrete objects.

14)

A. **Correct.** Equivalent fractions with common denominators must be used to add fractions. The LCM helps the student find the equivalent fraction.

B. Incorrect. Fractions can easily be added with unlike numerators, as long as they have common denominators.

C. Incorrect. Multiplying fractions does not require a common denominator.

D. Incorrect. Dividing fractions does not require a common denominator.

15)

A. **Correct.** Estimation allows students to use mental math to get an approximate answer.

B. Incorrect. The associative property addresses the way a multiplication or addition problem is grouped.

C. Incorrect. Ratios compare two things.

D. Incorrect. Probability calculates the likelihood that something will happen.

16)

A. Incorrect. The associative property is a part of order of operations and must be understood to master it.

B. Incorrect. The associative property may help with simplifying two-step equations.

C. **Correct.** The associative property addresses grouping addition or multiplication problems. To understand the associative property, students should know how to add and multiply.

D. Incorrect. While some associative property problems may involve fractions, most will involve whole numbers.

17)

A. Incorrect. The numerator, or top number of a fraction, represents a part of the whole.

B. **Correct.** The denominator, or bottom number of a fraction, represents the whole.

C. Incorrect. A whole number is not a fraction.

D. Incorrect. A natural number is not a fraction.

18)

A. Incorrect. Cartesian coordinates are used to graph on a plane, not a number line.

B. **Correct.** When graphing inequalities on a number line, students should understand positive and negative numbers, as well as the concept of zero.

C. Incorrect. Prime and composite numbers are used to calculate LCM and GCF.

D. Incorrect. Percentages would not be represented on a number line.

19)

A. **Correct.** The distributive property involves multiplying whole numbers.

B. Incorrect. The distributive property does not use division.

C. Incorrect. Whole numbers should be taught before multiplying by decimals.

D. Incorrect. The distributive property does not use division.

Go on →

20)

A. Incorrect. To find the perimeter, the sides should be added, not multiplied.

B. Incorrect. Jack is calculating the area of the triangle.

C. **Correct.** Perimeter is found by adding all sides of a shape.

D. Incorrect. Matthew seems to be attempting to calculate the area, but should not be using the hypotenuse of the triangle.

21)

A. Incorrect. Pounds and seconds are standard units of measure.

B. **Correct.** Pounds per second is the customary unit of measure for mass flow rate.

C. Incorrect. The metric unit of measure for weight is the kilogram.

D. Incorrect. Elapsed time is measured in hours, minutes, and seconds in the metric and customary systems.

22)

A. Incorrect. The average number of bus riders during a particular week does not provide enough information about the relationship between bus ridership and weather.

B. Incorrect. The number of rainy days does not matter.

C. Incorrect. The number of students who walk home from school is extraneous information.

D. **Correct.** The students need to know the average number of bus riders on rainy days and compare that quantity to the average number of bus riders on days with fair weather.

23)

A. Incorrect. Standardized tests are summative assessments.

B. Incorrect. Benchmark tests are summative assessments.

C. **Correct.** A ticket out the door is an informal, formative assessment.

D. Incorrect. End-of-unit assessments are summative assessments.

24)

A. **Correct.** Math symbols and numerals are abstract.

B. Incorrect. Drawing is a representation.

C. Incorrect. Dividing objects is concrete.

D. Incorrect. Using number cubes (dice) could be concrete or a representation, but not abstract.

25)

A. Incorrect. If the majority of the class understands fractions, they do not need to be retaught.

B. Incorrect. If only six students are struggling with a concept, it should not be retaught to the entire class.

C. Incorrect. Small group instruction would be the correct strategy, but this group is not struggling with multiplication.

D. **Correct.** The error the students are making is that they are adding, rather than multiplying, the numerator. If only six students have this problem, it should be retaught to the small group of students that need it.

Social Studies Practice

Content Knowledge

1

Which of the following events contributed to the United States' entry into World War II?

A. Germany's unrestricted submarine warfare
B. the attack on Pearl Harbor
C. the Battle of Britain
D. the Battle of the Bulge

2

Which of the following factors might contribute to inflation?

A. high interest rates and a low amount of printed currency
B. high unemployment rates
C. a decrease in supply and a low amount of printed currency
D. a decrease in supply and a large amount of printed currency

3

Luther and Barbara wanted to start a business in the engineering field. They were trying to decide between hiring one staff member and using the leftover money to purchase new inventory, or hiring two staff members to increase their marketing reach. These choices would be an example of

A. needs.
B. scarcity.
C. opportunity cost.
D. supply and demand.

4

Which of the following continents is located in both the Eastern and Western Hemispheres?

A. Europe
B. Africa
C. North America
D. A and B

5

Which of the following events is recognized as the beginning of the American Civil War?

A. the Battle of Palmito Ranch
B. the Battle of Fort Sumter
C. the Missouri Compromise
D. the Battle of Yorktown

6

Which of the following most contributed to the fall of the ancient Egyptians?

A. the death of Cleopatra
B. Alexander the Great conquering their land
C. severe droughts
D. Canaanite settlers entering Egypt

7

Which of the following is most likely a lasting influence ancient Romans had on modern society?

A. the development of direct democracy
B. the usage of columns in architecture
C. the development of republican democracy
D. literacy

8

Which of the following presidents was responsible for the New Deal?

A. Herbert Hoover
B. Rutherford Hayes
C. Franklin D. Roosevelt
D. Jimmy Carter

9

Which of the following is NOT a true statement about the ancient Greek civilization?

A. Men and women lived in different parts of a house.
B. They built aqueducts to carry water to public toilets.
C. Greek cities had an agora.
D. Socrates was a famous Greek philosopher.

10

Which of the following terms describes the economic principle of allowing industry to grow without any government intervention?

A. interdependence
B. free-market economy
C. communism
D. monopoly

11

Which of the following would be the most useful for studying population patterns within the state of Texas over a period of time?

A. a bar graph detailing population numbers over a period of 30 years
B. a map with the number of people living in different parts of Texas in the year 2000
C. a photograph showing how many people were at a state fair
D. a bar graph detailing population percentages compared with other states

12

Which of the following does NOT describe gender roles?

A. Gender roles feature behaviors considered appropriate for each sex by society, which generally acknowledges only male and female.

B. There is a consensus that gender roles are socially constructed.

C. Gender roles center on the ideas of masculinity and femininity.

D. Prevailing gender roles have been challenged.

13

Which of the following constitutional amendments is NOT considered part of the Bill of Rights?

A. the right to bear arms
B. the right to address witnesses arranged by the government when on trial
C. the right to equal protection under the law
D. freedom of speech

14

Antitrust law strengthens market forces to prevent monopolies. Which of the following terms best describes the implementation of antitrust law?

A. social regulation
B. economic regulation
C. health regulation
D. social security

15

Which of the following is NOT a responsibility of the executive branch?

A. approving laws
B. making laws
C. implementing laws
D. enforcing laws

16

Which of the following describes a significant effect of the depletion of the ozone layer?

A. people get darker skin
B. more UV rays enter the earth
C. increased skin cancer rates, build-up of greenhouse gases, and increased UV levels
D. increased build-up of greenhouse gases

17

Which of the following is a positive effect of urbanization?

A. increased tenement housing
B. sanitary conditions
C. political machines
D. increased employment opportunities

18

Asking citizens to be civil minded and independent and making the people as a whole sovereign is characteristic of

A. republicanism.
B. government.
C. economics.
D. communism.

19

Which of the following is an example of human geography?

A. studying climate

B. studying the spread of Christianity across the world

C. studying the effect of land features on animals and plants

D. studying continental movement over a period of time

20

A map of France shows a small box around Nice. Nice is portrayed in greater detail in a box at the bottom. Which of the following terms describes this box?

A. legend

B. inset

C. compass

D. insert

21

Which of the following did NOT contribute to the outbreak of the American Revolution?

A. the Boston Tea Party, in which colonists threw 298 chests of tea into the sea

B. Britain banning further westward expansion with the Proclamation of 1763

C. General Thomas Gage ordering troops to capture Thomas Jefferson and Samuel Adams

D. Charles Townshend taxing glass, oil, lead, and paint

22

Which of the following is an event that successfully ended the Cold War?

A. the August coup

B. the fall of the Berlin Wall

C. the Cuban missile crisis

D. the success of the Sputnik program

23

Which of the following established the concept of judicial review?

A. the John Peter Zenger trial

B. *Marbury v. Madison*

C. the Dred Scott case

D. the Scopes Monkey trial

24

Which of the following is an example of the separation of powers?

A. No members of Congress can serve in another branch of government.

B. The president cannot vote on legislation.

C. checks and balances

D. all of the above

25

Which of the following is a significant contribution of ancient China?

A. Mahjong

B. toothbrushes

C. gunpowder

D. the animal zodiac

26

Which of the following best exemplifies a global marketplace?

A. A US freelancer goes on vacation in Paris and does remote work for a US client.

B. A business in the United States orders parts from Taiwan, India, and Mexico, then assembles the final product in Germany.

C. A commercial website purchases inventory from China.

D. Appliances share a standardized electrical system.

27

Which of the following periods contributed to advancements of mathematics in ancient Greece?

A. the Classical period (500 – 336 BC)

B. the Early Bronze Age (2900 – 2000 BC)

C. the Hellenistic period (336 – 146 BC)

D. Archaic period (750 – 500 BC)

28

Which of the following is a responsibility of a citizen of the United States?

A. to treat others with kindness

B. to join after-school clubs

C. to suffer the consequences of breaking a law

D. to start a business

29

Fred wants to write a paper on Benjamin Franklin and his influence on science. He wants to include Franklin's theories about electricity. Which of the following resources should he use?

A. a chart depicting what devices used electricity after the invention of the lightbulb

B. an essay about the effects of lightning

C. a newspaper report on Franklin's many inventions

D. a draft of a scientific report Franklin wrote on electricity

30

Which of the following lands was acquired during the Louisiana Purchase?

A. the land roughly bordered by the Rocky Mountains, the Mississippi River, and the Rio Grande River

B. the land roughly bordered by the Rocky Mountains, the Mississippi River, and the northern border of modern day Texas

C. the land between the Rocky Mountains and the Mississippi River, and modern day Georgia

D. the land roughly bordered by the Rocky Mountains and the Mississippi River, including modern day New Mexico

Go on

31

Which of the following major events in US history led to a decline in immigration?

A. the Immigration Act of 1965
B. the Immigration Act of 1924 and the Great Depression
C. World War I, the Great Depression, and the Immigration Act of 1924
D. the Great Depression only

32

Which of the following was NOT a consequence of the scarcity of oil that led to the energy crisis in the 1970s?

A. The president urged US citizens to heat only one room in their homes in the winter.
B. The automotive industry suffered as Japan created more fuel-efficient vehicles.
C. Political leaders asked gas stations to close for one day a week.
D. Oil prices were high for most of the decade.

33

Which of the following were part of the New England colonies?

A. New York, Connecticut, and Massachusetts
B. Connecticut, Massachusetts, and New Hampshire
C. New Hampshire, Massachusetts, and New Jersey
D. New York, New Jersey, Pennsylvania, and Delaware

34

Which of the following is not a responsibility of the president of the United States?

A. setting foreign policy
B. writing legislations
C. delivering the State of the Union address
D. pardoning felons

35

A sign on the freeway indicates that you are 150 miles from the city of Pittsburgh. This shows your

A. absolute location.
B. physical geography.
C. geographic feature.
D. relative location.

36

Why did Congress pass the Neutrality Acts?

A. only to prevent the United States from loaning any money to nations at war
B. to help the United States have the best chance of winning a foreign war
C. to prevent the United States from engaging in civil war
D. to prevent direct and indirect US involvement in foreign conflict

37

Which of the following emerged during World War I?

A. penicillin
B. aircraft carriers
C. radar
D. nuclear power

38

Which of the following was a method people used to prevent risk of discovery when helping slaves escape through the Underground Railroad?

A. Escape routes were usually indirect in order to confuse pursuers.

B. Escape routes were usually direct to get slaves to freedom more quickly.

C. Children stayed with their mothers.

D. Information about routes was passed along by small notes.

39

Which of the following historical figures was a major architect of the US Constitution?

A. Thomas Jefferson
B. George Washington
C. James Madison
D. Patrick Henry

40

A student completes a research project on significant events of the American Revolution. Which of the following is an appropriate method to determine the credibility of the resources he or she has used to conduct research?

A. checking the author and date of research
B. reviewing website design and writing style
C. assuming all online resources are not credible
D. reviewing website design and domain name

41

Which of the following protects freedom of religion in the United States?

A. separation of powers
B. the First Amendment
C. power of eminent domain
D. popular sovereignty

42

Which of the following amendments prevents the government from quartering troops in private homes?

A. the Seventh Amendment
B. the Fourth Amendment
C. the Third Amendment
D. the Ninth Amendment

43

A project in which students research and explore significant contributions made by their community is an example of

A. questioning only
B. collaboration
C. data interpretation only
D. inquiry-based learning

44

Which of the following examples could be used to describe the theme of respect to elementary school students?

A. defending one's beliefs even when they are unpopular
B. paying a parking ticket
C. returning a library book on time
D. foregoing an opportunity to cut a line

45

Which of the following are considered geographical features on a map?

A. plains, plateaus, valleys, and mountains

B. continents, plateaus, cardinal directions, and mountains

C. bodies of water, plains, plateaus, and countries

D. plains, plateaus, areas depicting agricultural products, and mountains

46

Which of the following ideas from Thomas Hobbes influenced the US Constitution?

A. Individual rights should take priority over collective rights.

B. People should give up some of their rights and form a government to ensure order in society.

C. Communism is the only way to govern people.

D. People should create a utopia to avoid the evils of government.

47

Which of the following is considered a negative consequence of the Civil War?

A. sharecropping in the South

B. the South was forgiven for leaving the Union

C. adding amendments to the Constitution to address equal protection for people under the law

D. the Union helped the South rebuild roads and farms

48

Which of the following statements best describes Reconstruction in the US after the Civil War?

A. Debates over legalizing slavery in the US were ongoing.

B. During its military occupation of the South, the Union developed Black Codes to appease disaffected Southern aristocrats who had lost slaves.

C. Northern troops occupied the South to ensure that laws were being followed, and to help reunite the country after the Civil War.

D. President Lincoln led Reconstruction efforts.

49

Which of the following is true about the Trail of Tears?

A. The Trail of Tears drove Native Americans to Indian Territory (later, Oklahoma) because white settlers no longer required their assistance in agricultural production.

B. Removal treaties were enacted fairly and peacefully.

C. The Indian Removal Act of 1831 began the forced relocation of Native Americans that year.

D. The Cherokee Nation was forced to give up land east of the Mississippi River during Andrew Jackson's presidency.

50

The framers instituted a system of checks and balances because they were concerned about

- A. one branch of government gaining too much power.
- B. mob rule.
- C. the military taking over the government.
- D. the states overpowering the national government.

Curriculum, Instruction, and Assessment

1

A teacher reads a biography about Harriet Tubman, a slave who helped others escape to freedom via the Underground Railroad. Which of the following would be most relevant to have students consider in a discussion about citizenship?

A. honesty
B. courage
C. responsibility
D. love

2

Students in fourth grade are studying a map of the Nile during ancient Egyptian times and answering questions related to landmarks and places. Which of the following social studies skills is being assessed in this exercise?

A. understanding spatial relationships
B. understanding historical timelines
C. using topographical maps
D. understanding physical geography

3

Which of the following graphic organizers would help students compare and contrast Greek and Roman culture?

A. a KWL chart
B. a spider map
C. a tally chart
D. a Venn diagram

4

Which of the following is a primary reason for a teacher to discuss authority figures with students?

A. to teach them that they must obey authorities
B. to help them understand the role of an authority figure in government and how to assess whether a candidate is appropriate for that role
C. to help students understand why they should follow direction from their teachers
D. to prepare students to fill positions of authority in the future

5

Third-grade students are studying the history of their state. Which of the following would be considered a primary source on the topic?

A. a textbook chapter detailing major landmarks of the state
B. a letter from a previous resident of the state describing his or her experiences to a friend in another state
C. an interview in a newspaper with the owner of a new local restaurant
D. a chart outlining population patterns over a period of 50 years

6

Which of the following lessons helps students develop an understanding of a market economy?

A. Students explore economic competition in their area and identify local business competitors.

B. Students explore making smart buying decisions by comparing prices of goods.

C. Students work together to decide what is necessary to rebuild a community.

D. Students explore how individuals generate income.

7

Half of a class does not understand the concept of supply and demand. Which of the following lessons would be the most appropriate to re-teach this concept?

A. asking students to study varied economics-related vocabulary for a mid-unit test

B. teaching the same lesson students were initially exposed to

C. rephrasing the definition of supply and demand, then providing students with different examples and restating why the laws of supply and demand are important to economics

D. moving on to another concept and hoping that repeated exposure to the words will help the students gain an understanding of the issue

8

Which of the following would be best assessed using an analytic rubric?

A. the overall quality of a student's assignment

B. appropriate use of vocabulary in an assignment

C. a student's understanding of the causes and consequences of the major battles of World War I

D. student performance based on a student's understanding of the aftermath of World War I and its influence on World War II

9

Which of the following describes the most appropriate method for assessing a student's knowledge of the names and dates of major battles of the Civil War?

A. a multiple-choice test

B. a research report

C. a debate

D. a portfolio

10

Which of the following would be the most appropriate lesson for teaching the concept of communication?

A. studying the impact of bullying in school

B. studying how communities use transportation to move from place to place

C. studying the reasons for migration

D. studying how leaders are elected in the United States

11

Which of the following would be the most appropriate question for students to consider in preparing a debate on industrialization?

A. What were the major inventions of the Industrial Revolution?

B. Which invention created during the Industrial Revolution influenced society the most?

C. Why did the Industrial Revolution happen?

D. What factors contributed to poor living conditions for workers during the Industrial Revolution?

12

Which of the following would NOT be an effective way to create a democratic classroom?

A. The teacher is the only member of the class who is allowed to create rules for the classroom.

B. Students test out different classroom routines and vote on which one they think is the most effective.

C. Students choose to rotate classroom responsibilities on a weekly basis, such as cleaning desks and marking attendance.

D. At the end of a unit, students fill out a feedback form detailing what they thought was effective and suggestions on how to improve lessons in the classroom.

13

A teacher shows students a diary entry by a Confederate soldier during the Civil War and a textbook chapter about the Battle of Gettysburg. He then asks students to look at each source and choose which one they would use to help determine what happened during the Battle of Gettysburg. Which of the following best describes the purpose of the activity?

A. teaching students how to look for facts in a secondary source

B. helping students understand the different reasons to use primary and secondary resources and how both can help students gain a better understanding of the topic studied

C. helping students to understand the significance of the Battle of Gettysburg

D. helping students develop reading comprehension skills

14

Which of the following is an appropriate unit of study for students learning human geography in the upper elementary grades?

A. studying volcanoes around the world

B. comparing and contrasting differences in state laws

C. studying the New York City subway system and how it links people and places

D. studying successful, local, small businesses

15

Which of the following would be the most effective method to teach students about voting?

A. Students read a book about the drafting of the US Constitution.

B. Students read a document about antipathy in the South toward the Union during the Reconstruction period.

C. Students learn about why a president can only serve for two terms.

D. Students follow news about the current presidential election and discuss the importance of developing an informed opinion on each candidate.

16

A fourth-grade teacher is planning a lesson on the theme of interdependence. Which of the following activities would be the most appropriate to introduce to students?

A. Students identify what they ate for lunch.

B. Students identify different jobs in the school.

C. Students draw pictures of items found in the classroom.

D. Students name several businesses in the community that produce goods or provide a service, and identify how they rely on other goods and services.

17

Which of the following is true when teaching students to evaluate sources?

A. Students should only consider internet sources.

B. Students need to determine the credibility and contemporaneity of the source.

C. Students in the lower elementary grades should only look at secondary sources.

D. Students can include biased resources in their research.

18

A teacher is grading student essays on the types of inventions they thought were the most significant in the twentieth century. Which of the following responses would demonstrate a student's ability in drawing conclusions?

A. The student identifies the printing press as a significant invention and states that it helped to increase communication around the world

B. The student identifies the computer as the most significant invention of the twentieth century.

C. The student identifies the automobile as the most significant twentieth-century invention because it allowed people to travel farther in less time.

D. The student discusses why the twentieth century was the best time for inventions.

19

An elementary school teacher plans to take her students on a field trip to a candy factory. Which of the following units in the social studies curriculum would best accompany this activity?

A. Power, Authority, and Governance

B. Individuals, Groups, and Institutions

C. Civics: Ideals and Practices

D. Production, Distribution, and Consumption

20

Which of the following questions addresses the theme of Power, Authority, and Governance found in the National Curriculum Standards for Social Studies?

A. Why do oil prices fluctuate?

B. How is the system of checks and balances maintained?

C. How can I become a more informed voter?

D. Where were the major battles of the American Revolution?

21

Which of the following would be the most appropriate resource for a lesson on the aftermath of Germany after World War I?

A. a description of the Treaty of Versailles

B. a photograph of Adolf Hitler

C. a chart detailing the total deaths of soldiers from different countries

D. a video of the first nuclear explosion

22

A formative assessment in the middle of a unit on rainforests reveals that a student believes them to be located in both North America and Europe. What is the most appropriate next step the teacher should take?

A. The teacher should give an oral quiz on rainforest facts.

B. The teacher should ask the student to identify plants commonly found in the rainforest.

C. The teacher should show the student a map of rainforests around the world.

D. The teacher should teach a lesson on boreal forests.

23

A social studies class is studying the laws of supply and demand in economics. The teacher asks the students to look at a supply and demand curve to determine the relationship between oil and gas prices over a month. According to Bloom's Taxonomy, which of the following levels of thinking must students use to accomplish this activity?

A. knowledge

B. application

C. synthesis

D. analysis

24

Which of the following activities would be the most appropriate for students in understanding the unique features of their community?

A. learning about local resources
B. mapping out historical landmarks in their community
C. mapping out the number of banks in their community
D. learning about the different types of chain stores in their community

25

A teacher overhears a US-born student repeating a derogatory term for undocumented immigrants. Which of the following class activities would best reinforce the civic value of tolerance while communicating the relevance of history to students' lives today?

A. studying discrimination against Irish immigrants in the nineteenth and early twentieth century
B. a lesson about the economic contributions of temporary seasonal workers who have historically crossed the border from Mexico into Texas and the Southwest to work on farms
C. a class discussion about Chinese New Year, followed by refreshments
D. a class debate about immigration issues in the United States today

Answer Key

Content Knowledge

1)

A. Incorrect. Unrestricted submarine warfare occurred in 1917, during World War I.

B. **Correct.** On December 7, 1941, Japan bombed Pearl Harbor, hoping to prevent the US from interfering with its intent to invade Southeast Asia and other territories such as Guam and Hong Kong.

C. Incorrect. The 1940 Battle of Britain was the first major battle of World War II; the US was still technically a neutral party (although it was effectively supporting Britain through the Lend-Lease Act).

D. Incorrect. The Battle of the Bulge took place after the United States entered World War II.

2)

A. Incorrect. High interest rates and a low amount of printed currency usually contribute to deflation.

B. Incorrect. High unemployment rates do not lead to price increases.

C. Incorrect. A decrease in supply and a low amount of printed currency usually contribute to deflation.

D. **Correct.** Inflation occurs when prices increase. Both of these factors contribute to inflation.

3)

A. Incorrect. This situation describes a choice, not a need, which is something a person absolutely requires.

B. Incorrect. Scarcity refers to situations when there is not enough supply to meet demand, which does not apply to this situation.

C. **Correct.** Opportunity cost refers to the cost of the loss of one option when it is rejected for another (in this case, if Luther and Barbara choose to hire one staff member, they lose the marketing potential another employee would make possible, whereas if they choose to hire two, they lose the leftover money).

D. Incorrect. Supply and demand refers to the number of goods and their demand, which isn't the case here.

4)

A. Incorrect. The Eastern and Western Hemispheres are divided by the Prime Meridian, which intersects the European countries of the United Kingdom, France, and Spain. Furthermore, Ireland and Portugal are located in the Western Hemisphere, so Europe is indeed in both hemispheres. However, there is a better answer choice.

B. Incorrect. The Eastern and Western Hemispheres are divided by the Prime Meridian, which intersects the African countries of Algeria, Mali, Burkina Faso, Togo, and Ghana. Furthermore, Morocco, Western Sahara, Mauritania, Senegal, the Gambia, Guinea, Guinea-Bissau, Sierra Leone, Liberia, Côte d'Ivoire, and Cape Verde are located in the Western Hemisphere, so Africa is indeed in both hemispheres. However, there is a better answer choice.

C. Incorrect. North America is located entirely in the Western Hemisphere, which is divided from the Eastern Hemisphere by the Prime Meridian and the 180th Meridian.

D. **Correct.** Europe and Africa are located in both the Eastern and Western Hemispheres.

5)

A. Incorrect. The Battle of Palmito Ranch, the final encounter between Union and Confederate forces, is considered the end of the Civil War.

B. **Correct.** On April 12, 1861, the Confederate army attacked the Union-controlled Fort Sumter in Charleston, South Carolina, triggering the US Civil War.

C. Incorrect. The Missouri Compromise, also known as the Compromise of 1820, contributed to divisions between the North and the South; however the war did not begin until 1861.

D. Incorrect. The Battle of Yorktown was the last battle of the American Revolution.

6)

A. **Correct.** After Cleopatra's death, ancient Egypt became part of the Roman Empire.

B. Incorrect. The Egyptians welcomed him, and the new administration was based on an Egyptian model.

C. Incorrect. Severe droughts started in 2200 B.C.

D. Incorrect. The Canaanite settlers accepted Egyptian governance.

7)

A. Incorrect. Athenian democracy is the first known example of direct democracy; furthermore, the Romans did not practice this form of government.

B. Incorrect. The Greeks developed columns; the Romans adopted them.

C. **Correct.** Before it was an empire, Rome was a republic led by senators elected to the Senate.

D. Incorrect. The earliest known written language is cuneiform, developed by the Sumerians.

8)

A. Incorrect. President Hoover was president during the Great Depression.

B. Incorrect. Rutherford Hayes served from 1877 to 1881.

C. **Correct.** Franklin D. Roosevelt supported laws that helped those unemployed and impoverished due to the Great Depression.

D. Incorrect. Jimmy Carter served from 1977 to 1981.

9)

A. Incorrect. In ancient Greece, women lived in the back and upstairs part of the house, away from men.

B. **Correct.** The ancient Romans, not the ancient Greeks, built aqueducts and developed public toilets.

C. Incorrect. An agora was a central marketplace where the ancient Greeks could meet and conduct business.

D. Incorrect. Socrates was a Greek philosopher whose thinking was the foundation for later Greek and much modern Western philosophical thought.

10)

A. Incorrect. Interdependence describes the circumstances in which economic actors rely on each other to meet their needs.

B. **Correct.** In a free-market economy, the prices of goods and services are determined by sellers and consumers.

C. Incorrect. Communism is an economic and social system in which resources are collectively owned.

D. Incorrect. When one business dominates an entire industry, it holds a monopoly.

11)

A. **Correct.** A bar graph that features the population over a number of years would help researchers analyze population patterns.

B. Incorrect. While a population map may help, it only details one year; more information is needed to analyze population patterns.

C. Incorrect. This photograph does not indicate the population in the whole of Texas.

D. Incorrect. Researchers would use this to compare the population of Texas with that of other states.

12)

A. Incorrect. Gender roles are behavioral norms that influence human behavior.

B. **Correct.** There is debate over the degree to which gender is defined by physical features, social and cultural expectations, or both.

C. Incorrect. Femininity and masculinity are the main concepts of gender.

D. Incorrect. Notions of gender roles, gender identity, and inequality continue to be debated in public discourse.

13)

A. Incorrect. The Second Amendment guarantees the right to bear arms.

B. Incorrect. The Sixth Amendment states that the people have a right to confront witnesses arranged by the government.

C. **Correct.** The Bill of Rights is composed of the first ten amendments. The Fourteenth Amendment guarantees equal protection under the law.

D. Incorrect. The First Amendment ensures freedom of speech, religion, and assembly; the right to petition the government; and freedom of the press.

14)

A. Incorrect. Social regulations deal with how businesses behave, such as prohibiting harmful behaviors.

B. **Correct.** Antitrust law breaks up monopolies to allow fair competition within the economy.

C. Incorrect. Any health regulations would be classified as social regulation.

15)

A. Incorrect. The executive branch has the power to approve laws—the president signs or vetoes a bill once it has passed through Congress.

B. Correct. While the executive branch can approve them, only Congress can make laws.

C. Incorrect. The executive branch has the power to implement laws.

D. Incorrect. The executive branch has the power to enforce laws, and federal law enforcement agencies are part of the executive branch.

16)

A. Incorrect. This is not a significant effect.

B. Incorrect. More UV rays do enter the earth, but there are more significant effects of ozone layer depletion.

C. Correct. All of these are consequences of the depletion of the ozone layer.

D. Incorrect. An increase in build-up of greenhouse gases is not the only significant effect of ozone layer depletion.

17)

A. Incorrect. Tenement housing created poor living conditions due to its unsanitary conditions.

B. Incorrect. Diseases were common because of rapid population increases and poor living conditions.

C. Incorrect. Corrupt politicians would provide services to immigrants only if people voted for them.

D. Correct. Urbanization itself is the development of urban areas due to the arrival of job seekers; employment opportunities are themselves pull factors.

18)

A. Correct. Republicanism also stresses natural rights as central values.

B. Incorrect. There are many forms of government that do not necessarily welcome a civil-minded or independent populace.

C. Incorrect. Economics is the study of the production and consumption of wealth.

D. Incorrect. Communism stresses that all property is owned publicly by a classless society.

19)

A. Incorrect. Studying climate only addresses the earth's physical processes.

B. Correct. Human geography studies the relationship between humans and the physical world; studying how Christianity spread worldwide would need to address this relationship.

C. Incorrect. Studying the effect of land features on animals and plants does not address humans and so is physical geography.

D. Incorrect. Studying the movement of continents is an example of physical geography.

20)

A. Incorrect. A legend explains the symbols on a map.

B. Correct. An inset features details that are considered important on a map.

C. Incorrect. A compass depicts the cardinal and intermediate directions on a map.

D. Incorrect. As insert is not a cartographic feature.

21)

A. Incorrect. Colonists were enraged that Britain adjusted the Tea Act to benefit the Crown.

B. Incorrect. The Great Proclamation was at odds with colonial desire for expansion.

C. **Correct.** While troops were ordered to capture Samuel Adams, they were not asked to capture Thomas Jefferson.

D. Incorrect. The Chancellor of the Exchequer imposed these duties in 1767.

22)

A. **Correct.** This 1991 event in which members of the Soviet government attempted to take control from Mikhail Gorbachev contributed to the dissolution of the USSR, effectively ending the Cold War.

B. Incorrect. The fall of the Berlin Wall dissolved communism in Germany.

C. Incorrect. The Cuban missile crisis was in 1962, at the height of the Cold War.

D. Incorrect. This event happened at the height of the Cold War.

23)

A. Incorrect. This colonial trial helped to establish the freedom of the press in the United States.

B. **Correct.** This case established judicial review.

C. Incorrect. Dred Scott was a slave who sued for his freedom; the case did not establish judicial review.

D. Incorrect. This trial revolved around the question of teaching evolution in schools.

24)

A. Incorrect. Members of Congress can only serve in one branch of government during their term; however, all of the options presented are also applicable.

B. Incorrect. The president can only sign or veto legislation. He or she cannot vote on it in Congress; the executive branch is separate from the legislative branch. However, this is not the best answer choice.

C. Incorrect. Checks and balances show the importance of the separation of powers; no one part of the government controls decision making. However, there is a better answer choice here.

D. **Correct.** All choices are different examples of the separation of powers.

25)

A. Incorrect. Although this was an ancient Chinese invention, it was not a significant one.

B. Incorrect. The toothbrush was invented by the ancient Egyptians.

C. **Correct.** Gunpowder is one of the most important inventions of ancient China.

D. Incorrect. Although the animal zodiac was an ancient Chinese invention, it is not as globally significant as gunpowder.

26)

A. Incorrect. The freelancer is still a resident of the United States; despite the freelancer's location, he or she is exchanging services within the US market, not internationally.

B. **Correct.** A global marketplace involves the exchange of goods and labor around the world.

C. Incorrect. It is unclear where the commercial website is based, so it is unclear whether the purchase is international.

27)

A. Incorrect. The Classical period is most known for its development of the principles of democracy.

B. Incorrect. The early Bronze Age is most known for its invention of bronze.

C. **Correct.** This period in time saw advancements such as the Pythagorean Theorem and the calculation of the circumference of the earth.

D. Incorrect. The Archaic period is most known for its development in pottery and sculpture.

28)

A. Incorrect. While being kind is likely to help a citizen strengthen personal relationships, it is not his or her responsibility.

B. Incorrect. Joining after-school clubs is voluntary.

C. **Correct.** Citizens have a responsibility to understand laws and pay the consequences if they break them.

D. Incorrect. Starting a business can help a citizen generate wealth, but it is voluntary.

29)

A. Incorrect. This example does not address Franklin's thoughts on electricity.

B. Incorrect. An essay about the effects of lightning does not address Franklin's thoughts on electricity unless he wrote it himself, and it is not clear from this example that he did.

C. Incorrect. A newspaper report on Franklin's inventions is a secondary resource that only talks about Franklin's inventions, not his thoughts on electricity.

D. **Correct.** This is a primary resource that delves into the thought process behind Franklin's theories on electricity.

30)

A. Incorrect. The Louisiana Purchase did not include land as far south as the Rio Grande; this territory (mainly Texas) belonged to Spain.

B. **Correct.** Napoleon sold this section of land in 1803 to finance his European wars.

C. Incorrect. Georgia was not included in the Louisiana Purchase; it was one of the original colonies and first states.

D. Incorrect. New Mexico was not part of the Louisiana Purchase; the Southwest was controlled by Spain at the time.

31)

A. Incorrect. The Immigration Act of 1965 encouraged more immigration in order to attract skilled labor and reunite families.

B. **Correct.** Both the Immigration Act of 1924 and the Great Depression discouraged immigration to the United States.

C. Incorrect. World War I did not contribute to declining immigration.

D. Incorrect. This was only one contributing factor to declining immigration; furthermore, it was a global event not isolated to the United States. There is a better answer choice.

32)

A. **Correct.** The British prime minister recommended limiting heat usage in winter; the US president did not.

B. Incorrect. The US automotive industry slowed down because it produced larger cars that required more fuel.

C. Incorrect. In an effort to limit overwhelming lines at gas pumps and to conserve gasoline, political leaders asked that gas stations close for one day a week.

D. Incorrect. Scarcity (in this case, oil scarcity) results in higher demand and thus higher prices.

33)

A. Incorrect. New York was not part of the New England colonies.

B. **Correct.** All three were part of the New England colonies.

C. Incorrect. New Jersey was not part of the New England colonies.

D. Incorrect. These were all part of the Middle Colonies.

34)

A. Incorrect. The president has the Senate's consent to carry out foreign policy.

B. **Correct.** The president is responsible for enforcing law, not creating it.

C. Incorrect. The president periodically reports on the state of the nation, in what has become known as the annual State of the Union address.

D. Incorrect. Presidents can pardon felons convicted of federal crimes.

35)

A. Incorrect. Absolute location refers to a specific location based on geographic coordinates.

B. Incorrect. Physical geography is the study of the earth's natural processes, not location.

C. Incorrect. A geographical feature refers to a location's physical features.

D. **Correct.** Relative location refers to the location of a place relative to another, in this case Pittsburgh.

36)

A. Incorrect. This stipulation was only part of the Neutrality Act.

B. Incorrect. The Neutrality Acts were meant to prevent US involvement in foreign wars.

C. Incorrect. The Neutrality Acts were meant to keep the United States out of foreign wars.

D. **Correct.** The purpose of the Neutrality Acts was to prevent direct and indirect US interference in armed conflict overseas.

37)

A. Incorrect. Penicillin was discovered and used during World War II.

B. **Correct.** The first time an airplane flew from a ship was in 1912.

C. Incorrect. Radar was developed and used during World War II.

D. Incorrect. Nuclear power was developed, weaponized, and used during the Second World War.

38)

A. **Correct.** Routes were indirect to thwart pursuers chasing escapees and their allies.

B. Incorrect. Direct routes posed too great a risk; pursuers could more easily catch fugitives.

C. Incorrect. Sometimes children were separated because they were unable to keep up with their groups; furthermore, women were rarely able to escape the plantation unnoticed.

D. Incorrect. Information was transmitted verbally in an effort to maintain confidentiality.

Go on

39)

A. Incorrect. Jefferson drafted the Declaration of Independence.

B. Incorrect. Washington was the commander-in-chief of the Continental Army during the American Revolution and later became the first president of the United States.

C. Correct. Madison not only advocated for the ratification of the Constitution; he had also helped to write the Federalist Papers.

D. Incorrect. Henry was an anti-Federalist who opposed the ratification of the Constitution.

40)

A. Correct. Checking the author and date of research helps to determine if the information is credible and up-to-date.

B. Incorrect. Website design and writing style may provide indications as to the credibility of a source, but they alone do not determine legitimacy.

C. Incorrect. There are many credible online resources.

D. Incorrect. A domain name can indicate the legitimacy of a source, but website design is not always indicative of a credible source.

41)

A. Incorrect. Separation of powers is meant to prevent any one branch—executive, legislative, or judicial—from dominating government.

B. Correct. The First Amendment protects freedom of religion as well as freedom of speech, assembly, the press, and the right of the people to petition the government.

C. Incorrect. Eminent domain refers to the government's ability to seize private property for public use in certain situations. According to the Fifth Amendment, private property cannot be taken for public use without proper compensation.

D. Incorrect. Popular sovereignty is the concept that government is a social contract, legitimized only by the consent of the people.

42)

A. Incorrect. The Seventh Amendment states that civil cases may be tried by a jury.

B. Incorrect. The Fourth Amendment protects citizens from searches and seizures without a warrant.

C. Correct. The Third Amendment forbids the government from quartering troops in homes, an abuse suffered by Americans under British rule.

D. Incorrect. The Ninth Amendment states that citizens may enjoy rights other than those outlined in the Constitution, and that the Constitution does not override those rights.

43)

A. Incorrect. Questioning is only one aspect of inquiry-based learning. This project asks students to draw conclusions as well.

B. Incorrect. The description of this project does not specify whether the students work in groups.

C. Incorrect. This project involves data interpretation, but it requires other steps as well.

D. Correct. In inquiry-based learning, students gather relevant sources and interpret them in order to develop their own conclusions.

44)

A. Incorrect. Defying unpopularity exhibits courage, a theme of citizenship.

B. Incorrect. Paying a parking ticket is a responsibility, an element of citizenship.

C. Incorrect. It is responsible to return a library book on time; responsibility applies to citizenship.

D. **Correct.** Respect, another aspect of citizenship, involves taking into consideration the feelings of others.

45)

A. **Correct.** Geographical features depict the physical aspects of a place on a map.

B. Incorrect. Cardinal directions are not considered geographical features.

C. Incorrect. Countries are considered political features.

D. Incorrect. Agricultural products are not considered a geographical feature.

46)

A. Incorrect. Hobbes believed in collective rights; otherwise, he believed, individuals would only address their own needs, to the detriment of others.

B. **Correct.** Hobbes advocated for governments to create and ensure social order.

C. Incorrect. Hobbes believed that a monarchy was the best way to govern people.

D. Incorrect. Hobbes believed that people were naturally negative, and that a utopia would be impossible to construct.

47)

A. **Correct.** Sharecropping enabled landowners in the South to maintain control of former slaves.

B. Incorrect. Forgiving the South for their actions helped to unite the nation as a whole.

C. Incorrect. Equal protection as addressed in the Fourteenth Amendment was a positive outcome of the Civil War.

D. Incorrect. Rebuilding the South benefitted the country as a whole.

48)

A. Incorrect. Slavery was illegal according to the Thirteenth Amendment of the United States Constitution, of which ratification was a requirement for readmission into the Union.

B. Incorrect. Southern governments developed Black Codes in an effort to continue oppression of freed black Americans.

C. **Correct.** During Reconstruction, there were efforts to rebuild the devastated South, which was under Union military occupation following the Civil War.

D. Incorrect. While Lincoln did make some plans for Reconstruction, he died before he had a chance to implement them.

49)

A. Incorrect. White settlers wanted to grow cotton on Native American land themselves; they never employed Native American workers.

B. Incorrect. President Jackson and the government frequently ignored the legal rights of Native Americans.

C. Incorrect. The Indian Removal Act was passed in 1831, but the forced migration of the Cherokee and other tribes did not occur that year.

D. **Correct.** This series of incidents happened in 1838 and 1839.

50)

A. **Correct.** The purpose of checks and balances was to prevent tyranny in any branch of the government.

B. Incorrect. While there was some concern among the founders about the dangers of a pure democracy, checks and balances do not address the relationship between the government and the people.

C. Incorrect. Separation of powers kept the military in check. Also, with a civilian commander in chief, the military remains accountable to civilian authority.

D. Incorrect. Checks and balances do not refer to the relationship between the state and national governments.

Curriculum, Instruction, and Assessment

1)

A. Incorrect. Honesty is not the main theme of Harriet Tubman's story.

B. **Correct.** Harriet Tubman showed extreme courage when she returned to the South at great personal risk to help enslaved people escape.

C. Incorrect. Tubman took on great responsibility, but it is not the main theme of her story.

D. Incorrect. While Tubman likely had a personal love for freedom and compassion for enslaved persons, students should understand that love is not necessarily applicable to citizenship.

2)

A. **Correct.** Introducing maps allows students to acquire an understanding of the world around them. They can use this knowledge to create their own maps.

B. Incorrect. Studying maps does not help a student understand historical timelines.

C. Incorrect. Using a topographical map involves studying elevation.

D. Incorrect. Since the students are focusing on landmarks and since the map is specific to ancient Egypt, it is reasonable to assume that the students are studying human, not only physical, geography.

3)

A. Incorrect. A KWL chart outlines what the students know or want to learn about a given topic.

B. Incorrect. A spider map expands on a given topic; it does not compare and contrast two topics or concepts.

C. Incorrect. A tally chart simply tallies a number of different categories.

D. **Correct.** A Venn diagram can help students identify a given topic's similarities and differences.

4)

A. Incorrect. Students should not be taught to blindly obey authorities; rather, they must develop a critical understanding of an authority figure's purpose in society.

B. **Correct.** Understanding the role of an elected official helps students understand what is demanded of a person to take on that role and to understand the responsibilities of voters in electing public officials.

C. Incorrect. Students should learn the roles and responsibilities of all authority figures, not just teachers.

D. Incorrect. Understanding authority figures does not mean students must fill those roles.

5)

A. Incorrect. A textbook includes reported information, so it is a secondary source.

B. **Correct.** Such a letter is a primary source because it offers a firsthand account of a set of circumstances.

C. Incorrect. A newspaper article is a secondary source because it is a secondhand account of events.

D. Incorrect. Data like population patterns is considered a secondary source because it is reported information.

6)

A. **Correct.** Competition in business is an aspect of the market economy.

B. Incorrect. This would be an appropriate lesson for opportunity cost.

C. Incorrect. This would be an appropriate lesson on taxes or communities.
D. Incorrect. This would be an appropriate lesson on wealth and income.

7)
A. Incorrect. Re-teaching a concept does not involve any other topics.
B. Incorrect. Repeating the same lesson twice does not address what confused the students in the first place.
C. Correct. When re-teaching a concept, the teacher should break down what confused students and restate learning targets and learning objectives.
D. Incorrect. Moving on in a unit does not address student needs, and students who do not understand may fall further behind.

8)
A. Incorrect. An analytic rubric assesses various specific elements of an assignment; assessing the overall quality of the assignment would require a holistic rubric.
B. Correct. An analytic rubric assesses a student's understanding of more detailed skills, in this case appropriate vocabulary.
C. Incorrect. A general rubric would be used to assess knowledge on a broad topic like understanding the causes and developments of major battles; on the other hand, an analytic rubric addresses specific factors.
D. Incorrect. A general rubric is more appropriate for assessing a student's reasoning skills, in this case how World War I influenced the events of World War II.

9)
A. Correct. A multiple-choice test would quickly assess student understanding of content knowledge.
B. Incorrect. A research report would be more effective for assessing reasoning and research skills in addition to content knowledge.
C. Incorrect. A debate would assess a student's ability to synthesize information to form an opinion and defend it.
D. Incorrect. A portfolio of work is most appropriate for assessing a student's progression in skill development over time, not necessarily his or her content knowledge.

10)
A. Correct. This lesson examines the consequences of interpersonal behaviors in school.
B. Incorrect. This lesson focuses on spatial relationships and human geography.
C. Incorrect. This lesson is an example of human geography.
D. Incorrect. This lesson focuses on the topic of democracy.

11)
A. Incorrect. This question only covers content knowledge; it does not provide students with an opportunity to exercise the critical thinking skills essential for a debate.
B. Correct. This question asks students to form their own opinions based on their knowledge of inventions during the Industrial Revolution and their contributions to society.
C. Incorrect. This question is likely too broad for a classroom debate.
D. Incorrect. This question does not require students to construct a persuasive argument; a number of

commonly agreed-upon factors may be listed (environmental pollution, overcrowding, long workdays, etc.).

12)
- **A.** **Correct.** This signifies that the teacher is the only member of the class allowed to make decisions, unlike a democracy in which all people (ideally) can regularly participate in the decision-making process.
- **B.** Incorrect. In this case, the class is making group decisions democratically.
- **C.** Incorrect. Since students make this choice as a group, they are working democratically.
- **D.** Incorrect. Here, students have the opportunity to state their opinion, which is one element of a democracy.

13)
- **A.** Incorrect. The activity involves looking at both primary and secondary sources.
- **B.** **Correct.** Studying a wide variety of sources gives students an opportunity to understand why different types of sources are used in social studies.
- **C.** Incorrect. This activity's main purpose is to look at different resources, not necessarily to examine the significance of the precipitating event itself.
- **D.** Incorrect. This activity assumes the student already has solid reading comprehension skills.

14)
- **A.** Incorrect. Studying volcanoes is a lesson in physical geography.
- **B.** Incorrect. Comparing state laws is appropriate for a class in civics or government, not geography.
- **C.** **Correct.** Building and using public transportation shows how humans relate to and change their environment.
- **D.** Incorrect. Studying successful, local, small businesses is appropriate for a class in economics, not geography.

15)
- **A.** Incorrect. The Constitution addresses the democratic government of the United States, but there are aspects of the document that are unrelated to voting.
- **B.** Incorrect. This historical period is unrelated to voting in general.
- **C.** Incorrect. Learning why the president can only serve for two terms is useful knowledge for a voter, but it does not directly address the importance of voting or how to vote responsibly.
- **D.** **Correct.** Studying candidates and issues helps students understand how to vote responsibly.

16)
- **A.** Incorrect. This activity does not necessarily identify how the student depends on others for a good or service. Students could have cooked the meal and produced the food themselves.
- **B.** Incorrect. This activity helps students understand services people provide, but not how these people or services depend on one another.
- **C.** Incorrect. This activity identifies different types of goods, not how the production of these goods is interdependent.
- **D.** **Correct.** Interdependence is when a person or a group of people rely on one another to satisfy their own economic wants and needs.

17)

A. Incorrect. Students should consider a wide variety of sources.

B. Correct. It is the researcher's responsibility to ensure credibility and contemporaneity of sources; it is essential for teachers to ensure that students understand this.

C. Incorrect. Students should research a wide variety of sources, both primary and secondary.

D. Incorrect. Students should seek out unbiased sources.

18)

A. Incorrect. The student failed to identify a twentieth-century invention. The printing press is a fifteenth-century invention.

B. Incorrect. The student failed to justify the argument and thus did not demonstrate the ability to draw conclusions.

C. Correct. Here, the student argued that the automobile was a significant invention, using reasoning to support his or her conclusion.

D. Incorrect. The student failed to specify which invention in the twentieth century was the most significant.

19)

A. Incorrect. Visiting a factory does not address the philosophical or political roots of different forms of authority.

B. Incorrect. While a factory is one type of institution, this visit does not address the way individuals and groups relate to institutions in general.

C. Incorrect. A factory is generally not illustrative of democratic processes.

D. Correct. Learning how a factory works involves the study of how goods are produced, distributed, and consumed.

20)

A. Incorrect. This question explores the theme of Production, Distribution, and Consumption.

B. Correct. This question explores the topic of government structures and how they function, which is typical of this theme.

C. Incorrect. This question explores the theme of Civic Ideals and Practices.

D. Incorrect. This question explores the theme of People, Places, and Environments.

21)

A. Correct. The Treaty of Versailles had huge implications for the future of Germany.

B. Incorrect. This photograph does not describe the consequences of World War I for Germany.

C. Incorrect. This resource might be appropriate for understanding the aftermath of World War I, but it does not specifically focus on Germany.

D. Incorrect. This would be an appropriate resource for a lesson on World War II; the nuclear bomb was not used in the First World War.

22)

A. Incorrect. A quiz on rainforest facts does not help the student understand where rainforests are located.

B. Incorrect. This question only tests student understanding regarding the composition of the rainforest; it does not clarify where rainforests are located around the globe.

C. Correct. The initial assessment has revealed that the student does not understand where rainforests are located; consequently, the teacher should address this misunderstanding.

D. Incorrect. Lessons about different types of forests may teach the student that certain locations do not contain rainforests, but this lesson does not necessarily clarify where rainforests are located.

23)

A. Incorrect. This activity already assumes the student knows the laws of supply and demand.

B. Incorrect. This activity does not ask students to apply the law of supply and demand in a different context.

C. Incorrect. This activity does not ask students to organize different types of information because they are only looking at one supply and demand chart.

D. **Correct.** This activity requires students to take their knowledge of the laws of supply and demand and find evidence of it in oil and gas prices.

24)

A. Incorrect. Local resources may not be unique.

B. **Correct.** Landmarks are unique features of a place.

C. Incorrect. Banks are not unique to most communities.

D. Incorrect. Chain stores are not unique to most communities.

25)

A. **Correct.** Considering a historical example that mirrors current events forces students to think critically about issues facing their own society today. Despite facing discrimination, Irish Americans overcame enormous odds to make great contributions to the United States, and countless other immigrants continue to do the same. Such a lesson would reinforce the importance of tolerance and teach students the importance of learning history to develop their own values and conclusions.

B. Incorrect. Historically, thousands of non-US citizens have and continue to temporarily work on US farms, contributing to economic production. However, this lesson does not directly address discrimination and tolerance. Furthermore, guest workers do not necessarily immigrate.

C. Incorrect. Such a discussion would likely be enriching and fun; however, even though they would be learning about the traditions of an important immigrant community in the United States, students would not necessarily learn about discrimination, tolerance, or thinking in historical context.

D. Incorrect. A class debate could result in hurt feelings and even bullying; it might also unfairly single out any students from immigrant families or who are immigrants themselves.

Science Practice

Content Knowledge

1

Which of these is a biome?

A. a desert
B. a cornfield
C. a herd of bison
D. a beehive

2

Which planet orbits closest to Earth?

A. Mercury
B. Venus
C. Jupiter
D. Saturn

3

Which tool is used to measure the mass of an object?

A. a thermometer
B. a graduated cylinder
C. a balance
D. an abacus

4

Which organism has cells that contain mitochondria?

A. whale
B. mushroom
C. tulip
D. all of the above

5

Which condition can be diagnosed by an electrocardiogram (EKG)?

A. diabetes
B. torn ligaments
C. cancer
D. tachycardia

6

What are the negatively charged particles inside an atom?

A. protons
B. neutrons
C. electrons
D. ions

7

What is the name of the phenomenon when a star suddenly increases in brightness and then disappears from view?

A. aurora
B. galaxy
C. black hole
D. supernova

8

What term describes the resistance to motion caused by one object rubbing against another object?

A. inertia
B. friction
C. velocity
D. gravity

9

Which action is an example of mechanical weathering?

A. Calcium carbonate reacts with water to form a cave.
B. An iron gate rusts.
C. Tree roots grow under the foundation of a house and cause cracks.
D. Bananas turn brown after they are peeled.

10

Organisms in the same class are also in the same_____.

A. phylum
B. order
C. genus
D. species

11

Which type of rock forms when lava cools and solidifies?

A. igneous
B. sedimentary
C. metamorphic
D. sandstone

12

Which unit measures pressure?

A. kilometers
B. grams
C. grams per second
D. pounds per square foot

13

Which organism regulates its body temperature externally?

A. lobster
B. dolphin
C. whale
D. pelican

14

Which organism is a decomposer?

A. apple trees
B. mushrooms
C. goats
D. lions

15

Which pH level is classified as a base?

A. 2
B. 4
C. 6
D. 8

16

Which body system is responsible for the release of growth hormones?

A. digestive system
B. endocrine system
C. nervous system
D. circulatory system

17

Which example illustrates a physical change?

A. Water becomes ice.
B. Batter is baked into a cake.
C. An iron fence rusts.
D. A firecracker explodes.

18

Which energy source is nonrenewable?

A. water
B. wind
C. coal
D. sunlight

19

How long does it take the earth to rotate on its axis?

A. one hour
B. one day
C. one month
D. one year

20

Which organism is a reptile?

A. crocodile
B. frog
C. salamander
D. salmon

21

By what process do producers make sugars and release oxygen?

A. digestion
B. chloroplast
C. decomposition
D. photosynthesis

22

Which type of wave is a longitudinal wave?

A. surface wave
B. light wave
C. sound wave
D. electromagnetic wave

23

Which example demonstrates refraction?

A. rainbow
B. echo
C. mirror
D. radio

24

Which factor is an abiotic part of an ecosystem?

A. producers
B. consumers
C. water
D. decomposers

25

Which organelle makes proteins?

A. mitochondria
B. cytoplasm
C. vacuole
D. ribosomes

26

What term describes a relationship between two organisms where one organism benefits, to the detriment of the other organism?

A. mutualism
B. parasitism
C. commensalism
D. predation

27

Which statement is true?

A. Earth is much closer to the sun than it is to other stars.
B. The moon is closer to Venus than it is to Earth.
C. At certain times of the year, Jupiter is closer to the sun than Earth is.
D. Mercury is the closest planet to Earth.

28

Which metal attracts magnets?

A. iron
B. copper
C. silver
D. gold

29

Which statement is true?

A. Mass and weight are the same thing.
B. Mass is affected by gravitational pull.
C. Weight is affected by the gravitational pull.
D. Mass is related to the surface area of an object.

30

In which part of a plant does photosynthesis take place?

A. the roots
B. the stem
C. the leaves
D. the flower

31

Which example demonstrates electrostatic attraction?

A. Items in a car continue to move forward when the car stops suddenly.
B. Tides are affected by the moon.
C. The moon revolves around Earth.
D. Plastic wrap sticks to a person's hand.

32

Which example has the least amount of kinetic energy?

A. a plane flying through the sky
B. a plane sitting on the runway
C. a ladybug flying toward a flower
D. a meteorite falling to Earth

33

What term describes the speed and direction of a moving soccer ball?

A. velocity
B. momentum
C. mass
D. energy

34
Which of the following is caused by geothermal heat?

A. geysers
B. glaciers
C. tsunamis
D. tornadoes

35
Which term describes space weather?

A. supernova
B. black hole
C. volcanic lightning
D. solar flares

36
Which gas is found in large quantities in Earth's atmosphere?

A. carbon monoxide
B. bromine
C. nitrogen
D. fluorine

37
Which term describes an element?

A. atom
B. molecule
C. proton
D. ion

38
When Earth moves between the moon and the sun, it is called a

A. solar eclipse.
B. lunar eclipse.
C. black hole.
D. supernova.

39
Which element is most common in the universe?

A. carbon
B. lithium
C. potassium
D. titanium

40
Which storm is least likely to form over ocean water?

A. hurricane
B. typhoon
C. cyclone
D. tornado

41
Which substance can be used to neutralize an acid spill?

A. sodium bicarbonate
B. citric acid
C. cat litter
D. water

42
Which gas is produced by burning fossil fuels?

A. helium
B. oxygen
C. nitrogen
D. carbon dioxide

43
A warm air mass moving into a cold air mass is called a

A. warm front.
B. cold front.
C. isobar.
D. tornado.

44

Which of the following is NOT a cause of extinction?

A. poor reproduction
B. climate change
C. habitat conservation
D. overexploitation by humans

45

Which term describes the top layer of the earth's surface?

A. stratosphere
B. lithosphere
C. atmosphere
D. biosphere

46

Which substance is a good thermal conductor?

A. plastic
B. rubber
C. porcelain
D. aluminum

47

Which example demonstrates body systems working together to maintain homeostasis?

A. Jessica's tracheotomy opened a breathing obstruction.
B. Max's muscles, tendons, and ligaments allow his joints to bend.
C. Kevin's bones thicken from an excessive production of growth hormones.
D. Stacy shivers from the cold.

48

What is the primary role of amino acids in cells?

A. break down carbohydrates
B. break down fats
C. build proteins
D. filter waste

49

What part of the atom flows through a circuit to power a lightbulb?

A. protons
B. neutrons
C. electrons
D. nucleus

50

Which simple machine is shown in the following picture?

Figure 17.1. Simple Machine

A. inclined plane
B. pulley
C. screw
D. wedge

Curriculum, Instruction, and Assessment

1
Which experiment could be used to teach students about buoyancy?

A. mixing colors
B. tornado-in-a-bottle
C. sink-or-float
D. Mentos in Coca-Cola

2
Which skill are students using when writing a hypothesis before conducting a science experiment?

A. predicting
B. classifying
C. analyzing
D. solving

3
What is the safest way for students to observe a solar eclipse?

A. to look directly at the sun
B. to wear sunglasses
C. to use a pair of binoculars
D. to use a pinhole projection

4
Which lesson can best introduce a geology unit about the layers of the earth?

A. a lesson on hydroponics
B. an discussion on geothermal energy
C. a lecture about solar energy
D. a class on hydropower

5
Mr. DeJulius opens a soda bottle and places a balloon over the top of the bottle. The class observes the bottle every ten minutes. Which concept is the experiment demonstrating?

A. force and motion
B. magnetic attraction
C. acids and bases
D. states of matter

6
A student is identifying patterns in data collected on crystal formation at different temperatures. Which stage is this in the problem-solving process?

A. researching
B. writing a hypothesis
C. testing a hypothesis
D. analyzing data and drawing conclusions

7
Which safety precaution must be observed during an experiment to determine which substance is the best conductor of heat?

A. wearing protective gloves
B. keeping students ten feet away from the heat source
C. conducting disaster drills before beginning the experiment
D. requiring that students be accompanied by a parent

8

Which science should be taught with a geology unit about layers of the atmosphere?

A. meteorology
B. paleontology
C. seismic activity
D. food chains

9

Which physical science lesson can teach the formation of precipitation?

A. states of matter
B. magnetism
C. chemical reactions
D. force and movement

10

If a student is interested in astronomy, which career might the student pursue?

A. doctor
B. conservationist
C. marine biologist
D. aeronautic engineering

11

Which activity would teach students about photosynthesis?

A. creating a leaf rubbing
B. placing one plant in a windowsill and another in a dark closet to observe the effects
C. measuring the heights of different types of plants
D. collecting leaves on a nature walk and graphing the lengths of the leaves

12

Which career might a student who is interested in geology explore?

A. paleontologist
B. pilot
C. pharmacist
D. computer programmer

13

Which occupation requires an understanding of genetics and evolution?

A. firefighter
B. electrician
C. veterinarian
D. architect

14

Which activity can be used to explore density?

A. a sink-and-float station at a water table
B. sorting living and nonliving things
C. refracting light using a prism
D. an experiment with speed using toy cars and a ramp

15

How does a student know if an attempt to neutralize an acid and a base is successful?

A. The solution would taste sour.
B. The solution would have a soapy consistency.
C. The solution becomes flammable.
D. The solution turns into salt water.

16

Which activity demonstrates a chemical change?

A. dissolving drink mix in water
B. slicing an apple
C. cooking an egg
D. melting an ice cube

17

Which lesson could be used to teach students about the Doppler Effect?

A. recording the sound of a hair dryer moving toward and away from a microphone
B. graphing data on temperature changes in weather disturbances
C. collecting samples of precipitation
D. using a rope to demonstrate the movement of sound waves at different amplitudes

18

Which science works to improve farming practices?

A. oceanography
B. agrology
C. meteorology
D. astronomy

19

Which measurement system do scientists use?

A. the metric system
B. the US customary system
C. nonstandard units of measure
D. the ancient cubit

20

Which activity could be used to demonstrate Newton's Third Law of Motion?

A. hitting the 8-ball with the cue ball in billiards
B. rolling two balls of different masses down a ramp
C. dropping a ping-pong ball
D. swinging a pendulum

21

Which characteristic must be part of a good hypothesis?

A. A hypothesis must match the conclusion of an experiment.
B. A hypothesis must be from an unknown branch of science.
C. A hypothesis must be scientifically proven.
D. A hypothesis must be capable of being tested.

22

What type of furniture should be in a science lab?

A. individual student desks
B. tables with reclining chairs
C. modular desks
D. flat tables with tall stools

23

Which type of assessment would be used to guide small-group instruction?

A. a summative assessment
B. standardized tests
C. a formative assessment
D. end-of-unit tests

24

Anecdotal records and benchmark tests show that the students in Mr. Howell's class understand physical science concepts, but their standardized test scores are poor. What might be a reason for the difference?

A. Benchmarks are not aligned with instruction.
B. Instruction is not aligned with standardized tests.
C. The standardized test information is invalid.
D. Anecdotal records and benchmarks are invalid.

25

Which activity would be most effective for teaching about sound waves?

A. playing music on an iPod
B. demonstrating waves with a Slinky
C. creating a poem
D. drawing a diagram of the ear

D. Incorrect. Sandstone is a type of sedimentary rock.

12)
A. Incorrect. Length is measured in kilometers.
B. Incorrect. Mass is measured in grams.
C. Incorrect. Mass flow rate is measured in grams per second.
D. **Correct.** Pressure is measured in pounds per square foot.

13)
A. **Correct.** The metabolic rate of crustaceans is too low to regulate their temperature. Crustaceans use behavioral techniques, such as moving to shallow water, to maintain body temperature.
B. Incorrect. Dolphins are mammals. Mammals are endothermic, meaning they have a mechanism to regulate body temperature internally.
C. Incorrect. Whales are mammals.
D. Incorrect. Birds are endothermic.

14)
A. Incorrect. Plants produce their own food through photosynthesis, making them producers.
B. **Correct.** Mushrooms are fungi. Fungi break down organic material left by dead animals and plants, making them decomposers.
C. Incorrect. Goats eat producers, such as grass, making them primary consumers.
D. Incorrect. Lions are carnivorous animals that feed on primary consumers and secondary consumers, making them secondary or tertiary consumers.

15)
A. Incorrect. Acids have a pH between 0 and 7.
B. Incorrect. Acids have a pH between 0 and 7.
C. Incorrect. Acids have a pH between 0 and 7.
D. **Correct.** Bases have a pH between 7 and 14.

16)
A. Incorrect. The digestive system turns food into energy.
B. **Correct.** The endocrine system releases hormones, including growth hormones.
C. Incorrect. The nervous system is a network of communication cells.
D. Incorrect. The circulatory system delivers nutrients to cells and removes wastes from the body.

17)
A. **Correct.** When water changes form, it does not change the chemical composition of the substance. Once water becomes ice, the ice can easily turn back into water.
B. Incorrect. The chemical composition of the substance changes and cannot be reversed. Baking a cake is an example of a chemical change.
C. Incorrect. Rusting is an example of a chemical change.
D. Incorrect. Setting off fireworks causes a chemical change.

18)
A. Incorrect. Water can generate hydropower, which is a renewable energy source.
B. Incorrect. Wind is a renewable energy source.
C. **Correct.** Coal is nonrenewable because once coal is burned, it cannot be quickly replaced.
D. Incorrect. Solar energy is a renewable energy source.

19)
- A. Incorrect. One hour is 1/24 of the time it takes for the earth to rotate on its axis.
- **B. Correct.** Earth takes approximately 24 hours to rotate on its axis.
- C. Incorrect. The moon takes approximately one month to revolve around the earth.
- D. Incorrect. The earth takes approximately one year to revolve around the sun.

20)
- **A. Correct.** Reptiles like crocodiles have scaly skin, are hatched from eggs on land, and are cold-blooded.
- B. Incorrect. Amphibians like frogs are hatched from eggs in water, have gills but develop lungs, and become land animals as they mature.
- C. Incorrect. Salamanders are amphibians.
- D. Incorrect. Fish like salmon live in water; they also have a backbone, gills, scales, and fins.

21)
- A. Incorrect. Digestion is the process whereby large food particles are broken down into small particles.
- B. Incorrect. A chloroplast is the part of the cell where photosynthesis takes place.
- C. Incorrect. Decomposition is the process where substances are broken down into smaller parts.
- **D. Correct.** Photosynthesis describes the process by which plants convert the energy of the sun into stored chemical energy (glucose).

22)
- A. Incorrect. Waves on the surface of the ocean are transverse waves.
- B. Incorrect. Light waves are transverse waves.
- **C. Correct.** Sound waves are longitudinal waves because the vibrations travel in the same direction as the energy.
- D. Incorrect. Electromagnetic waves are transverse waves.

23)
- **A. Correct.** The light of the sun hits rain droplets and bends into a band of colors. The bending of waves is refraction.
- B. Incorrect. Echo is an example of sound reflection.
- C. Incorrect. A mirror is used to show light reflection.
- D. Incorrect. A radio is an example of sound waves reflecting off layers in Earth's atmosphere.

24)
- A. Incorrect. Producers are living things, which are biotic factors.
- B. Incorrect. Consumers are biotic factors because they are alive.
- **C. Correct.** Non-living things in an ecosystem, like air and water, are abiotic factors.
- D. Incorrect. Living things are biotic factors.

25)
- A. Incorrect. Mitochondria release chemical energy from glucose to be used by the cell.
- B. Incorrect. Cytoplasm provides support to the cell.
- C. Incorrect. Vacuoles store water.
- **D. Correct.** Ribosomes are responsible for production of proteins.

26)

A. Incorrect. In mutualism, both organisms benefit.

B. Correct. Parasitism describes a relationship in which one organism benefits from another organism, to the detriment of the host organism.

C. Incorrect. Commensalism is when one organism benefits from another without causing harm to the host organism.

D. Incorrect. Predation is killing and consuming other organisms for food.

27)

A. Correct. The sun is the only star in our solar system. The sun is about ninety-three million miles from Earth; the next closest star is about twenty-five trillion miles away.

B. Incorrect. The moon orbits Earth.

C. Incorrect. Even when Jupiter is closest to the sun and Earth is farthest from the sun, Earth is always closer to the sun than Jupiter is.

D. Incorrect. Mercury is the closest planet to the sun, and Venus is closer to Earth.

28)

A. Correct. Magnets readily attract iron.

B. Incorrect. Not all metals are attracted to magnets; copper is not.

C. Incorrect. Magnets do not attract all metals; for example, they do not attract silver.

D. Incorrect. Gold is not attracted to magnets.

29)

A. Incorrect. Mass is the amount of matter in an object. Weight is a measure of the gravitational pull on an object. Weight changes in space, but mass does not.

B. Incorrect. Weight is affected by gravitational pull, not mass.

C. Correct. Weight is affected by gravitational pull.

D. Incorrect. The surface area or size of an object does not indicate the mass of that object.

30)

A. Incorrect. Roots extract water and minerals from the soil.

B. Incorrect. The stem transports nutrients to other parts of the plant.

C. Correct. Through photosynthesis, leaves use the sun's energy to convert carbon dioxide into glucose (food).

D. Incorrect. The flower is the reproductive part of a plant.

31)

A. Incorrect. Newton's First Law is that *objects in motion stay in motion*.

B. Incorrect. Tides are affected by the gravitational pull of the moon. Gravitational force is the attraction between two masses.

C. Incorrect. The moon revolves around Earth because of the gravitational pull between the two masses.

D. Correct. Electrostatic force is an attraction between charged surfaces.

32)

A. Incorrect. A plane flying through the sky would have kinetic energy because of its mass and velocity.

B. Correct. Something that is not moving has zero velocity; therefore it has no kinetic energy.

C. Incorrect. Even though it has a low mass and a low velocity, a ladybug does have a small amount of kinetic energy.

D. Incorrect. A meteorite falling toward Earth would have a large amount of kinetic energy because of its mass and velocity.

33)

A. **Correct.** Velocity is the speed of an object in a certain direction.

B. Incorrect. Momentum is calculated by multiplying the velocity of an object by its mass.

C. Incorrect. Mass refers to the amount of matter in an object.

D. Incorrect. Energy describes the capacity to do work.

34)

A. **Correct.** Geysers are caused by geothermal heating of water underground.

B. Incorrect. Glaciers are formed when snow and ice do not melt before new layers of snow and ice are added.

C. Incorrect. Tsunamis are caused by earthquakes on the ocean floor.

D. Incorrect. Tornadoes are caused by instability of warm, humid air in the lower atmosphere mixing with cool air in the upper atmosphere.

35)

A. Incorrect. A supernova is a huge explosion of the core of a star that marks the end of the life cycle of the star. Since supernovas occur outside our solar system, they are not considered space weather.

B. Incorrect. Black holes occur outside our solar system, so they are not considered space weather.

C. Incorrect. Volcanic lightning is a lightning storm that occurs during a volcanic eruption when positively charged lava is launched into the negatively charged atmosphere. This does not occur in space; therefore, volcanic lightning is not considered space weather.

D. **Correct.** Solar flares are huge explosions on the sun. Space weather refers to conditions in the solar system that could potentially affect the work of astronauts in space and cause auroras on Earth.

36)

A. Incorrect. Carbon monoxide is a rare gas.

B. Incorrect. Bromine is a rare gas.

C. **Correct.** Nitrogen makes up 78 percent of Earth's atmosphere.

D. Incorrect. Fluorine is a rare gas.

37)

A. **Correct.** An atom is the smallest unit of an element.

B. Incorrect. A molecule is the simplest form of a compound, consisting of two or more atoms.

C. Incorrect. A proton is a positively-charged particle in the nucleus of an atom. A proton by itself will not make an element.

D. Incorrect. An ion is an electrically charged atom or group of atoms.

38)

A. Incorrect. A solar eclipse is when the moon moves between the sun and Earth.

B. **Correct.** A lunar eclipse is when Earth moves between the moon and the sun.

C. Incorrect. A black hole is a collapsed star with tremendous gravitational pull.

D. Incorrect. A supernova is an explosion of the core of a star.

39)

A. **Correct.** Carbon is a common element found in every organic compound and in the atmosphere of some planets.

B. Incorrect. Lithium is highly reactive and is found in small amounts in igneous rocks.

C. Incorrect. Potassium is found in Earth's crust and is essential to plant growth.

D. Incorrect. Titanium makes up less than 1 percent of Earth's surface.

40)

A. Incorrect. Hurricanes form over warm ocean water. Depending upon where a hurricane forms, it can also be called a *typhoon* or a *cyclone*.

B. Incorrect. A hurricane that forms in the western Pacific Ocean is called a typhoon.

C. Incorrect. A hurricane that forms in the Indian Ocean is called a cyclone.

D. **Correct.** Tornadoes occur when warm air masses collide with cold air masses over land.

41)

A. **Correct.** Sodium bicarbonate, which is a base, will neutralize an acid.

B. Incorrect. Citric acid neutralizes a base spill.

C. Incorrect. Once the spill is neutralized, cat litter may be used to absorb it.

D. Incorrect. An acid spill needs to be neutralized before water is used.

42)

A. Incorrect. Helium is found in large quantities on the sun. It is an inert, colorless, tasteless gas.

B. Incorrect. Oxygen makes up about 20 percent of Earth's atmosphere.

C. Incorrect. Seventy-eight percent of Earth's atmosphere is made of nitrogen, and nitrogen is essential for all living organisms.

D. **Correct.** Carbon dioxide is formed when fossil fuels containing carbon are burned. Excess carbon dioxide is responsible for global warming.

43)

A. **Correct.** A warm front is when a warm air mass moves into a cold air mass.

B. Incorrect. A cold front is when a cold air mass moves into a warm air mass.

C. Incorrect. An isobar is a contour line indicating locations of equal barometric pressures.

D. Incorrect. A tornado is caused by unstable air.

44)

A. Incorrect. Poor reproduction is one of the identified causes of extinction. If a species is not able to reproduce, it will eventually die out.

B. Incorrect. Climate changes, such as the Ice Age and global warming, are responsible for the extinction of a species.

C. **Correct.** Habitat conservation restores the natural habitat of organisms, protecting a species.

D. Incorrect. Overexploitation by humans through hunting for sport, animal testing, and illegal trapping has caused the endangerment of many species.

45)

A. Incorrect. The stratosphere is a layer of the earth's atmosphere.

B. **Correct.** The lithosphere is the top layer of the earth's surface.

C. Incorrect. The atmosphere refers to the layer of gases that surrounds the earth.

D. Incorrect. The biosphere is the part of Earth where life exists; the biosphere includes the atmosphere, the oceans, and the life-supporting areas above and below Earth's surface.

46)

A. Incorrect. Plastic is an insulator. Insulators block the flow of heat from one object to another.

B. Incorrect. Rubber is an insulator.

C. Incorrect. Porcelain is an insulator.

D. **Correct.** Aluminum is a good thermal conductor because heat energy can move easily through it.

47)

A. Incorrect. A tracheotomy is not a body system reaction; it is a medical intervention.

B. Incorrect. Max's muscles, tendons, and ligaments are part of the muscular system. The bending of joints is a normal function, not a way to maintain homeostasis.

C. Incorrect. Excessive production of growth hormones is an example of disease.

D. **Correct.** Homeostasis refers to body systems working together to ensure that temperature, pH, and oxygen levels are optimal for survival. Sensors in Stacy's nervous system trigger her muscular system to shiver in an attempt to warm her body.

48)

A. Incorrect. Amino acids do not break down carbohydrates.

B. Incorrect. Fats (lipids) are insoluble in cells.

C. **Correct.** Ribosomes make proteins by building amino acid chains.

D. Incorrect. Lysosomes in the cytoplasm filter waste from a cell.

49)

A. Incorrect. Protons remain in the nucleus of an atom.

B. Incorrect. Neutrons remain in the nucleus of an atom.

C. **Correct.** Electrons are negatively charged subatomic particles that exist outside the nucleus of an atom. A power source forces moving electrons through a circuit.

D. Incorrect. The nucleus is the part of an atom that contains protons and neutrons.

50)

A. **Correct.** An inclined plane is a flat surface raised to an angle so that loads can be easily lifted.

B. Incorrect. A pulley is a wheel with ropes that change the direction of the force in order to lift an object.

C. Incorrect. A screw is a rod-shaped object with a spiral groove.

D. Incorrect. A wedge is a type of inclined plane, such as an axe, that has both a wide and a thin end.

Curriculum, Instruction, and Assessment

1)
- A. Incorrect. Mixing colors teaches students how to make new colors by combining primary colors.
- B. Incorrect. Tornado-in-a-bottle teaches students about weather.
- **C. Correct.** Sink-or-float experiments teach students about buoyancy.
- D. Incorrect. Mentos in a Coca-Cola can teach about chemical bonding, pressure, or volcanic eruptions.

2)
- **A. Correct.** Prediction is used to develop a hypothesis.
- B. Incorrect. Classifying is to divide things into groups.
- C. Incorrect. Analyzing is to look for patterns.
- D. Incorrect. Solving is providing a correct explanation for something.

3)
- A. Incorrect. Looking directly at the sun can cause retina burns and is not safe.
- B. Incorrect. Wearing sunglasses will not protect the eyes from direct sunlight.
- C. Incorrect. Binoculars and telescopes are more dangerous for the eyes than looking directly at the sun.
- **D. Correct.** Pinhole projections are the safest way to observe a solar eclipse. Making a hole in a piece of cardboard will project the image of the sun onto a piece of paper where it can be viewed safely by students, who keep their backs to the sun.

4)
- A. Incorrect. Hydroponics deals with plant life.
- **B. Correct.** Geothermal energy is a renewable energy source that comes from the heat within the earth. A discussion about geothermal energy would be a good setting to introduce a geology unit on the layers of the earth.
- C. Incorrect. Solar energy is from the sun, not the earth.
- D. Incorrect. Hydropower comes from moving water, not the layers of the earth.

5)
- A. Incorrect. Force and motion, such as speed, velocity, mass, and momentum, are not part of the experiment.
- B. Incorrect. Magnetic force is not used in the experiment.
- C. Incorrect. Although soda contains carbonic acid, the experiment does not involve bases.
- **D. Correct.** Mr. DeJulius is showing different states of matter by illustrating the transition between the solid, liquid, and gas forms. The balloon will collect carbon dioxide gas that was once dissolved in the soda.

6)
- A. Incorrect. Collecting background information enables a student to develop a reasonable hypothesis.
- B. Incorrect. A hypothesis is an inference that needs further investigation to be proven either true or false.
- C. Incorrect. When testing a hypothesis, a student is performing an experiment and collecting data.
- **D. Correct.** Once data has been collected, a student analyzes the

7)

- A. **Correct.** In addition to gloves, wear goggles, close-toed shoes, and aprons. Hair should be tied back, and loose clothing and jewelry secured.
- B. Incorrect. If students are ten feet away, they will not be able to view the experiment. If students cannot be kept safe, a different activity should be selected.
- C. Incorrect. Conducting disaster drills before beginning an experiment of this magnitude is unnecessary.
- D. Incorrect. Parent volunteers can be a wonderful resource, but 100 percent participation during the school day is not always possible, and it is unfair to students who miss out on learning because a parent is unavailable.

8)

- A. **Correct.** Meteorology, or the science of weather, is related to atmospheric conditions.
- B. Incorrect. Paleontology is the study of fossils, and so is not very relevant to coursework on the atmosphere.
- C. Incorrect. Seismic activity is related to earthquakes and the earth's layers, not atmospheric layers.
- D. Incorrect. Food chains would be taught with life or environmental science, not geology.

9)

- A. **Correct.** Evaporation and condensation play important roles in the formation of precipitation.
- B. Incorrect. Magnetism is unrelated to precipitation.
- C. Incorrect. Precipitation is a physical change, not a chemical one.
- D. Incorrect. Gravity does pull precipitation to the ground, but force and movement are not related to the formation of precipitation.

10)

- A. Incorrect. Doctors work in the biological sciences.
- B. Incorrect. Conservationists are interested in environmental science.
- C. Incorrect. Marine biologists are interested in oceanography and biological science.
- D. **Correct.** Aeronautic engineers work on rockets, satellites, and other atmospheric and aerospace equipment.

11)

- A. Incorrect. A leaf rubbing may be fun and artistic, but it does not teach photosynthesis.
- B. **Correct.** This is a great experiment for demonstrating that a plant needs sunlight to make food.
- C. Incorrect. Measuring height is a math activity that does not explain photosynthesis.
- D. Incorrect. Students need to understand graphing, but this activity teaches nothing about photosynthesis.

12)

- A. **Correct.** Geology is the study of rocks and fossils, and paleontology is the study of fossils.
- B. Incorrect. Pilots are part of the aerospace industry.
- C. Incorrect. Pharmacists study chemistry and biology.
- D. Incorrect. Computer programmers study technology.

13)

- A. Incorrect. Firefighters must study chemistry and physics.

- B. Incorrect. Electricians study physical science.
- C. **Correct.** Veterinarians need to know about genetic disorders in plants and animals.
- D. Incorrect. Architects have backgrounds in mathematics, engineering, and art.

14)
- A. **Correct.** Sink-and-float stations can be used to test buoyancy and density.
- B. Incorrect. Understanding the difference between living and nonliving things applies to biology, not physical science.
- C. Incorrect. Light is not density.
- D. Incorrect. Force, motion, and energy are not density.

15)
- A. Incorrect. Solutions in a laboratory should never be tasted, but one characteristic of an acid is a sour taste.
- B. Incorrect. Lye, which can be used to make soap, is a base.
- C. Incorrect. Some acids are flammable, but some are not.
- D. **Correct.** Neutralization of an acid with a base results in a salt and water.

16)
- A. Incorrect. Dissolving drink mix in water is a physical change. The drink mix and water can be separated through evaporation.
- B. Incorrect. Slicing an apple is a physical change. The apple is still an apple.
- C. **Correct.** Cooking an egg is a chemical change. The heat changes the composition of the egg in an irreversible way.
- D. Incorrect. Melting an ice cube is a physical change. The water can be turn back into ice by freezing it.

17)
- A. **Correct.** The Doppler Effect is a phenomenon that makes sound waves change frequency. A hair dryer or other instrument that makes sound can be used to demonstrate the Doppler Effect.
- B. Incorrect. Doppler radar should not be confused with the Doppler Effect.
- C. Incorrect. The Doppler Effect is not related to samples of precipitation.
- D. Incorrect. The greater the amplitude of a sound wave, the louder the sound.

18)
- A. Incorrect. Oceanography is the study of the ocean.
- B. **Correct.** Agrology is the study of soil to improve farming.
- C. Incorrect. Meteorology is the study of weather.
- D. Incorrect. Astronomy is the study of space.

19)
- A. **Correct.** Scientists use the metric system.
- B. Incorrect. While students may use the US customary system, the metric system should be used in science classes.
- C. Incorrect. Nonstandard units of measure should be used in math classes when students are first learning about measurement.
- D. Incorrect. The ancient cubit was used in Egypt around 2700 B.C. It is not used today.

20)

A. Correct. Newton's Third Law of Motion states that for every action there is an equal and opposite reaction. When the cue ball hits the 8-ball, the cue ball stops, and the 8-ball moves.

B. Incorrect. Rolling two balls of different masses down a ramp would test Newton's Second Law of Motion, $F = ma$.

C. Incorrect. Dropping a ping-pong ball would test Newton's Law of Gravity.

D. Incorrect. This exemplifies Newton's First Law: objects in motion stay in motion, unless acted upon by an outside force.

21)

A. Incorrect. While a hypothesis should be reasonable, a hypothesis does not have to be correct.

B. Incorrect. A hypothesis could be new information, or a retest of an experiment under new conditions.

C. Incorrect. A hypothesis does not have to be scientifically proven. An experiment will provide results that may or may not prove something.

D. Correct. A hypothesis must be reasonable and testable by experiment.

22)

A. Incorrect. In science class, students need to work together in small groups.

B. Incorrect. Reclining chairs can potentially be dangerous. Students need steady, stable furniture.

C. Incorrect. Modular desks have limited surface areas.

D. Correct. Young scientists need flat-topped tables with tall stools that provide a good vantage point for making scientific observations.

23)

A. Incorrect. Summative assessments are end-of-learning tests.

B. Incorrect. Standardized tests are a type of summative assessment.

C. Correct. Formative assessments take place throughout the school day to guide instruction.

D. Incorrect. Unit tests are summative assessments.

24)

A. Incorrect. Students are scoring well on benchmarks and anecdotal records; therefore the benchmarks must be aligned with instruction.

B. Correct. Students are learning, but may not be learning the information or learning it to the level of rigor that is required by the standardized test.

C. Incorrect. Standardized assessments have been proven valid.

D. Incorrect. The anecdotal records and benchmarks are valid.

25)

A. Incorrect. This might be a fun transitional activity, but students will not be able to understand sound waves using an iPod.

B. Correct. A Slinky can demonstrate how sound waves travel and transfer energy.

C. Incorrect. A poem may be an enrichment activity, but will not teach students what they need to know about sound waves.

D. Incorrect. A diagram of the ear can help students understand how the ear receives sound after learning about sound waves.

Art, Music, and Physical Education Practice

1
Which of the following are not complementary colors on a color wheel?

A. blue and orange
B. red and blue
C. purple and yellow
D. red and green

2
Which of the following is a non-locomotor skill?

A. skipping
B. bending
C. throwing
D. leaping

3
Which of the following activities would most likely be achieved independently by first-grade students?

A. catching a ball
B. skipping
C. walking
D. leaping

4
Which of the following descriptions best describes timbre in music?

A. Timbre refers to the different sounds of various instruments.
B. Timbre refers to the loudness of an instrument.
C. Timbre refers to the pitch of an instrument.
D. Timbre refers to combining melody, harmony, and rhythm.

5
A student is critiquing an art piece. She talks about the artwork and how it reminds her of a sad time in her life. Which of the following areas of art criticism is she using?

A. description
B. judgment
C. interpretation
D. analysis

6

A teacher shows students several paintings by Monet, Renoir, and Cassatt. He explains that these painters used short brushstrokes and primary colors to create scenes that the artists witnessed at the very moment of their execution. Which of the following style of art are the students learning?

A. realism
B. impressionism
C. cubism
D. post-impressionism

7

Which of the following is not true about music notation?

A. A bass clef or treble clef is placed at the beginning of the stave.
B. It is a method of writing music.
C. Notes are read from left to right.
D. Notes must only fit on the stave.

8

Which of the following will most likely reduce the number of accidents in a physical education class?

A. posting signs on proper etiquette
B. incorporating a warm-up period to prevent injuries during activities
C. asking students to monitor one another during class
D. asking students to arrive on time for class

9

Which of the following reasons best describes why a teacher would introduce the recorder to students in an elementary class?

A. It can help students learn proper breathing techniques.
B. It allows teachers to teach a wide variety of songs and ensembles effectively.
C. It is appropriate for students who may not have well-developed motor skills.
D. It helps teachers show students pitch and rhythm.

10

Which of the following statements most appropriately describes the purpose of teaching game skills?

A. Game skills help students increase their awareness of their own bodies.
B. Game skills provide an opportunity for students to understand the connections between the games they play and motor skill development.
C. Game skills help students understand the role of stress in their bodies.
D. Game skills teach students to respect others.

11

Which of the following sports or activities is not appropriate to teach in second grade?

A. kickball
B. football
C. freeze tag
D. simple obstacle courses

12

Which of the following best describes why students should study art history?

A. A strong grasp of art history helps students improve their skill in art techniques.

B. A knowledge of art history helps students understand art criticism.

C. Studying art history gives students a break from creating art.

D. Art history helps students understand how an artwork addressed its contemporaneous society.

13

Which of the following methods is NOT an appropriate activity for teaching students about the benefits of nutrition?

A. showing students a picture of the USDA food plate and creating a balanced meal using the guidelines

B. showing students a picture of the food pyramid and creating a balanced meal using the guidelines

C. showing students possible side effects when they eat too much sugar

D. showing students the types of food that can help to fight disease

14

Which of the following would be an appropriate activity for first graders during a simple lesson on rhythm?

A. The teacher makes loud and soft sounds on a drum.

B. The teacher plays a pattern on the drum, and students try to repeat it.

C. Students listen to different percussion instruments.

D. The teacher plays music at different speeds and students clap to indicate the tempo.

15

What is the most appropriate reason for a teacher to use a skills checklist during physical education lessons?

A. A skills checklist allows the teacher to look at numerous skills at once.

B. A skills checklist is a tool for summative assessment.

C. A skills checklist helps the teacher record individual student progress and note when students have mastered specific skills.

D. A skills checklist allows the teacher to plan lessons.

16

Which of the following types of media is not appropriate for younger elementary students to use independently in an art class?

A. tempera paints

B. hot glue gun

C. scissors and white glue

D. crayons

17

Which of the following responses would be the most appropriate in providing effective feedback when reviewing an art portfolio during a student conference?

A. "You used a wide variety of colors in this painting."

B. "This is my favorite drawing of yours so far."

C. "All of the shadows are very dark and are in the same direction, which shows me you understand the direction of light. Great job!"

D. "You just need to practice your painting skills."

18

Which of the following types of instruments is most appropriate to use in a younger elementary music class?

A. Students shouldn't play instruments at a young age.

B. xylophone

C. flute

D. double bass

19

Which of the following questions would be most appropriate to ask students during a lesson on aesthetics?

A. If a piece of work is in a museum, should it be considered a work of art?

B. What are the elements and principles of art?

C. How is this piece of artwork displayed?

D. Why did the artist paint still-life subjects?

20

A teacher develops lessons in which students act out peer pressure situations relating to tobacco use. Which of the following topics does this address?

A. nutrition

B. healthy choices

C. substance abuse

D. making friends

21

A teacher hands out a quiz featuring questions about the types of notes and rests. Which of the following would the teacher most likely be assessing?

A. rhythm

B. pitch

C. recognizing familiar songs

D. musical notation

22

A physical education teacher is teaching students how to pitch, run, and stop at a specific distance; the teacher is also demonstrating how to strike a ball when it is thrown at the body. What sport is the teacher most likely preparing to teach next?

A. basketball

B. baseball

C. tennis

D. soccer

23

Which of the following instruments is a part of the brass family?

A. trombone, trumpet, and clarinet
B. trombone, trumpet, and French horn
C. piccolo, trumpet, and French horn
D. violin, double bass, and guitar

24

A student is gathering materials for a portfolio to prepare for a conference with his teacher. Which of the following types of materials would a teacher suggest he collects for feedback on improving his realistic drawing techniques?

A. completed handouts, finished paintings, and rubrics for past projects
B. still-life sketches, completed shading exercises, and photographs of subjects he wants to include in his drawings
C. photographs of subjects he wants to include in his drawings
D. shading exercises

25

Which of the following is the most appropriate way to explain visual communication to students?

A. It is a way to use symbols in art.
B. It helps to make art beautiful.
C. It is a way for viewers to talk about art.
D. It is a way to use pictures to communicate a message well.

26

Which of the following anecdotal notes would be appropriate to write down during a class?

A. how well a student scored on a quiz
B. a student's failure to recognize rhythmic patterns three classes in a row
C. a teacher's opinion on why a student is not able to throw a ball successfully
D. ideas for future lessons

Answer Key

1)

A. Incorrect. Blue and orange are complementary colors.

B. Correct. These colors are not directly opposite on the color wheel.

C. Incorrect. Purple and yellow are complementary colors.

D. Incorrect. Red and green are complementary colors.

2)

A. Incorrect. Skipping is a locomotor skill.

B. Correct. Non-locomotor skills, like bending, are usually movements that tend not to require moving through space.

C. Incorrect. Throwing is a manipulative skill.

D. Incorrect. Leaping is a locomotor skill.

3)

A. Correct. Students in first grade can demonstrate different skills that involve moving and staying still.

B. Incorrect. Skipping is mastered in the later elementary grades.

C. Incorrect. Walking should have already been mastered in the early years.

D. Incorrect. Leaping is mastered in the later elementary grades.

4)

A. Correct. Also called tone, timbre is used to distinguish between instrumental sounds.

B. Incorrect. Loudness of an instrument refers to the dynamics of a piece of music.

C. Incorrect. An instrument's pitch refers to the location of notes on a music staff.

D. Incorrect. Combining melody, harmony, and rhythm refers to the texture in a composition.

5)

A. Incorrect. In describing artwork, critique addresses art as objectively as possible.

B. Incorrect. In using judgment, the critic justifies his or her opinion on the artwork.

C. Correct. Interpreting artwork entails discussing the unique qualities of a piece and how the piece reminds a person about events in his or her own life.

D. Incorrect. In analysis, a critic describes how a work of art is organized.

6)

A. Incorrect. Realism depicts subjects as accurately and as truthfully as possible; such a depiction may not always include primary colors.

B. Correct. Impressionism developed as a reaction to the photography medium and focused on expressing an artist's emotions.

C. Incorrect. Cubism depicts subjects in small, tilted planes set on a flat space.

D. Incorrect. Artists like Van Gogh rejected the idea of subjects based on observations and created ones of personal significance.

7)

A. Incorrect. A clef at the beginning of the stave indicates the pitch and name of notes.

B. Incorrect. Music notation helps composers communicate how they want their music to be performed.

C. Incorrect. Reading notes from left to right is the correct method.

D. Correct. Notes can be placed on ledger lines if they are of a very high or low pitch.

8)

A. Incorrect. Posting signs will not necessarily prevent accidents.

B. Correct. A teacher should incorporate activities into the lesson to ensure the safety of all students.

C. Incorrect. A teacher should monitor students to prevent any accidents.

D. Incorrect. Punctuality does not necessarily prevent accidents.

9)

A. Incorrect. Other instruments can help students learn proper breathing techniques.

B. Correct. Using the recorder is a great way to teach songs and ensembles without teaching a new instrument every time.

C. Incorrect. Students must be able to physically play the recorder, so they must have developed motor skills.

D. Incorrect. Students can learn the concepts of pitch and rhythm through many ways other than the recorder.

10)

A. Incorrect. All physical education activities help students be aware of their own bodies.

B. Correct. Game skills help students master skills beyond physical development, including making decisions as a team.

C. Incorrect. Students learn about physical stress through the study of health, not by learning game skills.

D. Incorrect. Respect for others can be taught through any subject in school.

11)

A. Incorrect. Students in second grade have the motor skills to play kickball.

B. Correct. Second graders may not be coordinated enough to play football; furthermore, the sport poses numerous safety hazards.

C. Incorrect. Freeze tag is an appropriate activity for refining second-grade students' running and dodging skills.

D. Incorrect. Completing simple obstacle courses is an appropriate activity for second graders.

12)

A. Incorrect. Studying art history can help students recognize and evaluate how other artists apply different techniques; it does not necessarily help students improve their own skills.

B. Incorrect. There are numerous other ways to help students understand art criticism, including understanding how to describe artwork.

C. Incorrect. This is not the most appropriate reason to study art history.

D. **Correct.** Studying art history helps students to understand why an artist created the artwork they did.

13)

A. Incorrect. The USDA food plate is a useful tool to illustrate healthy food choices.

B. **Correct.** The food pyramid was replaced by the My Plate guidelines to demonstrate healthy food choices.

C. Incorrect. Teaching about the side effects of sugar would be an appropriate lesson in nutrition; it shows the impact of food choices on the body.

D. Incorrect. Discussing the benefits of various foods is an appropriate lesson; students are learning the value of good nutrition.

14)

A. Incorrect. Making loud and soft sounds on a drum is an activity best suited for teaching dynamics.

B. **Correct.** Teaching patterns is an appropriate introduction to the concept of rhythm.

C. Incorrect. Students could listen to percussion instruments during a lesson on timbre.

D. Incorrect. This would be an appropriate activity during a lesson on tempo.

15)

A. Incorrect. Checklists should only be used to review and assess one skill at a time.

B. Incorrect. Checklists can be used *in* summative assessments, but they cannot be summative assessments by themselves.

C. **Correct.** Checklists are most appropriate for giving immediate feedback and assessing mastery of skills.

D. Incorrect. Checklists can help teachers plan future lessons, but only if the teacher can gather enough consistent feedback.

16)

A. Incorrect. Tempera paints are appropriate for younger elementary students to use.

B. **Correct.** Using a hot glue gun could potentially be a safety hazard for younger students.

C. Incorrect. Students should have been practicing their cutting skills in preschool, so younger elementary students may use scissors and white glue.

D. Incorrect. Even younger students have the motor skills to use crayons.

17)

A. Incorrect. This feedback does not specifically address actions a student took that highlighted his or her strengths or weaknesses.

B. Incorrect. This phrase is the teacher's opinion, not feedback.

C. **Correct.** This feedback addresses specific actions the student took and highlighted the behavior the teacher wants repeated.

D. Incorrect. This is not feedback because it does not address the student's strengths.

18)

A. Incorrect. Students can learn instruments as long as they have the appropriate motor skills to play them.

B. **Correct.** Orff instruments are appropriate for younger students as they develop the fine muscle control that will enable them to play more complex instruments later.

C. Incorrect. Students may not have practiced the proper breathing techniques necessary to play a woodwind instrument.

D. Incorrect. Students may not have the appropriate motor skills to play a double bass.

19)

A. Correct. The study of aesthetics involves students discussing the nature of art.

B. Incorrect. Using art-related vocabulary helps students describe art, not necessarily to make judgments about it.

C. Incorrect. This question assumes that a piece of work is already art; it does not trigger debate over whether this is the case.

D. Incorrect. This question refers to the reasons an artist created a work, not on the nature of art itself.

20)

A. Incorrect. The lesson in question does not address how food and other substances work in the body; it addresses social interaction and does not address food at all.

B. Incorrect. Certainly, understanding the impact of tobacco use is integral to learning to make healthy choices; however, these lessons specifically address peer pressure as well.

C. Correct. Teaching lessons on substance abuse involves showing students how to make decisions based on the use of illegal substances, which often involve peer pressure.

D. Incorrect. Understanding the difference between healthy friendships and peer pressure is important, but these lessons directly address a substance abuse issue.

21)

A. Correct. Rhythm refers to the duration of a note and where it is placed within a musical composition.

B. Incorrect. Assessing pitch would require students to identify notes in relation to their placement on the staff.

C. Incorrect. Assessing whether students recognize familiar songs would most likely require them to review parts of a melody.

D. Incorrect. Assessing musical notation requires students to do more than just recognize the names of notes and rests. Students should understand ledger lines and the difference between the bass clef and the treble clef.

22)

A. Incorrect. Basketball requires students to dribble a ball, not to strike one thrown at them.

B. Correct. Baseball requires students to catch and throw a ball, run to bases, and strike a ball with a bat.

C. Incorrect. Students do not need to learn how to throw a ball to master tennis.

D. Incorrect. Soccer requires students to kick a ball with their feet.

23)

A. Incorrect. The clarinet is part of the woodwind family.

B. Correct. These are all instruments from the brass family.

C. Incorrect. The piccolo is part of the woodwind family.

D. Incorrect. These are all instruments from the string family.

24)

- A. Incorrect. None of these items show evidence of realistic drawing skills.
- **B. Correct.** All of these examples provide evidence of student progression, which helps the teacher give specific feedback.
- C. Incorrect. Photographs alone do not show the teacher the student's current skill level in realistic drawing.
- D. Incorrect. Shading exercises alone will not give the teacher a general or accurate picture of the student's ability to create realistic drawings.

25)

- A. Incorrect. Using symbols is one aspect of visual communication, but this explanation does not clarify why an artist would use them.
- B. Incorrect. The purpose of visual communication is not necessarily to create beautiful images.
- C. Incorrect. While visual communication can offer students a means to talk about art, this description does address its use as a way for students to understand an artwork's purpose.
- **D. Correct.** Visual communication uses imagery to effectively inform, persuade, or entertain viewers.

26)

- A. Incorrect. Anecdotal notes should be based on observations.
- **B. Correct.** Anecdotal notes are usually written in response to a series of observations in class.
- C. Incorrect. Anecdotal notes should be as objective as possible.
- D. Incorrect. Anecdotal notes should focus on student behaviors and skills, not lesson planning.

Made in the USA
Monee, IL
24 January 2025

10846238R00234